Untying
the
Knot

Untying *the* Knot

Making Peace in the Taiwan Strait

RICHARD C. BUSH

BROOKINGS INSTITUTION PRESS
Washington, D.C.

Library of Congress Cataloging-in-Publication data

Bush, Richard C., 1947–
    Untying the knot : making peace in the Taiwan Strait / Richard C. Bush.
        p.   cm.
    Summary: "A comprehensive analysis of the paradoxical relationship
between Taiwan and China, characterized by social and economic interaction
and political and military tensions, and the diplomatic diffidence of the
United States in the face of its high strategic stakes"—Provided by publisher.
    Includes bibliographical references and index.
    ISBN-13: 978-0-8157-1288-6 (ISBN-13, cloth : alk. paper)
    ISBN-10: 0-8157-1288-X (ISBN-10, cloth : alk. paper)
    1. Taiwan—Relations—China. 2. China—Relations—Taiwan. I. Title:
Making peace in the Taiwan Strait. II. Title.
    DS799.63.C6B87 2005
    327.951249051—dc22   2005012008

9 8 7 6 5 4 3 2 1

The paper used in this publication meets minimum requirements of the
American National Standard for Information Sciences—Permanence of Paper
for Printed Library Materials: ANSI Z39.48-1992.

Typeset in Minion

Composition by OSP, Inc.
Arlington, Virginia

Printed by R. R. Donnelley
Harrisonburg, Virginia

For Marty

Contents

Foreword

Of all the potential flash points in the world today, none poses more of a threat to international peace and more of a challenge to the United States than the Taiwan Strait. And of all the American experts on that issue, none is more qualified than Richard Bush to explain its origins, analyze its implications, and propose realistic but imaginative recommendations for its resolution.

Richard is, quite simply, America's leading Taiwan hand. He has a doctorate in political science from Columbia University and served for nineteen years in two branches of the U.S. government—the executive and the legislative—where he concentrated on East Asia in general and Taiwan in particular. He rose to senior positions, including those of National Intelligence Officer for East Asia and chairman of the board of the American Institute in Taiwan. That assignment was as sensitive and important as it was anomalous, since it made him responsible for the conduct of policy toward a country with which the United States does not have formal diplomatic relations.

Richard came to Brookings in 2002 as a senior fellow in our Foreign Policy Studies program and as director of our Center for Northeast Asia Policy Studies (CNAPS). He is what around here we call a "player/coach": he not only supervises the CNAPS visiting fellows program and two annual conferences, he also finds time to write. Just last year, he published *At Cross Purposes: U.S.-Taiwan Relations since 1942*, and now he gives us *Untying the Knot*, which explains why the dispute between China and Taiwan has been so resistant to solution despite the ethnic ties between the two, the complementarity of their economies, and their interchange in the fields of sport, culture, education, and religion.

In the early 1990s, China and Taiwan made a tentative—and, it turned out, short-lived—attempt to translate economic and social convergence into political reconciliation. Today the mutual mistrust is more corrosive than ever. Richard traces the dispute to its core, which he believes is not the separatist intentions of Taiwan's leaders; rather, it is a lose/lose dynamic that has developed between China and Taiwan as a result of the interplay of domestic politics on both sides of the Strait, competition between them in the international arena, and serious substantive differences on the issues of sovereignty and security.

While China and Taiwan have tied cross-Strait relations into a knot of Gordian complexity, Richard has some ideas about how the two parties might untie it, with a bit of help from the United States. Having spent much of his career on precisely this issue, he emphasizes the importance of the United States playing a supporting, not a starring, role. Washington, he cautions, can be most effective by facilitating reengagement between Beijing and Taipei, then retreating to the sidelines. Finally, he offers recommendations on how to manage the dispute if a permanent solution is impossible.

All in all, this is a model Brookings book: it combines a scholar's understanding of history and current events, a practitioner's sense of diplomacy as the art of the possible, and a natural writer's mastery of expository prose.

Moreover, we're glad to be bringing out this book right now. With presidential elections in the United States and Taiwan and the next leadership transition in China several years off, the complicating factor of domestic politics in the three countries involved has receded somewhat. As a result, this year—2005—may give policymakers in China, Taiwan, and the United States a chance to test some of the ideas that Richard advances here.

As this book went to press, the leaders of Taiwan's two opposition parties made highly publicized visits to China and met with leaders of the Communist Party. The full impact of those initiatives remains to be seen, but Richard's analysis provides the proper lens for assessing them.

STROBE TALBOTT
President

May 2005
Washington, D.C.

Acknowledgments

I am deeply indebted to many people for helping me write this book. Their contributions have made it a better work.

Much of my gratitude goes to my colleagues at the Brookings Institution, which provided a haven for me after nineteen years of U.S. government service. Strobe Talbott, the institution's president, and James Steinberg, vice president and director of Foreign Policy Studies, both encouraged me to undertake this project and helped ensure that the result met high standards. My colleagues at the Brookings Center for Northeast Asian Policy Studies— Sharon Yanagi, Kevin Scott, and Nina Palmer—took an extra administrative burden upon themselves to give me more time to think and write. Kevin and the center's interns over the last two years—Sheena Chestnut, Daphne Dung-Ning Fan, Alisa Frohman, Derek Grossman, Caleb O'Kray, Justin Wu, and Nina Zhan—provided a variety of research assistance. The center's visiting fellows provided much intellectual stimulation; professors Wilson Wai-ho Wong of the Chinese University of Hong Kong and Zhu Wenhui of Hong Kong Polytechnic University were especially helpful. My colleagues in Foreign Policy Studies were very supportive, Philip Gordon in particular. The Brookings library staff cheerfully tracked down every bibliographic request. Bob Faherty, director of the Brookings Institution Press, oversaw the project, and Janet Walker supervised the publication process. Eileen Hughes was an outstanding editor.

Beyond Brookings, I have been fortunate to be a member of the community of China and Taiwan scholars and analysts, both inside and outside the U.S. government, who have provided me with a constant stream of intellectual stimulation. Three of their number reviewed my manuscript, thereby saving me from various major and minor errors, for which I am deeply grateful. John Tkacik of the Heritage Foundation kindly provided his detailed chronology concerning cross-Strait relations. I am also pleased to acknowledge again the role that Steve Solarz played in redirecting my career toward Taiwan and cross-Strait relations in the mid-1980s. His recognition that international disputes must be understood in depth if they are to be solved is reflected in these pages.

For their financial support of this project, I am thankful to the Education and Culture Foundation of the Taiwan Semiconductor Manufacturing Corporation and the corporation's chairman, Morris Chang; the late Dr. C. F. Koo; Mr. Fan Jenfei, president of Taiwan Meiji Company; and Mr. Hong Ching-son, chairman of Kitai Contractors. Last but certainly not least, I am grateful to my family, both immediate and extended, for their love and encouragement. My wife Marty took a leap of faith almost forty years ago in agreeing that China was a career worth pursuing. That I still specialize in China today is due in no small measure to her support. It is to her that I dedicate this book.

Untying
the
Knot

China and Taiwan

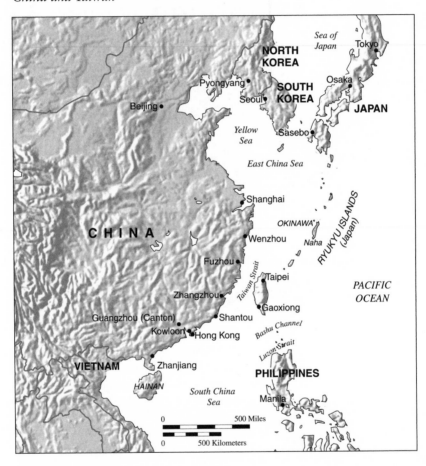

1

Introduction

In June 1995, Lee Teng-hui, the president of Taiwan, visited the United States, where he spoke at Cornell University, his alma mater, about the island's democratic transformation after decades of authoritarian rule. To show its displeasure, Beijing suspended the semiofficial contacts that it had developed with Taiwan's government and engaged in various displays of military power. Because Washington had allowed Lee to visit in the first place, Beijing also downgraded its relations with the United States.

In March 1996, when Taiwan was holding elections, China mounted even more aggressive displays of military force. The most provocative was launching unarmed ballistic missiles at targets outside the island's ports. The United States, concerned that war might occur through accident or miscalculation and that China might misread U.S. resolve to protect Taiwan, sent two aircraft carrier battle groups to the Taiwan area.

In July 1999, Lee Teng-hui stated in an interview with the press that the relations between the two sides of the Taiwan Strait were between two states (or countries—the Chinese term that Lee used is ambiguous). China then unleashed a barrage of propaganda against Lee, and Chinese fighter aircraft patrolled further into the Taiwan Strait than usual. To prevent tensions from escalating, the United States sent diplomats to both Beijing and Taipei to encourage restraint.

In March 2000, it became clear that Chen Shui-bian, the candidate of the Democratic Progressive Party (DPP), might win the Taiwan presidential election. Historically, the DPP had advocated establishment of a republic of Taiwan completely separate from China. At a press conference a few days before voters were to cast their ballots, China's premier, Zhu Rongji, declared

1

in threatening tones that "Taiwan independence means war." Because Beijing had already in effect declared that Chen was the independence candidate, Zhu's bluster suggested that a Chen victory would be a *casus belli*. Chen did win the election, and Washington again sent envoys to urge restraint.[1]

In 2002 and 2003, as part of his campaign for reelection, Chen made a series of statements that Beijing again interpreted as evidence that he was preparing to disrupt the status quo. It believed that his proposals to institute referenda and write a new constitution signaled that—under the cloak of democratizing Taiwan—he would seek to make the country independent. In response, China issued increasingly shrill warnings. The United States sought in various ways to dissuade Chen from any such course, and on December 9, 2003, President George W. Bush declared in the presence of China's premier, Wen Jiabao, that "we oppose any unilateral decision by either China or Taiwan to change the status quo. And the comments and actions made by the leader of Taiwan indicate that he may be willing to make decisions unilaterally to change the status quo, which we oppose."

Yet the Taiwan Strait area is not always as tense as it was or appeared to be in the summer of 1995, March 1996, July 1999, March 2000, or late 2003. However, those episodes demonstrate with exceptional clarity that the China-Taiwan dispute is dangerous and could erupt in war. They show just as clearly that if war broke out, the United States might be one of the warring parties if it decided that its own national interests required it to defend Taiwan against China—which happens to possess nuclear weapons. They also reveal that this is an odd sort of quarrel, one in which China's hostile reactions are not a response to a military threat but to the political threat that Beijing perceives in the travel and comments of Taiwan's leaders and in certain outcomes of its elections.

Indeed, from a broader perspective, it seems implausible that there would be much of a conflict at all. Other regional conflicts in the news—in Northern Ireland, the Balkans, Cyprus, and the Middle East, for example—have a set of common characteristics. They involve populations that are socially distinct but live in close physical proximity. Often there are multiple divisions among these populations, including differences in religion, language, ethnicity, and social customs. A mutually beneficial economic division of labor is lacking, and one group often dominates the other. Long, bitter memories of past conflict infuse current hostilities with what is an almost fight-to-the-death intensity. Paramilitary forces (Hamas, the IRA) that see it in their political interest to use violence to undermine and destroy efforts to resolve a conflict peacefully often are among the actors in these tragic dramas.

Because people live cheek by jowl, such violence results in at least a low-level civil war. Moreover, each of the conflicts mentioned has been the object of vigorous international and U.S. peacemaking efforts. In Northern Ireland and the Middle East, plans emerged that seemed to secure a foundation for an enduring peace but then collapsed to some degree in the process of implementation. In the case of Bosnia, the jury is still out.

The conflict between China and Taiwan certainly began in a similar way. After Mao Zedong's People's Liberation Army seized control of the Chinese mainland from Chiang Kai-shek's Nationalist Party—following years of high- and low-level conflict that began in the late 1920s—Chiang's army retreated to Taiwan. From 1949 until the 1980s, the two sides continued to be locked in a bitter military and ideological struggle that precluded any kind of economic or social cooperation. Mao sought to "liberate" the island; Chiang sought to mount a "counterattack" to retake the mainland. Chiang's Republic of China (ROC) fought to preserve its international recognition as the government of all of China; Mao's People's Republic of China (PRC) fought just as hard to wrest that status from it. The United States was caught in the middle. Clearly, the political conflict in the Taiwan Strait did not begin in the era of presidents Lee Teng-hui and Chen Shui-bian.

Yet the Taiwan Strait conflict today is very different from some other regional conflicts, both in its underlying configuration and in its prospects for resolution. First of all, China and Taiwan are separated by about 100 miles of water, removing the opportunity for easy infiltration (à la North Vietnam into South Vietnam) and the sort of communal conflict endemic in the Middle East and in Northern Ireland until the late 1990s. To be sure, the two sides have formidable military capabilities, and they are acquiring more. But this is a case in which a tall fence, in the form of the Taiwan Strait, makes it possible for them to be better neighbors.

Second, the people involved are socially and culturally the same. The population of Taiwan is made up of two major groups, both of which came from China. The first are descendants of people who migrated to the island from southeastern China beginning in the sixteenth century (the so-called Taiwanese); the second were refugees who arrived before 1950 as the government and armed forces of Chiang Kai-shek's Nationalist Party fled the Chinese mainland after being defeated by the communists (the so-called mainlanders).[2] Taiwan and the PRC share a common written language; differences in the spoken language are merely dialectical deviations from a common base. Religion is not a source of conflict at all. Politics aside, people in China and Taiwan have much in common.

Most important, the two sides found compelling reasons to set aside some of their ideological differences for the sake of pragmatic cooperation. In order to remain globally competitive, Taiwan companies moved production from the island to the mainland beginning in the late 1980s. China welcomed the investment, which created jobs and contributed to its own economic development, in the process of which Chinese factories became a link in the global supply chain.

The Cross-Strait Knot

And so a paradox presents itself. The economic and social interaction between Taiwan and China is broad and deep, yet a bitter political conflict that could take a violent form continues. The two societies have much in common, and their economies are complementary. Taiwan companies use mainland production facilities to maintain their profitability, and Chinese workers, engineers, and officials benefit as a result. Such interaction fosters some mutual understanding among certain sectors of the two societies, and yet political leaders in Beijing and Taipei mistrust each other's motives and intentions. Each side arms itself against any attempt by the other to irreversibly change the status quo. Through weapons systems such as submarines, cruise and ballistic missiles, and long-range bombers, China acquires the capacity to deploy its military power well beyond its borders and so deter Taiwan from moving toward de jure independence. Taiwan acquires advanced defensive systems to deter a mainland attack and to defend the island if deterrence fails. The absence of direct dialogue aggravates their mutual suspicion. Although each side understands that it has little or nothing to gain and much to lose from military conflict, war could come through accident or miscalculation if not deliberate action. Some hope that economic interdependence will be the prelude to political reconciliation. Others claim that Taiwan cannot resist an increasingly powerful China and should cut the best deal it can. Yet both reconciliation and Taiwan's submission to China's power seem remote possibilities.

Another curious feature of the conflict in the Taiwan Strait is the role of the United States. To be sure, for decades Washington has emphasized its "abiding interest" in a peaceful resolution of the dispute. It sells advanced weapons to Taiwan to maintain something of a military balance, and it has signaled that under certain circumstances it would come to Taiwan's defense if the PRC attacked the island. Yet unlike in the Balkans, the Middle East, or Northern Ireland, the United States has been reluctant to play a central role in reducing the risk of war by trying to foster a settlement. Washington has sought to contain the situation in the Taiwan Strait and create a positive environment in which progress might occur, but it steers clear of special envoys, shuttle diplomacy, and mediation. Despite the real possibility that the United States might be drawn into a war between China and Taiwan, it has kept a cautious distance.

What explains the mismatch between Taiwan and China's economic cooperation and their political-military stalemate, between America's strategic stakes and its diplomatic diffidence? If human interchange in a variety of fields were not occurring, the conflict between Taiwan and China would be more understandable. But the economic and social interaction between the countries is quite robust. Why is the political dispute so difficult to resolve that it has become increasingly militarized? Will economic and social interaction attenuate the political disagreements and so facilitate a more stable and less conflict-prone relationship? Is there a mutually acceptable basis on which Beijing and Taipei might resolve their differences? Is there anything that the United States, which is inextricably a part of the dispute, can do to mitigate it? Or is this a problem that is likely to endure in spite of any countervailing forces?

Those are the questions that this book seeks to address, and it is important to address them. Whether the goal of U.S. policy is to resolve the Taiwan Strait dispute or only to try to manage it, U.S. decisionmakers must understand why it is so intractable. If Washington, without properly understanding the problem, decides to break with past policy and attempt to facilitate a solution, it could easily make the situation worse. Even if the goal is just to avoid conflict and preserve some measure of stability, knowing where to strike a balance requires a clear sense of what motivates the two contending forces in the first place.

By way of background, chapter 2 provides an overview of Taiwan's history and its relations with both China and the United States until the late 1980s. Chapter 3 presents the paradox in more detail. It charts on one hand the growing economic and social interaction across the Strait and on the other the development of the political stalemate that has existed since the early 1990s. Beijing's explanation for the impasse is that the island's leaders have sought to permanently separate Taiwan from China. For more than two decades, the PRC has offered a formula for unification—"One country, two systems"—that would give Taiwan home rule but reserve for itself the status of exclusive sovereign, including the right to represent China in the international community. Beijing has interpreted Lee Teng-hui's and Chen

Shui-bian's words and deeds as evidence of a separatist agenda. I reject that view as a misunderstanding of their fundamental positions and argue instead that although both opposed the PRC's formula for unification, they were not against unification in principle. Rather, they focused on the terms and conditions of any reassociation. Specifically, they sought a formula for unification that accepted Taipei's claim that its government was sovereign and that it had, among other things, the right to participate in the international system. In effect, Lee Teng-hui and Chen Shui-bian were as worried about *how* Taiwan was to be a part of China as *whether* it was. Or, to be more precise, they focused on the legal identity of the government in Taipei and its relationship to the Chinese state.

Chapters 4 and 5 address two issues that form the substance of the dispute between Taiwan and China: sovereignty and security. Chapter 4 elaborates on the previous discussion, exploring in more depth the concept of sovereignty and the related idea of the state and how the two pertain to the dispute. Taiwan does score well on a number of the formal criteria for statehood and sovereignty. The one where it is most deficient—participation in the international system through diplomatic relations with other countries and membership in international organizations—is the one where the PRC has used its considerable leverage to exclude Taiwan. Taiwan's case also is complicated by confusion over what territory its government claims as its sovereign domain. This analysis of sovereignty pinpoints the two questions that would have to be answered in any settlement of the dispute. First, would the government of Taiwan have a right to rule the territory under its jurisdiction except in those areas where it chose to cede that right? Second, would it have the right to participate as a full member of the international community? How Beijing applied the one-country, two-systems formula in Hong Kong—where it has rigged the political system to prevent outcomes that it opposes—is particularly relevant in attempting to answer the first question. Also germane, in a negative sense, is how Taiwan's situation is different from that of Western Europe, where countries have been willing to delegate and pool their sovereignty in the interest of closer economic integration. Unlike those nations, which were recognized as sovereign states at the outset, Taiwan is fighting for Beijing's acceptance of its claim to sovereignty in the first place and resisting Chinese efforts to undermine that claim.

The other core issue, security, is addressed in chapter 5. I argue that the two sides are locked in a security dilemma in which each fears that the other threatens its fundamental interests and so acts to counter the threat. Moreover, each fears that if it takes the initiative to break the stalemate by offering concessions, the other will exploit its goodwill, leaving it more vulnerable. In an important sense, of course, the dilemma that traps China and Taiwan is not the classic one of international relations literature, in which the mutual threat is military. In this case, it is Taiwan's potential political actions that create insecurity in Beijing. But to forestall such actions, China acquires advanced systems from Russia and improves the fighting capability of the People's Liberation Army. Taiwan's armed forces respond by seeking to purchase as much defensive weaponry as they can from the United States. The political character of the problem is magnified by Taiwan's reliance on Washington not only for arms but also for its commitment to come to Taiwan's defense if attacked, which is an obvious source of resentment and insecurity in Beijing. But that commitment is not an unqualified advantage for Taipei either. Like the junior partner in any alliance, it worries that the United States will abandon it; Washington, on the other hand, fears that Taipei might entrap it in a conflict that it does not want. Taiwan's insecurity, its dependence on the United States, and its fundamental mistrust of China's intentions dictate that Beijing would have to do a lot to persuade Taipei to give up its alliance with the United States.

The sovereignty and security issues are the two substantive strands of the cross-Strait knot. They are twisted strands, because Taiwan's claim of sovereign status strengthens its justification for U.S. security assistance. Three aggravating factors tighten the knot, making the substantive issues even more difficult to resolve.

The first, discussed in chapter 6, is domestic politics in each country. In Taiwan, history, the politics of opposition, and how the democratic system currently functions all constrain the freedom of its leaders to bargain with Beijing. Harsh Nationalist Party rule after 1949 created among the Taiwanese the strong sense that they were different from mainlanders. They also began to conceive of Taiwan as a separate country and to develop an intense fear of outsiders. Their sense of having an exclusively Taiwanese identity plus their grievances after decades of repression at the hands of the Nationalist Party fueled their opposition to its rule and, in some quarters, gave rise to the desire for a Taiwan independent of China. It was the Democratic Progressive Party, the party of Chen Shui-bian, that led the opposition, and to this day the DPP has a clause regarding Taiwan's independence in its charter.

Yet Taiwanese identity politics has focused more on securing a democratic system and gaining international respect than on creating a separate state, a Republic of Taiwan totally independent of China. And, dialectically, the democratic system that emerged in the 1990s forced the opposition DPP to moderate its goals relating to Taiwan's independence in order to secure public support. Politics nevertheless has solidified an island-wide consensus *against* the one-country, two-systems proposal. But as a practical matter, it also makes it hard to secure broad approval of a package that addressed the sovereignty and security issues in a manner more to Taiwan's liking, if the PRC were ever to offer one. The electoral system has fostered the representation of radical views and the fragmentation of political parties, and constitutional defects complicate relations among the various parts of the governmental system. The rules of the legislature give small minorities a veto over controversial proposals, and the constitution requires a three-quarters margin to enact constitutional amendments.

On the mainland, nationalism and politics within the elite have had a similar effect. Policy is refracted through a personalized leadership system in which principal officeholders must build consensus for their initiatives, and their freedom of action varies by issue and over time. Taiwan is a particularly radioactive matter because the lack of resolution of the cross-Strait impasse has long deferred China's national unification. Any top leader who mishandles the issue is vulnerable to attacks from his competitors and key institutional groups like the military. Those responsible for PRC policy on Taiwan are reluctant to stray too far from the default position (the one-country, two-systems approach formulated more than two decades ago) and remain alert to any sign that Taipei is moving toward a permanent separation.

Politics within the communist leadership can be particularly delicate at times of a major succession, which is usually a gradual affair. Those in the retiring generation seek to keep their hand in important policy issues, none of which is more important than Taiwan. Members of the rising generation are reluctant to reveal their preferences on key policy issues, particularly regarding Taiwan, for fear of derailing their bid for power. Thus Jiang Zemin, who dominated Taiwan policy since the mid-1990s, was slow to cede control of decisionmaking to his successor, Hu Jintao.

Public opinion in China can also affect the handling of Taiwan policy. The "public" has different layers, with intellectuals who have connections with the party-state often having more influence on policy than the general population. Yet as the mass media become more competitive, popular nationalist sentiment can become more extreme than the regime propaganda that inspired it and so place limits on the leadership. That is especially true if the leadership is divided on an issue like Taiwan; if U.S.-China relations are poor; and if public opinion is mobilized by particular events. Periodic crises in cross-Strait relations have evoked flurries of Chinese commentaries and proposals whose recurring theme is that Beijing must be more resolute in dealing with Taiwanese (and American) perfidy. The danger for the paramount leader, of course, is that opponents will seek to use public criticism of his policies to mount a challenge to his leadership.

The second factor aggravating cross-Strait relations, discussed in chapter 7, is the decisionmaking process in both Beijing and Taipei. The policy process in each capital is more pluralistic and institutionalized than was the case twenty years ago, particularly when neither government is in a state of crisis. Still, each government is institutionally prone to read the worst into each other's intentions and into those of the United States. Moreover, because the cross-Strait issue is crucial to the survival of leaders in both Taiwan and China, top leaders still tend to control it, particularly in times of tension, and that centralization increases the possibility of misinterpretation. Thus at various points China has misread the motivation behind Taiwan's initiatives and exaggerated the threat that they pose to China's core interests. At a minimum, such misconceptions limit Beijing's willingness to make constructive concessions; at worst, they foster a tendency to overreact, which then deepens Taiwan's sense of insecurity. The Taipei government has had similar problems.

The third complicating factor, covered in chapter 8, is the attempt of each side to gain advantage over the other. Taiwan exerts significant effort to reenter, in some capacity, the international organizations that it was forced to depart twenty or thirty years ago. Having engineered that departure, China is ever vigilant in blocking Taipei's efforts to reenter. In addition, China takes advantage of the openness of Taiwan's political system to advance its interests. As in Hong Kong, China pursues a united front strategy in Taiwan, using the business community and the political parties opposed to Chen Shui-bian to check him and, in the long-run, create a better climate for unification on its terms. The zero-sum quality of this game complicates any effort to ameliorate the dispute.

A special object of the leverage game is U.S. policy, and the role of the United States is addressed in chapter 9. Taiwan devotes considerable energy to preserving the support it receives from the United States and to securing a stronger and more reliable U.S. commitment—which includes cultivating friends in Congress as a check against unfavorable actions by the executive branch. Beijing works to dilute administration support for Taiwan so that the latter will be in a less advantageous negotiating position. The core of Washington's "one-China policy," however, is to emphasize process, particularly peaceful means to resolve cross-Strait problems, rather than the substantive issues that divide China and Taiwan. It thus has sought to restrain China from using force and Taiwan from taking political initiatives that China might conclude justify the use of force. The United States has, on the other hand, eschewed any formal role as mediator.

What are the prospects of resolving this dispute, of untying this twisted and tightened knot? There is, of course, the possibility that China's strategy of economic enticement and its united front tactics will wear down Taiwan's resistance and produce an agreement based more or less on China's terms. Chapter 10 assumes such a scenario to be unlikely into the foreseeable future because of the strength of Taiwan's national identity; it examines instead whether there are ways to reconcile the substantive issues at play and ameliorate the aggravating factors. Regarding the sovereignty issue, some type of confederation would in the abstract satisfy the minimum objectives of each side: Beijing would get a form of unification and Taiwan would preserve its claim that its government retains sovereignty within a national union. And indeed, various Taiwanese political forces have suggested such an approach, although so far the PRC has rejected it. On the security side, there appears to be no simple *substantive* formula that would allay Taiwan's sense of insecurity, certainly not enough to lead it to cut its ties to the United States; it also seems that so far China has preferred to exacerbate Taiwan's sense of insecurity rather than relieve it. It is more feasible to begin a process of taking conditional and reciprocal steps (involving, for example, confidence-building and arms control measures) that over time would give Taiwan sufficient assurance that Beijing would not renege on any commitments that it made. As for the aggravating factors, if there is to be any mitigation of the corrosive effects of the leverage game, Beijing and Taipei would have to agree to a truce in the international arena and Beijing would have to pledge not to meddle in Taiwan's politics. With respect to China's domestic politics, national leaders might have a hard time selling a change in the one-country, two-systems concept after having sung its praises for so many years. But the larger political problem probably lies in Taipei, where a system that creates radical minorities and then gives them veto power might well fail to approve a substantive offer from Beijing that if viewed objectively would be seen to work in Taiwan's favor. To even start the process of negotiation, Beijing would have to abandon the preconditions it has imposed, and given Taiwan's sense of insecurity, it would have to accept a gradual process to produce a series of interlocking agreements rather than one grand bargain. In sum, if there is a deal to be had based on the current positions of the two sides,

China would have to make more concessions to get the process going and to bridge substantive differences. Taiwan, with its choice-averse political system, would have the harder job securing ratification of any agreements produced.

Such a negotiation process appears to dictate a limited role for the United States, and neither side necessarily trusts Washington's credibility enough to allow it to play a more central role. Beijing in particular has opposed internationalizing the dispute, except when it decides that it needs U.S. help to block Taiwan's actions. Taiwan could mobilize its influence in the U.S. political system to block any trend in negotiations that it did not like, even if it sought U.S. involvement in the process at the outset. Moreover, the United States is a party to the dispute, since it is the sole source of Taiwan's security and thus much of its psychological confidence. That support would be a key issue in negotiations between Taiwan and China, and how it was addressed would determine whether the security dilemma was resolved. In that respect alone, it is hard to see how Washington could be an honest broker and maintain both Taipei's and Beijing's confidence.

Nor is it clear what substantive value the United States might contribute to untying the cross-Strait knot. Given the positions of the two sides, the contours of the content necessary for any agreement are fairly apparent. What is missing is the political will on each side to make the necessary concessions, the mutual confidence that each side will keep its part of a bargain, and the domestic political capacity, particularly in Taiwan, to ratify any agreement. Those are not gaps that Washington can—or should—fill; direct dialogue between the two parties is far more likely to succeed in that regard. However, the United States may be able to play a useful role that speaks to the defects of the decisionmaking process on each side—that is, Washington might act as intellectual facilitator, interpreting the views of one side to the other, in order to reduce the possibility of misperception. In addition, there inevitably would be discussions between Washington and Taipei when security issues were under negotiation. Finally, the United States might serve as a guarantor of whatever agreement was reached to improve the chances that the two parties would live up to their obligations.

What the three parties should do if the knot cannot be untied is the subject of chapter 11. There is, of course, the possibility that over time the PRC's basic strategy will work and Taiwan will accommodate itself to the reality of China's power. Economics will trump political principles and military insecurity. Given the strength of the Taiwanese national identity and the defects of the political system, that seems unlikely. The task then will be to stabilize the situation to prevent future crises. For example, during his campaign for reelection, President Chen Shui-bian proposed that Taiwan write a new constitution and ratify it by referendum. Beijing judged that proposal to be tantamount to creating a new state, which it vowed to oppose by force if no other checks were placed on Chen. Once he had won another term and after encouragement from the United States, Chen retreated from his proposal and pledged to pursue only domestic political reform and do so according to established procedures. The PRC nevertheless believed that his restraint was more apparent than real and that his goal remained the permanent separation of Taiwan from China. It warned the Bush administration that Washington would have to impose strict limits on Chen in order to guarantee that China would not resort to military action against him.

The prospects for a military conflict in Chen Shui-bian's second term probably are not as dire as China initially believed. Preventing conflict will require Chen to manage domestic politics so that institutional reform remains his agenda and Beijing comes to understand that such an agenda does not threaten its fundamental interests. The United States will have to continue to emphasize dual deterrence, encouraging restraint on Taiwan regarding the content of a revised constitution and on the PRC regarding its response.

Such mutual restraint would reduce the chance of a conflict, but it would not ensure that one would not erupt through accident or miscalculation. Any war would have horrific consequences for China and Taiwan and pose enormous challenges for the United States and other nations in the international community. Nor would a truce concerning the revision of Taiwan's constitution foster stability. That, it seems, would require China to adopt a new approach to how to protect its equities and Taiwan to change its view of what is most important. Beijing's current strategy—ignoring the Chen administration and depriving it of policy successes, quarantining Taiwan in the international community, increasing Taiwan's insecurity by building up China's military, and meddling in Taiwan's politics—is yielding diminishing returns. It would gain more by initiating a limited engagement with the Chen administration, which could reduce misunderstanding about both sides' intentions; facilitate the opening of transportation links (so far blocked by the sovereignty dispute); and allow Taiwan more international space. Such steps would have a positive impact on public opinion in Taiwan, particularly among the approximately half of the population that favors some accommodation of China.

Taiwan, in addition to showing restraint on its cross-Strait initiatives, needs to emphasize substance instead of symbols. There is an all-too-common tendency on the island to focus on status and terminology instead of the underlying sources of national power. Because China's power will continue to grow, Taiwan must take steps to strengthen itself economically, diplomatically, psychologically, militarily, and politically. Certainly it should do so if the dispute with Beijing is likely to continue, but self-strengthening would be valuable even if there was the promise of settlement. And if the stalemate persists, the United States should continue what has been its usual policy: dual deterrence. That is, Washington would try to restrain Beijing from using military force and Taipei from taking political initiatives that might lead Beijing to react militarily.

Whether or not the Taiwan-China knot can be unraveled, all parties concerned must understand how the strands are twisted, tied, and tightened. Better understanding of the dispute is the first step toward making it less dangerous—and away from exacerbating it through bad analysis of the nature of the problem, including how each party views the intentions of the other. This study seeks to contribute to that understanding.

2

Getting to the Present

The mountainous, leaf-shaped island of Taiwan sits on the edge of the Asian continental shelf. About the size of Connecticut and New Hampshire combined, it is home to around 23 million people, most of whom live on the flatter, western side of the island. The great majority are ethnic Chinese. The government goes by the name of Republic of China. It also controls the Penghu archipelago, to the west of the main island, and several islands just off the coast of China.

Taiwan, around ninety miles from mainland China at the closest point, became a part of the Chinese cultural world only gradually. The original inhabitants were members of aboriginal tribes; ethnic Chinese—pirates, traders, and fishermen—made their first appearance only around the fourteenth and fifteenth centuries. Farmers from southeast China began to move to Taiwan in substantial numbers in the seventeenth century, bringing with them their folk culture and displacing the indigenous peoples in the process. The Dutch and Spanish established outposts on the island at the same time, but they soon left. In the middle of the century, Taiwan was a base of ethnic Chinese opposition to the new Manchu (Qing) dynasty and so acquired a special place in Chinese historical memories of political division and unification. In 1683, however, the Qing dynasty prevailed, and the island became a frontier of the Chinese imperial system. It was a fairly violent place, plagued by conflicts among ethnic Chinese groups and between them and the aborigines. Gradually, however, a more settled Chinese society that looked very much like that in the southeastern part of the mainland took hold. An upper class of landlords and merchants emerged, and, like local elites all over China, it responded to the incentives offered by the imperial system for upward social and political mobility.[1]

Taiwan's people would have continued to adapt to the late imperial system relatively undisturbed had it not been for the island's location in the sea lanes of East Asia. The commercial center of Danshui on the northern end of the island became a treaty port after the Anglo-French war with China in the late 1850s, and Taiwan was opened to international trade. Foreign vessels frequently ran aground on Taiwan's western coast, and local inhabitants often mistreated the stranded sailors, whom they considered invaders, so creating diplomatic incidents. Moreover, the island became a tempting prize for foreign powers seeking to secure a stronger position in the region. The Japanese occupied parts of Taiwan in 1874, and French forces briefly seized the Penghu Islands west of Taiwan (called the Pescadores in Portuguese) in 1883. In 1885 the Qing court decided that Taiwan needed more imperial attention and so elevated it to the status of province. The first governor embarked on a program to build basic infrastructure and rationalize the tax system, but he was in office too briefly to have a lasting impact. In 1895 Japan, having defeated China in a war over Korea, demanded Taiwan and the Pescadores as part of the peace settlement. It wanted the status of colonial power, the economic resources the islands might provide, and a southern defensive shield. Annexation was accomplished through the Treaty of Shimoniseki, whose validity Chinese nationalists to this day refuse to recognize.[2]

Japanese colonial rule began badly. With the hidden agenda of remaining under Chinese rule, groups on the island rebelled and declared Taiwan a republic. Japanese military forces put down the initial insurgency with little trouble but then spent more than two decades trying to consolidate their control. After World War I, Tokyo decided to put greater emphasis on the economic development of the island, appointing civilian technocrats rather than generals or admirals as governors. The colonial government built transportation and communications infrastructure, established an education and a public health system, and, in an early "green revolution," modernized agriculture through the use of scientifically bred seeds. Agricultural processing industries sprouted. Through a police force that penetrated Taiwanese society much deeper than any agency of the Chinese government ever had, the Japanese maintained strict social control, deflecting or suppressing Taiwanese appeals for greater political participation. And they tightened the screws when war with China began in 1937. Taiwan became an economic and recruitment base for the Japanese war effort and later a platform for attacks on Southeast Asia, including those against the Philippines, then a U.S.

colony. Taiwanese were pressured to become culturally more like Japanese. Despite the harshness of wartime colonial rule, some elderly Taiwanese in the late twentieth century would retain a certain nostalgia for the Japanese period because of both the progress that took place during that time and the oppression that came after.[3]

Even after Japan invaded China, Taiwan did not loom large in the Chinese consciousness. In the late 1930s, both Chiang Kai-shek, who headed the mainland's Republic of China government and the ruling Nationalist Party (Kuomintang), and Mao Zedong, leader of the Chinese Communist Party, regarded the island as a separate entity. It was like Korea in that it deserved to be free of Japanese rule, but it was not like Manchuria, which had to be returned to China. Taiwanese exiles living in areas under Nationalist government control in China argued that reversion of Taiwan should be one of China's war aims, but that did not become a real possibility until Japan attacked Pearl Harbor, when the United States entered the war and became an ally of China. Chiang then became more ambitious. By late 1942, he publicly demanded that Taiwan, which he termed one of China's "exterior fortresses," be returned to China at war's end; privately, he offered the United States the opportunity to set up joint military bases there. Although the U.S.-ROC alliance was riven with disputes over military strategy, allocation of resources, and whether U.S. personnel should work independently with Chiang's communist rivals to fight Japan, Taiwan was one issue where Chiang Kai-shek and Franklin Roosevelt saw eye to eye. FDR had his own plans for the island, and allowing international trusteeship of the island and a plebiscite to elicit the wishes of its people was not one of them. In his vision for postwar peace and security, "four policemen"—the United States, Britain, the Soviet Union, and China—would insist on disarmament by most other countries and enforce it through a system of military bases. Thus China and the United States would ensure that no country in Southeast Asia and the Pacific would rearm, and they would use Taiwan as a base from which to challenge noncompliance through naval blockades and aerial bombardment. FDR seems to have thought that since Taiwan was to play such a critical role in this program, it made perfect sense to return it to China. He made that decision no later than February 1943 and had it ratified at the Cairo Conference in December 1943. The previous month, U.S. airplanes had begun bombing targets on Taiwan, and for a while the U.S. Navy regarded Taiwan as a major stepping-stone in the rollback of Japan in the Pacific, developing plans that would have delayed the ROC government's takeover of the island. But in the end, for a variety of reasons, Roosevelt opted for a landing in the Philippines. Taiwan was bypassed, the Navy's plans were abandoned, and it was an ROC general that accepted the Japanese surrender on the island. At that point, the residents of the island welcomed its reversion to China.[4]

Internal Repression, Cold War Deadlock

The happy homecoming was short lived, however. Taiwan's new rulers were incompetent at best and inclined to abuse and alienate the Taiwanese population. In February 1947, after an altercation between a cigarette vendor and tax officials, popular discontent erupted into a full-scale rebellion. Local elites remonstrated with provincial officials to undertake reforms so that the actions of the "government" would be more acceptable to the island's population. But Chiang Kai-shek sent in reinforcements, which quickly suppressed the insurgency and engaged in the indiscriminate killing of local residents. The uprising, during which thousands of people were killed, became known as the 2-28 incident, in reference to its first day, February 28. Its suppression embittered the Taiwanese toward the ROC government for decades.[5]

The alienation on Taiwan only deepened as Chiang Kai-shek's Nationalists lost political and military ground to the communists on the mainland. By the end of 1948, it was clear that the contest was lost. Taiwan quickly emerged as Chiang's only refuge, and the island was soon flooded with 2 million refugees, both soldiers and civilians. The government itself relocated in December 1949, bringing with it a paranoia about threats from within. Chiang Ching-kuo, Chiang Kai-shek's son, was put in charge of reforming the Kuomintang (KMT) and purging it and the society at large of communists and other seditious elements, including any people who called for Taiwan's independence from China. This was the "white terror."

Immediately after Japan's surrender, the focus of U.S. China policy had been on the looming civil war on the Chinese mainland. With a mandate from President Truman, George Marshall tried to mediate between the Nationalists and the Communists, but mutual mistrust and the tendency of both Chinese parties to try to secure a tactical advantage soon brought Marshall's peacemaking effort to an end. Fighting between the Nationalists and Communists resumed, just at the time of the 2-28 incident. The United States did provide various kinds of assistance to Chiang's forces but soon became convinced that the KMT regime was too corrupt and ineffective to stave off a Communist military victory no matter how much aid it provided. Nevertheless, because Chiang's government had succeeded in garnering support in the U.S. Congress and the American media, particularly among anticommunist opponents of the Truman administration, the administration's decision to distance itself from Chiang met with domestic resistance. The Nationalists' allies in Congress ensured that the regime continued to get some military assistance, and they would continue to exert significant influence on U.S. policy toward the ROC government in the future. However, the general trend of U.S. policy in the late 1940s was clear: disengagement from Chiang and his government.[6]

Once the Nationalist cause seemed lost, Washington focused on the vulnerability of Taiwan, to which the KMT was retreating. Ever since the Cairo Declaration of December 1943, Mao Zedong and his revolutionary colleagues had set their sights on seizing the island as well as the mainland, and Taiwan became one part of their mission of national recovery and unification. That their civil war rivals, whom they termed the "Chiang Kai-shek reactionary clique," planned to mount a last ditch stand on Taiwan was all the more reason to take the island.

In the Truman administration in 1949, there was a consensus that a Communist takeover was both likely—again because of the Nationalists' political and military ineptitude—and detrimental to U.S. security interests. On the other hand, the United States lacked the military assets to defend Taiwan. Various schemes were considered and abandoned. There was hope that not coming to Taiwan's defense would encourage the new People's Republic of China (PRC) to maintain some independence from Moscow. President Truman announced in January 1950 that the United States would not intervene and that he considered Taiwan to be a part of China.

North Korea's invasion of South Korea in June 1950 saved Taiwan and the ROC. Washington—afraid that the invasion of South Korea was part of a larger campaign by the communists to extend their control and wanting to end the ROC's continuing minor attacks against the mainland—deployed the 7th Fleet to the Taiwan Strait to prevent the PRC and the ROC from attacking each other. The net effect, however, was to ensure Chiang's survival. The ROC was able to retain its seat in the United Nations and diplomatic relations with a majority of the world's countries. The Truman administration justified its policy reversal by saying that because there had been no peace treaty with Japan to dispose of "ownership" of Taiwan, its legal status (whether it was indeed part of China) had not been determined; thus its security was an international issue, not a purely domestic one.[7]

Over time, Taiwan became an important link in the U.S. chain to contain communism. The United States provided significant security assistance to the ROC's armed forces, and the intelligence agencies of the two countries cooperated closely. In late 1954, the two governments concluded a mutual defense treaty, which served to guarantee that relations between China and the United States would be hostile for a long period of time.[8] China had not given up its nationalistic ambition to bring Taiwan under its control. In Beijing's eyes, the civil war with Nationalists had not ended and it was only U.S. military support for Chiang that ensured Chiang's survival. Although China lacked the military capability to take Taiwan, it did probe for weaknesses in the KMT's position and in the U.S.-ROC alliance.

The KMT regime used that breathing space to consolidate its harsh, repressive rule on Taiwan. Mainlanders from China, who constituted around 15 percent of the population, ruled over the native Taiwanese majority. The KMT justified its minority rule on the grounds that it was the government of all of China. It maintained that because it was not possible to hold elections in districts throughout China, the membership of the Legislative Yuan and the National Assembly had to be frozen and Taiwanese representation in those bodies limited more or less to Taiwan's share of China's total population. The KMT also asserted that because a state of emergency "to suppress the communist rebellion" was in effect, political freedoms had to be severely restricted. Taiwanese who engaged in political dissent lost their lives or their freedom, and the rest regarded their rulers with silent hostility. The United States offered economic assistance to promote a successful program of export-led growth, but successive administrations decided that promoting political liberalization was either inappropriate (because of the ROC's strategic importance in the U.S. fight against communism, which might be undermined if the regime were challenged) or impossible. A further constraint, of course, was the ROC's continuing support among American politicians, which it did everything to cultivate.[9]

Taiwan's authoritarian system aside, the alliance was still a case of "same bed, different dreams." Chiang pursued a policy of "counterattack" against the mainland and hoped that the United States would help. American presidents, on the other hand, sought to restrain such adventurism. In 1954 and 1958, Chinese artillery shelled the ROC-controlled offshore islands of Jinmen and Mazu (Quemoy and Matsu), primarily to test the ROC's resolve to keep the islands. The Eisenhower administration knew that the islands had no strategic value but understood that their loss would be a serious psychological blow to Nationalist morale and to U.S. credibility. If China were serious about taking them, the United States might need nuclear weapons to save them. In any case, Washington certainly did not want to get drawn into a major war with China because of provocative actions by Chiang's armed forces. It therefore imposed limits on ROC's offensive actions against the mainland, which only prompted arguments with Chiang over how big an action had to be to be offensive. (Moreover, Washington recognized that limited diplomatic contact between the United States and China would help in managing conflict.) Chiang resented American control, which he believed called the legitimacy of his government into question. Then, as more third world countries emerged from colonial rule and began to recognize Beijing, the ROC's position in the United Nations became increasingly vulnerable. The Kennedy and Johnson administrations urged Chiang to pursue a more pragmatic approach that would permit the PRC's entry into the United Nations, on the condition that the ROC also remain. Ideologically rigid, Chiang rejected these "two-China" suggestions.[10]

The 1970s: A Dramatic Shift

Richard Nixon and Henry Kissinger transformed the foundation of U.S. policy toward Taiwan. They saw China as a counterweight to the Soviet Union, and China's price for cooperation was destruction of the pillars of the relationship between Taiwan and the United States. In the first stage of its campaign, Beijing sought U.S. affirmation that there was one China, not two; that Taiwan was part of China, not an entity of undetermined status; that the United States would not support the Taiwan independence movement and that the United States would recognize the PRC as the government of China. Nixon and Kissinger arguably moved in that direction in 1972 by issuing the Shanghai communiqué, which marked the beginning of rapprochement between the United States and China, and they were more explicit in private conversations. In return, they sought without much success to gain the PRC's acceptance of the principle that the Taiwan Strait issue should be resolved peacefully. Nixon could pull off rapprochement with "Communist China," in spite of the opposition of the ROC's American supporters, because he had begun the venture in secret, because the strategic rationale rang true, and because he had impeccable anticommunist credentials. None of that was any consolation for Taipei, to whom Nixon had pledged, "I will not sell you down the river." To make matters worse, Beijing's supporters in the United Nations succeeded in October 1971 to seat the PRC at the ROC's expense. And over the rest of the decade, most countries would switch their recognition from the ROC to the PRC.[11]

Those setbacks fostered political ferment on Taiwan, as critics of the regime challenged its legitimacy and political monopoly. Chiang Kai-shek had designated his son, Chiang Ching-kuo, as his heir-apparent and gradually was vesting him with power over the Nationalist state, including all security, military, party, and government institutions. The younger Chiang, who would become president in 1978, pursued a domestic political strategy that differed from the hard authoritarianism of his father (who died in 1975) and was more suited to the ROC's declining international position. He expanded the representation of native Taiwanese in the Kuomintang and began grooming some of their number for high office. He relaxed the hitherto tight controls on political freedom and competition in order to use limited expression of political opinion and elections as a barometer of KMT performance. The number of seats in the Legislative Yuan elected from districts in Taiwan grew in accord with increases in the island's population. Elections were not totally free and fair, and because the permanent members of the legislature remained, the KMT's majority was never threatened. Still, the ruling party had to appeal to the electorate, and it saw election results as a measure of its performance.[12]

The slow pace of liberalization was not fast enough for the regime's opponents, who began calling for a democratic system. Mainlander intellectuals mounted an initial, rather polite challenge in 1972 and 1973 but then backed down when the regime reached the limit of its tolerance. Taiwanese dissidents would later act more aggressively, exploring the formation of an opposition party, in violation of KMT restrictions. Throughout the 1970s and 1980s, Taiwanese politics would exhibit a cyclical pattern marked by a series of events wherein the regime relaxed controls, the opposition overreached, the security services cracked down, and a new experiment with relaxing controls began.[13]

The U.S. effort to create a geopolitical alignment with China resumed in 1978 during the Carter administration. Beijing made clear that if the United States wanted diplomatic relations, it would have to cut its ties with Taiwan. Specifically, it demanded that Washington break diplomatic relations with Taipei, end their mutual defense treaty, and withdraw remaining U.S. military personnel and facilities. Washington agreed. It also acknowledged "the Chinese position that Taiwan was a part of China" and pledged to conduct relations with the island on an unofficial basis. Although the administration concluded that it would be fruitless to seek a PRC pledge to use peaceful means to resolve the Taiwan Strait issue, it did insist on making a unilateral, uncontested statement of the abiding U.S. interest in a peaceful resolution.

While Washington thought that it had Beijing's understanding that it could continue arms sales to Taiwan, it found that Deng Xiaoping, China's new paramount leader, thought that the sales were ending. Indeed, Deng argued, unless they ended, Taipei would resist a peaceful reconciliation and so make China's use of force more likely. In the end, he agreed that normalization of relations between China and the United States should go ahead, but he reserved the right to reopen the issue.

The Carter administration had hoped that the breakthrough in normalization would be sufficient to reduce opposition from the ROC's congressional supporters, but a political firestorm erupted anyway. In drafting the Taiwan Relations Act (TRA) to create a structure for postnormalization relations with Taiwan, Congress sought to redress what it regarded as Carter's failure to ensure Taiwan's security. The law stated that it was U.S. policy to consider "any effort to determine the future of Taiwan by other than peaceful means, including by boycotts and embargoes, as a threat to the peace and security of the Western Pacific area and of grave concern to the United States." It authorized arms sales to ensure that Taiwan's military had a "sufficient self-defense capability" and required the executive branch to "inform the Congress promptly of any threat to the security or the social or economic system of the people on Taiwan and any danger to the interests of the United States arising therefrom." Although the PRC saw the TRA as inconsistent with the actions that the executive branch had taken, the law neither mandated arms sales to Taiwan nor provided a security guarantee to fully compensate for the termination of the mutual defense treaty. The TRA was more a statement of political commitment than a set of legally binding requirements, but it did reflect the strong support that the ROC still enjoyed in the United States.[14]

A Political Fencing Match

China now had the advantage. After having been at loggerheads with the United States for two decades over Taiwan and virtually everything else, Beijing got Washington to give up at least the formal trappings of its relationship with Taiwan in return for China's geopolitical alignment with the United States. The PRC had also beaten the ROC in the international arena. It had diplomatic relations with all but about thirty countries, and it now took its seat in the international organizations within the United Nations system. Having placed Taipei squarely on the defensive, Deng then sought to resolve the Taiwan issue once and for all. China lacked the ability to impose a military solution—and to do so would have alienated its new American partners—so he sought a political settlement. On New Year's Day 1979, the PRC announced a new policy of "peaceful unification" (instead of "liberation"), proposed discussions to end the state of cross-Strait confrontation and the opening of direct economic links with Taiwan, and promised to take Taiwan's "realities" into account and to respect the status quo. Chiang Ching-kuo's immediate response to the offer was to declare that there would be no contact, no negotiations, and no compromise with the PRC. If unification was to occur, he said, it would be on the basis of the anticommunist principles of Nationalist ideology.

In addition to Deng's peace overture, Chiang had to cope with a domestic challenge to his power. Opposition politicians sought to exploit U.S. derecognition of the ROC as grounds for attacking the KMT's legitimacy as the government of all China and so the basis of its denial of political power to the Taiwanese. They fashioned a network of legal magazine offices into an opposition organization (political parties were still illegal) and undertook a variety of public activities criticizing the regime. Chiang tolerated them for a while, but conservative forces soon convinced him that the situation was getting out of hand. The security services used a confrontation in the port city of Gaoxiong in December 1979 as an excuse to arrest most of the opposition leaders. A new period of openness had led to a new round of repression.

With the election of Ronald Reagan, China feared that the United States was going to reverse its policy, robbing Beijing of the advantage that it had gained vis-à-vis Taiwan. Deng had a two-pronged response. In September 1981, the PRC made a new peace overture to Taipei. In addition to reiterating its proposal for direct economic links and welcoming Taiwan's investment on the mainland, China offered a more detailed unification proposal. Once Taiwan came back into the fold, it would be a special administrative region of China with a high degree of autonomy. It could keep its economic and social system and its nongovernmental ties with foreign countries, even its armed forces. Taiwan's leaders could take positions in the Chinese government. This formed the conceptual core of the one-country, two-systems formula that China would elaborate for Hong Kong and Macau and continues to offer to Taiwan to this day. Taipei rejected the proposal then and continues to do so now.

One month later, Deng revealed the second prong. Beijing demanded that the United States end arms sales to Taiwan, on the grounds that Chiang Ching-kuo would have no incentive to respond to Beijing's new offer as long as they continued. China was prepared to end cooperation with the United

States unless Washington complied, and the Reagan administration was seriously divided between those who emphasized China's strategic value and those who were loath to sacrifice Taiwan's interests. In the end, the administration took the PRC's new peace offer as sufficient reason to agree in a communiqué issued in August 1982 to cap the quality of weapons it sold to Taiwan and to reduce their total dollar value, sending shock waves through Taiwan's government. Washington would later find ways to lessen the impact of the communiqué, but as of 1982 another pillar of Taiwan's survival was apparently weakening.[15]

Simultaneously, the United States posed yet another challenge to Taipei's position, this time to the KMT's political monopoly in Taiwan. This one came from liberals in Congress, urged on by Taiwanese American exiles. That was somewhat ironic, since Congress had always been Taipei's main instrument for restraining unfavorable initiatives by the executive branch, an instrument that it had fortified with tangible incentives to its friends on Capitol Hill. Now, Taiwanese Americans were providing similar support to members of Congress like Steve Solarz, Claiborne Pell, and Ted Kennedy, who publicly criticized KMT rule, gave moral support to the opposition, and suggested that a democratic Taiwan would better merit American support. The KMT regime used its influence to resist their efforts, but it ended up its own worst enemy. Exposure of a long-standing program of Taiwan's security services to monitor Taiwanese American political activity—and especially two egregious political killings, one in Taiwan in 1981 and another in the United States in 1984—seriously harmed the government's image in the United States. Neither the Reagan administration nor the ROC's friends in Congress would defend the regime.[16]

Chiang Ching-kuo was facing a different kind of pressure from within. Taiwan's business interests wanted to be able to trade with and invest in the mainland. There was a natural complementarity between the two economies, and wages were gradually rising on the island, reducing the competitiveness of its labor-intensive industries. U.S. pressure on Taiwan in 1987 to appreciate the value of the new Taiwan dollar would only increase the incentives for companies to move production offshore. So in spite of government prohibitions against any type of economic interaction, Taiwan companies were quietly testing the limits. The government knew that it was futile to try to stop them entirely and so embarked on a strategy of relaxing the limits gradually.[17]

Chiang Ching-kuo was getting advice from both reformers and conservatives on how to respond to these pressures. Conservatives argued that he should hold the line; reformers called for an economic opening to the mainland and liberalization of the political system. Chiang himself came to the counterintuitive conclusion that the KMT could better maintain its hold on power by opening up the political system than by continuing its repression of opposition activity—and that it could secure stronger support from the United States in the process. As early as 1982 he signaled that he had four goals for the rest of his tenure: democratization, Taiwanization, economic transformation to preserve prosperity, and opening up to China. The question for Chiang was not whether to liberalize but how fast to do it. By promoting his agenda, he also bought time for Taiwan to cope with the challenge that China presented. Within a few years he acted on his goals. In 1985, the government signaled that "indirect" trade with China—whereby goods had to be shipped through a third place, for example, Hong Kong— was acceptable. Then, in October 1986, Chiang did not order a crackdown when the opposition announced formation of the Democratic Progressive Party (DPP). He also revealed that he planned to end martial law. And in 1987 he officially allowed residents of Taiwan to travel to the mainland to visit their hometowns and relatives. Thus the KMT gradually removed the barricades of its cold war with the mainland and its barriers to political freedom at home.[18]

In January 1988, Chiang Ching-kuo died, his reform program still in its early infancy. Succeeding him was Lee Teng-hui, a Taiwanese scholar and technocrat who had been co-opted by the KMT but who retained a deep bitterness about how the regime had treated the native population. Initial assessments overestimated the strength of the conservative forces around Lee and underestimated his political skill. Within six years, Lee was able to dismantle the remaining props of authoritarianism and build the institutions of a democratic system. Democratization would broaden the spectrum of discussion within Taiwan about the island's relationship with China. The DPP would soon be free to advocate an independent Taiwan overtly and to test the idea with the voters.[19] All of those changes created anxiety in Beijing.

Two other developments were significant. The first was the Tiananmen Square incident in China, which shattered the consensus in the United States that maintaining a positive relationship with China was in U.S. interests and led some members of Congress to try to impose economic sanctions on China. It also removed a reason for limiting U.S. ties with Taiwan. Second, East European countries began to throw off Moscow's yoke, and soon the Soviet Union itself dissolved. That removed what had been the initial rationale for rapprochement between Washington and Beijing, although it was a waning justification by the mid-1980s anyway. It also had a profound practical effect. The end of the cold war created a global buyer's market for arms. The Soviet Union was desperate for customers for its defense industrial complex, and the Chinese military quickly seized the chance to acquire advanced air and naval systems. Those acquisitions foreshadowed a change in the military balance in the Taiwan Strait, so Taipei presented itself as a ready customer to American and European defense contractors, who themselves were looking for new buyers. The American firms in turn pressed the Bush administration to ease the decade-long policy of restraining arms sales to Taiwan.

The old order was coming to an end. Taiwan businesses were exploiting opportunities for trade with and investment in China while Taiwanese politicians were questioning whether China was where the island's future lay. American politicians began to question whether the past balance that Washington had struck between Beijing and Taipei still served U.S. interests. Beijing worried that shifts in Taiwan politics and U.S. policy would deny China its long-sought national unification. Those forces would combine to make the 1990s a decade of economic convergence and political deadlock, of coexistence and conflict.

3

Economic Cooperation, Political Deadlock

From 1949 until the mid-1980s, the Taiwan Strait was a no-man's-land. There was virtually no social or economic contact between mainland China and Taiwan, and the ideological gulf between the two was deep. Although there was usually little danger of war, the KMT regime maintained military vigilance toward the mainland and continued to repress the island's Taiwanese majority. Since the late 1980s, however, the story line has taken two very different paths: economically and socially, what was a no-man's-land is now a superhighway of cross-Strait trade and travel, while politically and militarily the two sides are locked in a stalemate of mistrust and hostility. Each side fears that the other threatens its fundamental interests, and the danger of war is higher now than it was twenty or thirty years ago. But it is a new sort of stalemate, shaped by the end of ideology on both sides of the Strait and by democratization on Taiwan, which has allowed the public an unprecedented voice in political issues and fostered the development of a uniquely Taiwanese identity.

The first of these stories—the product of economic and political imperatives on both the mainland and Taiwan—is easily told. Its phases have been defined by the inexorable transfer of manufacturing from Taiwan to the Chinese mainland and by the increasingly sophisticated technology of the products that Taiwan firms produce or assemble there.

The second story is more complex. It is the tale of China's effort to entice Taiwan into a national union and Taiwan's growing reluctance to comply in spite of their burgeoning economic ties. This story begins with Beijing's unification proposal, the same one-country, two-systems formula that was offered to Hong Kong. It continues with a series of responses from Taiwan, which became more reserved as time went on. At the center of this story are Taiwan's two recent presidents—Lee Teng-hui (1988–2000) and Chen Shui-bian (2000 to the present)—who have dominated Taiwan's cross-Strait policy within the context of Taiwan's democratic system. The tragedy of this tale is Beijing's belief that Lee and Chen wanted to permanently separate Taiwan from China and frustrate its goal of national unification. For Beijing, therefore, the reason that the cross-Strait conflict has persisted is their perfidy. Yet I conclude that in fact Beijing's belief has been a misinterpretation of Lee's and Chen's intentions. If my view is correct, then one must look elsewhere to explain why the dispute remains unresolved.

This chapter tells these two stories as they evolved over the 1990s. The economic and social tale is covered briefly. The political one is told at greater length and provides the context for the analysis of the current cross-Strait deadlock in later chapters.

Economic and Human Interaction

By the late 1970s, after four decades of failed policies, the Chinese Communist Party faced public alienation. Under the leadership of Deng Xiaoping, it decided that fostering economic growth was the only way to restore its legitimacy, but growth that was rapid enough to employ the burgeoning Chinese workforce required massive amounts of foreign investment. Taiwan business owners were an obvious source, because they had capital and because they were culturally Chinese. On Taiwan, meanwhile, companies that manufactured goods for the international market were losing their competitiveness because of the rising cost of land and labor, growing demands for environmental protections, and the appreciation of the new Taiwan dollar. Moving production offshore was an obvious way to prevent their goods from being priced out of the global market, and the mainland presented the best alternative production platform: the society was Chinese, local governments were providing special investment incentives, and the cost of land and labor was low. Moreover, someday the mainland might become a place to sell finished goods from Taiwan. There was a political dimension, of course. Beijing hoped that Taiwan investment would improve the climate for reunification, and Taipei feared that it would increase the island's political vulnerability to takeover by China.

The movement of production west across the Strait occurred in several waves. The first, in the late 1980s, was dominated by labor-intensive small and medium-sized enterprises (SMEs) that turned out products like gar-

Table 3-1. Taiwan's Investment in the PRC, 1989–2003
Millions of dollars

Year	Number of cases	Contracted investment	Realized investment	Cumulative contracted investment
1991	1,735	1,389	466	. . .
1992	6,430	5,543	1,051	6,932
1993	10,948	9,965	3,139	16,897
1994	6,247	5,395	3,391	22,292
1995	4,847	5,849	3,162	28,141
1996	3,184	5,141	3,475	33,282
1997	3,014	2,814	3,289	36,096
1998	2,970	2,982	2,915	39,078
1999	2,499	3,374	2,599	42,452
2000	3,108	4,042	2,296	46,494
2001	4,196	6,904	3,158	53,398
2002	4,853	6,741	3,971	60,139
2003	4,495	8,560	3,380	68,699
2004	4,002	9,310	3,120	78,009

Source: 1991–2003 data: www.chinafdi.org.cn/chinese/article_view.asp?id=1086 (April 15, 2005); 2004 data: http://tga.mofcom.gov.cn/aarticle/d/200501/20050100338608.html (April 15, 2005).

ments, shoes, and basic consumer electronics. The second wave occurred in the mid-1990s, as larger Taiwan firms in sectors such as petrochemicals and food processing joined the SMEs. One reason was to get behind Chinese tariff barriers and so continue to provide cheap raw materials to their Taiwan SME customers or, in the case of food processing, to market goods in China itself. The third wave surged in the late 1990s as information technology (IT) firms, which had become the dominant sector of Taiwan's economy, moved to the mainland to maintain the competitiveness of their low-end products. The recession that began in 2000, which hit the global IT industry especially hard, only accelerated the trend. By 2003, half of the 1,000 top Taiwan companies had investments in the PRC. Investment projects approved by Taiwan's government have surpassed $30 billion, and as table 3-1 suggests, the total contracted amount is double or triple the approved figure. By one estimate, the PRC accounted for 74 percent of Taiwan's total foreign direct investment from 1991 to 2002.[1]

Investment drove trade. The bulk of the products that Taiwan shipped to the mainland were components for assembly; the bulk of the products that

Table 3-2. Cross-Strait Trade, 1990–2004
Millions of dollars

Year	Total	PRC imports from Taiwan	PRC exports to Taiwan
1990	2,574	2,254	320
1991	3,964	3,369	595
1992	6,588	5,890	698
1993	14,395	12,934	1,461
1994	16,326	14,084	2,242
1995	17,880	14,785	3,095
1996	18,990	16,186	2,804
1997	19,834	16,435	3,399
1998	20,560	16,694	3,866
1999	23,478	19,528	3,950
2000	30,534	25,494	5,040
2001	32,350	27,344	5,006
2002	44,672	38,082	6,590
2003	58,367	49,362	9,005
2004	78,320	64,780	13,540

Source: 1990–2003: International Monetary Fund, *Direction of Trade Statistics* (Washington: 1996, 2003, and 2004); 2004: "2004 Nian Liangan Maoyi Touzi Qingkuang," Ministry of Commerce of the People's Republic of China, Department of Taiwan, Hong Kong, and Macao Affairs, January 25, 2005 (http://tga.mofcom.gov.cn/aarticle/d/200501/20050100338068.html).

went from the mainland to Taiwan were finished or almost finished goods. Two-way cross-Strait trade totaled $78.3 billion in 2004—$64.8 billion in exports from Taiwan; $13.5 billion in exports from the mainland. In 2004, 25.8 percent of Taiwan's exports went to the PRC, making it the island's primary trading partner, ahead of even the United States.[2] Table 3-2 charts the trends in cross-Strait two-way trade.

The networked character of Taiwan companies makes the migration more complicated than it might seem. You-tien Hsing's study of the migration of the Taiwan shoe industry, which occurred during the initial phase of this transition, provides an excellent example of this complexity.[3] Shoe making is a highly competitive industry. Manufacturers must not only reduce costs as much as possible but also respond constantly to changes in fashion while meeting tight delivery schedules. Taiwan's shoe industry is composed of horizontal networks of producers that specialize in a variety of products and of vertical networks that link product development and production, manufacturers and suppliers (upstream and downstream), manufacturers and subcontractors, and manufacturers and trading companies that link Asian products to international markets.

After the mid-1980s, some parts of those networks, but not all, moved to the mainland. Indeed, a complex and shifting geographic division of labor evolved within the industry that was determined by where each task could be performed most efficiently and effectively. As of the mid-1990s, 80 to 90 percent of activities related to information collection, product development, product design and testing, research and development, and marketing and sales were concentrated in Taiwan. Two-thirds of production was done on the mainland, but the rest was still done on Taiwan. Some information collection, marketing, and sales activities were done overseas. Such an arrangement could not work without the special management skills of the firms involved and the cooperation of local mainland officials, which usually was willingly offered.[4]

The second and third waves of investment have linked economic actors in Taiwan and China more tightly into global supply chains that include Japan, Europe, and especially the United States. Their collaboration represents an adjustment by each to the imperatives of globalization. For example, Taiwan companies have taken the middle position in the information technology chain. Generally, American firms provide the brands, the sophisticated technology and components, and marketing services. Their Taiwan partners provide some technology, advanced components, and management services. The Taiwan operations on the mainland do much of the manufacturing and assembly that used to be done on the island. This is a mutually beneficial arrangement. By cutting costs, Taiwan firms remain the supplier of choice for brand-name companies such as Dell and Compaq, which also benefit from the management and other skills of the Taiwan firms in providing access to China's market. Chinese partners likewise get valuable access to the international market through the services of these firms.[5]

Taiwan's personal computer (PC) industry, which was built on a foundation of experience in electronics manufacturing, the talents of engineers, and government assistance, offers a good example of a complex and evolving global supply chain at work.[6] Personal computers are assembled from a much larger number of components than shoes are, and some of them—logic integrated circuits, memory integrated circuits, chip sets, smaller liquid crystal displays, cathode ray tubes, and motherboards, to name just a few—are very sophisticated. PCs also require midstream peripheral items like keyboards, monitors, image scanners, PC mouses, and power supply units. Taiwan PC companies did not seek to manufacture all of these components in house but instead created an "extensive network of vertical linkages within the industry . . . ranging from upstream electronic components and parts . . . to the final assembly of desktop and portable PCs."[7] Because PCs were produced primarily for the export market and because of the constant pressure to cut costs, over time Taiwan's main PC firms moved some elements of their networks to the mainland and other locations in order to remain competitive and maintain their middle position in the supply chain. Small suppliers producing only a few items on a small scale moved first. Then more differentiated, medium-sized firms moved some operations while upgrading others on the island. The large manufacturers that make a large variety of items—and whose production outside of Taiwan is an integral but supplemental part of their overall strategy—were the last to move, and they do so on a selective basis.[8]

The shift of production from Taiwan in the IT industry and other sectors only accelerated at the end of the twentieth century. Several factors were at work. The recession in the IT industry created downward pressure on production prices. If Taiwan companies were to remain competitive, they had to squeeze costs in products like laptop computers. Simultaneously, the entry of Taiwan and China into the World Trade Organization foreshadowed lower trade barriers between the two. The transfer of power on Taiwan from the Kuomintang to the Democratic Progressive Party fostered some uncertainty about the investment climate on the island, and the DPP's political stance toward China would affect the fortunes of companies that had tied their futures to the mainland.

In a hypercompetitive global environment, reducing costs was not the only challenge for Taiwan's IT companies; they also had to ensure quality control and on-time delivery. They could not guarantee timeliness if the Taiwanese subcontractors who provided components remained on the island, and they could not count on new Chinese subcontractors on the mainland for quality. The only solution was for the whole network of supplier firms to move to the mainland to support the core company. As Terry Cooke concludes, "This, more than any other factor, explains the rapidity and scale of the migration of IT manufacturing across the Taiwan Strait in recent years. Individual firms were not making the decision to relocate. Instead, entire supply chains or sub-ecosystems were moving *en masse*." There was a side benefit for Taiwan firms: not only did they preserve their share in international markets, but by being on the mainland, they also obtained better access to the Chinese domestic market.[9]

With investment came human interaction. Several hundred thousand Taiwan people are now living in Shanghai and its suburb Kunshan, in Dongguan in Guangdong province, and in other Chinese urban areas. Because the employment situation on Taiwan was rather gloomy, young people looked across the Strait for jobs. A 2004 survey found that 30 percent of those surveyed expressed "a high interest" in working on the mainland while 15 percent considered moving there permanently.[10] According to Taiwan government estimates, there have been more than 200,000 cross-Strait marriages (half of which have endured).[11] Taiwan schools have been established in Dongguan and Kunshan to cater to the children of the Taiwan people in those areas. More significant is the flow of sophisticated talent among Silicon Valley in California, Hsinchu in Taiwan (where a science-based industrial park is located), and Kunshan, much of it made up of ethnic Chinese of various nationalities. U.S.-educated Taiwan engineers have fostered the movement of technology, capital, and expertise between the United States and Taiwan and the development of productive business partnerships. As Taiwan companies move more production to China, they put their younger Taiwan-raised executives in charge of mainland operations and recruit talented Chinese engineers. Young Taiwan IT entrepreneurs build relationships with China's young entrepreneurs and the children of high-ranking officials, and they may attend Chinese business schools. In turn, Silicon Valley is a magnet for talented engineers from both China and Taiwan.[12]

Such human interaction has proliferated beyond the economic arena into just about all realms of social life. Take, for example, contacts reported in the press in June 2001:

—Museum curators from Taiwan's National Museum of History and the Henan provincial museum jointly produced a catalogue of bronze objects from the tomb of a Western Zhou nobleman, Prince Zeng. The objects were excavated in the early twentieth century, and some of them probably were removed to Taiwan before the KMT's retreat to Taiwan in 1949.

—Pilgrims from a Taoist temple in Yunlin County, Taiwan, made a pilgrimage to the mother temple in Quanzhou, Fujian province. Taiwan temples have organized many such pilgrimages since the late 1980s to restore spiritual bonds that were cut after 1949.

—Taiwan's universities have had extensive exchange programs with their mainland counterparts. National Taiwan University has had links with Peking, Nanjing, Fudan, and Qinghua universities and with the University of Science and Technology of China. The Yuan Ze University has had ties with Qinghua, Beijing, Jiaotong, and Hefei science and technology universities. During June 2001, educators from both sides held a conference on adult education in Taipei.

— Three thousand Taiwan students have studied at mainland universities in the fields of law; finance; accounting; Chinese literature, history, and religion; and Chinese traditional medicine.

—Through the major Taiwan charitable organization, the Tzu Chi Foundation, Taiwan donors have provided bone marrow to mainland patients suffering from leukemia. As of June 2001, eighty-six such donations had been made.

—In the latest example of sports exchanges (including baseball, basketball, and swimming), athletes from China and Taiwan participated in a long-distance race to promote China's bid to host the 2008 Olympics. Taiwan cyclists finished a week-long cycling tour on the mainland.

—The Taipei and Shanghai municipalities held a nine-day city cultural exchange.

—In the realm of maritime disaster relief, Taiwan's coast guard rescued fishermen from a Chinese freighter that ran aground.

—Through the interaction of the Red Cross societies of the two sides, Taiwan sent back a number of illegal immigrants from the mainland and eight PRC nationals who high-jacked airplanes to Taiwan. The PRC transferred to Taiwan four criminals wanted on the island.[13]

Yet it is easy to exaggerate the extent of cross-Strait human interaction. Emerson Niou has discovered that a significant majority of the Taiwan population has had little or no direct exposure to the PRC. Based on recent polling, 67.8 percent have not traveled at all to the mainland since 1987 and an additional 12.7 percent have visited only once. Only 13.1 percent of Taiwan respondents or their family members have gone to study, work, do business, or reside in the PRC.[14]

Moreover, not everyone in Taiwan regards the growing interaction with the mainland to be an unalloyed blessing. The island's growing economic dependence on China in particular fosters fears about the PRC's potential leverage. T. J. Cheng and Denny Roy have offered analyses of the three most important forms of possible Chinese influence. The first is the "hostage effect," the possibility that Beijing might impose economic sanctions on Taiwan to achieve political ends or that a significant economic downturn in an unstable China would automatically hurt Taiwan. The second is the "hollowing out effect," whereby the economy on the island becomes progressively weaker because manufacturing migrates to the mainland and China simultaneously becomes more technologically proficient and economically competitive because of Taiwan's help. The third is the "fifth column effect," in which Taiwan businesses with a presence in China might promote their interests in ways that are biased in favor of Beijing—or Chinese agents and saboteurs might take advantage of cross-Strait economic and social interaction in order to infiltrate Taiwan.[15]

Cheng concludes that these three modes of Chinese influence are not likely to work as feared. Economic sanctions probably would be counterproductive because China depends on Taiwan companies for investment, employment, and export markets.[16] China's emergence as the key manufacturing center in East Asia and the movement of Taiwan production there do pose a challenge to the island's economy, in that it will have to find new competitive niches to ensure high-wage, full employment on the island. Although that is a serious challenge, the political leverage that it creates for China is indirect at best. And Taiwan business interests have been careful not to promote Beijing's agenda actively (but more on that later). Roy argues that Taiwan's entrepreneurs, not its government, should do the risk assessment regarding the Chinese economy.

Two realities are at work in Taiwan's anxiety over economic interdependence with the mainland. On one hand, even if Taipei wanted to stop the flow of investment and the transfer of production across the Strait, it would be hard pressed to do so. Lee Teng-hui tried during the late 1990s, under his "no haste, be patient" policy, which restricted investment in larger projects, such as power plants. In the event, a lot of manufacturing was moved to the mainland nevertheless, and when necessary Taiwan companies moved funds through third parties. On the other hand, even if the concerns about closer cross-Strait economic integration are unjustified, the fact that some Taiwan people have them makes them politically relevant—which is only one of several elements of the stalemate between Taipei and Beijing.

Political Deadlock

Why has such a generally positive and mutually beneficial interaction not led to political reconciliation? To answer that question—and so illuminate why the Taiwan Strait issue is so hard to resolve—it is necessary to examine in detail how the two sides have bargained over the terms under which unification might occur. The bargaining has taken place in several stages. The first, in the early 1990s, held the greatest promise. Each side had some confidence in the intentions of the other; Taiwan was prepared to put forward ideas of its own; and the two met at a high level concerning nonpolitical issues. The second stage, in the mid-1990s, was a time of tension. Lee Teng-hui became increasingly frustrated with Beijing's failure to accommodate his fundamental views on unification. Tensions were highest in 1995 and 1996, after Lee Teng-hui's visit to the United States. The third stage occurred in the late 1990s, as cross-Strait dialogue resumed and political negotiations became a live possibility. In advance of those talks, Lee Teng-hui sought to better define Taiwan's position, but he misplayed his hand and negotiations never occurred. The fourth stage came with the victory of Chen Shui-bian in the March 2000 presidential elections; over the next two years, he signaled a desire to engage Beijing, to no avail. The fifth stage comprised the campaign for the March 2004 elections, when Chen was seeking a second term.

The purpose here is not to provide a full history of cross-Strait relations over the past ten years or more but to explore the PRC's explanation of why reconciliation has not occurred: that Lee Teng-hui and Chen Shui-bian were in fact separatists and were not interested in unification. That judgment has become part of the conventional wisdom on cross-Strait relations, and it is one possible explanation for the political stalemate. Yet it should be subjected to objective evaluation rather than accepted at face value. Careful analysis of Lee's and Chen's authoritative statements leads me to conclude that China's allegations are not justified. That is not to say that Lee and Chen did not contribute to the deadlock but that the reason for stalemate does not lie in their fundamental goals. Rather it is a function of the interaction of three factors: their serious substantive concerns about China's approach to unification; Beijing's relatively inflexible response to their concerns; and an increasingly competitive political environment on the island. It was that interaction that produced conceptual deadlock and a spiral of mutual antagonism and mistrust.[17]

One Country, Two Systems

The one-country, two-systems formula had its roots in ideas on unification that the PRC conveyed secretly to Taipei in the 1950s.[18] They lay dormant for almost two decades before being revived in the late 1970s, and by the mid-1980s they had crystallized into a set of proposals that persist to this day.

The first step in that crystallization occurred on New Year's Day 1979, two weeks after the announcement of the normalization of relations between the United States and the People's Republic of China. As Taipei was still absorbing the shock, the standing committee of China's National People's Congress (NPC) issued a "message to Taiwan compatriots." The statement asserted that "the world in general recognizes only one China, with the Government of the People's Republic of China as the sole legal government," thereby rejecting the ROC's claim that it was the—or even a—government of China. It also asserted that the "reunification of China" was "the general trend of development" and that "no one can stop this trend." Besides that definition of the situation, the message contained several additional elements of importance. First of all, the word "reunification" replaced the term "liberation," which has a more aggressive connotation. Second, the statement announced an end to the every-other-day ritualistic shelling of the offshore islands of Jinmen and Mazu and called for talks to end the existing "state of military confrontation" between the two sides. Third, the call for talks identified the two sides as the "Government of the People's Republic of China" and "the Taiwan authorities" (*dangju*). That is, the two had very different statuses: Beijing was a legal government and Taipei was something less. Fourth, the message said that China's leaders would "take present realities into account, ... respect the status quo on Taiwan and the opinions of people in all walks of life there and adopt reasonable policies and measures in settling the question of reunification." Finally, the statement called for the early establishment of transportation and postal services in order to facilitate "people-to-people interaction" and claimed that "there is every reason for us to develop trade between us." Although the message did not go beyond these basic issues, the seeds of the one-country, two-systems formula were sown.[19]

The first major elaboration of the statement came on September 30, 1981, delivered by Ye Jianying, a Communist Party elder who was the chairman of the NPC's standing committee. Among his "nine points," he stated that

—the Chinese Communist Party (CCP) and the KMT should hold talks "on a reciprocal basis" to facilitate cooperation for national reunification.

—the two sides should make arrangements and conclude an agreement on cross-Strait postal service, trade, air and shipping services, visits, and various kinds of exchanges.

—after unification, Taiwan would be able to "enjoy a high degree of autonomy as a special administrative region" and that "the central government" would not interfere with "local affairs on the island."

—Taiwan would be able to retain its armed forces.

—Taiwan's current socioeconomic system, as well as its way of life and economic and cultural relations with foreign countries, would remain unchanged. Property rights would not be encroached upon.

—various Taiwan "people in authority and representative personages" could take up PRC leadership posts.

—Taiwan people who wished to settle on the mainland could do so and would not suffer discrimination.

—Taiwan industrialists and businesspeople would be welcome to invest and engage in business ventures on the mainland, with guarantees of their legal rights, interests, and profits.[20]

Ye Jianying's offer put flesh on the bones of the 1979 message. Most of the elements of the one-country, two-systems concept were included: preservation of Taiwan's socioeconomic system, Taiwan's right to maintain its military, articulation of the concept of a special administrative region with a high degree of autonomy, noninterference by the central government in "local affairs," the establishment of various economic and people-to-people links, and appeals to Taiwan companies to invest in China. The political relationship between the two was defined as that between a central government (Beijing) and a subordinate region. And, unlike with the 1979 proposal, wherein the PRC government and the "Taiwan authorities" were to negotiate an end to hostilities, discussions of unification were to be conducted on a party-to-party basis, another way of downgrading the legitimacy of the ROC government.

In January 1982 Deng Xiaoping reportedly used the phrase "one country, two systems," for the first time, indicating that the systems he was talking about were economic systems: socialism on the mainland and capitalism on Taiwan.[21] Deng next discussed unification in June 1983, with Seton Hall University professor Winston Yang. He repeated many of Ye's points but added a few elements. Completely new was the idea that on judicial matters, Taiwan could exercise independent jurisdiction and the right of final judgment "need not reside in Beijing." He specified that Taiwan authorities could administer "party, governmental, and military systems" but warned that the armed forces could not be a threat to China. He made clear that after unification Taiwan's government would be a local one and that complete autonomy was impossible: "Complete autonomy means two Chinas, not one. Different systems may be practiced, but it must be the People's Republic of China alone that represents China internationally."[22]

The one-country, two-systems model took even more definite form in December 1984, when Great Britain and China signed a joint declaration on Hong Kong. It contained both familiar elements and new elaborations:

—establishment of the Hong Kong Special Administrative Region (HKSAR), "directly under the authority of the central government"

—a high degree of autonomy, except in foreign affairs and defense, which were the responsibility of the central government

—vesting in the HKSAR of executive, legislative, and "independent judicial power" and a promise that existing laws then in place would remain unchanged unless amended by the HKSAR

—continuation of the current social and economic systems

—constitution of the HKSAR government by "local inhabitants" (selected according to guidelines that were included as annexes to the joint declaration)

—specific guidelines on the maintenance of the HKSAR's economic and cultural relations with other countries and Hong Kong's participation in international organizations and agreements under the aegis of the PRC

—protection of private property, ownership of enterprises, right of inheritance, and foreign investment.

The joint declaration included two completely new elements. First, it mandated that internationally recognized human rights and freedoms would be ensured by law. That provision was not surprising since civil liberties were part of Hong Kong's system and arguably one element of continuity, but London probably had insisted on it in order to forestall criticism in Hong Kong, Britain, and around the world. Second, the Chinese National People's Congress would enact a "Basic Law" for the HKSAR that would embody all these policies.

At its core, the one-country, two-systems proposal was an offer of home rule. The central government, to which all special administrative regions were subordinate, was in Beijing. Under the leadership of local residents, SAR governments had the authority to administer local political, economic, and other affairs. As a PRC legal scholar would write about Hong Kong in 2004: "State sovereignty is the premise of local power. Local autonomy . . . is merely a pattern of power distribution within a sovereign state. . . . The political, economic and legal systems of Hong Kong are part of the national system instead of independent ones out of the national system."[23] The central government was the exclusive sovereign, the representative of China in the international system. SARs could have economic and cultural relations with other countries, but their external activities were conducted at the discretion of the sovereign and could not undermine its rights and prerogatives.

Phase One: Taiwan's Positive Response

Lee Teng-hui became the president of the Republic of China in January 1988, after the death of Chiang Ching-kuo. Soon thereafter, he offered his views on the PRC's one-country, two-systems formula, and not surprisingly they were consistent with Taipei's customary position—that unification could occur only in accordance with the Three Principles of the People, enunciated by the KMT's founder, Sun Yat-sen: nationalism, democracy, and the equal distribution of wealth. The ideological gap between the communist mainland and anticommunist Taiwan was simply too great for

Taiwan to concede on the issue. Also unacceptable from Taipei's point of view was Beijing's use of united front tactics to exert pressure and its refusal to renounce the use of force.

That Lee's early statements aligned with the conventional ROC position was understandable. He was politically weak, a Taiwanese among a leadership that was still dominated by mainlanders. His reelection in March 1990 was not ensured. The opposition within the KMT was such that Lin Yang-kang would challenge him for the presidency, and students would demonstrate for reform. Even though he won reelection, he had to agree to install General Hau Pei-tsun as premier. Moreover, Lee's initial instinct was to pursue democratization on Taiwan before moving to cross-Strait issues. Yet his initial statement identified two key issues that would define the Taiwan Strait issue for the duration of his presidency: the one-country, two-systems proposal was unacceptable because, as he put it, its underlying objective was "localizing the ROC government" and because Beijing had not renounced the use of force.[24] Still, his views were very general, and no ideas on how these issues might be negotiated were suggested.

Once elected, however, Lee had more freedom to change Taiwan's political system and reshape its policy toward the mainland in a way that was more systematic and forward-looking than his previous statements indicated. Lee was under some pressure from Taiwan business executives who wanted to expand trade and investment in China, and they used Taiwan's increasingly democratic system to promote their interests.[25] But Lee still did not have a free hand; he had to accommodate others in the leadership. Most important, he had changed his view on whether to emphasize the domestic or the cross-Strait front, concluding that he had to maintain a balance among domestic politics, cross-Strait relations, and Taiwan's international role. Instead of pushing domestic political change first, as he had proposed in the late 1980s, Lee sought in the early 1990s to achieve a breakthrough with Beijing in order to speed constitutional reform and democratization. His logic was that a reduction in the Taiwan sense of threat from the mainland would make it easier to justify removing past restrictions on domestic political expression and competition.[26]

Lee presented his new approach at his inauguration in May 1990. Taiwan and the mainland, he said, "are indivisible parts of China" and all Chinese were "compatriots of the same flesh and blood" who together should seek peaceful and democratic means to achieve the "common goal of national unification." Noting the global democratic tide, Lee offered the following proposal to the PRC:

If the Chinese communist authorities can recognize the overall world trend and the common hope of all Chinese, implement democracy and a free economic system; renounce the use of military force in the Taiwan Strait and do not interfere with our development of foreign relations on the basis of a one-China policy, we would be willing, on a basis of equality, to establish channels of communication, and completely open up academic, cultural, economic, trade, scientific, and technological exchange, to lay a foundation of mutual respect, peace, and prosperity. We hope then, when objective conditions are right, we will be able to discuss our national reunification, based on the common will of the Chinese people on both sides of the Taiwan Strait.

For the first time, Taiwan offered its ideas on how the two sides might get to the goal that they both claimed to want. Lee specified three things that the PRC would have to do to open the lines of communication and exchange: democratize, renounce the use of force, and exercise diplomatic restraint. He also insisted that contacts occur on an equal basis—a concept that later would be defined more precisely. And he promised talks on unification when conditions were right. [27]

Beijing recognized the possibility of progress represented by Lee's new approach, and a complex courtship between the two sides ensued. Much was conducted in public, visible to domestic audiences and the United States, but there also were secret meetings between representatives of the top leaders in Beijing and Taipei.[28] Although neither side gave up the competition for international influence and a variety of nettlesome procedural and substantive issues were in play, there was confidence that a political settlement might be possible. Both sides set up institutional structures to conduct cross-Strait relations. In late 1990 and early 1991, Taiwan created a three-tier structure: the National Unification Council (NUC), chaired by Lee Teng-hui, to set broad policy parameters; the Mainland Affairs Council (MAC), established within the Executive Yuan (cabinet), to set policy guidelines and supervise implementation; and the semiofficial Straits Exchange Foundation (SEF), which, under MAC guidance, would interact with the PRC and solve practical problems. The PRC's counterpart to the MAC was the Taiwan Affairs Office, a joint agency of the State Council (the top governmental body) and the Central Committee of the Chinese Communist Party. The analogue to SEF was the Association for Relations across the Taiwan Strait (ARATS), which was established in December 1991. Beijing ultimately would create the Leaders' Small Group on Taiwan Affairs as something of a counterpart to the NUC. The creation of SEF and ARATS was particularly important, for it gave the two sides a way to meet, even at a symbolically high level, without violating each other's political principles.

In February 1991, the NUC formalized Lee's approach in the National Unification Guidelines (NUG), which the Executive Yuan adopted in March of the same year. The guidelines stated a single goal—to establish a democratic, free, and equitably prosperous China—and established four principles:

—The mainland and Taiwan were parts of China and unification was the responsibility of all Chinese.

—Unification should be done for the people's welfare and not become a subject of partisan wrangling.

—Unification should promote Chinese culture, human dignity, fundamental human rights, democracy, and the rule of law.

—Unification should ensure the rights, interests, security, and welfare of the people of the "Taiwan area" and should be achieved in gradual phases under the principles of reason, peace, parity, and reciprocity.

The NUG also altered some of the details of the process that Lee had suggested in May 1990. The first, short-term, stage was to promote exchange and reciprocity. Taipei and Beijing would eliminate their mutual state of hostility, solve all disputes through peaceful means under the one-China principle, not deny the other's existence as a political entity, and respect each other in the international community. That done, the two sides would create the institutional and legal structure for cross-Strait exchanges and reduce limits on contacts. In the meantime, Taiwan would speed up its constitutional reform effort and the PRC should continue its reform process, ultimately allowing freedom of expression and implementing democracy.

The NUG also changed Lee's three conditions for beginning the first stage. Democratization in China was no longer a precondition; instead, each side had only to respect the other as a political entity. The other conditions were softened. Each was stated as a parallel and reciprocal obligation (*both* should resolve disputes peacefully; *each* should promote democracy), and all obligations were to be assumed during the course of the first phase, not prior to it. In particular, Taipei would later claim that it had formulated the "political entity" concept in order to foster cross-Strait interaction. The term was "quite broad," the government asserted: "It can be applied to a state, a government, or a political organization." It was a type of creative ambiguity.[29]

Lee's inaugural address had set forth only two stages in the unification process, but the NUG proposed three. "Mutual trust and cooperation" was the essence of the NUG's second phase, in which official communications and direct postal, transportation, and commercial ties (the PRC's "three links") would begin. High-ranking officials would undertake mutual visits, and they would collaborate within international organizations. The third phase would be similar to Lee's original second stage: the two sides would create a consultative organization to discuss unification and map out a constitutional system for a unified China.[30]

In the spring of 1991, Taiwan's National Assembly passed a number of amendments to the constitution and terminated the "period of national mobilization" declared by the KMT government. On April 30, 1991, Lee announced that Taiwan "will not use force to achieve national unification." From now on, he declared, "We shall regard the Chinese Communists as a political entity ruling the mainland area" and no longer as a "rebel regime." In effect, Taipei renounced its attitude of hostility toward Beijing. Lee also endorsed the work of the NUC and its guidelines and restated his view that the ROC was a sovereign country. He also put Beijing on notice. If it did not want Taipei to "regard the Mainland as an antagonistic political entity," then it would have to renounce force and stop its quarantine of Taiwan in the international community. Still, he was prepared to be patient if Beijing's immediate response was not positive. Finally, he described the dispute with the PRC as one of a "divided nation."[31]

In short, the government of Taiwan had reaffirmed the goal of national unification. Moreover, it had laid out a process for reaching that goal, one that was more detailed than anything Beijing had offered. It made a virtue of the reality that the use of force was not a practical option for Taiwan, and it clarified the issues that would be the keys to progress: the legal identity of Taiwan's government, its right to participate in the international system, and the PRC's renunciation of the use of force.

The PRC rejected Lee's approach. In June 1991, it restated its opposition to Taiwan's independence ("two Chinas"); refused to renounce the use of force; and stated that negotiations would have to be conducted between the KMT and the CCP (Taipei had rejected party-to-party talks as inconsistent with its view that the two sides were separate political entities).[32] China also sought to use nonpolitical issues to achieve political gains. The burgeoning economic and human contacts between Taiwan and the PRC created the need for at least semiofficial contacts and understandings. When Taipei, through the SEF, sought to reach such understandings, Beijing demanded that draft agreements on practical issues like smuggling and piracy, notarization of documents, and tracking lost mail had to include reference to the "one-China principle." Taiwan was reluctant to comply because doing so might constitute acceptance of Beijing's claim that Taipei constituted a local government. That most countries in the world and the United Nations regarded the PRC government as the sole legal government of China intensified Taipei's caution. So, fearing a political trap, it rejected Beijing's demand.

Positive momentum resumed in July 1992. In a secret meeting, Wang Daohan, the head of ARATS, and Su Zhicheng, a key aide of Lee Teng-hui, decided that the way out of the impasse was for Wang to meet his counterpart, Koo Chen-fu, chairman of SEF, in Singapore. In preparation for the meeting, there was movement through the summer and fall toward reaching a side understanding on how to deal with the problem of the one-China principle as it pertained to SEF-ARATS agreements so that progress could be made in functional areas. As part of that process, Lee and his government decided to define "China" more precisely. On August 1, 1992, the National Unification Council, which Lee chaired, passed a significant resolution. It reaffirmed adherence to the one-China principle and the position that the geographic entities of the mainland and Taiwan both were parts of China. It made clear that the two governments had conflicting definitions of the meaning of "one China." Beijing's position, the resolution said, was that China was the PRC and that Taiwan after reunification would have the same, subordinate status as Hong Kong. For its part, Taipei made a three-part assertion:

—China meant the ROC, which was founded in 1912 and was by implication a successor state to the Qing dynasty.

—The ROC's sovereignty still covered all of China but its government's "political power" (jurisdiction) covered only Taiwan, Penghu, Jinmen, and Mazu. (To say that Taiwan's sovereignty was confined to Taiwan, Penghu, Jinmen, and Mazu would have been even more objectionable because Beijing might have taken it as asserting the existence of a separate Taiwan state.) This point would resurface in a controversy in 2003.

—China therefore was a divided country, with two political entities ruling their respective side of the Strait.[33]

Events on other fronts in late summer probably complicated the quest for a Koo-Wang meeting. Beijing continued its campaign to marginalize Taipei in the international arena and won a victory on that front in August 1992, when it established diplomatic relations with South Korea, long a diplomatic partner of the ROC. Taiwan, on the other hand, scored some successes in the global buyer's market for advanced arms, securing U.S. approval for 150 F-16 aircraft in September 1992 and French approval for sixty Mirage fighters in November of the same year. In October, at the Chinese Communist Party's Fourteenth Congress, General Secretary Jiang Zemin presented a view on cross-Strait relations that constituted a rejection of Taiwan's August statement on one China. In his political report to the congress, Jiang declared, "We resolutely oppose 'two Chinas,' 'one China, one Taiwan,' or 'one country, two governments' *in any form*. We resolutely oppose any attempts and actions designed to make Taiwan independent." This was an outright rejection of Taipei's concept of a divided country. Jiang also reiterated the call to move toward talks on "the formal end of hostilities and gradual realization of peaceful reunification." But those talks would be between the CCP and the KMT (not the PRC government and the Taiwan authorities, as in the 1979 offer), thus denying the ROC its status as a sovereign government.[34]

Still, the two sides chose to paper over their differences and ignore outside distractions in order to go forward with the April 1993 meeting between Koo Chen-fu and Wang Daohan. Beijing set aside its requirement that the one-China principle be mentioned in the texts of the technical agreements to be signed. In the fall of 1992, there emerged through an exchange of communications an understanding that permitted the meeting to go forward. In the final exchange, the ARATS formulation of the "consensus" was that "both sides of the Taiwan Strait uphold that One-China principle and strive to seek national unification. However, in routine cross-Strait consultations, the political meaning of 'One China' will not be involved." SEF stated that "although the two sides uphold the One-China principle in the process of striving for cross-Strait national unification, each side has its own understanding of the meaning of One China." Thus ARATS and SEF both stated that the two sides upheld the one-China principle (which was factually true at the time), but they differed on whether their differences on the issue were procedural or substantive. ARATS said that the political meaning of one China need not be addressed in routine consultations; Taiwan asserted that the two sides disagreed on what the concept meant.[35] This understanding was little noted at the time, but it later became famous as the "1992 consensus" (see chapter 9).

Mutual adjustments made it possible for Koo Chen-fu and Wang Daohan to finally meet, in Singapore in April 1993, where they approved four agreements, including one on regular meetings between SEF and ARATS. The meeting was probably the high point of cross-Strait interaction, and SEF and ARATS continued to meet on routine issues. But the disagreement over the one-China principle foreshadowed the political deadlock to come.

Phase Two: A Tougher Taiwan Line and the Cornell Crisis

Lee Teng-hui's approach to the PRC shifted in 1993. The key components of his prior approach persisted: the PRC must acknowledge the ROC as an equivalent political entity; it must accommodate Taipei's role in the international system; and it must renounce the use of force.[36] But he changed his emphasis, tone, and style, moving from ambiguity toward greater clarity.

Domestic politics was one reason for the shift. With the support of progressives in his own party and moderates in the Democratic Progressive Party, he had engineered a fundamental change in the membership of the Legislative Yuan and the National Assembly. The elderly members who had run for office on the mainland in the late 1940s were retired. Elections would be held in geographically defined districts on Taiwan to pick most of the new members, with the rest of the new members picked by the political parties according to their share of seats in the geographic districts. In the National Assembly election of December 1991, the DPP had overestimated popular support for declaring a Republic of Taiwan and had done badly. But it moderated its appeal in campaigning for the Legislative Yuan election of December 1992 and was able to expand its political power to a new level. The DPP won 36 percent of the vote and 50 of 162 seats in the legislature, which gave it more opportunities to criticize the government.

To check the opposition's growing momentum, Lee sought to co-opt its issues. Taiwan's global status and role—or lack thereof—was probably the issue that most required a response. People on Taiwan were frustrated by the island's exclusion from international organizations, and since 1990 the public had responded positively to the DPP's proposal that Taiwan try to join the United Nations. That response had given the DPP a weapon with which to challenge the Kuomintang, so in 1993 the government co-opted the issue and began a formal UN campaign. Its action was consistent with Lee's longstanding demand that Taiwan have a greater international role, his belief that an expanded role could stimulate positive cross-Strait relations, and his willingness to be flexible on what Taiwan should be called. The PRC, on the other hand, argued that Taiwan did not deserve any international role and that its quest for one was an obstacle to better cross-Strait relations—a stance that would only harden Lee's stance toward Beijing.[37]

At the same time, the DPP was raising questions about the direction of cross-Strait relations. In the spring of 1993, for example, it charged that the government was not consulting the public sufficiently on the Koo-Wang talks that were to be held in Singapore at the end of April and that it might betray the public's interests. To blunt the charge, the government limited the agenda of the talks to functional and technical issues.[38]

Lee, of course, had unleashed the opposition by continuing the process of democratization. He believed that he should respond to the views of both the elites and the public, but he also believed that a more open political system would pay instrumental benefits as well. It brought new ideas to Taiwan's political discourse and guaranteed that the voters would have a say on any cross-Strait arrangements that the two governments concluded. Lee also increasingly believed that he could strengthen his leverage vis-à-vis Beijing by releasing the island's populist forces, which would demand a greater international role for Taiwan. As he said in early 1994: "A successful foreign policy might be termed a bargaining chip in our mainland policy. If both are done well, they can be complementary." Moreover, democratization was only one of several defenses that Lee erected against a dangerous trend that he believed to be emerging. He feared that as business ties across the Strait proliferated, popular sentiment for a too-easy accommodation of Beijing would grow in Taiwan's immature democracy. To prevent any such outcome, he focused on fostering a distinctly Taiwan identity by revising textbooks, reopening cases of KMT repression of the people of Taiwan, and asserting that the people of Taiwan shared a common fate. He also sought more international space and held to a firm negotiating position. As he put it, "I believe that before we do anything else, Taiwan has to get its own house firmly in order. If Taiwan's identity is not completely clear to its people, how can we deal with mainland China?"[39]

As the DPP increased its pressure on Lee, pressure from conservatives within the KMT receded. In February 1993, Hau Pei-tsun left the premiership. Lee soon gained more control over mainland policy than he had exercised before and placed people who were more responsive to his wishes in charge of the relevant organizations. In August, KMT conservatives who doubted Lee's commitment to unification left to form the Chinese New Party.[40]

But political dynamics were not the only reason that Lee toughened his cross-Strait position; substantive issues were at work as well. He concluded that Jiang Zemin, the rising star in the Beijing leadership, was not as flexible as he had believed. In 1991 and 1992, Lee had crafted a flexible mainland policy that included a symbolic commitment to one China in the hope that Beijing would accommodate his political imperatives.[41] But Jiang did not reciprocate. Instead, as noted above, his October 1992 political report rejected various formulas whose essence would be more appealing to Taipei: "two Chinas," "one China, one Taiwan," "one country, two governments," and China as a divided country.

That China continued to talk of Taiwan as a subordinate unit left Lee increasingly annoyed, and he therefore made increasingly explicit what was implicit in the NUG's references to "parity" and "political entity." In January 1993, he spoke of the two sides as "real, equal political entities." He explained in May 1993 that this greater clarity was necessary because ties between the two sides of the Strait were proliferating, making the "question of national identity" more serious. Indeed, he said that the definition of the two sides of the Taiwan Strait had become "a big problem." One element of that problem was "the trap of 'one country, two systems.'" He reiterated the point in 1994. Beijing's refusal to recognize the fact that Taiwan and China were "separate entities ruled by two different governments" and to "treat the ROC *as an equal*" [emphasis added] had stalled cross-Strait interaction. Also that year, he referred to the ROC as "a nation within a divided China." In private, Lee began to talk more skeptically about one China.[42]

Beijing formalized its rejection of Lee's overtures in a long essay on cross-Strait relations entitled "The Taiwan Question and the Reunification of China."[43] The essay was probably China's response to Taipei's decision to mount an official effort to rejoin the United Nations. It restated the standard elements of the one-country, two-systems formula and called again for establishing the three links. For Beijing, there was one China, Taiwan was a part of it, and the Chinese central government was in Beijing. Unification had to occur on that basis. The essay restated Jiang's proposal of negotiations—now by "the two sides"—to end the state of hostility and offered some flexibility regarding the mode of negotiation. "Anything" could be discussed, but only on the premise of the one-China principle. Beijing showed no flexibility on Taipei's fundamental principles—equality, renunciation of force, and Taiwan's international role.[44]

Lee acted on his growing frustration over the PRC's diplomatic blockade of Taiwan. Because it was virtually impossible to get Taiwan into international organizations where the PRC was already a member, Lee turned to an arena where Beijing had less power to block him, securing visits to friendly countries with which the ROC did not have diplomatic relations.

Lee had begun his "visit diplomacy" in early 1989 with a trip to Singapore, which at that time did not have relations with either Taipei or Beijing. He was willing to ignore the concerns of KMT conservatives over terminology—what term would be used to refer to him, for example—because travel to countries outside the ROC's limited diplomatic orbit was popular with the public. Through his trip, Taiwan was at last getting some of the recognition it deserved. Moreover, he believed that cross-Strait relations would improve as Taiwan's international role expanded, and he wanted to improve his bargaining power with Beijing.

Lee refrained from high-profile overseas travel for the next five years but resumed it with a trip to the Philippines, Indonesia, and Thailand in February 1994. It was no accident that this venture came after a year of mounting frustration with Beijing's rigid approach to unification and its international quarantine. Unlike Singapore five years before, all three of those countries had diplomatic relations with the PRC. And at the end of his Southeast Asian visit, he indicated that he had set higher sights for his diplomatic efforts: "I'd like to visit the United States most. But not just the United States, the United Kingdom, France, Germany, or Japan would be fine, too. Given the chance, I'd hold discussions with the U.S. president, Japanese prime minister, British prime minister, or French president."[45]

Three subsequent events clouded the atmosphere. First of all, in March 1994 twenty-five Taiwan tourists vacationing on Qiandao Island in Zhejiang province were robbed and murdered. The local authorities' investigation did nothing to inspire confidence among Taiwan's people or to satisfy their intense desire for answers. The quick arrest and execution of three "suspects" failed to calm the outrage on Taiwan and only stimulated latent negative feelings about the mainland.

Second, Lee did an interview in April 1994 with Japanese journalist Shiba Ryotaro that PRC commentators often cite as evidence of Lee's separatist intentions. Beijing was particularly annoyed that Lee described the KMT as a regime that "came from outside" (*wailai*), spoke of the "sorrow of being Taiwanese," and compared himself to Moses (suggesting, they charged, that he was going to lead Taiwan's people out of China). Yet Beijing exaggerated Lee's remarks. The interview reflects his change in tone, but it does not represent a new direction in his substantive thinking. In referring to Moses and the Exodus, for example, Lee cited the 2-28 incident—that is, he saw himself as leading the people of Taiwan out of past repression, not out of China. Many of his other responses to Shiba were consistent with comments he was making around the same time. Yet they helped make the case for those in China who wanted to see the worst in his intentions and did not bother to read carefully.[46]

Third, Lee planned to stop over in Hawaii in April 1994 on his way to visit countries in Latin America with which Taiwan had diplomatic relations. He wanted to stay the night and play golf, but the Clinton administration, under some pressure from China, permitted only a refueling stop. Lee was furious at his treatment, but his resolve to visit the United States was strengthened. Because his Foreign Ministry was opposed to any such undertaking, he hired a lobbying firm, Cassidy and Associates, to mount a campaign to secure U.S. permission. Beijing saw that as yet another challenge.

In sum, the years 1993 and 1994 were a period in which Lee was freed from the constraints imposed by KMT conservatives but subjected to greater pressure from the DPP—and one in which his search for greater international space for Taiwan raised concerns in the PRC about his motives. It also was when he was preparing to run in Taiwan's first direct presidential election, scheduled for March 1996. This was uncharted territory for all of Taiwan's politicians. Initiatives like visiting the United States would, he felt, appeal to the public's desire for a wider international role and deprive the DPP of issues in the election.

Politics aside, what is significant for the purposes of this analysis is that the substance of Lee's approach to mainland policy remained basically unchanged. His formal statements convey his continuing strong objection to the specific kind of unification that Beijing was proposing. A China in which Taiwan was a subordinate unit with little or no role in the international community was not the kind of China that Lee wanted Taiwan and the ROC to be a part of. Jiang had ignored Taiwan's proposals and gestures, so Lee emphasized the Taipei government's essential equivalence to Beijing by defining what Taiwan was and by pursuing a more aggressive international agenda. Reviewing those years in a July 2003 interview, he said, "I changed my tactics, not my principles."[47]

EIGHT POINTS, SIX POINTS, CORNELL. On January 30, 1995, Jiang Zemin made his first major speech on China's Taiwan policy, his famous "eight points."[48] By and large, the address reiterated many of the staples of the one-country, two-systems proposal, including opposition to Taiwan's effort to expand its international role and refusal to renounce the use of force because, he said, Taiwan might respond to such a pledge by declaring independence. In addition, Jiang ruled out formulas like "two Chinas over a certain period of time," thus rejecting Taipei's assertion that its government was a sovereign entity. He urged negotiations on ending the state of hostilities.

But Jiang's speech was not simply a rehash of past offerings. His tone was different, and the speech suggested new flexibility in terms of process. Consultations to prepare for talks on ending hostilities would be on "an equal footing." He proclaimed that "Chinese should not fight fellow Chinese." He said that "leaders of the Taiwan authorities are welcome to pay visits in appropriate capacities" and that the PRC's leaders were ready to accept invitations to visit Taiwan. Those statements indicated an effort to move rhetorically in Taipei's direction.

Still, all of them were made under the rubric of "the principle of one China," which would be the basis for any agreement to end the state of hostilities and to resolve the issue of Taipei's international role. Adherence to that principle would be "the basis and premise for peaceful reunification," a condition that constituted a qualification of Beijing's promise that "anything could be discussed." Hence the definition of that principle was crucial, and Taipei feared that the definition would negate its sovereignty. Finally, saying that Taiwan's leaders could come to China "in appropriate capacities" also raised the issue of the Taipei government's status.

Lee Teng-hui's response to Jiang's eight points came on April 8, 1995, in a "six point" address to the National Unification Council. He chose to restate past policy and lay the blame for the slow pace of "peaceful reunification" at the door of Beijing, which refused to accept the "84-year existence of the ROC government," insisted on sovereignty and jurisdiction ("ruling rights") over Taiwan, and blocked Taiwan from taking its rightful place in the international community. Lee called on Beijing to renounce the use of force and urged it to accept the reality of "the two shores of the strait being split and separately governed." Only then would there be movement on unification and broader consensus on what "one China" meant.[49]

Thus, in the early 1995 exchange, each leader repackaged past positions but did not really break any new ground. Jiang was restrained by the strength of the one-country, two-systems orthodoxy, linked as it was to Deng Xiaoping's prestige. Lee had his own reasons to stand his ground. On one hand, Jiang had not shown any creativity on matters of substance. On the other, he saw greater advantage in securing success internationally than in accommodating Beijing right away—specifically, by making a visit to the United States, which he thought would both enhance public support for his reelection and increase his leverage against Beijing. His campaign to mobilize congressional pressure on the Clinton adminstration to approve a visit to Cornell University, his alma mater, had already begun. For Lee, Jiang's eight points were too little, too late.

Beijing responded to Lee's visit to the United States by canceling a second Koo-Wang meeting scheduled for July and suspending cross-Strait dialogue; suspending dialogues with the United States on human rights and military issues; withdrawing the PRC ambassador to Washington; and, most ominously, conducting two rounds of military exercises, one in the summer and fall of 1995 in advance of Taiwan's Legislative Yuan elections and the other in March 1996 before the presidential elections. It was not the first time that Beijing had used military exercises to make a point when Taiwan was holding elections. But those two rounds were larger in scale and closer geographically to Taiwan (especially the March round) than any before. The Clinton administration warned China not to move beyond displays of force and responded to the second round of exercises by sending two aircraft carrier battle groups to the Taiwan area to reduce the chances of accidental conflict. It also counseled Taipei to avoid actions that might cause a negative PRC reaction, and it urged them to resume dialogue.

Most Western scholarship on the Cornell episode concludes that PRC actions from July 1995 to March 1996, particularly the military exercises, were a *response* to Lee Teng-hui's initiatives. According to that view, Beijing had concluded from those initiatives that Lee was intent on permanently separating Taiwan from China and that his separatist aims (and U.S. complicity in them) constituted a threat to China's vital interest in unification. The leadership therefore chose to engage in coercive diplomacy to demonstrate China's serious resolve to counter the recent drift of events. Its goals were to compel Taiwan and the United States to reverse course; to create a measure of panic among the Taiwan people; and to deter other countries from following the U.S. lead in allowing visits by Lee.[50] Furthermore, Beijing asserted that if there were to be a return to the status quo ante, Lee would have to "return to the one-China principle." Cornell had ended the conciliatory tone and flexibility in process suggested by Jiang's eight points.

Lee Teng-hui pursued his Cornell visit because he was frustrated that Beijing had been unresponsive to his approach to unification and wanted to improve his bargaining power and political position at home. To be sure, the Taipei government aggravated the situation by creating the impression in Washington and perhaps Beijing that the focus of Lee's remarks would be his Cornell years and Taiwan's economic reform. In fact, the speech had an overtly political character, and both the United States and China felt betrayed.[51]

But was Cornell proof positive that Lee Teng-hui wished to create an independent Taiwan, as the PRC and some Americans believe?[52] His tactics certainly did nothing to endear him to either Washington or Beijing, but China had given him reason to play hardball. The content of the speech itself, however, does not justify the conclusion that he was engaged in a separatist project. He did, to be sure, introduce the concept of popular sovereignty in the discussion of Taiwan's legal status. The people of Taiwan—and they alone—had chosen all of the members of the National Assembly for the first time in 1991 and those of the Legislative Yuan in 1992. Moreover, the new National Assembly had amended the constitution further so that direct election of the president would occur for the first time in 1996.

Those reforms, taken together, provided a wholly new justification for the claim that the ROC was a sovereign state. The previous justification—that the ROC was the successor to the Qing dynasty and had existed since 1912—was more in line with traditional international law. The new, additional justification, which was more in line with ideas on state-creation fostered by the French Revolution, was that the people of Taiwan had, through free elections, constituted their government. Lee also asserted that a sovereign state and a successful democracy like Taiwan merited better treatment by the international community. Yet none of that was inconsistent with the views that he had expressed since the beginning of his presidency on the legal character of the ROC government.[53]

The other intellectually innovative concept that Lee presented at Cornell was his claim that Taiwan had global political significance—that is, that Taiwan's experience of democratization should serve as an example for the rest of the world and particularly for China. In making that claim, he sought to secure the moral high ground for Taiwan and to reject the idea that the PRC was on the right side of history. In his mind, Taiwan was not just a part of China; it was the *best* part of China. Addressing cross-Strait relations in this way was indirect, but it was no less profound, and it reflected his commitment to a certain kind of unification.

Beijing chose to go to the mat over Cornell not only because of what Lee had said but also because he said it in the United States. His American visit created concern not only because more high-level travel might be in the offing, but also, and more important, because Beijing chose to include within its definition of separatism any Taiwan efforts to gain international support for the idea that the Republic of China existed as an equal Chinese government.

INAUGURATION CONCILIATION. In his second inaugural address, delivered on May 20, 1996, Lee reprised his Cornell themes of popular sovereignty and Taiwan's rightful leadership of the modernization of China. He also justified his promotion of a distinctly Taiwan identity on the grounds that "fifty years of a common destiny forged in fortune and misfortune have united us all into a closely bound and interdependent community." He further reaffirmed that Taiwan would continue to promote pragmatic diplomacy because it needed international space and, as a democracy, deserved respect. And he took a conciliatory stance on cross-Strait relations.[54]

Alluding to Jiang Zemin's eight points, Lee deplored the century-long tragedy of Chinese fighting Chinese and stated that "Chinese should help each other." He asserted that Taipei's strategy during his first term was based on "*expanding cross-Strait relations, leading to eventual national unification* [emphasis added]." Beijing, however, had "refused to admit the very fact that the Republic of China does exist" and undertaken propaganda attacks and military exercises to intimidate the ROC.

Lee restated Taiwan's basic principles regarding dialogue and political reconciliation. The ROC was a sovereign state; the two sides were separate jurisdictions that were pursuing eventual unification; Beijing had to accept these "facts"; and an agreement to terminate the state of hostilities was a priority. But he also offered something new. He sought to reassure the PRC by saying that Taiwan need not declare independence because it already had independent status. Lee was trying to address Beijing's stated anxiety about such a declaration, and he did so by playing on different meanings of the word "independent," which could be used to indicate the creation of a new state (which was not on the agenda) or simply to describe the reality that Taiwan was not subordinate to the PRC. He was prepared to make a "journey of peace" to the mainland to meet there with Beijing's leaders. Most significant, he did not restate his previous precondition that the PRC renounce the use of force, although he did note that renouncing force was, along with democracy, human rights, and peace, one of the values of the new international order. But it was no longer an immediate obstacle to cross-Strait progress.

Phase Three: On-Again, Off-Again Dialogue

Beijing canceled cross-Strait dialogue in response to Lee Teng-hui's visit to the United States, stating that it would not resume unless he returned to the one-China principle. For two years thereafter, the two sides fenced over the terms on which resumption of talks could occur. Lee did not alter his fundamental position during that period, and his discussions of cross-Strait relations replayed old themes. He particularly emphasized the need for Beijing to recognize the political reality of the ROC's existence. Only once—in July 1997—did he repeat the demand that Beijing renounce the use of force.[55]

In early 1998, in the context of improving U.S.-PRC relations and stable U.S.-Taiwan ties, the two sides took incremental positive steps. Beijing reduced its emphasis on the one-China principle, and Taiwan signaled for the first time that it was willing to discuss political issues. (The Koo-Wang talks in April 1993 had addressed only functional issues.) Reinforcing those overtures was their deepening economic interdependence: annual two-way trade was then on the order of $25 billion, and Taiwan firms had more than $20 billion in realized investment in China. Lee sought to push things along with his July 1998 speech to the National Unification Council, where he referred to "one divided China" and declared that "China must be reunified." The result was Koo Chen-fu's visit to Shanghai and Beijing in October for meetings with Wang Daohan, Vice Premier Qian Qichen, and others. No new substantive ground was broken, and Koo was under instructions to stress the significance of Taiwan's democratization. The main achievement of his trip was an agreement that the process of reengagement should continue and that Wang would visit Taiwan in 1999.[56]

On July 9, 1999, three months before Wang's visit, Lee granted an interview to reporters from the German international broadcasting service, Deutsche Welle. Asked his reaction to what the journalists described as Beijing's view that Taiwan was a renegade province of China, he responded as follows:

> Historic facts are as follows: Since the PRC's establishment, the Chinese communists have never ruled Taiwan, Penghu, Jinmen, and Mazu, which have been under the jurisdiction of the Republic of China. In 1991, our country amended its Constitution. . . . Consequently, the state organs subsequently formed will only represent the Taiwan people. The legitimacy of the administration of state power can only be authorized by the Taiwan people and has absolutely nothing to do with the people on mainland China. Since our constitutional reform in 1991, we have designated cross-Strait ties as nation-to-nation (*guojia yu guojia*), or at least as special state-to-state ties (*teshu de guoyuguo de guanxi*), rather than internal ties within "one China" between a legitimate government and a rebellion group, or between central and local governments.[57]

Lee's statement sparked immediate tensions between Taiwan and the PRC. Beijing mounted an intense propaganda barrage. There was increased air activity over the Taiwan Strait by both sides. The Clinton administration worried about the risk of conflict erupting through accident or miscalculation and was annoyed that Lee had not informed Washington in advance that he would offer that formulation, which was new in that it was at least a more explicit statement of the relationship between the two sides. Compounding the problem were the different connotations of the Chinese words *guojia* and *guo*: country, nation, and state. Why did Lee feel moved to make this statement?

A number of reasons have been offered. Lee wanted to influence the campaign for the March 2004 presidential election. He wanted to strengthen his legacy. In the summer of 2003, Lee told me that international lawyers whom his subordinates had consulted in the previous few years had concluded that Taiwan, or the ROC, was not a state and that his remarks were a response to that assessment.[58] In other words, he concluded that it was necessary to define the identity of Taiwan and its governing authorities precisely in terms of international law, in preparation for political negotiations with Beijing. The policy of ambiguity that he had adopted for nonpolitical talks was no longer appropriate. Indeed, Lee's focus on the need for clarity was not new. As early as May 1993, as noted previously, Lee had observed that "the definition of the two sides of the Taiwan Straits became a big problem." In July 1997, he had said that "China is a divided nation, ruled by two *distinct* political entities. . . . Only if Taiwan has a *definite* international status [emphasis added] can it commence talks with Beijing on an equal footing to discuss the problem of reunification." In June 1998, he had said, "Two sides should talk about international law. In doing that, we would also be talking about sovereignty."[59]

Yet whatever Lee's motivation, he misplayed his hand. As described in chapter 7, he impulsively decided to make this formula public without consulting key members of his foreign policy team or the United States. A better strategy would have been to deploy it privately in whatever political negotiations might have occurred. Instead he gave Beijing a propaganda advantage.

Tactics aside, how does Lee's July 1999 formulation contrast with previous ones? Was this a new departure—as Beijing put it, "an attempt to fundamentally change the status of Taiwan as a part of China"?[60]

It is reasonable to conclude that Lee was making explicit what had been implicit in Taipei's position for almost a decade: that the government of Taiwan possessed sovereignty, just as the Beijing government did. Note in particular what Lee was using this new formulation to oppose: he was challenging the idea that Beijing's relationship to Taipei was, as he put it, one "between a legitimate government and a rebellion group, or between central and local governments." This was consistent with Taiwan's long-standing rejection of the one-country, two-systems formula, which, in Taiwan's view, assigned subordinate status to special administrative regions.

Moreover, Lee did not reject the idea that Taiwan was a part of China or suggest that unification was no longer an objective. Instead, he focused on the status of Taiwan in international law and on the terms of its relationship to that China—and *Beijing's* relationship to that China. His formulation addressed *how* Taiwan was a part of China—or, to put it more precisely, the relationship of Taiwan's government to the postunification Chinese state.

It is also possible to interpret Lee's state-to-state formula as asserting something entirely new. It was not his use of the words *guojia* and *guo*, which can have a range of more or less provocative meanings in China. Rather, there is the clear possibility that Lee and his advisers were asserting that Taiwan was, under international law, a state totally separate from the Chinese state. Taipei's view before 1991 was that the ROC was the sole legal government of the Chinese state. Thereafter, under Lee's initiative, Taipei held that the Chinese state was divided, with two sovereign governments—the ROC and the PRC.

The intimations of innovation can be seen in Lee's focus on the point that constitutional changes had limited the territory of the ROC government to the islands of Taiwan, Penghu, Jinmen, and Mazu. Why might this be relevant? The Montevideo Convention defined five explicit criteria for statehood: a permanent population; an effective government; the capacity to enter into relations with other states; independence; and a defined territory.[61] Taiwan indubitably satisfied the first four criteria, but its stance on "defined territory" was ambiguous. The NUC's August 1992 statement claimed that ROC's sovereignty covered all of China but that its jurisdiction was confined to the four islands cited above. Lee's advisers may have wanted to create a stronger justification for the ROC's sovereign status by removing the ambiguity over the scope of reach of its sovereign territory and so remedy the one criterion for statehood that Taiwan did not meet: defined territory. They did so by going through the ROC constitution as amended to find provisions that supported the idea that the Taipei government had a well-defined territory. Moreover, Lee may have been trying to meet an additional, implicit criterion of statehood: the leaders of the political entity in question must assert that it is a state for it to be one under international law. His July statement thus met that requirement as well.[62]

Phase Four: Chen Shui-bian Wins the Presidency

Among those who believed that Lee Teng-hui and he alone was impeding progress and creating tensions in cross-Strait relations, there was hope that another KMT president might break the cross-Strait stalemate. And Beijing thought so too. But the results of the March 2000 election came as something of a shock: the traditional KMT vote was split between its official candidate, Vice President Lien Chan, and James Soong Chu-yu, a party stalwart who had bolted because he had wanted the nomination himself. As a result, Chen Shui-bian, the candidate of the opposition Democratic Progressive Party, was able to squeak out an unexpected win, beating Soong by a mere 300,000 votes. Beijing had realized only late in the game that Chen might win and feared that he might act on his party's traditional advocacy of creating an independent Republic of Taiwan. It therefore issued a series of verbal threats, among them PRC Premier Zhu Rongji's warning that "Taiwan's independence means war!"

Chen won the election first and foremost because of Soong's defection from the KMT. He also was able to play on his record as mayor of Taipei Municipality from 1994 to 1998, on public dissatisfaction with the KMT after its fifty-five years of rule on Taiwan, and on growing political corruption. But Chen Shui-bian also succeeded because, modeling himself on Bill Clinton in the United States and Tony Blair in Britain, he had deliberately tried to move the rather ideological DPP toward the more pragmatic center of the political spectrum in order to win power. This was most obvious and necessary concerning cross-Strait policy, because the public had doubts about the DPP's ability to manage the China issue. Chen sought to reassure the public that he would not act rashly. As he said, echoing Lee Teng-hui, Taiwan did not need to declare its independence from China because it already was independent. Unlike some in the DPP, he favored establishing direct links and broadening cross-Strait economic relations in order to gain the confidence of the business community. He also knew that the United States had concerns about the direction of his policies, and he took steps to assuage them. This shift was evident in the evolution of the DPP's and Chen's public position on an independent Taiwan.

Chen's first venture into the complexities of cross-Strait relations had come after a visit to Beijing in 1990, when he drafted a "peace agreement" between China and Taiwan, which by implication was between two countries. A year later, he got involved in a debate with the DPP over how much to emphasize independence in the election campaign for a new National Assembly. The more radical New Tide faction pushed for a plank that called for an independent Republic of Taiwan. Chen Shui-bian was able to water down the position somewhat, but it was still the most far-reaching position the DPP had taken. The provision read as follows:

> In accordance with Taiwan's actual sovereignty, *an independent country should be established* [emphasis added] and a new constitution promulgated in order to create a legal and political system appropriate to the realities of Taiwan society, and to return to international society in accordance with principles of international law. . . . Based on the principle of popular sovereignty, the establishment of a sovereign, independent and self-governing Republic of Taiwan and promulgation

of a new constitution should be carried out by all residents of Taiwan through a national referendum.[63]

Thus the DPP stated its explicit goal of establishing an independent country, and it was not long before the voters registered their verdict. DPP candidates won only 24 percent of the vote, a recent record low. The debate over how much to emphasize independence continued for another eight years, but a turning point was reached in 1996, when radical elements left the DPP to form the Taiwan Independence Party. Not unlike the formation of the Chinese New Party (the name was later shortened to New Party) by KMT members dissatisfied with Lee Teng-hui, this defection freed those who remained in the DPP to explore more centrist positions.

That process, which took place over almost three years and which Chen Shui-bian dominated, culminated in the May 1999 adoption of a party resolution on cross-Strait relations. The resolution read as follows:

> Taiwan is a sovereign and independent country. . . . Taiwan, although named the Republic of China under its current constitution, is not subject to the jurisdiction of the People's Republic of China. Any change in the independent status quo must be decided by all residents of Taiwan by means of plebiscite. . . . China's growing might and consistently stubborn hegemonic thinking presents the greatest obstacle to Taiwan's future. Given the unpredictability of international politics and the complicated web of interests, the DPP believes that Taiwan must take a safe, cautious, gradual and well-examined approach to China.[64]

This represented a significant retreat from the charter language of 1991, although in a formal sense the charter still took precedence. The party placed more emphasis on process than on ultimate outcomes (as it had in the 1980s) and placed the onus for the unstable situation on Beijing. The explicit goal of establishing an independent Republic of Taiwan in the future had disappeared. Replacing it was a formulation of Taiwan's current status that was fairly similar to that of the KMT (an "independent sovereign state"). There was, however, an important difference: this description applied to Taiwan, not to the ROC. In a first for the DPP, there was a backhanded acceptance of the term "the Republic of China" ("although named the Republic of China under its current constitution"). And there was the emphasis on caution and gradualism.

Between the lines, one sees an effort to balance the traditional goals of the party and a more pragmatic vision. KMT formulations were borrowed but then altered in ways that DPP fundamentalists could tolerate. The purpose of this new position, which was reaffirmed in most of Chen Shui-bian's campaign statements in the 2000 presidential campaign, was to remove a vulnerability that had dogged the DPP for almost a decade—the claim that it could not be trusted with power. As Shelley Rigger summarized the DPP's evolution: "A careful reading of DPP statements on the [independence] issue reveals a party struggling through a protracted search for a position that both preserves its commitment to Taiwan's autonomy and identity while acknowledging the political realities beyond the party's control. Many DPP members still dream of an independent Taiwan, but individually and collectively they now recognize that this is not a dream they can realize unilaterally or soon."[65]

Some in the DPP were going beyond simply adjusting the party's rhetorical positions. They toyed with the idea of removing the Republic of Taiwan clause in the party charter. And, realistic about the prospects for complete independence and about the importance of China to Taiwan's economic well-being, they began to quietly explore conceptions of China—other than the PRC's one-country, two-systems proposal—with which they as Taiwanese would be comfortable. Because some in the party still adhered to the true faith, they had to do this rather quietly, but they believed that such flexibility was imperative. Chen himself did not object to a discussion of one China as an issue but refused to accept it up front as a principle, as Beijing insisted.[66]

Yet Chen Shui-bian did not have a totally free hand. He had moved the DPP away from its origins as the independence party for the sake of electoral victory, and some observers speculated that he could persuade his party to accept a cross-Strait settlement in ways that a KMT president could not— just as anticommunist Richard Nixon had secured the support of his fellow conservatives for his opening to China. But many in the DPP had not given up their fundamental goal of establishing a Republic of Taiwan. For this "fundamentalist" faction, gaining power was yet another step toward their long-cherished goal, not the goal itself. These people also were aware of the Nixon analogy and were reluctant to go along. So Chen had to be somewhat cautious in his initiatives, testing the limits of the fundamentalists' tolerance.

Chen had other handicaps as well. First of all, he had not expected to win in March 2000; his goal had been only to do well in the election as a trial run for 2004. Consequently, he had made no plans for a transition of government. Second, the DPP lacked the personnel, in terms of both numbers and executive talent, to run a complex government like Taiwan's. Indeed, Chen decided to name a cabinet of "all the people," including KMT members and outsiders. Third, over the years the DPP had perfected the skills of criticizing and obstructing the government as part of its strategy for gaining power, but its leaders were unprepared for being in the hot seat themselves—for having the responsibility for developing a policy agenda, winning public and parliamentary support for it, and implementing related programs. To make matters worse, the KMT and the People First Party (PFP), which James Soong formed after the 2000 election, refused to give the DPP a honeymoon and were relentless in their criticism of it. Together the parties still had a comfortable majority in the legislature, which they would soon use to block Chen's agenda and otherwise make life difficult for him. It was said that the DPP was slow to learn how to be the ruling party and that the KMT and PFP were slow to learn how to be the opposition. And finally, a global recession began in the summer of 2000, just after Chen took office, creating a new set of problems. The DPP was about to experience all the difficulties inherent in being an opposition party coming to power for the first time in a new democracy.

As far as the PRC was concerned, the past defined how it approached the Chen presidency. The DPP's historical association with the goal of Taiwan's independence was far more significant to Beijing than Chen's adjustment of the party's approach. His resistance to China's one-country, two-systems resolution of the cross-Strait conflict and the separatist intentions that Beijing inferred in explaining his resistance were more important than the possibility that he might be Taiwan's Nixon. And so the PRC defined Chen and the DPP as the "Taiwan independence" party during the 2000 election campaign and declared that it would not resume dialogue with Taiwan unless Chen accepted the one-China principle. Moreover, Beijing may have felt that it was unnecessary to deal with Chen because he had won with only 40 percent of the vote against a divided field—and that by employing united front tactics it could prevent his reelection in 2004. Once he became president, Beijing saw little reason to probe the possibility that his signals might represent something worth pursuing.

THE FIRST TWO YEARS. Chen Shui-bian reaffirmed his stance of moderation and conciliation in his inaugural address of May 20, 2000:

> The people on the two sides of the Taiwan Strait share the same ancestral, cultural, and historical background. While upholding the principles of democracy and parity, building upon the existing foundations, and constructing conditions for cooperation through good

will, we believe that the leaders on both sides possess enough wisdom and creativity to jointly deal with the question of a future "one China."

I fully understand that, as the popularly elected 10th-term president of the Republic of China, I must abide by the Constitution, maintain the sovereignty, dignity and security of our country, and ensure the well-being of all citizens. Therefore, as long as the CCP regime has no intention to use military force against Taiwan, I pledge that during my term in office, I will not declare independence, I will not change the national title, I will not push forth the inclusion of the so-called "state-to-state" description in the Constitution, and I will not promote a referendum to change the status quo in regard to the question of independence or unification. Furthermore, there is no question of abolishing the Guidelines for National Unification and the National Unification Council.

Chen sought to reassure the PRC about his intentions, with some qualifications. He asserted the common heritage of the people on the two sides of the Strait (which was heresy to those in the DPP who believe that the Taiwanese were a totally distinct nation). He identified himself as the president of the Republic of China. He pledged to abide by the constitution (which Beijing could have taken as an implicit acceptance of the one-China principle). On the condition that the PRC had no intention to use force, he promised not to do several things that Beijing feared (which, again, it could have taken as proof that he was not a separatist). On the premise of "democracy and parity" and with the acknowledgment that there was a past record of interaction ("building upon the existing foundations"), he expressed confidence that the two leaderships could deal with the question of one China. Chen cited the principles of sovereignty, parity, and abjuration of the use of force, as Lee had before him, but he also expressed confidence that a "future 'one China'" was an achievable objective.[67]

The PRC quickly rejected his efforts at conciliation. Within hours of Chen's inaugural speech, the Taiwan Affairs Office issued an authorized statement that accused Chen of being evasive, ambiguous, and insincere regarding the one-China principle. It said that the principle was the "touchstone" for whether he "safeguards national sovereignty and territorial integrity or continues to stubbornly push the separatist policy of 'Taiwan independence'"—quite an either-or distinction.

Beijing warned that on Taiwan there were still people who "stubbornly stick to the separatist position that 'Taiwan is a sovereign and independent country' in an attempt to split Taiwan from China. This is a serious crime of dividing the country and endangering the people. It will unavoidably undermine Taiwan's social stability and economic development, *provoke conflicts* between compatriots across the strait and within Taiwan, [and] *endanger peace* in the Taiwan Strait and the Asia-Pacific region [emphasis added]." Since Chen had associated himself with the sovereign-and-independent-country position, the warning was clearly aimed at him. The statement also restated China's preconditions for the resumption of dialogue: Taipei had to explicitly promise not to pursue the "two-state theory" and to adhere to the "consensus" ARATS and SEF had reached in November 1992 prior to concluding various technical agreements.[68]

Other parts of the PRC statement would make Chen naturally reluctant to accept the 1992 consensus and the one-China principle, which supposedly was at its heart. On one hand, the PRC's declaration asserted that in regard to cross-Strait relations and negotiations prior to reunification, "upholding the principle of one China means upholding that there is only one China in the world, that Taiwan is part of China, and China's sovereignty and territorial integrity brook no cutting apart." That formulation was problematic in three respects. First of all, any prohibition against dividing China's sovereignty would arguably deny sovereignty to the government on Taiwan. Second, Taipei knew full well that Beijing claimed to be the only government representing China in the international community, a claim that would deny it any role. And third, Taipei had an aversion to accepting any PRC "principle" because of its fear that in any future negotiation the PRC would manipulate that principle to its advantage. It was far better, in Chen's view, to reach a mutually acceptable consensus on what the one-China principle meant than to accept the PRC's version without having fully clarified its substantive ramifications.[69]

The theological character of the issues, the intensity of DPP politics, and the difficulty of conducting delicate diplomacy in public were all on full display in late June. At a meeting with a delegation of the Asia Foundation, Chen said that his government was willing to accept the 1992 consensus as Taiwan understood it: "one China, respective interpretations." He also criticized China's interpretation, "the one-China policy, which downgrades the Republic of China to a local-level government under the People's Republic of China—something that is unacceptable to the people of Taiwan." Because Beijing insisted on its own, unacceptable interpretation, Beijing was responsible for the negotiating stalemate. Taiwan, Chen asserted, hoped to resume negotiations in order to establish common ground to find a mutually acceptable definition of "one-China."[70]

The fundamentalists in his party, who felt that Chen already had made too many concessions to the PRC, ignored the qualifications in his statement and focused instead on his general willingness to accept the 1992 consensus. A firestorm of opposition erupted. An editorial in the pro-DPP *Taipei Times*, for example, characterized the statement as "outrageous . . . either an amazing mistake, or a sign of weakness." Chen's statement, the editorial asserted, suggested that he had acknowledged that the PRC was the "one China" in question. Moreover, the paper charged, Chen had yielded once again to Beijing without getting anything in return. "Chen is giving away the entire game before time. . . . While most people were concerned about rash provocations [by him], rash concessions are equally dangerous. Chen has demonstrated that he understands the former point. Now it is high time to learn the latter." Within a few hours, Tsai Ing-wen, chairman of the Mainland Affairs Council, issued a clarification to the effect that Chen had said nothing new, that the consensus was that each side could have its interpretation of one China, that there had never been a consensus on the one-China principle, and that Beijing's version of the principle was the obstacle to progress. The episode led Chen to be more cautious in his statements and Beijing more suspicious about his intentions.[71]

Chen sought after his inauguration to foster a consensus of another kind—within Taiwan on mainland policy. He formed a cross-party task force and recruited Lee Yuan-tseh, head of Academia Sinica, to be its chairman. The KMT and the new People First Party, headed by James Soong, chose to boycott the group, so undermining its very purpose and probably giving fundamentalists in the DPP a stronger voice. The task force issued its final statement in late November 2000. Two key premises were that the ROC and the PRC "neither belong to nor represent each other" and that any change in the status quo should occur with the consent of the Taiwan people. It made several recommendations to Chen. First, the cross-Strait relationship, particularly with regard to how he responded to the PRC's "one China," should be "managed in accordance with the constitution of the Republic of China." Second, the PRC should respect Taiwan as a member of the international community and renounce the use of force against it. Third, the effort to foster consensus within Taiwan on mainland policy should continue. Note that either explicitly or implicitly, the first two points replicate the main demands that Lee Teng-hui had made of Beijing: sovereignty, international space, and renunciation of force. Yet domestic politics—the refusal of the KMT and the PFP to participate in the consensus-building effort—again thwarted Chen's efforts to make progress on cross-Strait relations.

On occasions Chen suggested that he maintained an open mind on China. Asked during a June 2000 press conference about the idea of a confederation with China, Chen responded positively: "I do not think we have any preconceptions on such an idea, nor do we have any pre-established premises or conclusions on the subject. Instead, we are trying to keep our minds open on the entire matter in order to leave plenty of room for the opinions of leaders on the Chinese mainland side. . . . Such a proposal is just one of the kind that could eventually be formulated into a working plan based on the development of future cross-strait relations. Whether or not it would work will rely heavily upon the decision of the people." Similarly, in a September interview with the *New York Times*, he criticized the KMT for making unification the only option for Taiwan's future, because such an arbitrary process not only violated democratic principles but also was inconsistent with the views of Taiwan's people, who were broadly opposed to the one-country, two-systems proposal. By implication, he indicated that the right kind of unification was an option.[72]

Despite signaling, the mutual mistrust was too great, and Chen had to spend much of his time fending off pressures from various directions. A negotiating stalemate soon formed, and an opportunity for the two sides to engage and perhaps explore the potential for reconciliation slipped away. The danger persisted that, in an increasingly militarized environment, the political dispute between Beijing and Taipei might deteriorate into armed conflict.

But then, in late 2000, Beijing took a new and more moderate tack, but not because it was changing its substantive position. Rather, it had concluded that Chen was so weak that he would last only one term, and it therefore pursued a strategy of ignoring him, denying him any political victories, and aligning with his opponents in order to undermine him from within. It sought to exploit Taiwan's recession-related difficulties by luring even more Taiwan companies to the mainland. Those companies in turn exerted pressure on Chen's government regarding policies that impeded greater economic integration, such as investment controls and the absence of direct transportation links. Beijing also sought to cultivate the opposition parties, the KMT and the PFP, and at least the KMT sought China's aid in keeping Chen in a weak position. That the major media were inclined toward unification helped shift the public debate on Taiwan in the PRC's direction. Its strategy, it appeared, was to wait Chen out as long as he did not do anything truly provocative. It would build a united front against the DPP in the expectation that his successor would be more accommodating. Exerting political and economic leverage would better protect China's interest than engaging in intimidation, which would bring in the United States, or negotiating on any terms that Chen would find acceptable.

At the same time, Beijing continued to build up its military capabilities. It was producing short- and medium-range ballistic missiles domestically at a rate of more than fifty a year and developing air- and land-attack cruise missiles, but it also purchased from Russia power-projection systems that it could not produce itself. Those included advanced fighter aircraft, submarines, destroyers, and longer-range air defense systems, which had two purposes. The first was to deter any irreversible moves by Taiwan's leadership in the direction of independence; the second was to increase its ability over time to perhaps compel Taiwan to negotiate on the PRC's terms. By mid-2003, the U.S. Department of Defense had concluded that China's military acquisitions might reflect its desire not just to deter what it feared (independence) but to compel Taiwan to do what it wanted (negotiate unification on its terms). Some scholars did not doubt the buildup, but they downplayed the ability of the People's Liberation Army to bring Taipei to heel, either through surgical air strikes, a naval blockade, or an amphibious landing, even without U.S. intervention.[73]

Yet Chen continued to make tantalizing statements that suggested an openness to certain kinds of unification. Most interesting was one of his 2001 New Year's messages:

> It has always been my belief that the people on the two sides of the Strait share the same roots as well as the common goal of coexistence and co-prosperity. Since both sides have expressed the wish to live under the same roof, it is necessary to show understanding for and help each other. Neither side should try to undermine or destroy the other. We appeal to the government and leaders on the other side to respect the ROC's living space and dignity in the world arena by publicly renouncing the threat of force and by transcending the current dispute and stalemate with the most profound tolerance and far-sightedness. We appeal to the government and leaders on the other side to gradually build trust between the two sides, starting from the integration of cross-strait economic, trade, and cultural affairs and then jointly searching for a new framework of lasting peace and political integration between the two sides, thereby working together to explore the space of unlimited possibilities in the utmost interests of the people on the two sides of the Strait.

This statement is important in several respects. Most significant is Chen's identification of "political integration" as a potential outcome. He was drawing on the European experience, the gradual but increasingly close union of sovereign entities. That was, of course, much different from the one-country, two-systems approach, but it was a form of unification all the same. And Chen developed a new Chinese term to apply to his concept of integration. It was *tonghe*, which joined the first character of the PRC word for unification (*tongyi*) with another character (*he*) that has the meaning "to combine." Moreover, Chen had identified a process by which political integration could occur, which would begin in the realms of economics, trade, and culture and later move into the realms of security and politics. And he called on each side to understand and not to try to undermine or destroy the other—as he thought Beijing was trying to do to Taiwan—appealing to Beijing to renounce the use of force, allow Taiwan some international space, and generally show tolerance.[74] The implication of Chen's approach was that the entities that would take part in this process of integration would be sovereign and independent, like the members of the European Union.

In an interview with a Japanese magazine in early 2001, Chen also revisited the 1992 consensus, opining that setting preconditions was unhelpful and that the two sides differed in their understanding of the consensus.

> In their view on the other side of the Strait, the consensus is just another expression of the one-China principle, a point on which they lay special stress. For Taiwan, however, the official interpretation Taiwan has chosen about the consensus is that the one China could take two different expressions, one for the one side and another for the other side. This interpretation has been denied on the mainland.

He said that there was room for the two sides to negotiate a common meaning of "one China" and come to a final consensus through mutual concessions and compromise.[75]

As if to confirm Chen's moderation toward Beijing, more ideological figures associated with the DPP quickly attacked his remarks on integration. Li Thian-Hok, a Taiwanese American, charged that Chen's concept of political integration betrayed a lack of understanding of Taiwan's unique history and a worldview that was "narrowly focused on China." It was clear, Li charged, that "Chen aims to give up Taiwan's de facto independent status in exchange for peace and a high degree of autonomy, perhaps an improved variant of the 'One Country, Two Systems' model. . . . . Chen Shui-bian's DPP government shares with Beijing a common vision of a prosperous future 'One China.'" He also criticized Chen's pledges of restraint in his inaugural address because they unilaterally limited Taiwan's sovereign status. "By forfeiting these powers," Li said, "Chen has diminished and marginalized Taiwan's status as a fully independent sovereign state, without consulting the wishes of the Taiwanese people."[76]

Beijing's strategy of exerting economic and political leverage while building up its armed forces suffered two setbacks during 2001. The first was the new course set by the Bush administration, which believed that the Clinton administration should have been tougher on China and more solicitous of Taiwan. Moreover, many of its senior officials believed that a rising China posed a more general challenge to U.S. dominance of the East Asian region and that Taiwan would be a litmus test of American resolve. The collision of a U.S. EP-3 reconnaissance aircraft with a Chinese fighter ten weeks after Bush's inauguration only aggravated that concern. The new administration therefore improved the treatment of Taiwan officials, for example, during high-level transits of the United States.[77] And in April 2001, President Bush approved both a robust package of arms sales to address China's military buildup and stated with greater clarity that the United States would come to Taiwan's defense if the PRC attacked.

Beijing's second setback was the December 2001 elections on Taiwan for the Legislative Yuan. It had hoped that economic problems and the DPP's mistakes in governing would keep the party in a minority position, but the DPP won more seats than predicted and the KMT suffered greater-than-expected losses. Meanwhile, a small party created by Lee Teng-hui—the Taiwan Solidarity Union (TSU)—did well in its first outing. The end result was that the KMT and the PFP (the so-called Blue forces, after the color of the KMT flag) had just a few more seats than the DPP and the TSU (the so-called Green forces, after the color of the DPP flag). Beijing's united front strategy was not paying immediate dividends. The stalemate, it appeared, would continue.

RETREAT FROM MODERATION. As the March 2004 presidential election neared, Chen gradually abandoned what he regarded as his conciliatory stance. He worked under the assumption that the KMT and the PFP would field a single ticket instead of the divided field that allowed him to squeak to victory in 2000. An essential first step in meeting that challenge was to mobilize his political base, which had been unhappy with his performance. His frustration over Beijing's refusal to engage with him reduced his inclination toward moderation.

In May 2002, Chen did repeat his reassuring formulation of New Year's 2001 about economic and cultural integration as the first step toward political integration, pledging that "we will not deviate from this goal, and this policy will not change." But in July, right before he was to assume the post of DPP party chairman, Beijing announced the establishment of diplomatic relations with the tiny Pacific country of Nauru, which broke ties with Taipei. Chen responded by declaring that Taiwan would "go its own way." Then on August 3, speaking by teleconference to an audience of overseas Taiwanese supporters, he created new questions about his intentions. Expressing his frustration with the PRC, he said, "Taiwan is our country, and our country cannot be bullied, downgraded, marginalized, nor treated as a local government. Taiwan is not a part of any other country, nor is it a local government or province of another country. Taiwan can never be another Hong Kong or Macau because Taiwan has always been a sovereign state. In short, *Taiwan and China are standing on opposite sides of the strait, there is one country on each side (yibian yiguo)* [emphasis added]. This should be clear."[78]

Chen's words evoked memories of Lee Teng-hui's special state-to-state (*teshu guoyuguo*) formulation, but the similarities of their remarks were more evident in Chinese than in translation. In Lee's case, *guo* was rendered "state," carrying that word's connotations in international law. In Chen's case, *guo* was translated "country." Because the Chinese word is the same, that amounts to a distinction without a difference. In any case, without further elaboration of what Chen meant it is hard to tell what the difference between "state" and "country" might be, and if one goes to the core of each concept—both refer to sovereign entities—then any differences are insignificant. His assertion that "Taiwan is not a part of any other country" certainly contradicted Beijing's position. Yet his rejection of subordination to another authority and his specific focus on Hong Kong and Macau as the negative point of reference were not inconsistent with Taiwan's past positions. To say that China and Taiwan were each countries was no doubt offensive to Beijing, but it did not in and of itself rule out certain kinds of national unions, although it did rule out the one-country, two-systems arrangement.

But the damage was done. Chen's statement dashed the hopes of those in China who may have held a slender hope that he would not test Beijing's tolerance, and it reconfirmed the beliefs of those who thought he could not be trusted.[79]Another source of worry for Beijing was his call for serious consideration of legislation to enable the holding of referenda, which was a long-standing objective of the DPP; China, however, feared that he was creating a mechanism for declaring independence. A vicious cycle was at work. Chen was frustrated by Beijing's treatment of him and felt the need to appeal to the DPP's traditional supporters as the next presidential election neared.

The *yibian yiguo* episode solidified China's mistrust of him and its inclination to prepare for the worst.

Chen did not totally abandon a moderate approach on the question of mainland relations. He offered his most extensive and substantive views on Taiwan and cross-Strait relations in a January 22, 2003, session with a delegation of the Foreign Policy Research Institute. He began by criticizing the PRC's policy of threatening Taiwan militarily, isolating it politically, and trying to downgrade its status to that of a local government—and all the while engaging it economically. He asserted that the ROC—not Taiwan, to which he and other DPP leaders usually referred—was a sovereign state, with jurisdiction over Taiwan, Penghu, Jinmen, and Mazu. He denied that he was being provocative by making that assertion. Indeed, he felt compelled to do so by virtue of his constitutional position as the president of the Republic of China—and to remind the international community that Taiwan was not a part of the PRC. He acknowledged that the people of Taiwan and China "share the same blood, culture, and historical background" but rejected the idea that Taiwan was subordinate to China or a part of the PRC. He placed the blame for the cross-Strait stalemate on the PRC. It had engaged in "unfriendly behavior while Taiwan had tried to take positive steps." He called on Beijing to resume dialogue. He repeated his proposal for economic and cultural integration as the starting point for building trust and a framework for peace and political integration.[80]

As the March 2004 election approached, Chen took new initiatives that raised concerns about his ultimate intentions. In May 2003, he called for referenda to address such controversial issues as nuclear power, the size of the legislature, and whether Taiwan should be allowed to participate in the World Health Organization. The last issue was particularly sensitive for China because, depending on how the question was worded, it could touch on Taiwan's legal identity. In September he called for a new constitution to rectify problems in Taiwan's political system (for some of the problems, see chapter 6) and, as he put it, to make Taiwan a normal country. Increasingly, he equated the one-China principle with the one-country, two-systems formula and its subordinating effect on Taiwan: in October he asserted that "under the 'one China' principle, Taiwan cannot be an independent, sovereign country; it is nothing more than a part, a local province, or a special administrative region of some other country." In December he referred to one China as a "myth" that Taiwan should abandon. There was talk in the DPP of holding referenda on the one-country, two-systems question and changing the name of the ROC to Taiwan. All of that increased Chinese and U.S. concern.[81]

Some observers believed that those initiatives were primarily election tactics, and that has been my interpretation. To win reelection, Chen had to mobilize a weak political base in a hotly contested race, and referenda and a new constitution were traditional goals of the DPP. He could also gain by putting the pan-Blue opposition on the defensive for its more accommodating, so-called "pro-unification" approach to China (hence his linking the one-China principle and the one-country, two-systems approach). Other analysts were more skeptical, seeing in his actions an effort to incrementally establish a basis for the permanent separation of Taiwan from China. Moreover, Chen's reaffirmation of his inaugural pledges was not reassuring, coming as they did with the qualification that they applied to his term in office as the tenth president of the ROC and only if Beijing did not intend to use force. The project for a new constitution was to occur after Chen's first term, and the PRC's military buildup could conceivably be interpreted as evidence of intention to use force. Moreover, the inaugural pledges did not rule out referenda or a new constitution. Excluded were referenda to choose unification or independence, to change the name of the country, and to include Lee Teng-hui's state-to-state formula in the constitution.

Whatever Chen's intention, one motivation for taking these steps cannot be ruled out—that is, that he was increasingly frustrated by the PRC's strategy of ignoring, isolating, and undermining him, which prevented him from achieving a record of performance that would help his reelection. Like Lee Teng-hui in 1993 and 1994, Chen concluded that goodwill and restraint had gotten him nowhere; he therefore had little incentive to exercise restraint, particularly when domestic politics dictated otherwise.

Summing Up

Beijing stated its position on Lee's actions and intentions most fully and categorically in its February 2000 white paper on the Taiwan Strait issue, where it alleged that

> Since the early 1990s, Lee Teng-hui has gradually deviated from the One-China Principle, trumpeting notions such as "two governments," "two reciprocal political entities," "Taiwan is already a state with independent sovereignty," and "At the present stage, the Republic of China is on Taiwan and the People's Republic of China is on the mainland." Moreover, he went back on his words, saying that "I have never said that there is only one China." In addition, he has connived at and provided support for the separatists who advocate "Taiwan independence" and their activities, thus helping the rapid development of the "Taiwan

independence" forces and the spread of the "Taiwan independence" ideology. Under the direction of Lee Teng-hui, the Taiwan authorities have adopted a series of measures toward actual separation. Since 1999, Lee Teng-hui has stepped up his separatist activities. In May, he published the book *The Road to Democracy*, which advocates the division of China into seven regions, each enjoying "full autonomy." On July 9, he went so far as to publicly distort the inter-Straits relations as "state-to-state relations, or at least special state-to-state relations," in an attempt to fundamentally change the status of Taiwan as a part of China, sabotage the relations between both sides of the Taiwan Straits, especially the basis for cross-Straits political dialogues and negotiations, and wreck the foundation for peaceful reunification.[82]

Among the "measures toward actual separation" that the white paper cited were reform of the political structure, seeking more international space, purchasing weapons from the United States, and creating a Taiwan identity, particularly among young people.

The white paper's indictment against Lee was absolute: "Lee Teng-hui has become the general representative of Taiwan's separatist forces, a saboteur of the stability of the Taiwan Straits, a stumbling-block preventing the development of relations between China and the United States, and a troublemaker for the peace and stability of the Asia-Pacific region."

Similarly, Beijing has asserted that Chen Shui-bian is also pursuing a "splittist" agenda. On the day of Chen's inauguration in 2000, the PRC's Taiwan Affairs Office announced that Chen's refusal to accept the one-China principle (which Beijing knew to be his position) was tantamount to pursuing "the separatist policy of 'Taiwan independence.'" In August 2002, after some remarks by Chen that Beijing found especially provocative, it declared that he had used "all possible means and pretexts to attain his 'Taiwan independence' goal in incremental fashion." It charged that, contrary to respecting the popular will, he had "imposed on the Taiwan people the separatist conspiracy of a very small number of 'Taiwan independence' diehards."[83]

Are those allegations really justified? Are Lee and Chen alone responsible for the cross-Strait impasse? If they are, then untying the Taiwan knot would require some way of changing the intentions and actions of the island's leaders. Or does the reason for the conflict lie elsewhere?

Based on Lee Teng-hui's many words about cross-Strait relations during the twelve years and four months of his presidency, several conclusions can be drawn. First of all, he did not advocate a Taiwan nation-state that was separate from the entity called China, Beijing's charges to the contrary notwithstanding. Throughout his years as ROC president, his primary goal was to define the terms and conditions under which unification should take place, not whether it should. As time went on, he refined those terms, making them more precise, but the stated objective remained the same. Even at the end of his last term, when he asserted explicitly that the Republic of China was a state on a par with the PRC, he portrayed that status as congruent with the unification of China.

Second, Lee's core principles were remarkably constant. He emphasized three basic points. First of all, if there was to be a unified China, the government in Taipei had to be recognized as possessing sovereignty and being essentially equal to the government in Beijing. Second, Taiwan had the right to play a significant role in the international community. Third, Beijing's growing military capabilities and its refusal to renounce their use was an obstacle to reconciliation. Those principles by definition ruled out a one-country, two-systems approach. The relative emphasis among them changed over time. The stress on international participation grew in the mid-1990s in response to domestic frustration over the island's isolation, as did attention to its Taiwan identity. Lee demanded that Beijing renounce the use of force as an immediate precondition for progress up until 1996 and then dropped it for a while. He announced his state-to-state formula after many years of referring to two equal political entities, probably in anticipation of negotiations on political issues. Yet those were shifts of emphasis in the midst of remarkable continuity.

Of course, Beijing and others will argue that Lee's claims for the ROC were inconsistent with unification or that they were a ploy to rule out unification. From the PRC's point of view, offering any proposal at odds with its one-country, two-systems arrangement—and any proposal premised on sovereignty of the Taipei government—is tantamount to permanently separating Taiwan from China. That inference is correct only if national unions cannot be created among sovereign entities, yet history has its share of confederations, federations, and commonwealths. Designing such a union for the two sides of the Taiwan Strait would not be easy, but that is different from concluding that Lee Teng-hui was a separatist simply because he asserted that the ROC was a sovereign entity. Similarly, Lee's approach got tougher as time went on, but there was a reason for that. The issues in cross-Strait relations were shifting from practical matters to political negotiations, and with the shift came the need to define more precisely the legal status of the Taiwan government.

There is some justification in concluding that Lee's special state-to-state pronouncement was a significant shift in position; it was, to be sure, a new way of talking about a long-standing issue. Undoubtedly, Beijing interpreted the statement in a very negative light.[84] I am inclined to believe that Lee was making explicit what had been implicit in Lee's and Taipei's views on the first of its three key, constant issues—the nature of the government in Taipei.

Lee did state his positions more provocatively than some other officials in his government. Rhetorical toughness—based on his belief that weakness on the part of Taiwan would only invite more Chinese aggressiveness—was a part of his negotiating style. In an October 1991 interview, for example, he complained that Beijing was a "bully."[85] And there is evidence that Lee made his state-to-state pronouncement in part because he had received information that Beijing would make an announcement framing cross-Strait relations in a way that would put Taiwan on the defensive. He therefore decided to preempt any such statement with one of his own.[86] More generally, some of Lee's initiatives constituted a frustrated response to Beijing's inflexible stance.

In the 1990s, Lee's position was right in the mainstream of Taiwan views on cross-Strait relations. Public opinion and all major political parties agreed with his basic principles. Lee opposed the one-country, two-systems arrangement for reasons that most people on Taiwan would support, and he used his influence to shape that consensus as one part of his strategy to prevent an unthinking, automatic accommodation of Beijing.[87] He was tapping strong and preexisting sentiments, which Beijing only made stronger through its steps to intimidate the Taiwan people.

Some might charge that whatever Lee said, his actions revealed a less-than-benign intent. The PRC white paper of February 2000 listed a number of his "measures toward actual separation," including reforming the political structure, creating a Taiwan identity, purchasing weapons from the United States, and seeking more international space. Yet most of those steps had a legitimate justification and were taken in response to demands from within Taiwan society. U.S. weapons were necessary to counter China's military modernization and buildup and its refusal to renounce the use of force. And each step was consistent with Taipei's definition of its status as a sovereign government. None was prima facie proof that Lee intended to permanently separate Taiwan from China—*unless the formula for unification rejected Taiwan's claim of sovereignty, as China's did.* And Lee's actions did not necessarily have the significance that Beijing attributed to them.

Some have suggested that Lee's behavior after he left office proves that he was a separatist during his time as president. Lee Teng-hui did shift toward a more radical course after he left the chairmanship of the KMT under pressure from conservative forces. He laid low for a while and then reentered politics. He fostered the emergence of the Taiwan Solidarity Union, which is the party most inclined toward independence and which often acted as an ally of the DPP. Freed from the constraints of office, he also promoted a vision that only reaffirmed Beijing's view of him. He supported changing the national title from the Republic of China to Taiwan—or even the Republic of Taiwan. He asserted that as a result of the constitutional amendments of the 1990s, a Second Republic already had emerged. And Lee certainly placed even more emphasis than before on the need for a strong Taiwan identity.

Yet this more radical stance was still defensive in character, a product of his concern that Taiwan was weak and needed to be stronger. He believed that the island's people had been victims of "alien rule" for more than two centuries and had unquestioningly absorbed the Chinese mentality. They had not been able to shape their own destiny; they even lacked the consciousness that they were "masters of this soil." He therefore recommended that the education system focus on Taiwan's history and the trend of globalization; that the economy be retooled to ensure competitiveness against a rising China *and* to strengthen Taiwan's identity; and that a constitution be adopted that was more compatible with the island's realities than the existing one, which was adopted on the mainland in 1947 and bequeathed Taiwan "a government system with the old China in mind." In short, Taiwan could face an increasingly strong China only if the people of Taiwan were able to strengthen their sense of themselves.[88]

Even to conclude that Lee was a separatist in retirement (his actual statements suggest more nuance than he is usually credited for) does not necessarily prove that he was one in office. What matters is what he said and did during the period that he was ultimately responsible for the people of Taiwan and was a participant in the decisionmaking process of the ROC government. His record does not confirm the allegation. If he was in fact a separatist all along, which I do not believe, then he repressed his intentions during his presidency. At the time that he had the most power and opportunity to attain his purported goal, the substance of his approach toward China did nothing to serve that goal—and he received no reciprocation from Beijing.

Chen Shui-bian's point of departure was very different from Lee Teng-hui's. He was a leading figure in the Democratic Progressive Party, which had long harbored the dream of a Taiwan totally separate from China, a Republic of Taiwan. And to retain the loyalty of his party, he had to bow to those sentiments—for example, by referring to China and Taiwan as different countries. He came into office after more than a decade of cross-Strait interaction, and the evolution of mainland policy under Lee Teng-hui would constrain Chen to some extent. Lee had not had a completely blank slate, to be sure, but he was less "path dependent" than Chen would be.

In some respects, however, Chen Shui-bian's political course has been similar to Lee Teng-hui's. Like Lee, he had come to realize that political imperatives required him to abandon past orthodoxy. Just as Lee Teng-hui had downplayed (but not abandoned) the goal of unification in order to secure political support in a democratic system, so Chen understood that the DPP would have to deemphasize its historical commitment to an independent Taiwan if it were going to become a ruling party. During the campaign for the 2000 elections, Chen tried very hard to reassure the electorate that he would not take any ideologically inspired actions that would threaten Taiwan's peace and prosperity. He did not object to discussing "one China" as an issue but refused to accept it a priori as a principle. Just as Lee had had to adjust what he said and did during his second term to take some account of U.S. views, so too Chen understood that he would have to modulate his position in order to secure U.S. support. Similarly, during the first years of his presidency, the more ideologically motivated members of his party constrained him from getting too far ahead of DPP orthodoxy, to the point that he chose to reverse course as his reelection campaign loomed. In part to respond to party pressure, he took steps to strengthen the Taiwan identity, as Lee had for different reasons. For example, in an episode recounted in chapter 6, he gave in to pressure from DPP fundamentalists to put the word "Taiwan" on the front of new ROC passports. Beijing saw this as part of a campaign of "creeping independence," but it could also be evidence of a delicate balancing act between domestic politics and external realities. And like Lee Teng-hui, Chen Shui-bian became increasingly frustrated with Beijing's rigid attitude and lost his incentive to exercise restraint.

Chen did not talk in as much depth as Lee Teng-hui on the substantive disagreement between Beijing and Taipei, in part because Beijing framed the discussion around the question of whether Chen would accept the one-China principle and in part because of political constraints. There is no question that Chen's approach took on a hard edge during his campaign for reelection and only confirmed Beijing's judgment that he was a separatist.

Yet that judgment is contradicted by a theme that runs through Chen's statements, affirming that certain kinds of unification are possible and that, like Lee Teng-hui, he is not opposed to unification per se. His proposal regarding a possible integration process, including political integration, is the clearest evidence of a more open-minded approach than Beijing gave him credit for, in spite of his domestic political constraints. And even in the heat of his reelection, when he emphasized most strongly that China and Taiwan were two different countries, he held open the possibility of some kind of union. Chen tried, in a *Time* magazine interview in mid-February 2004, to signal that the door to a union of some kind was not closing:

> My belief, my basic thinking of cross-strait relations throughout the 20 years of my political career has been that, since ancient times, a unified state or situation over a long period of time in the world will eventually give way to separation. Likewise, a long period of separation is bound to lead to unification again some day. Therefore, a country may be divided into a number of countries, while many countries may also unite into one. . . . Currently, there are two separate, independent countries across the Taiwan Strait, neither of which has jurisdiction over the other. But who knows if these two separate countries might become one over time?[89]

Neither Lee nor Chen was acting in a vacuum. Each in his own way was responding to a PRC offer whose fundamentals did not change during their presidencies, even when they, in their minds, sought to demonstrate an openness to some form of unification. In neither case did Beijing seek to engage Taipei, listen to Taiwan's views, and adjust its own accordingly. It chose not to probe Taiwan's ideas when the atmosphere was relatively conducive to dialogue and when doing so would have given it the opportunity to gauge Taiwan's true intentions and determine whether they actually were antithetical to its own approach. When times were bad, it cut off dialogue altogether and imposed a political price for any resumption. Lee and Chen responded to China's obstinacy with mounting frustration and then toughened their respective approaches, clearly making the situation worse. But if China does not like where Lee Teng-hui ended up and where Chen Shui-bian is going, it is not without blame. Moreover, Lee and Chen have had to operate in a democratic political environment that is characterized by intense, cutthroat competition, a still-evolving environment in which ideological followers hold pragmatic leaders to strict account and in which not everyone has learned how to play the game. More than a decade after this political system took shape, Beijing still does not understand it and or how to influence it.

It is not possible, of course, to know what Lee Teng-hui and Chen Shui-bian desire in their heart of hearts. They would probably take a Republic of Taiwan if they could get it without running serious risks. One can find things that they said and did that may justify the conclusion that they were separatists, as charged by Beijing, yet those "facts" must be weighed against other evidence that suggests another conclusion: that their respective approaches to China were more complicated and flexible than Beijing has given them credit for. Their substantive approaches were not fundamentally at odds with China's fundamental goal: ending the division between the two sides of the Strait. For both, however, the primary issue was the legal status of the government that they headed in a unified China. As leaders in a democratic system, Lee and Chen could not ignore domestic political pressures if they wanted to remain leaders. China's failure to seriously engage them, along with a variety of other alienating actions, shaped their views in profound ways. If we are to learn why the Taiwan knot is tied, we must look for explanations other than their alleged separatism.

The Taiwan Paradox

Taiwan, therefore, presents a paradox. Economically and socially, Taiwan is being pulled into China's orbit. The island can balance the mainland's magnetic force by enhancing its business ties with the United States, Japan, Southeast Asia, and so on, but only up to a point. If the island's companies are to survive, they have little choice but to take advantage of the incentives that the mainland has to offer. Globalization dictates that if Taiwan companies—even high-tech companies—are to remain competitive, they must locate some of their activities in the PRC. As former premier Vincent Siew has asserted, cross-Strait relations are critical to Taiwan's medium- and long-term development: "Taiwan," he said, "cannot afford to ignore the immense mainland market."[90] Socially, the urban areas of China's east coast are attractive to some Taiwan people because the middle-class society that Taiwan already has become is emerging there, without the costs and some of the turmoil.

This economic and social logic does not affect all residents of Taiwan—or even a significant majority. And the migration of production facilities does foster anxiety about hollowing out, fifth columnists, and becoming hostage to the PRC's economic sanctions. Still, the business imperative is fairly irresistible.

But nonetheless, the economic and social logic does not produce a corresponding logic in favor of political reconciliation. Quite the opposite—for two decades, Beijing and Taipei have been at loggerheads over the terms and conditions under which that reconciliation might take place. The PRC has insisted on its one-country, two-systems formula. Lee Teng-hui and Chen Shui-bian have rejected that formula and insisted that Beijing treat their government as an equal, sovereign entity with rights of participation in the international system and that it renounce the use of force, something that Beijing is unwilling to do. Moreover, Taiwan's resistance grew as the economic interdependence between the two deepened. What explains this paradox? Why is it that people of the same ethnic background who have many reasons to collaborate in the production of goods and services cannot find a basis for compromise when it comes to issues of power and authority—to the point that military conflict is not an implausible outcome?

One reason is that China apparently has misunderstood the fundamental position of Taiwan's leaders. From their statements and actions, Beijing has inferred that their goal is to permanently separate Taiwan from the entity called China and to obstruct unification. Those statements may be so interpreted if the point of departure is Beijing's constricted set of terms and conditions, which dictates that it construe Chen's and Lee's actions as separatist. Yet, as one can see, there are reasons to dismiss that explanation. A less narrow approach to the question of national union on China's part would yield a very different conclusion. A different approach to *how* Taiwan might be part of China would produce a more positive answer to the question of whether it *should be* a part of China. Because of its narrow perspective, Beijing thus has missed opportunities to make the objective of unification attractive to Taiwan's people and their leaders.

There is, of course, the possibility that Beijing understood Lee and Chen perfectly well but chose to reject their proposals for reasons that had nothing to do with the substance of their views. Perhaps the one-country, two-systems proposal was immutable because Deng Xiaoping was its author. Perhaps China feared that if it acknowledged that the Taiwan government possessed sovereignty—that sovereignty could be shared—then Hong Kong, Macau, Xinjiang, the Dalai Lama, and even Guangdong and Shanghai might seek to take advantage of the precedent. Perhaps it feared that Lee Teng-hui's approach to the Chinese state and its constituent elements might undermine the Chinese Communist Party's legitimacy and its claim to rule as the exclusive sovereign.[91] (And perhaps labeling Lee and Chen as separatists was a useful way to deflect attention from the real issues facing China).

Whether its judgment of Lee and Chen was a substantive misperception or something else, Beijing's definition of them as separatists has created a serious obstacle to any serious resolution of the Taiwan Strait issue, and it obscures a proper understanding of what really divides China and Taiwan.

Most in Taiwan, on the other hand, understand that the trends are not in their favor. China's economic attraction will grow, binding Taiwan companies even more tightly to the mainland. The People's Liberation Army will acquire even more effective capabilities and, with them, the potential for intimidating Taiwan. So the island faces a choice regarding how to cope with the challenges posed by China's proximity. Should it accommodate the economic logic or continue its resistance of the last decade? Ignoring this unhappy dilemma is not an option. Avoiding a choice is itself a choice.

Identifying this paradox does not explain it, specifically why political reconciliation has been so difficult. If the stalemate is not part of a separatist project on the part of Taiwan's leaders, as Beijing alleges, then what are the strands of this seemingly untiable knot? That is the focus of the next two chapters.

4

The Sovereignty Issue

Examination of Lee Teng-hui's and Chen Shui-bian's response to the one-country, two-systems proposal reveals two things. On one hand, they did not have a separatist agenda that would rule out all formulas for unification. On the other, they opposed the one-country, two-systems concept and rejected the idea that Taiwan was a part of the People's Republic of China. At the core of their opposition was their fundamental view of the legal character of the government in Taipei—that is, that it possessed sovereignty and that its status would have to be recognized if unification was to occur. Taipei's goal has not been to avoid being a part of China, as Beijing sought to frame it. Rather, the issue was *how* Taiwan might be part of China—or more precisely, how the governing authority in Taipei would be part of the state called China. Would the Taipei government be subordinate to the government in Beijing? Or would it be in some sense equivalent to the government, as part of a larger union?

Sovereignty is one of two substantive issues at the heart of the political dispute between Taipei and Beijing; security is the other. Sovereignty is a matter of principle, an either-or issue. If there is to be a union between the two entities, either the government of the PRC/mainland part of the union will have sovereignty over the ROC/Taiwan part or it will not. The Taipei government could voluntarily choose to cede elements of its sovereignty during negotiations if it had reason to do so. Fundamentally, however, resolving the conceptual stalemate will require *either* that Taiwan give up its claim that its government possesses sovereignty *or* that China significantly amend the one-country, two-systems formula. It is hard to see how disagreement on this core issue could be papered over for very long.

The possibility that Taiwan might drop its claim cannot be ruled out. Growing economic and social interaction between the two sides of the Strait over an extended period may make the PRC offer more palatable, particularly if military tensions are low. For now, however, that outcome appears to be an unlikely. The one-country, two-systems concept has not received broad public support on the island. The one member of the Legislative Yuan who endorsed it, Feng Hu-hsiang, was defeated in the 2001 elections. Moreover, the three leading political parties—the DPP, the KMT, and the People First Party (PFP) of James Soong—all endorse some version of the principle that the ROC is an independent, sovereign state. Even the PFP, which is said to favor unification, reaffirmed that principle in August 2000, when it rejected the idea that Taiwan was a part of the PRC, stated its opposition to the one-country, two-systems proposal, and asserted that each side of the Taiwan Strait "has its own rights and obligations concerning international affairs."[1]

This chapter explores the sovereignty issue in detail, beginning with a discussion of how the concept, along with the related concept of the state, is interpreted. Next it assesses the ramifications of the implementation of the one-country, two-systems model in Hong Kong for the preservation of sovereignty on Taiwan. Finally, it assesses whether the idea of sovereignty is outmoded when China and Taiwan are becoming increasingly interdependent.

Concepts: Sovereignty and the State

What is meant by *sovereignty*? What is meant by a related idea, the *state*? The concept of sovereignty emerged as a response to the overlapping lines of authority that existed during the High Middle Ages. Its core idea was territorial exclusivity, the discrete alignment of certain governmental units (states) with the territory and people over which those units ruled. In the Middle Ages, the relationship between rulers on one hand and territories and peoples on the other was highly ambiguous. Multiple authorities at various levels—feudal lords, kings, and rulers of the Holy Roman Empire—could claim the same territory and the people within it, along with the right to intervene in their affairs. A single ruler could be subject to several overlords. The Catholic Church asserted jurisdiction over the people and life of secular political units within Christendom (a nonterritorial construct). The ultimate authority in any one political system, its territory, and its people was therefore open to question.

The European political order that had emerged by the time of the Treaty of Westphalia in 1648 was, in contrast, a model of clarity. The primary actors in the international system were sovereign states, each of which had a well-defined territory and population. Competing lines of authority and the rights of suprastate actors like the Church were significantly reduced and restricted, if not eliminated entirely. Regarding politics within political systems, theorists like Bodin and Hobbes sought to define the ultimate source of authority, against which rebellion was not a legitimate act. States became the principal entities possessing international legal personality and the primary actors in the international system. States were the beneficiaries of the Westphalian norms of independence and noninterference in internal affairs. New states came into being by and large through the actions of existing states or with their assent. In the twentieth century, states created most of the world's international governmental organizations and in many cases limited membership in those organizations to other states.

This evolution from overlap to exclusivity and from ambiguity to clarity occurred over a long period, with other models of organization, such as the Hanseatic League, competing with the state for a time. But in the end, state sovereignty became the organizing principle of European—and soon international—political life. The concept refers to "supremacy over all other authorities within that territory and population" on one hand and "independence of outside authorities" and freedom from their intervention and interference in internal affairs on the other. Indeed, "many writers essentially equate sovereignty with independence, the fundamental authority of a state to exercise its powers without being subservient to any outside authority."[2]

Applying the concepts of sovereignty and the state requires operationalizing them. For the concept of the state, the best guide is the classic definition of statehood enunciated in Article 1 of the Montevideo Convention of 1933: "The State as a person of international law should possess the following qualifications: (a) permanent population; (b) a defined territory; (c) government; and (d) capacity to enter into relations with other States." Some specialists on international law argue that statehood is a more useful concept than sovereignty, regarding the latter as "a somewhat unhelpful, but firmly established, description of statehood."[3]

Stephen Krasner distinguishes four distinct dimensions of the concept of sovereignty.[4] The first he terms domestic sovereignty, which traditionally was the most important dimension and the concern of Bodin and Hobbes. This refers to how public authority is organized within the state and how it might be effectively exercised within the state's borders. Ideas about domestic sovereignty have evolved over time. Hobbes proposed the concentration of authority in a single ruler, while Locke and Montesquieu, among others, argued that authority would be enhanced by sharing power among institutions. But all addressed the question of who governs within.

The second is what Krasner calls Westphalian sovereignty, which refers to "political organization based on the exclusion of external actors from authority structures within a given territory." This is sovereignty in the sense of independence vis-à-vis outside parties. The issue here is whether the governing authorities of a particular territory, however they are organized, have the absolute right to rule within their domain, a right that is established when other states accept the norm of noninterference in that territory's affairs. Those authorities may choose to limit their powers through treaties with other actors or to delegate some to international organizations, but they do so voluntarily.

The third dimension is international legal sovereignty, which refers to the status of those entities that possess formal juridical independence and thus a "ticket of general admission to the international arena." Those entities are known as states in international law (more on that below). They establish their status by securing recognition as states from other states and membership in organizations like the United Nations that by charter are open to states only. The concern here is whether a government and the people under its jurisdiction may participate in the international system.

The fourth dimension is "interdependence sovereignty," which is "the ability of public authorities to regulate the flow of information, ideas, goods, people, pollutants, or capital across the borders of their state." It has become commonplace to note that globalization has degraded at least interdependence sovereignty, if not the other types as well.

Krasner notes that these four types of sovereignty do not necessarily correlate with each other. A government may be recognized as a state and a member of the United Nations but also face challenges to its domestic authority from internal opponents; it may have no control over its borders; and it may lack the ability to fend off intervention from external forces.[5] As discussed below, Taiwan is weak on international sovereignty and stronger on the others.

In applying the concepts of sovereignty and statehood, China and Taiwan have come up with conflicting results. And Taiwan's democratization has produced different views within the island's population itself.

The State

From a common-sense perspective, Taiwan meets—and it asserts that it meets—all the Montevideo criteria. It has a capable government that rules over a well-defined territory and permanent population. It conducts relations—at least substantive if not diplomatic relations—with other states. And from that standpoint, the ROC on Taiwan meets these qualifications much better than many of the member states of the United Nations, from which Taiwan is excluded because of pressure from the PRC. In Robert Jackson's terms, it possesses "empirical statehood" if not "juridical statehood."[6] Indeed, Taiwan is the prime example of a political entity whose governing effectiveness far exceeds its internationally recognized status.

The Taipei government has long used the formulation "independent, sovereign state" to describe itself. A gloss on the word "independent" is required. Does that imply that Taiwan (the DPP's preferred term) or the ROC (the KMT's preference) is a totally separate country? A careful review reveals a web of complexity. First of all, this formulation is not recent. Chiang Kai-shek's statement on the ROC's forced departure from the United Nations and Chiang Ching-kuo's response in December 1978 to the U.S. termination of diplomatic relations with Taiwan included this statement: "The Republic of China an independent, sovereign state." And neither of them can be charged with pursuing Taiwan independence.[7] Second, the Chinese version of that sentence—*Zhonghua Minguo shi yige zhuquan duli de guojia*—is different from the Taipei government's English rendition of it. A more precise English translation would be "The ROC is a state whose sovereignty is independent" or "whose sovereignty is independently derived." A simpler and more precise translation would be "The ROC is a sovereign state." Third, as noted above, international law specialists would argue that independence from any external authority is the defining characteristic of sovereignty.[8] So when the Taipei government uses the "independent, sovereign state" formulation, it can be read as a statement about the nature and status of the governing authority of what they call the Republic of China: that it is not subordinate to the PRC.

Beijing, on the other hand, has asserted that in 1949 the Republic of China ceased to exist as the government of the state called China and was replaced by the government of the PRC. Beginning in 1949, it asserted its right to represent China in the international community, and within three decades most other states around the world had agreed that the PRC was the sole legal government of China. Moreover, Beijing says, the territory of Taiwan was returned formally to the state called China in 1945. It bases that assertion on three grounds: the Cairo Declaration in 1943, which expressed the Allied Powers' intention to return Taiwan to China; the Nationalist takeover of the island in 1945; and, since 1949, the formal acknowledgment by most of the countries that have recognized the PRC that Taiwan is part of China. All that remains to be done is to end the division between the two sides of the Strait and bring political reality into accord with China's claim under international law. In Beijing's view, neither Taiwan nor the ROC—the former as a new state, the latter as a competing government of the long-existing state called China—has an international legal personality. Neither, therefore, is a state. Moreover, there is no international mechanism to authoritatively validate any claim to statehood that Taipei might make and to dismiss the counterclaim of the PRC that it is simply a subordinate unit of China. Without such a mechanism, China's power is sufficient to maintain the gap between Taiwan's capacity to govern and its legal status.[9]

Even if one accepts the general idea that Taiwan meets the functional criteria for statehood, some anomalies are at play here. The first stems from conflicting views over the origin and identity of the state in question. Under Kuomintang rule, the ROC government asserted that it was the government of the state called China and that it had existed since 1912, after the fall of the Qing dynasty, to the present time. The conventional view within the Taiwanese opposition was very different—that is, that Taiwan was a separate nation-state that was not in any way connected with the state called China. They note that whatever the intention stated in the Cairo Declaration, the transfer of title over the island from Japan back to China after World War II was never executed. KMT rule was illegitimate. Moreover, the popular sovereignty that comes with a democratic system has created an alternative basis for state formation. In its purer form, this was an argument for establishing a Republic of Taiwan.[10]

Over time, both the KMT and the DPP opposition, starting from different places, moved toward a rhetorical middle ground. Lee Teng-hui used the term "Republic of China on Taiwan"—more clearly identifying the ROC with the territory under its control—and began to stress popular sovereignty as the basis of the ROC's legitimacy. He asserted that Taiwan did not have to declare independence because it was independent already. The DPP, as it prepared in 1999 for Chen Shui-bian's campaign for the presidency, took the traditional ROC formulation and gave it a novel and significant twist. Its 1999 resolution on cross-Strait relations states: "Taiwan is a sovereign and independent country [or state, the Chinese word is the same]. . . . Taiwan, although named the Republic of China under its current constitution, is not subject to the jurisdiction of the People's Republic of China." Note that the entity that is sovereign and independent is Taiwan, not the Republic of China, which was only the current, constitutionally prescribed name of Taiwan. So the DPP was going further than the KMT in its assertion of statehood.

To be sure, politics was at work in these shifts. Lee Teng-hui wanted to maintain support among Taiwanese voters who might consider switching from the KMT to the DPP. Chen wanted to position himself so that he both retained the support of the true believers in the DPP and reached out to more moderate voters who feared that he would bring disaster on Taiwan. Both manipulated the terms "Republic of China" and "independence" for their respective purposes. Each proclaimed that the ROC, or Taiwan, was already independent. For both, the assertion of statehood was designed, in part, to reject subordination to the PRC. The core issue here is whether such a formulation closes the door on any sort of unification—and it does not, because there are political unions composed of sovereign states. So some flexibility remains.

A second anomaly concerns the territory over which the ROC government claims to be sovereign. If the essence of statehood is territorial exclusivity, then what territory belongs to the ROC? Within Taiwan itself there has been a disagreement. The ROC constitution of 1947 did not specify what the territory was, but the ROC government asserted that it included mainland China, Taiwan, the Pescadores, and, for complicated reasons, what is now the Republic of Mongolia.[11] After the KMT regime retreated to Taiwan in 1949, it maintained its position that it was sovereign over all of China, and it did not recognize the PRC's jurisdiction over the mainland. In the early 1990s, the Lee Teng-hui government shifted that position, reasserting the ROC's claim to sovereignty over all of China but confining its *jurisdiction* (the area of actual political and administrative control) to the islands of Taiwan, Penghu, Jinmen, and Mazu and acknowledging the PRC's jurisdiction over the mainland. Traditionally, the DPP held that the scope of Taiwan's sovereignty was confined to Taiwan, Penghu, Jinmen, Mazu.

Here again, there was some movement toward the middle. As observed in the last chapter, one interpretation of Lee's special state-to-state formulation in July 1999 maintains that he restricted the ROC's sovereignty *only* to Taiwan, Penghu, and the offshore islands in order to eliminate the ambiguity that had existed concerning the territory issue. Similarly, the DPP, in its May 1999 statement, used the lesser term "jurisdiction" to refer to those territories, not "sovereignty." And in February 2004, Chen Shui-bian said, "Some people ask if the territory of our state includes Outer Mongolia or even the mainland of China. There is the People's Republic of China on the mainland of China and the Republic of Mongolia in Outer Mongolia, both of which are members of the United Nations. We will not naively and ignorantly make a fool of ourselves internationally by saying that our territory includes the Republic of Mongolia and the People's Republic of China."[12]

The intersection of state identity and the question of territory creates a third anomaly. As Jacques deLisle cogently points out, there is an inconsistency in what the Taiwan government asserts the state to be. If it identifies with the historical ROC as the government of the state called China, it weakens its claim that it meets the Montevideo criteria because, arguably, its actual territory is ambiguous (is it really all of China?). If it argues that it meets the Montevideo criteria based on its rule of Taiwan and the associated islands, then it does so on behalf of a state, Taiwan, that no other party is willing to acknowledge. Thus, "Taipei best satisfies the 'assertion' test [that it is a state] with respect to an entity (the original, but diminished ROC) that is not the one which most clearly displays the other elements of statehood (a separate, 'new' state of Taiwan)."[13]

So the situation regarding statehood is muddled. The PRC insists that the ROC does not exist and that Taiwan will have subordinate status after reunification. Taiwan's assertions about its statehood certainly conflict with the one-country, two-systems formula, and some go further than others, but none, it appears, excludes the possibility of some kind of unification. Some students of international law have reached the conclusion that Taiwan is not a state.[14] Yet Taiwan's case is not frivolous, and on Taiwan there is a broad consensus that the Taipei government possesses a character that puts it much more on a par with the government in Beijing than with the Hong Kong Special Administrative Region.

Sovereignty

On Krasner's four dimensions of sovereignty—domestic, interdependence, Westphalian, and international—Taiwan also earns a mixed score. With respect to domestic sovereignty, the island's government has been coherent and effective since the ROC transferred its capital there in 1949. It has undergone a profound transformation from autocracy to democracy. From the late 1940s to the mid-1980s, with the KMT penetrating all major institutions, Taiwan was a party-state along Leninist lines. Dominated by a strong leader, it was not accountable to the people, whose demands it ignored, and it suppressed all dissent. Initially, the most powerful institutions (the armed forces, security services, and propaganda units) had the mission of preserving national security as the leader defined it. Over time, power was shared with a technocracy whose mandate was to facilitate economic growth and social modernization. Then in the mid-1980s, Chiang Ching-kuo began—and Lee Teng-hui later completed—a gradual process of liberalization and democratization that turned the party-state into an open and competitive political system. A set of representative institutions with a populist character—electoral parties and a genuine legislature—was superimposed on the national security apparatus, which has atrophied or disappeared in most respects, and the economic technocracy, which has yet to determine its new role. The culmination of the transformation process was the victory of Chen Shui-bian in the presidential election of 2000 and the winning of a plurality of seats in the Legislative Yuan by his Democratic Progressive Party at the end of 2001. The people that the party-state had seen as subversives were now running the government. As Lee said at his second inaugural address, "From now on, the people as a whole, rather than any individual or any political party, will be invested with the ruling power of the nation."

Similarly, regarding interdependence sovereignty, the Taipei government has a significant capacity to control its borders with respect to immigration, customs, quarantine, and capital flows (being an island helps). For more than a decade, however, there has been a problem with illegal immigration by people from the mainland. Moreover, the linking of business operations on each side of the Strait in global supply chains is eroding somewhat the economic segregation that previously existed. On an institutional level, one way that a government can maintain control over its borders is to collaborate with neighboring countries—for example, with their public health authorities in order to control the spread of infectious diseases. In the case of China and Taiwan, however, there is little or no interaction between the two governments.

With respect to Westphalian sovereignty, the Taiwan government has by and large had the absolute right to rule within the area of its jurisdiction without interference by any outside power. Whether autocratic or democratic, the island's central government has been in charge. But there have been exceptions. Arguably, the United States in the 1950s and 1960s leveraged its economic aid to Taiwan to restrain and redirect Chiang Kai-shek's actions. Washington succeeded in shifting Taiwan's economic policy emphasis from import substitution to export-led growth.[15] More recently, and particularly since Chen Shui-bian's election, there have been suggestions that the PRC is trying to penetrate Taiwan politics. Stanley Roth, former U.S. assistant secretary of state for East Asian and Pacific affairs, asserted in January 2001 that Beijing "has essentially embarked upon a very clumsy united front strategy, seeking to bring over elements of the opposition parties and key business leaders to the mainland side."[16]

It is in the area of international sovereignty that Taiwan is the weakest and most vulnerable. Conceptually, historically, and politically, the deck is stacked against it. The conceptual obstacle is the long legal tradition that states are the primary actors in the international system. There is a state called China, which is a member in most international organizations. The ROC held that position in the 1950s and 1960s, and its status was recognized by a majority of the world's countries. After a long struggle, Beijing gained the upper hand in the 1970s. Most countries now recognize the government of the PRC as the sole legal government of China and therefore the rightful holder of China's seat in international organizations like the United Nations. In no state-based international organization is there a member with the name "Taiwan." Most countries recognize in some explicit way that Taiwan is part of China. There are exceptions, most notably the United States. It has only "acknowledged the Chinese position that Taiwan was a part of China," without formally stating its position. Less than thirty countries now recognize the ROC, and the only exception to its exclusion from international organizations is its membership in organizations like APEC (Asia-Pacific Economic Cooperation forum) and the World Trade Organization (WTO), for which membership was not restricted to states but deliberately opened up by the United States and others to economies and special customs territories so that Taiwan could join.

Yet the fact that the ROC's international sovereignty is weak does not ipso facto dictate that it lacks sovereignty altogether. Nor does it restrict any formula for unification with Beijing to those that would place Taipei in a subordinate position. Taiwan scores high on other dimensions of sovereignty, arguably the ones that are relevant for forming a national union. Moreover, the ROC's international sovereignty has diminished only because Beijing has waged a relentless campaign to restrict it and because other countries have gone along. Moreover, Taiwan might have reason to believe that its Westphalian sovereignty might be in jeopardy if it accommodated the one-country, two-systems formula.

This disagreement over the legal identity of the governing authority on Taiwan—over whether it possesses sovereignty—surfaces in many of the disputes between Beijing and Taipei. For example, after Chen Shui-bian's election in March 2000, the PRC demanded that he accept the one-China principle in order to resume cross-Strait dialogue. Chen believed that to accept the one-China principle as China defined it would be to concede that his government did not possess sovereignty. He knew that Beijing defined the one-China principle in at least two ways, neither of them good for Taiwan. For purposes of the international system, the principle is that there is one China in the world, Taiwan is a province of China, and the government of the PRC is the sole representative of China in the international community. That negates Taipei's claim to international sovereignty. For purposes of cross-Strait relations, the principle is that there is one China in the world, Taiwan is a part of China (or, more recently, that the mainland and Taiwan both belong to China), and China's sovereignty and territorial integrity cannot be split.[17] The final element, the "unsplittability" of sovereignty, apparently negates Taipei's claim of Westphalian sovereignty. Given these definitions, Chen feared that to accept the one-China principle at the outset was tantamount to conceding a fundamental issue before the negotiations ever began.[18]

A shift in focus can illuminate the problem of sovereignty. Recall that the above discussion on domestic sovereignty—the organization of internal political power—was limited to the territory under the jurisdiction of the Taiwan government. But what if the focus were on the organization of power within a state called China, a state that, for the sake of argument, encompassed both the territories of Taiwan and the mainland and their respective governments? There would be many options of organizing that state. One would be Beijing's one-country, two-systems model, under which the PRC government alone would constitute the central, national government and the Taiwan authorities would be a subordinate unit, albeit with a measure of autonomy. Yet there might be other configurations of power within the Chinese state that permitted a sharing of sovereignty among constituent units that were equal in their legal character. A confederation, for example, is a national union composed of sovereign units (the European Union is an example). Such an arrangement for domestic sovereignty would have other implications as well. It might accommodate an international role for the constituent units and changes in the regulation of the borders between them. The heart of the matter is how the Taipei government might be part of the Chinese state.

As it does concerning the concept of the state, Taiwan can make a decent case that it is a sovereign entity in functional terms. Yet Beijing's rigid approach to these norms (ironic in a regime that once was part of a project to overturn the international system) has become an obstacle to the very goal that it seeks—unification.

Hong Kong

Hong Kong provides a useful basis for assessing the practical impact of the one-country, two-systems approach on Taiwan's sovereignty, particularly on its domestic and Westphalian sovereignty. Hong Kong, of course, has been the principal test-bed for the formula. For two decades, Beijing has calculated that if Hong Kong lost neither its prosperity nor fundamental freedoms after becoming a special administrative region of the PRC, then the Taiwan leadership and populace would be more likely to accept the formula themselves. If Taiwan were to decide that autonomy or home rule fully protected its interests, then it might abandon the claim that it was a sovereign government.

Yet a close examination of the political system of the Hong Kong Special Administrative Region (HKSAR) offers little reassurance to those in Taiwan who place a high premium on the legal identity of their government and the island's competitive democratic system and representative institutions. At least for now, the formal political process in Hong Kong makes it virtually impossible that the more anti-Beijing political forces will ever come to power. It thereby distorts the popular will.[19]

This is not to say that Beijing has not shown restraint in Hong Kong. It has not abused civil liberties. The press does criticize the administration and thereby ensures some measure of accountability. The civil service remains a strong and effective institution. The PRC has by and large made good on its pledge in the 1984 joint declaration with Britain to give the territory a high degree of autonomy and to allow Hong Kong's people to govern Hong Kong. But to say that Hong Kong more or less has home rule begs the question of who rules at home.[20] The HKSAR has a government that is for the most part responsive and effective, but it does not have a representative government. Those who govern do so free of the threat of replacement through popular elections that might spur them to improve their performance and make themselves accountable to the people they govern. From the outset, Beijing's strong preference for handling the postreversion HKSAR government was to continue the executive dominance that was the hallmark of British colonial rule.[21]

The UK-PRC joint declaration of 1984 provided the conceptual design for autonomy, or home rule, for Hong Kong under the one-country, two-systems model. The Basic Law of the HKSAR, which the PRC National People's Congress enacted in 1990, translated the concept of autonomy into concrete rules for playing the political game in Hong Kong. Early in the Basic Law drafting process, in April 1987, Deng Xiaoping ruled out the British parliamentary system, the U.S. congressional system, and any other form of separation of powers, noting that a legislature was useful only if it kept to "the right policies and direction." He also asserted that Beijing should have the power to intervene in Hong Kong in an emergency: "Isn't it possible that something could happen in the region that might jeopardize the fundamental interests of the country.... Can anyone imagine that there are in Hong Kong no forces that might engage in obstruction or sabotage? I see no grounds for taking comfort in that notion. If the Central Government were to abandon all its power, there might be turmoil that would damage Hong Kong's interests."[22]

Tiananmen Square became just such an event. The demonstrations in Beijing and elsewhere in the spring of 1989 startled much of Hong Kong's population. Some even sided with the Chinese dissidents, providing money, propaganda, and moral support and helping activists on Beijing's wanted list to escape. The crackdown created a radically new climate and became the point of reference from which all actors viewed the new Hong Kong political system.

The HKSAR Basic Law was written in the shadow of Tiananmen. With their siege mentality, China's leaders feared that Hong Kong might become a base of subversion against the mainland. Leading pro-democracy politicians in the former colony had a different concern. Could a regime that had indiscriminately killed thousands of its own citizens be trusted not to intervene in Hong Kong's affairs? For both camps, the drafting of the Basic Law thus took on critical importance. Beijing, already bent on preserving an executive-led system—something akin to British colonial administration under the PRC flag—wished to write the mini-constitution in a way that would prevent the political forces that they most feared from coming to power. Chief among those forces—those who expressed the strongest anxiety about China's intentions—were the United Democrats (later the Democratic Party) and the Hong Kong Alliance in Support of the Patriotic and Democratic Movement in Hong Kong. To be sure, some Hong Kong people participated in the drafting process, but most of them were disinclined to oppose Beijing's effort.

One critical issue was how the chief executive and members of the Legislative Council were to be chosen. Among the last things that China wanted, for example, was for Martin Lee, an articulate barrister and leader of the Democrats, to become head of the special administrative region or for his party and others like it to gain a legislative majority.

The Joint Declaration had prescribed that the chief executive would be picked either through elections or consultation. In the Basic Law, Beijing opted for election, but with a very limited franchise. Selection by universal suffrage was "the ultimate aim," but there remained the possibility that even when universal suffrage was attained there would be restraints on who could run. (It is not clear from the language of the provision whether a real contest was envisioned.) And that was all in the future. Through at least the first ten years following reversion, an election committee of 800 members would pick the chief executive. The body would be made up of 200 people each from business; the professions; the labor, social service, and religious sectors; and members of the Legislative Council, representatives of organizations at the local (district) level of the Hong Kong system, and the Hong Kong members of the PRC's National People's Congress and Chinese People's Political Consultative Conference (the supreme united front organization). Subsequent legislation dictated precisely how members would be picked from those various sectors and their component organizations, and in many cases they were picked by a very narrow franchise—for example, members representing a specific commercial sector would be picked by companies in that sector. Potential candidates required the support of at least 100 members of the election committee before their names could be placed in nomination. And any change in these procedures—in the direction of broader suffrage, for example—would need the support of two-thirds of the Legislative Council and the approval of the chief executive.

The effective result of this arrangement was an election committee whose members were biased toward the business community and other sectors favorably disposed to Beijing. For the first two "elections," in 1996 and 2002, candidate Tung Chee-hwa faced no opposition.

In those two cycles, Beijing further ensured that its candidate would be elected by signaling well in advance that it preferred Tung as chief executive. With Beijing having "tapped" Tung, it became difficult if not foolhardy for anyone to challenge him. For example, in September 2000, Chinese Vice Premier Qian Qichen privately counseled HKSAR Chief Secretary Anson Chan to support Tung Chee-hwa. Because Chan would have been the most formidable challenger to Tung, Qian's advice might be read as an effort to dissuade her from running. Then in October, both PRC Premier Zhu Rongji and Qian publicly expressed support for a second term for Tung. (When Hong Kong reporters asked Jiang Zemin if this was an "imperial order," he asserted that the journalists were being "simple" and "naïve.") Sixteen months later, in February 2002, Tung handed in a nomination form that had the signatures of more than 700 of the 794 eligible members of the Election Committee. Because any challenger would have to have had at least 100 signatures, there was no contest. Apparently, Tung and his allies did not wish to face even token opposition.[23]

With respect to the Legislative Council (LegCo), China had pledged in the Joint Declaration that the members would be determined by election alone. But the Basic Law created two types of seats—modern-day analogues of the pocket and rotten boroughs of eighteenth-century Britain—that greatly increased the representation of certain narrow sectors and so limited the impact of broad popular sentiment. In the first type, fully thirty of the sixty members of LegCo were to be selected from functional constituencies that represented the business, financial, legal, educational, and other sectors. All were picked on the basis of a limited franchise. Most came from sectors whose interests were consistent with those of China; barristers and teachers were the exception. (It should be noted that functional constituencies were begun by the British, as their part of their strategy to co-opt Hong Kong's elites.) For the second type of seat, ten members of the first Legislative Council, picked in 1998, were selected by the same Beijing-friendly election committee that chose the chief executive. The number of those seats would decline over time, to six in 2000 and to none in 2004.

The remainder of the seats in the Legislative Council—twenty in 1998, twenty-four in 2000, and thirty in 2004—are chosen in direct elections in geographic districts. As a result, popularly elected members constituted only half of the legislature after 2004; the rest were drawn from small functional constituencies, which tend to be defined by narrow interests.

Yet another feature of the postreversion electoral system has the effect of reducing strong opposition in the legislature: the proportional representation list system, which replaced single-member, first-past-the-post districts for LegCo district races. Single-member districts, instituted by the British right before reversion, gave an advantage to the Democratic Party, which throughout the 1990s was the most popular party in Hong Kong. If its candidates got the most votes in their districts, they and no one else would get a seat in LegCo. A proportional representation system gives smaller parties that would be shut out in a single-member arrangement a better chance of winning seats. If one of these parties secures a certain fraction of the vote (but less than half), they get a seat. In Hong Kong, this has worked to the advantage of the pro-Beijing Democratic Alliance for the Betterment of Hong Kong (DAB). Thus in 1995 the Democratic Party secured 60 percent of the seats with 42.3 percent of the vote, but it got only 45 percent of the seats with 40.2 percent of the vote in 1998. In 1995 the DAB got 10 percent of the seats with 25.3 percent of the vote, but in 1998 it scored 25 percent of the seats with 23.6 percent of the vote. As Lo Shui-hing concludes, "Above all, the proportional representation or list system that has been adopted since the 1998 LegCo elections paves the way for the pro-CCP groups to grasp some directly elected seats in the legislature . . . [and] enhanced the DAB's share of the seats."[24]

Once the members of LegCo are picked, those who won direct elections face another disadvantage. Any bill introduced by an individual member must secure the support of not just a majority of the entire Legislative Council (as is the case with government bills) but also of a majority of *both* the members in the functional constituencies *and* the members picked by direct elections and (until 2004) by the election committee. To make matters worse, individual members may not introduce bills that relate to public expenditures, political structure, or the operation of the government, and the chief executive must approve any other bills relating to government policies that an individual member might wish to introduce. Not only is the Legislative Council unrepresentative in a democratic sense, it also has only limited powers vis-à-vis the executive. In Lo's view, "Overall, the LegCo from 1998 to 2001 became more a symbolic opposition than a substantial check and balance against the government."[25]

The Legislative Council was not the only body whose elective character was diluted. Before reversion, Hong Kong had a set of municipal councils and district boards that were directly elected. The municipal councils had executive powers regarding public health, leisure, and recreation services; the district boards advised the government on district matters. The most important function of both was to serve as a training ground for future elected representatives: parties would groom their activists by running them in local elections. In 1999, however, the government secured legislation that abolished the municipal councils and added appointed members to the district boards, now termed district councils—and so eliminated one proving ground for rising political leaders.[26]

As two prominent Hong Kong political scientists concluded in early 2002, Hong Kong was a "partial democracy," "an experiment with limited suffrage in a liberal, self-governing society."[27] People on Taiwan therefore might have several reasons to fear that a Hong Kong–style political system under the one-country, two-systems proposal would significantly alter Taiwan's political institutions and so weaken the sovereignty of the island's government. The first is Beijing's underlying motivation for creating the Hong Kong system—to reduce to a low level the probability that the Democratic Party and its allies might come to power in Hong Kong. The Taiwan analogues of those parties are the DPP and the Taiwan Solidarity Union. By inference, and assuming that Beijing takes the same risk-averse stance, it would likely seek unification arrangements in Taiwan that would limit the already considerable influence of the DPP and the TSU (which claimed almost half of the seats in the Legislative Yuan election in late 2001).

As it happens, from 1949 to the early 1990s a majority of seats in Taiwan's legislature were not filled through direct elections. During the same period, the president was elected indirectly, by an unelected national assembly dominated by the KMT. The opposition to the KMT, led by the DPP after 1986, gained strength by challenging those unrepresentative structures, and one of the KMT's great achievements was to reform them. Any effort to reintroduce a version of Hong Kong's functional constituencies and election committee—as devices to keep the DPP from holding power—would only reconfirm Taiwan's suspicions about the PRC's intentions.

Second, the Hong Kong experience raises questions—again hypothetical—about other ways that Beijing might limit the power of the Taiwan parties and leaders that it fears. Because China begins with the premise that what it calls Taiwan independence is fundamentally inconsistent with unification as it defines it, what restrictions might it ask to have imposed on political forces that it associates with the independence objective? Would it ask the DPP and the TSU to alter their fundamental objectives, as embodied in party charters, to satisfy its concerns about their postunification intentions? Would it insist on restrictions on the formation of new political parties that advocate independence? Would it require constraints on freedom of expression and freedom of the press to exclude public discussion of these politically incorrect subjects? Who would decide when a line had been crossed and what happened next? Whatever bargain is struck, would it be only an intermediate stage in a longer struggle over the scope of democracy on Taiwan?

On this score, the Taiwan case is more complicated than that of Hong Kong. No one in Hong Kong mounted a serious challenge to the reversion of sovereignty to China, and no one does so now.[28] But there are people on Taiwan who are strongly opposed to unification, at least on Beijing's terms. The version of political correctness that Beijing applied to Hong Kong—patriotism—is vaguer than that applied to Taiwan by the one-China principle. Thus China probably has less inclination to tolerate a postunification setup on Taiwan that permits antiunification forces total freedom of action.[29]

The Hong Kong case provokes other questions. Would Beijing feel the need to find a leader of Taiwan who maintained and enforced its limits on political participation? If so, could that person expect to command any legit-

imacy from the broad majority of Taiwan's population, particularly the segment that most mistrusts Beijing? Or would the chief executive of a Taiwan
special administrative region end up being a polarizing figure in the island's
politics? It should be noted that PRC Vice Premier Qian Qichen modulated
the Chinese position somewhat in July 2001 when he reportedly said that
under the one-country, two-systems approach Taiwan would "continue to
maintain the existing government framework, and [that] the Taiwan government will make its decisions on personnel." The question, of course, is
how much of the framework was meant. Is it the institutional structure, or
are electoral arrangements and political participation included? After all,
Deng Xiaoping promised that "Hong Kong people would rule Hong Kong,"
but that did not stop Beijing from creating obstacles to prevent certain Hong
Kong people from gaining power.[30]

Finally, the arrangements for Hong Kong's role in the international system fall far short of what anyone in Taiwan would feel proper, and they are
inconsistent with the popular view that the ROC is a sovereign state. Specifically, representatives of the HKSAR government can participate in
diplomatic negotiations bearing on Hong Kong, but only as members of
the PRC delegation. In international organizations and conferences that are
limited to states and for issues relevant to Hong Kong, its representatives can,
again, be members of the PRC delegation. That is, Hong Kong is not a state.
Furthermore, it can participate in international organizations not limited to
states under the name "Hong Kong, China." With that same nomenclature,
the HKSAR can maintain relations and conclude and implement agreements with "states, regions, and international organizations" in appropriate
fields, particularly economic fields. Whether international agreements to
which the PRC is a party apply to Hong Kong would be decided by Beijing,
depending on Hong Kong's needs and the views of the HKSAR government.

There are other aspects of the PRC's approach to Hong Kong, discussed
in chapter 8, that also speak to the reality of the one-country, two-systems
model. Suffice it to say that at this point, Beijing's proactive redesign of the
Hong Kong political system plus its anxiety about the intentions of "pro-
independence" political forces on Taiwan suggest that it would consider
redesigning Taiwan's system if the island became a special administrative
region of China. If so, it would negate in a very concrete and consequential
way one critical dimension of the Taiwan government's sovereignty—the
exclusive right to rule in the territory under its jurisdiction or at least to
decide voluntarily how that right should be diminished. By defining what is
politically correct, it would limit political expression. By restricting who

rules at home, it would create only a façade of home rule. Sovereignty, therefore, is not a purely symbolic issue for Taiwan.

Sovereignty in an Era of Globalization

To some, it may seem a bit anachronistic that sovereignty should be a key obstacle in cross-Strait relations. After all, it might be argued, what is important is the substance of autonomy rather than an obsession with principle. Moreover, in an increasingly globalized era, economic and social interaction across borders is growing and intensifying and governments, in the interest of their countries, are choosing to cede some of their right to rule over the people within their territory. In the process, old conceptions of sovereignty are being modified. In the European Union, for example, gradual economic integration has made borders less relevant and required national governments to pool and delegate their sovereignty rather than insist on it.

As described in chapter 3, Taiwan and China are no exception to this global trend. Over the last two decades, businesses on both sides of the Strait in a variety of sectors have grown increasingly integrated. That integration would not have been possible if the two governments had not set aside their preoccupation with national security and rigid political orthodoxies. Indeed, the Taiwan government has found that it cannot control some forms of interaction even when it tries to. For example, in order to reduce what he saw as the increasingly dangerous economic dependence of Taiwan firms on the Chinese market and to limit the PRC's political leverage, Lee Teng-hui sought in the mid-1990s to restrict Taiwan investment in major projects on the mainland. The effort failed, however, because investors funneled their funds through shell companies in places like the British Virgin Islands. Such trends provoke the question of whether Taiwan's emphasis on sovereignty is appropriate today. What is there left to protect in its name? Is Taiwan's economic dependence on the mainland not so great that it should give up what has become a symbolic principle for the sake of its substantive well-being?

As was indicated at the outset, there is at least a theoretical possibility that Taiwan's people will decide that economics trumps politics instead of the other way around. As good Marxists, PRC's leaders certainly hope that they will. In the meantime, economic cooperation fosters a shared interest in peace and stability.[31] Yet global economic trends will not necessarily dictate the outcome in this case.

First, the economic interaction that is occurring between the two sides of the Strait is still between two customs territories. The single internal market that has emerged in Western Europe does not pertain there (indeed, one could argue that China itself is not a single internal market). Although Taipei is hard-pressed to control investment in the PRC and the entry of mainland Chinese into its territory, the customs authorities on both sides continue to do their job. That the frontier that they monitor is water only reinforces the segregation.

Second, as also observed in chapter 2, the economic interaction that occurs between China and Taiwan is part of a larger collaboration. This is not simply a case of the pairing of Taiwan firms and their mainland counterparts. Taiwan companies act as the intermediate link in global supply chains: on one side is China, which serves as a base for manufacturing; on the other is the United States, whose corporations drive innovation and whose market for goods and services is a powerful magnet. Taiwan is in the middle, making contributions that are both cost-effective and within its technological capability. For example, in today's information technology industry, American companies define the products of the future and provide the most sophisticated technology. Companies in Taiwan design and produce the semiconductor chips (particularly the higher-end ones) that are the heart of those products, and they provide a higher level of value-added services, like testing. The manufacture of lower-end components and most assembly takes place on the mainland. There is no inherent reason why such arrangements would necessarily undermine the Taiwan government's fundamental authority within its own territory or require that it concede sovereignty to Beijing.[32]

Third, there is a significant asymmetry in the political role of companies on each side. There is some validity in the point that cross-Strait economic players share an interest in stability. Yet some of the Chinese companies involved are state corporations, whereas far fewer of Taiwan's are. Moreover, Taiwan's political system is far more open to the influence of business interests than the PRC's.

Fourth, it is easier for countries to pursue integration at the expense of sovereignty if the idea of war between them is unthinkable and if together they live under the shadow of the threat of a potential aggressor, as European nations did after World War II. Europe had lost too much and gained too little from centuries of military conflict, and the Soviet Union posed a common security challenge. In the case of China and Taiwan, as the next chapter shows, Beijing believes that war may be necessary to fulfill its political objectives, and both sides have prepared for that possibility. And there is no outside threat to drive them together.

The issue of transportation links illustrates the complex interaction between economic integration and defense of sovereignty. It was China that first proposed direct transportation links, in 1979. Initially Taiwan resisted for ideological reasons, because the Chiang Ching-kuo government had committed itself to a policy of no direct contact. The economic interchange that was permitted after 1986, for example, had to remain at least nominally indirect. In the 1990s, Taipei held back because it sought to get something in return, most specifically the PRC's renunciation of the use of force. Taipei took a number of measures to ease the burden on its carriers, but shipping and air traffic still have to go through the motions of stopping at a third point. Chen Shui-bian came to office favoring the three links, but Beijing held back because it had grave doubts about his commitment to unification. It also thought that it could use the growing desire for direct links of Taiwan's shipping and air transportation companies and their clients to create political leverage on Chen. So Beijing insisted that any discussion of transportation links would have to be conducted either through SEF and ARATS, based on the one-China principle, or through private business associations.

As already mentioned, Chen feared that accepting the one-China principle without prior discussion of what it meant would be tantamount to making major concessions on the sovereignty issue before political negotiations even started. He has believed that the PRC proposal to work through private associations is only a not-so-subtle ploy to undermine the legitimacy of his government—and again, to accept it would be making a major concession in advance of political negotiations. The PRC's "private associations," after all, were actually under government control, whereas Taiwan's were not, at least to the same degree. Chen's initial demand, therefore, was that the talks on transportation links be on a government-to-government basis, which the PRC regarded as Taipei's way of securing what Beijing wants to avoid (recognizing Taiwan's sovereignty) and gaining political credibility for Chen in the process. Meanwhile, Taiwan's transportation companies, supported by opposition politicians, continued to urge him to concede. Subsequently, the Chen administration shifted to allowing private associations to formally take the lead as long as the substantive negotiations were conducted on a government-to-government basis. It was necessary, said MAC chairperson Tsai Ing-wen, "to practically and efficiently control such contacts between the two shores, to prevent a conflict of interests (especially that between private and public interests), and to guard against an erosion or loss of Taiwan's public power."[33] Legislation was passed in October 2003 that would permit private organizations to act on behalf of government agencies, but with government officials in the delegation and the Mainland Affairs Council still retaining ultimate authority, particularly over any agreements concluded.[34] (In early 2005, delegations from the two sides arranged direct charter flights for Taiwan business people on the mainland returning to the island for the lunar new year. The delegations were nominally led by the airline association on each side, although many members of the two delegations were officials of the relevant civil aviation authorities, serving as "advisers.")

This deadlock surfaced in other ways. For example, if the PRC government forbids its agencies from having contact with Taiwan on political grounds, then financial monitoring organizations cannot collaborate to ensure appropriate behavior by financial institutions that operate on both sides of the Strait. Conflicts over trademarks are hard to reconcile. As with the transportation issue, Beijing has suggested that trade associations resolve such impasses. But China and Taiwan law enforcement authorities cannot collaborate in catching criminals of any kind who operate on both sides, and collaboration through private academic or business organizations is ineffective. Public health authorities cannot work together to prevent the spread of disease by quarantining humans, animals, or plants. However, not all the effects of deadlock work to Taiwan's disadvantage. Agricultural producers on the island gain from this situation. They faced stiff competition from China because of the open markets requirement for accession to the World Trade Organization, but in cases in which communication between quarantine authorities is necessary—to enforce phytosanitary requirements, for example—agricultural products cannot enter Taiwan because Beijing is unwilling to permit the necessary consultations.[35]

If the ROC government has seen its sovereignty eroded in small and uncontrollable ways by cross-Strait economic relations, it has voluntarily conceded much more in multilateral and bilateral trade negotiations. At least in the field of foreign economic policy, it has given up the power to set quotas, tariffs, and other barriers to outside goods and services. It has done so in part because it believes that its own economic vitality depends on its participation in a liberalized international economic system and that it will suffer if it is excluded. It has done so also because the World Trade Organization was the one international institution in which it had a good chance at full membership, in contrast to organizations within the United Nations system, from which it was shut out. Moreover, as noted previously, membership in the WTO had been structured to allow "separate customs territories" to join so that Taiwan could do so without having to make political concessions to China. But based on its experience with organizations in the UN system, of which the PRC was already a member, Taipei knew that it if it waited to join the WTO until after China entered, it would be excluded or humiliated. So in order to increase its political standing in the international community—a manifestation of its sovereignty—it was willing to cede power and authority over important elements of its economic policy.

Finally, when it comes to the "pooling" of sovereignty, the European experience can be overinterpreted. It is true that economic integration was the focus in the early stages, in order to overcome the inability of a number of relatively small economies to survive in an increasingly competitive global economy—hence the movement toward an internal market. And the members of what became the European Union realized over time that success required not only that they abandon economic policies that were inconsistent with a single internal market but also, in order to foster mutual confidence, that they create supranational institutions and cede some sovereignty in the process. National parliaments in particular lost power as a result. It is one thing for all parties to give up bits of sovereignty gradually in a reciprocal way; it is another for Taiwan to give it up altogether and Beijing to give up nothing.[36]

Moreover, "pooling" and another mechanism, "delegation," of sovereignty have specific meanings within the European Union; they are not general metaphors, as often thought. Pooling involves decisionmaking arrangements such as qualified majority voting, as opposed to the unanimity rule. Delegation is to supranational actors, EU officials who are given the authority to take autonomous actions. These voluntary limitations on Westphalian sovereignty have gone further in economic policy than they have on political and foreign policy issues, to say nothing of the fundamental identity of member states. In cross-Strait relations, the priority, at least in Beijing, is very much on matters of politics and identity.

Even in Europe, there are cases in which sovereignty still matters. The Cyprus conflict pits the Turkish minority (supported by Turkey) and the Greek majority (supported by Greece) against each other. Efforts to resolve the dispute and create a unified, federal Cyprus composed of two politically equal communities with sovereignty over their respective territories had foundered over the demand of the Turkish Cypriot leader, Rauf Denktaş, that the sovereignty of the Turkish Republic of Northern Cyprus be recognized at the outset of negotiations on unification. That the Greek side had the advantage internationally only reinforced Denktaş in his determination to secure prior recognition. Through the facilitation of the United Nations, progress was made toward establishing a structure in which the two constituent states would take charge of their domestic affairs and a federal administration would be responsible for foreign affairs and the banking and legal systems. Although the Turkish community was smaller, it would have an equal say in executive and legislative functions, consistent with the notion of separate sovereignty. Greece and Turkey, which had previously backed their respective communities on the island, supported the plan. Turkey had a particular interest in doing so, for it would have speeded its entry into the European Union. In the end, although in 2004 Turkish Cypriots voted in a referendum to approve the plan, a majority of the Greek community opposed it, in part for economic reasons, in part because of its mistrust of the Turkish minority, and in part because it knew that the Greek Cypriot republic, which already enjoyed international recognition, would join the European Union whether unification occurred or not.[37]

It is one thing to cede sovereignty when it is universally acknowledged at the outset, as it is in western Europe. It is another thing to give it up when it is still in dispute, as in the case of Beijing and Taipei. There, the argument is over the nature of political power in Taiwan—and perhaps China itself. Recent history may have attenuated the emphasis on sovereignty in western Europe, but not completely. In China, for historical reasons, it remains an obsession. As Jacques deLisle observes, "Conventional notions of strong, nation-state-based sovereignty—ones rooted in Westphalia and coming to full fruition at the time of China's unhappy 19th-century encounter with the West—are particularly robust in contemporary China and continue to cast a long shadow over the politics of cross-Strait relations."[38]

The Duplex

The sovereignty issue combines several different elements: legal status, ownership of territory, jurisdiction and control, economic and social interaction, and the international environment. Using the duplex house as a metaphor for cross-Strait relations may help to capture those elements simultaneously.[39]

Duplexes were common in the American suburbs in the 1950s and 1960s. A duplex was a single physical structure comprising two separate dwelling units—each with its own living room, kitchen, bedrooms, and so on—that shared a common interior wall. Each unit was owned by a different family, and usually all that they had in common was the physical proximity of their respective living spaces.

Our imaginary duplex is known as China. The PRC "family" inhabits one dwelling and the ROC "family" the other. The evolution of cross-Strait relations can be traced by analogy, as follows: During the 1950s and 1960s, the heads of the two "families" each claimed ownership of the entire physical structure and regarded the other family as illegal occupants. There was no contact between the two families, each of which was ruled with an iron hand by its patriarch. The only thing that they both agreed on was that both dwellings were integral parts of the whole structure; they disagreed on who owned the structure. The ROC family was more successful in securing neighborhood support for its claim. Most other families acknowledged it as the owner of the whole house and honored its request to have no contact with the PRC family. They accepted it as the representative of the duplex in community affairs. The American family in the neighborhood protected the ROC family both physically and politically.

The tide of neighborhood opinion turned in the 1970s. As more houses were built in the community (as colonies became countries), their leaders agreed with the PRC family's view that it owned the duplex and should represent it in community affairs. They generally honored the PRC patriarch's request to have only low-level contact with the ROC family. Because it saw benefits in interacting with the PRC family, even the American family agreed to take these steps, but it chose to continue to be responsible for the safety of the ROC family.

Two things happened in the 1980s. First, the two families discovered that they shared doors in the structure's common interior wall. Gradually, they began to have contact with each other, sharing and exchanging their respective possessions. Family members began asking whether their positive interaction might mitigate the argument between the two patriarchs over who owned the structure. Indeed, the PRC patriarch even thought that this contact, plus the shift in neighborhood opinion, gave him the upper hand. He made an offer to the ROC patriarch: if the ROC patriarch would accept that the PRC family owned the entire structure, he would allow the ROC family to continue to occupy its dwelling undisturbed and to participate in some neighborhood activities. The hope was, of course, that the ROC family would so enjoy the interaction through the interior wall that it would forget its concerns about ownership of its dwelling and about how the family would interact with others in the neighborhood.

The other development took place within the ROC family. The patriarch decided to permit a more open approach to family decisions. Some members of the family, resentful of the autocratic treatment by previous patriarchs, offered a radically different approach: in their view, the family should stop making the absurd claim that it owned the whole structure.

Instead, the family should acknowledge that the PRC family was the rightful owner of its dwelling and its dwelling alone. The ROC family should rename itself Taiwan and claim ownership of its dwelling only, a property that had no legal connection whatsoever with the PRC property. Understandably, that new proposal did not sit well with the PRC family or with the members of the Taiwan family who still saw the family as the owner of the whole structure.

In the early 1990s, the patriarchs of the two families began talking to each other. They needed to resolve some practical matters arising from the comings-and-goings through the interior doors, and they also explored the possibility of resolving the ownership dispute. The ROC family head took an important step when he declared that he now acknowledged the PRC family head as the rightful owner of its dwelling and not as an illegal squatter. However, he argued that the two family heads were of equal status and that he was not prepared to acknowledge the PRC head as the sole owner of the entire structure. He also claimed the right to go out in the neighborhood and participate in community meetings and activities without the permission of the PRC head.

A new PRC family leader ignored his claims, so the ROC leader decided that he would go out into the neighborhood, where he made a visit to the American house. That caused some tension in the neighborhood, and the PRC family head came to believe that the ROC head was opposed to resolving the ownership dispute amicably but actually wanted to create two legally separate dwellings.

More and more, the Taiwan family has insisted that it is the sole and rightful owner of its dwelling. It has long maintained that its patriarch is legally equivalent to the patriarch of the PRC family. There are conflicting views within the ROC family on whether and how to resolve the ownership dispute. A few still hold on to the hope of dissociating the two properties from each other. Some have toyed with the idea of adopting some form of shared ownership, such as joint tenancy, tenancy in common, partnership, or holding company, which would end the ownership argument between the two family heads while acknowledging their equality.

The sovereignty issue is at the core of the cross-Strait dispute; unless it is resolved, the dispute will never be resolved. So far it has been an either-or issue. China has proposed an approach to unification that grants home rule to Taiwan, a formula that Taipei has consistently rejected. Taipei has asserted that it is a sovereign entity, an assertion that Beijing has labeled separatist. Such a fundamental split cannot be papered over; it must be reconciled in a conceptual and practical sense. Chapter 10 revisits this conundrum.

5

The Security Issue

Security—or the lack of it—has bedeviled cross-Strait relations since the late 1940s. But the military equation changed significantly in the 1990s, as the People's Liberation Army began to modernize in earnest. Beijing has since contemplated the use of force to stop what it has perceived (or mis-perceived) to be Taiwan's leaders' intention to mount a separatist challenge to unification. Meanwhile, Taiwan has struggled to acquire its own military assets to reduce Beijing's temptation to engage in coercion or warfare. At the heart of the security issue, of course, is the United States, which since 1950 has undertaken a varying responsibility for Taiwan's defense in the belief that any Chinese use of violence to determine Taiwan's fate would affect the fundamental U.S. interest in peace and stability in East Asia. Cross-Strait militarization increases the danger of conflict—conflict in which the United States would likely participate. It augments the need for each party to display an appropriate mix of warnings and reassurances to the other in order to reduce that danger, and the situation will become more complicated as over time China gains the ability to project power toward Taiwan.

The security factor is not just a source of instability; it is also a key obstacle to crafting a solution to the Taiwan Strait dispute. If this were merely a misunderstanding over Lee Teng-hui's and Chen Shui-bian's intentions or an abstract argument over the status of the Taipei government after unification (or both), wise people on both sides of the Strait might—with the right kind of communication and a little creativity—come up with ways to clarify perceptions and bridge conceptual gaps. However, the impasse is not simply a function of too little diplomacy. It is also a consequence of the profound vulnerability that each side feels regarding the other, although for

China, that vulnerability is more political than military. If there is to be a settlement, reducing their mutual sense of vulnerability will be essential.

This chapter explores the nature of the security issue, the second substantive issue at the heart of the Taiwan Strait dispute, the second strand of the knot. Taiwan and China are caught in a security dilemma. Each side sees the power of the other and how it might be used and finds that power threatening. Each takes steps to guard against the perceived threat, only to trigger a hedging response from the other. Compounding the dilemma is the mistrust that the actions of each engender in the other. That mutual mistrust severely complicates any effort to resolve the dispute. Each side fears that if it is conciliatory, the other will exploit its generosity, leaving it more insecure. That makes it particularly difficult to craft a political settlement that would eliminate the security dilemma altogether and with it the danger of war. To complicate matters further, this particular security dilemma has two special elements. The first is that China does not fear Taiwan's military power but the political initiatives of its leaders. The second is the role of the United States, on which Taiwan is utterly dependent.

If China and Taiwan had nothing to gain from finding a common way out of this dilemma, then there would be no reason to find a way to resolve it. On the face of it, however, they both have much to gain from a situation in which they can maximize the economic cooperation that already exists and minimize or eliminate the sense of mutual vulnerability that politics and militarization create. If Taiwan did not feel threatened by the PRC's military buildup, if Beijing did not have to worry that Taipei might act to secure total independence, if each had confidence in the stated goodwill of the other, and if Taiwan were not so utterly dependent on the United States, then an enduring peace might be possible. How, therefore, might the two sides find a way out of the trap of mutual vulnerability?

The Security Dilemma

As developed by Robert Jervis and others, the concept of the security dilemma begins with the idea that international politics is fundamentally anarchic. "In such a world without a sovereign," Jervis writes, "each state is protected only by its own strength."[1] And, John Herz observes, "Striving to attain security from . . . attack, [actors] are driven to acquire more and more power in order to escape the impact of the power of others. This, in turn, renders the others more insecure and compels them to prepare for the worst."[2] Three factors compound this vicious cycle and tempt states to choose war now over the possibility of greater danger later. First is the element of time: a state may fear that even if another state is friendly today, it may become an adversary tomorrow; the state may also fear that it will be less and less able to protect its interests as time passes. Second is the fact that many weapons systems can be used for offensive and defensive purposes, so that one side might regard any weapons the other acquires for its own protection as offensive arms. Third is an overlay of psychological factors. While one state may view the military buildup of another as reflecting aggressive intent instead of the desire for self-protection, it sees its own acquisitions as benign and ignores the possibility that the other may see them as hostile.[3]

Jervis elaborated on the security dilemma by considering more fully the role of offensive and defensive status. When the offense has the advantages of geography and technology or both, then the security dilemma is exacerbated because the defense will fear quick defeat. If the defense has the advantage, the offense's capabilities will be relatively less threatening. As noted above, when weapons can be used for offensive and defensive purposes, vulnerability increases. When one state's weapons are solely defensive, an adversary will feel more secure. When a class of weapons is solely offensive, agreements to control them can enhance mutual security.[4]

Arms are not the only way that states acquire the power to cope with a security dilemma. Having allies is another, and Glenn Snyder has explored the resulting dynamics. There are twin dangers in an alliance: abandonment and entrapment. The first refers to a state's fear that its ally will not fulfill explicit commitments, will not give support when expected, will adopt a neutral position, or will even align with its opponent. The second refers to a state's anxiety that its ally will draw it into a conflict in pursuit of interests that, to some degree, it does not share. The risks of these two dangers are inversely correlated. As one partner in an alliance has less fear that the other will abandon it, the other's fear of entrapment increases. A strong commitment to an ally will reduce a state's leverage over that ally. Important factors in the alliance security dilemma, all of which influence the risk of abandonment or entrapment, include the relative dependence of one ally on the other, the strategic interest that each has in defending the other, how explicit the alliance agreement is, past behavior, and how the stronger ally deals with the adversary. If it shows firmness, then the weaker ally will be reassured but more prone to entrap. If the stronger ally tries to conciliate the adversary, then the weaker will have greater fears of abandonment.[5]

Finally, a state does not necessarily have a perfect view of its vulnerability to an adversary or of any dilemmas that its alliances may entail. Therefore it may exaggerate—and act on—both the danger that an enemy poses and the commitment of a friend (this subject is examined in more detail in chapter 7).[6]

Insecurity in the Taiwan Strait

A security dilemma has dominated cross-Strait relations since 1949, when the ROC government moved to Taiwan. The PRC and the ROC read the worst into each other's efforts to build military power, and each probed the other's strength and resolve. Taiwan, of course, depended on its U.S. alliance, which had its own problems: Chiang Kai-shek feared American abandonment, and Washington was anxious about being entrapped in a war that it did not want.

In the 1970s, the United States saw anti-Soviet strategic value in rapprochement with the PRC, but Beijing demurred until Washington was prepared to cut its security ties to Taiwan. Among the PRC's preconditions was for the United States to end its mutual defense treaty with Taiwan, withdraw its remaining military personnel, and close its installations on the island, and the Carter administration accepted those terms. In Taipei's eyes, Washington had abandoned Taiwan in order to ally with its enemy. American support for Taiwan's security did not end completely, however. To compensate for the termination of the treaty, Congress sought to restore at least a modest, if not binding, defense commitment by passing the Taiwan Relations Act. And the Carter administration declared its intention to continue some arms sales to Taiwan.

Having weakened Taiwan's U.S. alliance in the hope that Taiwan would recognize its own growing vulnerability and capitulate, Beijing mounted a political offensive for unification under its one-country, two-systems formula. It also tried to further weaken the island militarily. In 1981, Deng Xiaoping reopened the issue of U.S. arms sales, which had not been resolved in normalization talks, and demanded an end to the transfers. His logic demonstrated a tough-minded approach to Taiwan's security problem. As he told Leonard Woodcock right before the normalization announcement, if Taipei continued to get arms from the United States, it would have no incentive to negotiate with China. By implication, Deng wished to make Chiang Ching-kuo feel as insecure as possible. He also sought to convince the United States that its own security interests would be best served by ending the arms sales. If the United States wanted the Taiwan issue resolved without force, as it said that it did, then it should deny Taipei the means to defend itself; Taiwan then would have no choice but to strike a deal. Deng warned that if Taipei were to refuse to negotiate because it continued to get U.S. weapons, Beijing would have to use force. It mattered little to Deng whether U.S. arms were offensive or defensive; transfers of any kind were a problem.[7]

Deng's logic no doubt was grounded in traditional Chinese statecraft and in the Chinese Communist Party's experience in the civil war. During the early 1949 siege of Beijing, for example, the People's Liberation Army had overwhelming power and the Nationalist armies under Fu Zuoyi lost all hope. They gave up without a fight; the use of force was unnecessary. Winning through coercion and intimidation was regarded as a "peaceful" outcome.[8] Such an outlook ignores, of course, the possibility that Taiwan might negotiate only when it had a certain sense of security.

Beijing and Washington reached an agreement of sorts on arms sales in a communiqué in August 1982. On the basis of policy statements by the PRC pledging to "strive for peaceful unification," the Reagan administration agreed to limit the sophistication of the weapons that it sold to Taiwan and gradually reduce the total dollar value of sales. There was a fresh sense of abandonment in Taiwan, which Washington sought to allay through political reassurances and a new approach to helping Taiwan preserve a qualitative advantage in its weapons systems. The Reagan administration encouraged Taipei to produce advanced systems, such as fighter aircraft, indigenously. Rather than sell Taiwan finished systems, the United States would provide the necessary technology and Taiwan would build arms and equipment itself.[9] At the same time, Chiang Ching-kuo tried briefly to hedge his security bets. He authorized resumption of a nuclear weapons program originally begun in the mid-1960s but terminated in 1977 under U.S. pressure. Washington discovered the later effort and shut it down in 1988.[10]

By the 1990s, other trends that increased the security dilemma were in play. There were growing political conflicts over Taiwan's approach to the unification of China. Lee Teng-hui, as described in chapter 3, became increasingly frustrated over the constraints of the one-country, two-systems proposal and Beijing's refusal to adjust its approach. He believed that he had come part way to meet Chinese concerns, only to find that the PRC refused to concede on the questions of sovereignty and Taiwan's international role. In his mind, China had exploited his goodwill. He therefore became more active in trying to expand the ROC's international space. For its part, the PRC saw Lee's effort to reinsert Taiwan in the international system as a serious threat and an act of bad faith. A subsequent effort to resolve political issues only reinforced underlying mistrust. Thereafter, each side would be more cautious.

The early 1990s was a time when both China and Taiwan sought to take advantage of the buyer's market in advanced weapons systems created by the collapse of the Soviet Union. In something of an arms race, Beijing and Taipei both sought to add new systems to their armed forces to counter the acquisitions of the other. China acquired the Sukhoi-28 advanced fighter aircraft from Russia, and Taiwan intensified its drive to secure F-16s from the United States and Mirage 2000s from France. Over the same decade, China bought Kilo-class submarines from Russia, and Taiwan requested diesel-powered submarines from the United States. China produced a growing force of short- and medium-range ballistic missiles indigenously, and Taiwan sought to acquire missile defense capabilities from the United States (it ultimately got Patriot missile batteries). In addition, Taiwan sought to improve its security relationship with the United States to provide better balance against China's growing military power.

Taiwan has been at something of a disadvantage in seeking a hedge against the PRC's buildup. The United States, its only significant source of arms, will sell the island only defensive weapons, in the belief that it might be destabilizing for the ROC armed forces to have the ability to strike targets on the mainland. One might think, therefore, that Beijing would feel relatively more secure because it can acquire offensive systems and Taiwan has had to confine itself to defensive systems. Recall that when one party to a security dilemma has the offensive advantage, it heightens the other party's sense of vulnerability.

But this asymmetry of acquisitions does not make Beijing feel more secure. The security dilemma here is not the classic dilemma described in the international relations literature. Although the two sides of the Strait are engaged in something of an arms race, it is not Taipei's recent arms acquisitions that make Beijing feel more vulnerable. What China dreads instead are any Taiwan political initiatives to permanently separate the island from China, or, as China might put it, to seize Chinese national territory by fiat rather than force. Taiwan's military power and its alliance with the United States become relevant not because they are inherently threatening but because they may be used to defend such political initiatives. In this case, defensive capabilities increase the security dilemma. It is at least to deter Taiwan from taking separatist steps and to counter its defensive military buildup that the People's Liberation Army acquires yet more capabilities. And supposedly it is to allay its fears of Taiwan's independence that Beijing has asked Taipei to reaffirm the one-China principle. The central political dimension of this security dilemma gives it an asymmetrical and perhaps unique character. As Thomas Christensen so elegantly puts it:

Security dilemma theorists have assumed that international security politics concerns merely defending sovereign territory from invasion and foreign acquisition. [But] to a large degree, the Taiwan question is one more of the island's political identity than of the PRC's territorial expansion. The danger to the PRC is that Taiwan might eventually move from de facto independence to legal independence, thus posing an affront to Chinese nationalism and a danger to regime stability in Beijing.[11]

There are other important political features of this unique security dilemma, aside from the challenge that Beijing believes that Taiwan poses to its security. First of all, during the 1980s and 1990s, each sought to acquire arms (or deny them to the other) not for the purpose of fighting a war but as political symbols that, it hoped, would weaken the resolve of the other side. This was not an arms race but an "awe race." Thus Beijing sought to end U.S. arms sales to Taiwan to make the latter feel weak and abandoned, leaving it with no reasonable choice but to negotiate on Beijing's terms. Taipei wanted to maintain defense cooperation with the United States to convey the impression to Beijing that it still had a powerful backer and therefore no reason to capitulate. The advanced systems that each side acquired in the early 1990s were as much political trophies as they were weapons of war. Whoever gained the advantage in this race to overawe the other would increase the other's insecurity.[12]

The second feature is the centrality of U.S. support for Taiwan and its impact on the political balance of power between Beijing and Taipei (a subject addressed in more detail in chapter 9). As former PRC Vice Premier Qian Qichen said in January 2001, "If foreign countries [that is, the United States] interfere in the Taiwan issue, the local Taiwan Independence factions will rely on this kind of foreign interference to stir up splittism, and cause the Taiwan problem to drag on forever. . . . If the American Government takes a stance of supporting peaceful reunification, then it will be of very great use."[13]

It was these *political* vectors that created the crisis of 1995 and 1996, which at its core was a PRC coercive response to a political initiative undertaken by Lee Teng-hui and U.S. support of it.[14] Lee's goal was to enhance Taiwan's international profile, which the PRC had worked hard over several decades to restrict, and to demonstrate his ability to secure U.S. agreement to his unprecedented visit. The PRC leadership believed that Lee's actions reflected his intention to pursue "Taiwan independence." In one line of argument, Lee was covertly pursuing independence while others were pursuing that goal overtly. Lee's alleged covert approach was of particular concern, because it was designed to reduce the risk of Chinese military action.

Just as vigorously, Beijing concluded that Washington was complicit in Lee's effort to break out of the political constraints that it sought to impose. He would not be able to conduct his activities, the Chinese leadership believed, if countries like the United States did not help him. Some in China also believed that Washington was using Taiwan as part of a much larger plot to contain China—to prevent it from becoming a great power, economically, politically, and militarily.[15]

Beijing regarded Lee's activities and U.S. complicity in them as a threat to China's vital interests. China's national mission, as the communist leadership defined it and propagandized it to the public, was to complete the unification of the country, including Taiwan. As the leaders were fond of saying—to American officials and scholars, most often in private—they could not survive in power if Taiwan was forever "lost." And if Taiwan was actively seeking permanent separation with U.S. help, then Beijing had to act to stop it. As Ross puts it, this was a "question of war and peace."[16] So the leadership employed coercive diplomacy to demonstrate China's serious resolve regarding the drift of events, hoping thereby to compel Taiwan and the United States to reverse course and to deter other countries from following the U.S. lead.

From the perspective of the United States, the 1995–96 episode revived all its old fears of entrapment by Taiwan. Lee had used his government's access to the U.S. political system, particularly Congress, to create pressure on the Clinton administration to grant him a visa. His visit had caused a sharp deterioration in relations with China, which the Clinton administration was in the process of repairing after a rough start. Then, when the PRC undertook more aggressive exercises in March 1996, before the Taiwan presidential election, the administration felt compelled to act. It sent two aircraft carrier battle groups to the Taiwan area in order to prevent a war from occurring through accident or miscalculation, but it also sought to restrain Taiwan from any future destabilizing actions.[17]

The key point here is that the insecurity that Taiwan created for Beijing was political, not military. It was the PRC's fear of "covert independence" and Washington's perceived willingness to facilitate that objective that drove it to take limited military action. That Beijing misperceived Lee's motives, as demonstrated in previous chapters, did not diminish the challenge that it thought his actions represented. Although the coercive character of its strategy was real enough, its targets were also political. It wished to reduce electoral support for Lee in the presidential elections and for his party in legislative contests; undermine the island's economy; and create psychological stress in the civilian populace. Sowing a certain level of panic among the people of the island would, Beijing hoped, bring home to Lee Teng-hui the stakes involved. China also wished to remind Washington that there were limits to its tolerance of Lee and that the United States had a responsibility to respect them.

Although tensions declined after Lee's inauguration in May 1996, the security dilemma in the Taiwan Strait continued. China accelerated its military modernization effort in order to try to deter future separatist actions. But the buildup only exacerbated anxiety in Taiwan, while China was disturbed by U.S. efforts, begun in the Clinton administration, to enhance Taiwan's military capability. And new political developments in Taiwan exacerbated anxiety in China. Lee Teng-hui's July 1999 "special state-to-state" declaration was followed by more aggressive Chinese air patrols over the Taiwan Strait, and the prospect of Chen Shui-bian's March 2000 election victory provoked a warning that Taiwan's independence meant war. Statements exchanged on May 20, 2000, the day of Chen's inauguration, manifested the security dilemma in concrete terms. As described in chapter 3, Chen pledged not to take certain steps that Bejing feared, but his pledge was subject to the condition that the PRC had "no intention to use military force against Taiwan," suggesting the fear that it had precisely that intention. A few hours after Chen's address, the PRC's Taiwan Affairs Office issued its own announcement, which, among other things, demanded that Chen allay China's concerns about his intentions by accepting the one-China principle and no longer engaging in any efforts to secure Taiwan's independence. It warned that if his government maintained the stance that Taiwan was a "sovereign and independent country," it would "provoke conflicts between compatriots across the Strait and within Taiwan, [and] endanger peace in the Taiwan Strait and the Asia-Pacific region."[18]

Again, it was Taipei's political stance that Beijing saw as a threat to China's national security and as justification to not engage Chen. And again, each side refused to make any big concessions, fearing that its goodwill would be exploited. Because China thought it had found a way to contain Chen politically—not because the two sides had found a way to reduce their mutual sense of insecurity—the tensions created by Chen's election would decline temporarily. But they would increase again in late 2003 and early 2004, when Chen's reelection campaign proposals again raised China's fears.

Behind the scenes, Chinese officials were more frank about the military dimension of the Taiwan Strait issue. Vice Premier Qian Qichen, in a speech to the Foreign Affairs College in the same month as Chen's inauguration, reminded his listeners that "Comrade Deng Xiaoping used to say that we should use 'two hands' in settling the Taiwan issue and not rule out any of the two ways: Doing as much as we can with our right hand to settle the issue peacefully because the right arm is stronger. However, in case this does not work, we will also use the left hand, namely military force." For his part, Chen Shui-bian thought that Beijing had exploited his goodwill. He had been led to believe that making certain statements in his inaugural statement would be taken as an implicit yet sufficient way of addressing the one-China issue and so result in the resumption of dialogue. He had made them, but nothing happened. As a result, he became more cautious.[19]

Indeed, the 1995–96 crisis, Lee's 1999 demarche, and Chen's election not only raised tensions and deepened mistrust but also transformed profoundly how the Chinese leadership, particularly the PLA, saw the role of military power in coping with the Taiwan question. That is, they began to feel that China could no longer use its increasing military advantage simply to deter Taiwan from undertaking provocative political initiatives through displays of force, no matter how imposing. Beijing came to realize that it might have to go to war to protect its Taiwan equities. The official PLA budget has grown at around 15 percent a year since 1989, and the increases have been offset by inflation only during the 1993–97 period. Moreover, the actual defense budget is at least twice the official one. The best, albeit rough, measure of China's acquisition of advanced power-projection systems is its trend in spending on foreign military equipment. The Stockholm International Peace Research Institute estimates that foreign deliveries to China of major conventional weapons totaled $2.58 billion from 1992 to 1995, $3.59 billion in 1995 to 1999, and $10.26 billion from 2000 to 2003.[20]

China's Military Posture

Today, three elements of the PRC's security policy foster both insecurity in Taiwan and concern in Washington. The first is the modernization of the People's Liberation Army, which allows more effective power projection, giving the PRC the ability to damage the island of Taiwan and its population, armed forces, and commerce. The second is an evolution in the PRC's intentions regarding the use of force. The third is growing evidence that the improvement in China's military capabilities is facilitating a shift in strategy, from deterrence to coercion and blocking U.S. involvement. These have created debates in both the United States and Taiwan on how to respond, as well as problems of alliance management. (The following discussion draws on two reports, one the annual report on Chinese military power by the U.S. Department of Defense (DOD), which would be responsible for helping to defend Taiwan if that was deemed necessary, and the other by a panel of scholars and former officials assembled by the Council on Foreign Relations.[21])

China's Military Capabilities

As China tried to cope in the 1990s with the political challenge that it believed Taiwan posed to its national security, it saw both an opportunity and a problem. The opportunity was the post–cold war buyer's market in international arms. The problem was the revolution in military affairs, which became obvious during the Persian Gulf War, when U.S. forces equipped with high-tech arms and equipment handily defeated an Iraqi force structure very similar to that of the PLA. It was made more obvious by subsequent U.S. actions in Kosovo, Afghanistan, and Iraq.

Since the early 1990s, therefore, China has carried out a military modernization program that American analysts have described as "ambitious" and "deliberate and focused." The goal has been to acquire over time the capability to project military power outside its borders and to fight short-duration, high-intensity conflicts. In general, the program has involved a shift from a purely continental orientation to one that includes a maritime focus; from a strategy of in-depth defense and wars of attrition to one of "active peripheral defense," offensive operations, and quick resolution; and from reliance on ground forces to developing air, naval, and missile forces. Increasingly, a particular focus has been to prepare to fight a war over Taiwan, a war that might pit Chinese forces against the United States.[22]

Funded by a budget that grew at a double-digit rate over most of the 1990s and that now amounts to between $44 and $70 billion (depending on how funds outside the official, published budget are counted),[23] the PLA has gradually acquired more advanced equipment, including

—about 500 short-range ballistic missiles of increasing accuracy and lethality

—more than 100 fourth-generation Russian combat aircraft (the Su-27 and Su-30), with more on the way

—two Russian Sovremeny-class guided missile destroyers, with two more on order

—four Kilo-class Russian submarines, with eight more on order

—improved air-defense facilities to expand the effective range of its combat aircraft

—improvements in command, control communications, computers, and intelligence

—improvements in electronic and information warfare.[24]

Cruise missiles and more advanced munitions also are under development.

The PLA has undertaken concerted efforts to improve personnel and training. The goal is to create a cadre of commissioned and noncommissioned officers who have the professional and technical qualifications to conduct modern warfare. Training has become more realistic, and it places greater emphasis on joint operations. Recent maneuvers have focused on small-scale specialized actions that address the type of high-intensity conflicts that the PLA would expect to fight, including defensive actions against a technologically superior foe. The navy has conducted longer sea patrols and exercises to prepare for airborne supply operations, antiship missile attacks, and open ocean operations. Drills for amphibious landings are done on a regular basis. All of these seem designed to prepare for what China regards as the real possibility of war over Taiwan.[25]

The PLA still has a number of weaknesses. The air force is limited in its ability to conduct ground and naval support operations, air-to-air interception, and ground attack. Pilot training, sortie generation, longer-range bombardment, in-flight refueling, command and control, and joint operations all need significant improvement. The navy's various elements are not integrated, and they are vulnerable to a variety of enemy attacks. Modern amphibious assets are lacking.

So there are limits on what China can do today. As an expert panel commissioned by the Council on Foreign Relations concluded, "The PLA currently has the ability to undertake intensive, short-duration air, missile, and naval attacks on Taiwan, as well as more prolonged air and naval attacks." Increasingly, it would be able to inflict costs on any U.S. forces that intervened to defend Taiwan. The outcome of air and naval attacks would depend both on American and Japanese actions and on Taiwan's political and military response. In assessing the various scenarios for a PRC campaign, the 2004 DOD report concludes that China's ability to conduct an attack from the air (with planes and missiles), a naval blockade, and information operations is improving. Both the Pentagon and the Council on Foreign Relations reports judge that the PLA would face major difficulties in attempting an occupation of the island.[26]

Thus what China can achieve with its current capability is a function of several interrelated factors: its objective, Taiwan's vulnerability, how long it would take to achieve victory (which affects the ability of the United States to intervene, if it chose to do so), and the risks involved. If China's objective were to destroy the ROC's capacity to wage a war and even occupy the island through a strategy of attrition, Taiwan probably has sufficient layers of defense to hold out until U.S. forces arrived in strength. As Michael O'Hanlon notes, a successful amphibious assault requires an attacker to do three things: achieve air superiority; use maneuver, surprise, and strength to land forces in a place where they outnumber defenders and their firepower; and strengthen its initial lodgment faster than the defender can bring forces to bear.[27] Moreover, if China could not meet those conditions, as would likely be the case, the costs of defeat, in terms of China's international position and the communist regime's legitimacy, would be profound.

A strategy of coercion, as opposed to domination, entails a different calculus. Here the target is not territory or Taiwan's war-fighting capability but factors like the population's will to resist and the military's command-and-control facilities. This strategy is more consistent with China's current capabilities, such as its increasingly accurate ballistic missiles and information warfare assets. Such a blitzkrieg strategy might succeed quickly (unlike a war of attrition in a domination strategy), before the United States could intervene. The rewards of a rapid victory would be high, but the risks of failure would again be serious.[28]

The PLA understands its weaknesses and can learn from the successes of the world's most powerful military, which would likely be its major adversary in a conflict over Taiwan.[29] It is serious about correcting its weaknesses over time, and the PRC government has demonstrated a willingness to commit significant resources to the modernization and institutional reform of the armed forces. China's military capabilities will only get better. Michael Swaine estimates that in the 2007–10 time frame, China could attain three significant power-projection capabilities that are relevant to a Taiwan scenario. It may be able to

—attack a wide range of civilian and military targets in the East Asian region with as many as 1,000 ballistic missiles and several hundred medium-range bombers armed with conventional ordinance and cruise missiles

—transport one to two divisions by sea and air transport as far as Taiwan

—conduct limited air and sea denial operations up to 250 miles from China's continental coastline (that is, keep U.S. forces away from Taiwan).[30]

China's Intentions

For decades, the PRC leadership identified a variety of circumstances that would compel it to use force against Taiwan. The constant was a declaration of independence, and acquisition of nuclear weapons was cited fairly often. These conditions had the virtue of being steps that Taipei would or would not take. Whether it did so would be clear and unambiguous.

In February 2000, one month before the Taiwan presidential election that Chen Shui-bian won, the PRC offered a new approach to the use of force. In a white paper on Taiwan policy, it announced: "However, if a grave turn of events occurs leading to the separation of Taiwan from China in any name, or if Taiwan is invaded and occupied by foreign countries, or if the Taiwan authorities refuse, sine die [without a clear timetable], the peaceful settlement of cross-Straits reunification through negotiations, then the Chinese government will only be forced to adopt all drastic measures possible, including the use of force, to safeguard China's sovereignty and territorial integrity and fulfill the great cause of reunification."[31]

This declaration is interesting for several reasons. First of all, there is the substance of the conditions, all of which Beijing might deem to apply today. The first condition refers not to Taiwan's declaration of independence but to circumstances that lead to the "separation of Taiwan from China in any name." Presumably, one of the names under which that separation might take place would be the Republic of China. The second condition seems inapposite, until one recalls that "invasion and occupation" were the words that the PRC used to describe the U.S.-ROC security relationship when the United States intervened in the Taiwan Strait at the beginning of the Korean War. By inference, there is a point at which the current U.S.-Taiwan military-to-military relationship might again meet that description and, in Beijing's mind, become the functional equivalent of a defense treaty. The third condition is Taipei's refusal after an indefinite period to settle the dispute with Beijing through negotiations. Apparently, Beijing rules out the possibility that Taipei might have objectively legitimate reasons not to accept its terms for such a settlement.

The second point of interest is that what actions by Taiwan might trigger the PRC's use of force are not clear-cut. In all cases, Beijing has the discretion to decide whether the conditions have been met. Third, at least the third condition is met not by Taipei taking an offending action (such as declaring independence) but by *not* taking action (settling the dispute).

The PRC did not repeat these conditions through most of Chen's presidency. In late 2003 and early 2004, concern mounted in China concerning Chen Shui-bian's project for a new constitution, which it saw as tantamount to declaring independence. Beijing worried that neither the political opposition on the island nor the United States would have the will or ability to stop Chen. Wang Zaixi, a vice-minister at the PRC's Taiwan Affairs Office, reiterated these "three ifs" in a speech to a Chinese-American audience in New York City in January 2004.[32]

Thereafter, momentum built in Beijing for a more authoritative expression of China's intentions concerning Taiwan, one that would show its seriousness and resolve. The result was the antisecession law passed in March 2005 by the National People's Congress. The relevant provision (Article 8) reads as follows: "In the event that the separatist forces of Taiwan independence should act under any name or by any means to cause the fact of Taiwan's secession from China, or that major incidents entailing Taiwan's secession from China should occur, or that the possibilities for a peaceful reunification should be completely exhausted, the state shall employ non-peaceful means and other necessary measures to protect the country's sovereignty and territorial integrity." As with the "three ifs" of February 2000, the conditions under which force would be employed are not clear-cut; they depend only on Beijing's subjective interpretation. With regard to the second condition ("major incidents"), Beijing no doubt did not wish to be too specific on what it opposed, for fear that leaders on Taiwan might do something provocative that had not been considered. In the process, however, Taipei had little guidance on where to show restraint. Whether enshrining these positions in law would actually change Chinese behavior was another question.[33]

Military Strategy

There is a good bit of disagreement among experts on Beijing's strategic calculus concerning Taiwan. The expert panel of the Council on Foreign Relations, for example, concluded that "the PLA is acquiring military capabilities designed to defend Chinese sovereignty and territorial interests and, in particular, to pose a credible threat to Taiwan in order to influence Taiwan's choices about its political future or, failing that, to prevent Taiwan from achieving political independence. These capabilities are also intended to deter, delay, or complicate U.S. efforts to intervene on behalf of Taiwan." Specifically, Beijing might try to compel Taiwan to resume dialogue on the PRC's terms or, in a crisis, undermine the island's economy through some sort of blockade. The Department of Defense basically agrees: "The PLA is focused on developing a variety of credible military options to deter moves by Taiwan toward permanent separation . . . . A second set of objectives, though no less important, includes capability to deter, delay, or disrupt third-party intervention in a cross-Strait military crisis."[34]

But the Pentagon report goes further. On the basis of the character of the PRC's military modernization, it concludes in effect that Beijing no longer seeks just to deter Taiwan from taking overt actions that China wishes to avoid but "if required, to compel by force the integration of Taiwan under mainland authority. . . . The PLA's determined focus on preparing for conflict in the Taiwan Strait . . . casts a cloud over Beijing's declared policy of seeking 'peaceful reunification.'" China's strategy is "fundamentally coercive." The most likely goal of Chinese force development is "to compel Taipei's acquiescence to a negotiated solution by promising swift and effective retaliation if it does not," both to crush the island's will to fight and to preclude U.S. intervention. As military modernization continues, China's ability to intimidate Taiwan will increase. A number of specific operations can be imagined: a sudden violent attack, including elimination of Taiwan's senior civilian and military leadership ("decapitation," in military jargon); gradual escalation of military pressure; information operations; an air and missile campaign; a naval blockade, and so on.[35] (Note the impact of a shift in strategy for the security dilemma. If Taiwan concludes that it needs to be able to defend against coercion with missile defense and antisubmarine warfare assets, China will conclude that it is actually preparing to secure the political initiative that China is trying to prevent.)

Taiwan's Response

Although it is difficult to predict how Taiwan's people would react to a Chinese strategy of intimidation, the PRC's military buildup and the growing possibility that its assets have more than a symbolic purpose have caused some anxiety on Taiwan and spawned a cottage industry of conferences and publications on the topic.[36] The Ministry of National Defense's July 2002 white paper offered a detailed official assessment. It hit many of the same points that the Pentagon report did (equipment procurement, a strategy of quick victory and area denial vis-à-vis U.S. forces, and so forth). It outlined the mounting military danger that China poses to Taiwan but also emphasized that the threat takes political, economic, and psychological forms as well. In short, it concluded,

> The urgency of resolving the 'Taiwan Issue' has prompted the PRC to redirect its military attention toward southeastern coastal areas—an act creating worries among the people on Taiwan and seriously affecting the ROC's psychological defense. . . . Thus, our survival and development are confronted with gruesome threats. . . . Under the cir-

cumstance, a crisis of military confrontation could still be triggered in the Strait.[37]

A report issued by the ruling DPP at the end of 2003 (in the midst of an election campaign) warned the public that Beijing was assembling the capabilities to launch a sudden strike against the island that would paralyze command-and-control operations, seize control of its air space, and so allow an amphibious landing—all before the United States would have a chance to intervene.[38]

The concern about the China threat is shared by civilian policy experts on Taiwan. In the summer of 2004, the Foundation of International and Cross-Strait Studies issued its "Quadrennial National Security Estimate Report," which reflected the consensus among leading scholars concerning Taiwan's national defense and foreign policy issues. The report concluded that the PRC is embarked on a "stunning" program of military modernization designed to project power into the western Pacific and restrict U.S. access to Taiwan in a conflict. The PLA has improved both its conventional capabilities (against which Taiwan has some ability to defend itself) and those termed "asymmetric" (against which there is little or no defense). Examples of the latter are electronic and information warfare and, of special concern, China's improving arsenal of missiles. These have "made it impossible for Taiwan to put up an effective defense. . . even to the point of being helpless against them." The report estimates that the PRC will become a "world level" military power by 2029 at the latest and that "by that time, [it] will be able to capitalize on the missile threat to force Taiwan to the negotiating table [and] seek to hold off any potential intervention by U.S. or Japanese forces." An attack strategy of "chopping off the head" [eliminating the civilian and military leadership and so wreaking havoc with command and control] cannot be ruled out." The report warns that Taiwan is not facing this threat squarely. Part of the public lacks "a sense of urgency" with regard to security issues, and its "defense consciousness" in a crisis is open to question. Growing public debt will limit the quality of future arms acquisitions. Finally, Taiwan's own actions affect the PRC's intentions: "The key factor that may determine the cross-Strait relationship is how Taipei strikes a balance between an emerging new Taiwan identity and the realities of world politics."[39]

The Taiwan public's sense of vulnerability is harder to gauge because of methodological limitations, but what information is available indicates that its fear is not insignificant. One indicator is a series of telephone surveys sponsored by the Mainland Affairs Council on whether the PRC is hostile to the Taiwan government or the Taiwan people (see figure 5-1). Over the six years between April 1998 and April 2004, respondents (Taiwan adults ages twenty to sixty-nine) felt a fluctuating degree of Chinese hostility toward both Taiwan's government and its people, usually correlating with the actual level of tension in the relationship at the time. As few as 38.3 percent acknowledged Chinese hostility to the people in February 2002 (just following Beijing's offer to have some contacts with DPP members), while 66.7 percent did so in August 1999 in the aftermath of Lee Teng-hui's special state-to-state announcement. Perceived Chinese hostility to the government was lowest in December 2002 (56. 8 percent of respondents) and highest in August 1999 (88.5 percent). On average, 48.5 percent (almost half) of respondents believed that the PRC was hostile to the Taiwan people and 66.8 percent believed that it was hostile to the government. Hostility toward the government was always deemed to be higher than hostility toward the people, with the difference as low as 8.1 percent in August 1998 (when preparations were under way for Straits Exchange Foundation chairman Koo Chen-foo's visit to the mainland) and as high as 23.1 percent in July 2002 (when the PRC was able to steal away Nauru, one of Taiwan's erstwhile diplomatic partners). This series of polls makes sense: the public's perception of China's hostility to Taiwan's people will always be less than its perception of China's hostility toward Taiwan's government because the positive economic and social benefits of the relationship are realized in the people-to-people arena. And the opinions expressed, of course, are highly influenced by events.[40]

The fluctuations in views on the single issue of differences in Beijing's hostility toward Taiwan's people and toward its government reflect a broader public disagreement. No one on the island denies the PRC's military buildup, but some sectors still view those developments through a nonmilitary lens. In a sense, Taiwan has shifted more slowly than the PRC from viewing security issues in purely political terms. Some observers on the island argue that economic interaction is a far more important indicator of the PRC's intentions than weapons acquisitions. Moreover, they believe that the policies of Lee Teng-hui and Chen Shui-bian have provoked China into acquiring advanced military equipment and that Chen aligned too much with the United States during 2000 and 2001.[41] This contrarian view has obstructed the effort to build support in the Legislative Yuan for funding the purchase of weapons systems approved by the Bush administration. Others accept the threat as real but remain unconvinced that it is necessary to build up the island's defenses to prepare for a possible war. They are confident, given Bill Clinton's dispatch of carrier battle groups in 1996 and George Bush's expres-

Figure 5-1. Beijing's Hostility

Percent

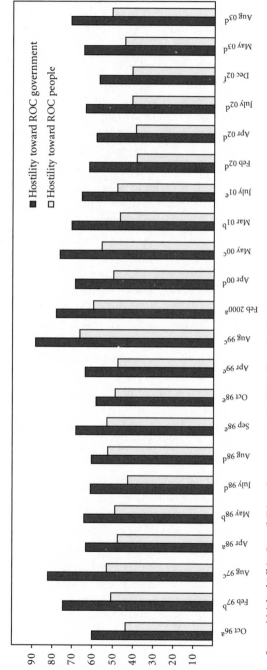

Source: Mainland Affairs Council, Taiwan (www.mac.gov.tw/english/index1-e.htm).

a. Burke Marketing Research, Ltd., Taipei.

b. Center for Public Opinion and Election Studies, National Sun Yat-sen University, Kaohsiung.

c. China Credit Information Service, Ltd., Taipei.

d. Election Study Center, National Chengchi University, Taipei.

e. Survey and Opinion Research Group, Dept. of Political Science, National Chung-cheng Univeristy, Chiyi.

f. e-Society Research Group, Taipei.

sions of support in April 2001, that the United States will come to Taiwan's aid under any circumstances. Still others believe that Taiwan should ensure its security not by relying on the United States, which will provide only defensive weaponry, but by the indigenous production of offensive systems that could attack targets on the mainland and so, it is thought, deter Beijing.

Complicating matters is the need to reform Taiwan's defense establishment. Long dominated by ground forces that received preferential access to resources, in the late 1990s the armed forces began a multifaceted reform to tailor the force structure to meet the need for air and sea defense, giving greater budget priority to the air force and navy, where the priority should have been. Streamlining command and control; rationalizing strategic planning and equipment procurement; and restructuring personnel management, logistics, training, and other functions to match the variety of advanced weapons systems were additional, complementary goals.

Disagreement at the political level over how much defense to acquire and the inevitable difficulties of simultaneously reforming Taiwan's military institutions has retarded the creation of a force that can match military modernization in China. The PLA faces many of the same challenges regarding institutional reform that Taiwan's armed forces do, but it faces fewer resource constraints and political obstacles. Taiwan is making progress, but it is not assembling defensive equipment as fast as China is assembling offensive equipment, and it lags behind China in transforming its equipment into capabilities by improving its military doctrine and training. As Michael Swaine concludes, "Yet it remains far from certain that [this progress] will reduce the threat of conflict with Beijing. The improvements in Taiwan's deterrent and war-fighting capabilities might not be large enough to influence greatly Beijing's overall political, diplomatic, and military strategy toward Taiwan—nor even to affect in any major way a specific decision to apply coercive measures or outright force in a crisis or military conflict."[42]

A more comprehensive and sophisticated poll, conducted in June 2004, provides probably the best sense of the Taiwan public's attitudes on the security situation.[43] By more than a two-to-one margin (59.3 percent and 26.6 percent), respondents believed that Taiwan lacked the power to "resist Chinese aggression" on its own. This sense of vulnerability was positively correlated with education and inversely correlated with age: 72 percent of college graduates and 74.6 percent of people 20 to 29 years of age agreed that Taiwan lacked the capacity to defend itself. On the other hand, only a small fraction—11.2 percent—believed that war was likely in the next three years without provocation by Taiwan; 64.5 percent thought it unlikely.

Views shifted when the poll factored in Taiwan actions that Beijing might regard as a *casus belli*. When asked whether war would occur if a new constitution is promulgated in 2006 (a Chen proposal during the campaign for the March 2004 election), 28.1 percent responded "yes" and 38.3 percent responded "no." If the provoking event was a declaration of independence, the proportion of those who thought that war would be likely rose to 58.3 percent, while 21.4 percent demurred. The concern that Taiwan's actions could provoke a war increased with the level of education. Those who identified themselves only as Taiwanese were much less worried that the promulgation of a new constitution would provoke a war than those who identified themselves as Chinese or both Taiwanese and Chinese.[44] Pollsters found that the older and less educated the respondents, the more likely they were to give a "don't know" response.

Furthermore, 47.6 percent of the public was unwilling to wage a war against China if independence was declared (34.7 percent was willing). Men were evenly split, but women were opposed by more than two to one. The young and the well-educated were evenly split. Concerning identity, 49.1 percent of those who identified themselves as only Taiwanese approved; of those who stated a dual identity, 58.6 percent were opposed, as were 65.7 percent of those who saw themselves only as Chinese.

Not surprisingly, therefore, a clear majority (52 percent) thought that the best way for Taiwan to survive in this complicated security environment was to maintain "friendly engagement" with *both* the United States and China. The public was divided over the issue of "the government spending large sums of money procuring weapons from abroad": 42.5 percent approved while 43.1 percent were against it. There was general confidence (52 percent versus 23.3 percent) that the United States would send troops to defend Taiwan. Unfortunately, the survey did not explore whether the United States would do so if Taiwan provoked the conflict.

In sum, the poll suggests that the Taiwan public does not treat the threat that the PRC poses to the island as seriously as defense officials and the scholars cited. It acknowledges that whether there is war or peace is a function of Taiwan's own actions and that it is in Taiwan's interests to maintain good relations with Washington and Beijing. Views on the need to acquire expensive weapons systems and the wisdom of fighting after a declaration of independence are mixed.

Not too much can be read into the results of a single survey, given the fluidity of the Taiwan public's opinions. Some results may simply have reflected the island's political polarization, and the use of hypothetical situations is always questionable. Yet both surveys demonstrate that the public understands the benefits of economic and social convergence with China—and, by extension, of a solution to the cross-Strait dispute—as long as Taiwan's security is protected. And both polls as well as government and scholarly views suggest that concerns about the PRC's capabilities and intentions will complicate any search for settlement.

Extrapolating forward, Taiwan's sense of vulnerability will likely deepen if it continues to lag behind the PRC in relative growth of military power. Taiwan need not, of course, match the PRC plane for plane, ship for ship, and defensive missile for offensive missile. What it must be able to create through its defense modernization is the confidence that it can do three things: deter Beijing from engaging in coercion; if deterrence fails, sustain a defense until the United States comes to the rescue (if it chooses to do so); and, if negotiations occur, conduct them without fear of intimidation. The belief of some on Taiwan that offensive capabilities could provide a sufficient deterrent is an illusion. Taiwan probably lacks the technological and budgetary resources to produce such weapons, and it would certainly lack the intelligence resources needed to use them effectively. Because the United States is the ultimate guarantor of its security, Taiwan must ensure that there is no strategic divergence that might lead Washington to conclude that its de facto ally is entrapping it in a conflict it prefers not to fight.

U.S. Views

The PRC's military modernization has also fostered a debate in the United States on how to calibrate policy actions in order to preserve stability and prevent both sides from miscalculating the intentions of the other or the risks involved. The 1995–96 crisis led some observers to urge Washington to restrain Taiwan's political initiatives. Robert Ross asserted that if the United States and China are going to "deal with" the Taiwan Strait issue satisfactorily, "Washington cannot permit American ideological support for Taiwan's democracy or Taiwan's democratic politics to undermine the polities of war and peace. . . . To avoid policy drift, future administrations will have to make policy that is in the interest of the United States, not Taiwan." Chas. W. Freeman wrote: "U.S. policy can no longer hope to deter war exclusively by keeping Beijing at bay. The United States must also discourage decisions and actions by Taipei that could leave Beijing with little choice but to react militarily."[45]

Other American observers, including many individuals who became part of the Bush administration's foreign policy team, took a very different view.

They believed that the Clinton administration had been slow to arm Taiwan in response to the improving capabilities of the PLA; moreover, it had given reassurances to Beijing that it should have given to Taiwan and shown resolve to Taiwan that it should have shown to Beijing. In the weeks after Lee Teng-hui's state-to-state formulation, they issued a statement that in view of the PRC's threats, "it [had] become essential that the United States make every effort to deter any form of Chinese intimidation of the Republic of China on Taiwan and declare unambiguously that it will come to Taiwan's defense in the event of an attack or a blockade against Taiwan, including against the offshore islands of Matsu and Kinmen. . . . The time for strategic and moral 'ambiguity' with regard to Taiwan has passed."[46]

It came as no surprise, then, that the Bush administration took several decisions to reorient U.S. policy just three months after Bush took office, in April 2001. First, to deter Beijing from attacking Taiwan and to improve the ability of the ROC armed forces to fight should that become necessary, it approved the sale of a number of advanced weapons systems to compensate for the PRC's improvements: Kidd-class destroyers for maritime air defense, P-3 Orion aircraft for antisubmarine warfare, diesel-powered submarines, mine-sweeping helicopters, and a mix of missiles and torpedoes. Moreover, it conducted a number of assessments of what further improvements were needed.

Second, it allowed closer collaboration between the U.S. and Taiwan defense establishments, expanding a process begun in the Clinton administration designed to ensure—through reform of areas like military doctrine, training, command and control, and logistics—that U.S. weaponry would be well used in the event of a conflict and that the two militaries could fight together effectively. The interaction now went well beyond that narrow orbit. As summarized by the *Washington Post*: "U.S. military representatives, once almost completely banned from visiting Taiwan, are currently involved in dozens of programs on the island, including both classroom seminars and training in the field. U.S. officers are advising Taiwan's military at all levels in policy, implementation and training. . . . In addition, the two militaries have established a hotline for communicating in case of an emergency. . . . Meanwhile, hundreds of Taiwanese military personnel are now undergoing training and education in the United States."[47]

Third, to reduce the chances that Beijing might miscalculate U.S. resolve in response to a PLA attack, the president signaled that the United States would come to the island's defense under just about any circumstances, which enhanced the confidence of Taiwan's armed forces that they would not have to fight alone.[48]

Still, as of early 2004, the Bush administration remained concerned that Beijing's systematic modernization program not only was creating options for the use of force but also "casts a cloud over Beijing's declared preference for resolving differences with Taiwan through peaceful means. . . . Taiwan's relative military strength will deteriorate, unless it makes significant investments into its defense." The sophistication of the PRC effort "calls for more strategic harmonization between the U.S. and Taiwan."[49]

Developments on Taiwan: Chinese and American Views

As might be expected in a security dilemma, China watched the U.S. initiatives with serious concern, for they foreshadowed a new military calculus should there ever be a conflict: Taiwan itself would be better able to resist, and the PLA would likely have to fight against the United States. Even in the absence of a conflict, closer ties between the U.S. and ROC militaries were unwelcome. As Vice Premier Qian Qichen said in early 2001, as the Bush administration was coming into office: "We must recognize that an attitude of enmity and considerable tension still exists across the Strait. The United States arms sales are just pouring oil on the fire. There was always a flicker of conflict there in the first place, and if you add to it, will that spark not flare up?"[50]

Beijing, of course, worried about the impact of U.S. arms sales on Taiwan's military capabilities relative to its own. For example, a robust missile defense for the island would negate to some degree the effectiveness of the PRC's arsenal of short-range ballistic missiles, its main tool for deterring any separatist moves. But the main focus of Chinese criticism was the integration between the U.S. and Taiwan militaries and how total U.S. security cooperation would affect the political intentions of the island's political leaders. A July 2002 article in the Chinese journal *Shijie Zhishi* began with a stark lead paragraph: "Everything that the U.S. government does makes the 'one China principle' hollow. This de facto military alliance between the United States and Taiwan causes reunification and the security environment to face grave challenges." The author, Wang Weixing of the Academy of Military Sciences, went on to catalogue, on the basis of press reports, all the indicators of a de facto alliance: increased arms sales; linking of command centers that would facilitate joint operations; a congressional mandate for a DOD plan on joint training; intensified exchanges, at a higher level; U.S. observers at Taiwan exercises; more Taiwan officers in U.S. military education institutions; congressional designation of Taiwan as on a par with NATO allies for certain programs; ending strategic ambiguity concerning the use of force; enhancing deployments in East Asia and the Western Pacific; building up facilities on Guam; and so on. The author concluded, "Obviously, the Americans are taking the Taiwan military by the hand to help them complete all predetermined plans." The United States was now "brazenly" violating the spirit of the commitment it made at the time of normalization concerning its security relationship with Taiwan. The American goal was to "publicly bolster 'Taiwan independence' forces, encouraging them to 'use arms to resist peace' and 'use arms to resist reunification,' thereby hindering the great cause of China's peaceful unification." (The use of the phrase "defend independence by force" became a staple of PRC analysis of Taiwan's defense policy, specifically its intentions, after 2000. The phrase, used no doubt to challenge the strong U.S. opposition to the use of force, also reflected China's anxiety about the shifting Taiwan challenge to its security.)[51]

Another Chinese commentator took some of the same evidence and drew conclusions about Chen Shui-bian's motives in "willingly playing the part of a 'generous moron' and the 'pawn' of the United States." He wanted to increase his political capital for resisting reunification and seeking independence, because "the 'Taiwan independence' elements regard the elevation of U.S.-Taiwan military relations as the best protective umbrella for pursuing 'Taiwan independence.'" In addition, he wished to build support for his reelection effort. Wang Weixing charged in 2003 that Chen had used these various links to "manipulate" the Taiwan armed forces so that they "have gradually degenerated into forces for 'Taiwan independence.'" Whether or not the evidence in these accounts is factually correct or the conclusions deduced from it are valid, they reflect the sense of greater insecurity that China feels about these trends. As Wang concluded in his 2002 article, "for a considerable period of time in the future, our strategic environment will have no cause for optimism."[52]

It was the Chen administration's political intentions that the PRC watched most closely, since the threat from Taiwan that China perceived was political (separatism). When Chen was elected, Beijing announced that it would take nothing for granted and vigilantly "listen to his words and watch his deeds" (*ting qi yan, guan qi xing*). Having been tripped up by Lee Teng-hui's "covert independence," China observed Chen like a hawk to ensure that, emboldened by American support, he did not challenge China's interests in an irreversible way.

One staple of the Chinese view of the issue was to assert a strong degree of continuity between Lee and Chen. Yu Keli, a scholar at the Taiwan

Research Institute of the Chinese Academy of Social Sciences, took this tack in arguing that the core of Chen's mainland policy was Lee Teng-hui's formulation, announced in July 1999, that cross-Strait ties were a "special state-to-state relationship." Yu found evidence to support his hypothesis in the Chen administration's opposition to unification, doctrine of integration (because it would freeze the status quo), efforts to "de-Sinicize" Taiwan (to create a Taiwan identity), support for overt proponents of independence, and efforts to secure U.S. support. The state-to-state relationship and independence were two sides of the same coin; the former was merely less provocative than the latter. As a result, "cross-Strait relations . . . remain strained" and "a serious crisis lies latent between the two sides and this aggravates a series of conflicts on the island"—a reference, no doubt, to the polarization that had occurred between Chen's political coalition and that of the opposition.[53]

Xu Bodong, an intellectual whose views are on the margin of the Chinese mainstream, took this logic one step further. He described how Lee Teng-hui had deviated from "the one-China principle" in the latter part of his administration and then played a key role in shifting power to Chen and the DPP in 2000. Once in office Chen was more conciliatory than the feisty Lee, but he "held on to his 'Taiwan independence' stance" and took advantage of Beijing's tolerance. Xu found this situation quite dangerous. "This means that the Taiwan side intends to change its original position toward itself and national identity. In other words, the Taipei authorities intend to unilaterally overturn the rules of the game between the two shores, abolish the prerequisite for 'peaceful unification' and, on the question of war and peace between the two shores, which is a major issue of principle, wittingly or unwittingly and foolishly opt for war."[54]

Chen Shui-bian's proposals during his campaign for reelection caused a quantum leap in PRC concerns that he would take political initiatives that would so challenge Chinese equities that it would require a military response. Beijing regarded Chen's August 2002 statement that there was one *guo* (usually translated "country") on each side of the Taiwan Strait (*yibian yiguo*) as worse than Lee Teng-hui's state-to-state relations, and it quickly responded to what it perceived as a threat to the national interest. An authoritative commentary by the Xinhua news service and *Renmin Ribao* (*People's Daily*) labeled Chen's comments as "gravely separatist 'Taiwan independence' remarks" and a "deliberate provocation to the compatriots on both sides of the Strait" that belied his supposed attempt in his inaugural speech to reassure China and others about his intentions. The commentary alleged that his statement followed a series of steps "to attain his 'Taiwan independence' goal in incremental fashion" and that "*yibian yiguo*" was a "vain attempt to change the status quo and split Taiwan from China and push Taiwan toward war," something that the PRC would not tolerate. "We warn the Taiwan independence forces that you are facing the choice of what kind of 'your own road' to follow, whether to stubbornly follow the road of 'Taiwan independence' or to rein in on the brink of the precipice." Retrospectively, Beijing concluded that its "get-tough" policy toward Chen was successful because it forestalled the "serious consequences of 'Taiwan independence.'"[55]

Chinese anxiety about Chen's intentions rose again during the fall of 2003, as he advocated a new constitution and referenda to mobilize the support of his base voters. Seeing a dangerous trend, Beijing began to issue stern warnings that Chen's political initiatives were encroaching on its "bottom line" and that if he crossed it, China would have to respond forcefully. Major General Peng Guangqian of the Academy of Military Science warned in early December, "We would pay whatever price we need to pay" to defend China's sovereignty and territorial integrity. China, he predicted, would be willing to give up the 2008 Olympic Games, the 2010 World Expo, plus, temporarily, foreign relations, foreign investment, the safety of coastal cities, and the country's economic development: "All these prices are affordable. It is worthwhile to earn the complete reunification of the country and revitalization of the nation by making temporary, localized sacrifices. If the 'Taiwan independence' elements and the international anti-China forces [that is, the United States] wanted to take a gamble, they would inevitably have to pay heavy prices and end in ignominious defeat."[56]

Chen's initiatives prior to the 2004 election also unnerved Washington, in the broader context of the Bush administration's revised assessment of China's strategic role. Up to that point, it no longer believed that a rising China would likely challenge a status quo United States, with Taiwan being the first point of conflict. Particularly after the September 11 attacks, it had come around to the view that it could work with Beijing and other powers to resolve difficult security problems that threatened their respective interests. North Korea and South Asia were the prime examples of this more cooperative approach, which provided U.S.-China relations with a strategic rationale, which they had lacked for more than a decade. The Bush administration worried that Chen might provoke China into a coercive response (through miscalculation or otherwise) and draw the United States into a conflict that it did not need (given North Korea, Iraq, and so on) with a country with which it wished to cooperate. Taiwan of course denied any provocative intent, but the U.S. fear of entrapment ultimately led President Bush in December 2003 to warn, "We oppose any unilateral decision by either China or Taiwan to change the status quo. And the comments and actions made by the leader of Taiwan indicate that he may be willing to make decisions unilaterally to change the status quo, which we oppose."[57]

At the same time—and not inconsistently—the Bush administration worried that Taiwan was not moving fast enough to modernize itself to meet the PRC challenge. In February 2004, Richard Lawless, the deputy assistant secretary of defense responsible for Taiwan matters, complained, "Economic trends, the domestic debate over defense strategy, national identity issues, service parochialism, all complicate Taiwan's force modernization, training, and jointness." Defense spending had declined in real terms and as a share of GDP over the prior decade. Many of the systems approved by President Bush in April 2001 had not been acquired by the end of his first term. The Pentagon believed that Taiwan needed to assign higher priority to readiness, including personnel management, logistics, maintenance, and training. It needed to strengthen its processes for strategic and force planning and foster interoperability among its services and those of "the United States and other potential defense partners."[58]

On the surface, these two concerns seem in conflict. Yet if Taiwan's leadership assumed that the U.S. commitment was unqualified and that it would come to the island's defense whatever the *casus belli*, there would be less reason for it to speed up its military transformation and little reason to exercise political restraint.

The Security Dilemma and the Cross-Strait Stalemate

The China-Taiwan security dilemma is relevant in two ways to the stalemate between them. It certainly aggravates the difficulty of maintaining stability and minimizing tensions in the current context. But it also complicates any effort to resolve the dispute in a mutually acceptable manner. Each side will be concerned that if it takes a step to reduce the other's sense of insecurity, the other may exploit the concession and leave it more vulnerable. If there is to be a settlement, the parties will need to find ways to assure each other that its goodwill will be reciprocated and that neither will use its power (military or political) to put the other's interests at risk. Given that the U.S. security commitment to Taiwan is the key to the island's assessment of the risks it might face, what would China have to offer Taiwan to convince it to cut that cord?

There have been attempts in the past to address the cross-Strait security dilemma, but their effect has been limited. Take, for example, Taipei's long-standing demand that Beijing renounce the use of force, which was an element of the first stage of the three-stage process laid out in Taipei's National Unification Guidelines. Lee Teng-hui reiterated the need for China to renounce force on a number of occasions thereafter. Chen Shui-bian pledged that he would not declare independence or take other steps that Beijing found extremely provocative only "as long as the CCP regime has no intention to use military force against Taiwan." China has sought to reassure Taiwan on this question, but only up to a point. Jiang Zemin declared in his January 1995 statement that "Chinese should not fight fellow Chinese," but Beijing has also been explicit in its refusal to renounce force. Jiang explained that Beijing's refusal was intended to guard against "the schemes of foreign forces to interfere with China's reunification and to bring about the 'independence' of Taiwan." Later authoritative PRC statements would also cite independence as a reason. The logic was that if Beijing renounced the use of force, then Taiwan would certainly declare independence. As Jiang told the *New York Times* in August 2001, "We cannot renounce the use of force. If we did, a peaceful reunification would become impossible."[59] Beijing believes that if it makes this concession, Taipei will take advantage of its goodwill.

There is also the concern on each side that the proposals of the other that purportedly would increase mutual security might actually contain traps that would leave it in greater danger. For example, Beijing has proposed that the two sides conclude an agreement to end the state of hostilities that has existed since the ROC lost the mainland in 1949. That offer was repeated on various occasions thereafter—for example, in Beijing's statement right after Chen Shui-bian's inauguration in May 2004. Early on, Taiwan responded positively to this proposal, most authoritatively in the National Unification Guidelines and Lee Teng-hui's 1996 inaugural address. But it got cold feet once the PRC began in January 1995 to insist that the discussions on such a pact be held under the one-China principle. From Taipei's point of view, to accept that principle might undermine its negotiating position on the issue of sovereignty. Conversely, Taiwan began to talk occasionally in the late 1990s in terms of a peace agreement. In July 1998 Lee Teng-hui told the National Unification Council that the two sides should sign "a peace agreement, thereby ending the state of hostility." For Taipei, that modality was consistent with its view that the dispute was between two equal sovereign entities. But Beijing believes that the conflict is a civil war between two belligerent forces, of which it is the only sovereign entity—which is why it did not respond to Lee's offer.[60]

The United States is often part of this conundrum, as illustrated by an offer that Jiang Zemin put forward when he met George W. Bush in Texas in October 2002. Jiang reportedly offered a trade-off: China would redeploy its missiles targeting Taiwan in return for a reduction in U.S. arms sales to the island's military. This was a significant innovation on Beijing's part, because it acknowledged a link between China's military deployments and U.S. arms sales to Taiwan. Still, there were a number of substantive problems with this offer. For example, the missiles in question are mobile and once redeployed could be deployed again. Also, the PLA has other assets that threaten Taiwan (advanced fighter aircraft, submarines, and so on). Most significant, however, is the very fact that Jiang was seeking to deal directly with Washington and so reduce the Chen government's confidence in its ally. Redeploying missiles would, to be sure, reduce Taipei's insecurity to some degree, but the price Taiwan would pay—in terms of fewer American weapons and fears of U.S. abandonment—would only render it more vulnerable and subject to intimidation by the PRC.[61]

The mutual mistrust that frustrates these failed efforts to stabilize the *current* situation would be multiplied many times in any effort to address security issues as part of a *future* overall settlement. The PRC's objective in such a project would be to minimize or eliminate Taiwan's freedom to again pursue what it regards as a separatist agenda. That is the core of the one-country, two-systems formula: Taiwan accepts the status of subordinate unit of the People's Republic of China and gets home rule in return. A likely corollary of that bargain would be the end of Taiwan's security relationship with the United States. In Chinese eyes, it is that tie that allows "separatism" in the first place. Yet even after such an agreement China would be unlikely to rest easy. There probably would be political forces on the island that— even if they did not harbor the goal of changing the status quo—remained highly suspicious of Chinese intentions, and Beijing would likely exaggerate their impact. That has certainly been the case in Hong Kong, where the PRC was unwilling to leave much to chance and imposed limitations on home rule in order to exclude the Democratic Party from significant power and where the advocates of greater democracy put Beijing on the defensive in 2003 and 2004. It would probably do the same in Taiwan. Moreover, if Taiwan were to retain residual security ties with the United States, Beijing would probably view them with some paranoia. So it would naturally seek safeguards as it negotiated an agreement.

Taiwan, of course, would seek to preserve its defense ties with the United States—the ultimate guarantee of its security—even more than Beijing would wish to end them. China will not stop acquiring advanced military capabilities if significant progress occurs on unification. That those capabilities are growing and that China has a history of using them for purposes of intimidation would create fear that China might use them in the event of a serious unanticipated conflict. How could Taiwan ensure that a stronger Beijing would not exploit its weakness in the absence of U.S. aid? How could negotiations even begin on unification if there were uncertainty about future Chinese intentions?

Note again the asymmetry of this situation. The threat that Beijing perceives from Taiwan is mainly political, whereas the threat that Taiwan perceives from China is primarily military. U.S. security support for Taiwan is absolutely vital for the government and people of Taiwan, whereas it is simply a source of frustration for China.

Note also that in any settlement between Taiwan and China there is an important link between the ultimate legal identity of the Taipei government—the focus of the last chapter—and how the ongoing security dilemma is addressed. If Taiwan accepted Beijing's position that Beijing is the exclusive sovereign of the national union and that Taipei possesses no residual sovereignty, that would likely discourage other countries from intervening in what the world would have come to see as a domestic matter.[62]

Beijing and Taipei have given relatively little attention to security issues as part of a settlement, in contrast to the sovereignty issue, which has been the focus of discussion for almost two decades. The only exception has been Beijing's proposal regarding the future of Taiwan's armed forces after unification. In his nine-point statement on unification of September 1981, Ye Jianying promised that Taiwan could retain its armed forces. Deng Xiaoping reiterated that pledge in June 1983, offering three elaborations: first, the central government would not station PLA troops on Taiwan; second, the Taipei authorities would administer "party, governmental, and military systems"; and third, the armed forces could not be a threat to China. In May 2000, Qian Qichen stated that Taiwan may have armed forces "of a certain size." In January 2001, echoing Deng, he said that "if the army in Taiwan can maintain *national* defense and security, then there is no problem."[63]

An ancillary question is how the Taiwan armed forces would equip themselves. Due to Beijing's pressure, few countries are willing to supply Taiwan militarily, and the United States is the only one that matters. There have been Chinese suggestions that the island could continue to acquire weapons systems from external sources. For example, a *People's Daily* article in July 1991 stated that "Taiwan may . . . purchase necessary weapons from other countries after establishment of a Special Administrative Region." However, that offer has never been made by a senior PRC official. And there are indications that Beijing would place limits on the implementation of this offer. There was Deng's proviso that the Taiwan military could not threaten the mainland, and the 1991 article mentioned above made clear that Taipei's postunification arms acquisitions "shall not harm the interests of the unified country." All this suggests that Beijing, as the exclusive sovereign under the one-country, two-systems proposal, would assert its right to authorize Taiwan's arms purchases and would be unwilling to allow the sort of weapons that would make Taiwan more secure.[64] In short, Beijing's pledges are unlikely to reassure the island. If, hypothetically, unification was to occur, only to be followed by a major dispute, then Taiwan would be more vulnerable to PRC intimidation than it is today because its armed forces would be weaker and the PLA's stronger. Whether Beijing would actually engage in such intimidation cannot be known, of course. Yet what is important here is what the people in Taiwan would fear, Chinese reassurances to the contrary notwithstanding, and whether they would believe that trusting Beijing's promises was a risk worth running.[65]

To address the security dilemma in the context of a settlement would be easier if the two sides were conscious that it exists. Yet that understanding is limited. When Taipei takes actions that, by any objective standard, China could reasonably regard as provocative and demanding an aggressive response, it often assumes that Beijing will give it the benefit of the doubt and respond in a measured way. And Iain Johnston concludes that China's leaders probably do not appreciate or accept the dynamic of the security dilemma either. That is, they do not realize that overtures that they craft as positive appeals to the Taiwan public do not always get a favorable response—that they actually are perceived as threatening—because they were not well designed. "Security dilemma arguments rarely have had appeal inside China because they require a recognition that China's own behavior has been counterproductive and has undermined its own security."[66]

A Game Theory Metaphor

The last chapter sought to illuminate the cross-Strait sovereignty conundrum through the metaphor of the duplex house. This chapter closes with a well-known "game" that international relations specialists have used to elucidate the security dilemma and explore why adversaries who have an objective reason to resolve their dispute (to "cooperate") refuse to do so because of mutual mistrust. This is the Prisoners' Dilemma.

In the Prisoners' Dilemma, the police have under arrest two individuals whom they suspect of having committed a major crime, but they have only enough evidence to convict the two on minor charges. They hope to induce one or both to incriminate the other on the serious charge. As the payoffs of the game are structured, if both prisoners remain quiet (if they cooperate with each other), each will get a light sentence. If both squeal (if both "defect" from cooperation), then both will get a moderate sentence. If only Prisoner A chooses to incriminate Prisoner B, then A is freed and B gets a heavy sentence (in the language of game theory, A "defects" and B "cooperates"). If Prisoner B alone chooses to incriminate A, then the rewards and punishments are reversed. In a one-round game, therefore, both A and B, each assuming that the other will talk, invariably squeal and take a moderate sentence rather than remain silent and trust the goodwill of the partner. The risk of being exploited is too severe. It is the combination of greed (the desire to go free) and fear (the anxiety that the partner will squeal) that produces a suboptimal outcome.[67] What is the rational course of action for each individual produces an outcome that is less positive than the one that the two could obtain together (if there were honor among criminals). The game is illustrated in figure 5-2. The scores represent the positive reward to each criminal (a high score equals a low sentence). For each criminal, the preference ordering is DC>CC>DD>CD. Each player stands to gain the most by defecting, whatever the other does. Consequently, both will defect, even though the theoretical rewards of mutual cooperation are greater than those of mutual defection. The outcome of their interaction, therefore, is mutual defection.

How does this metaphor apply to the quest for a solution to the China-Taiwan dispute? In the language of game theory, mutual cooperation (CC) represents a settlement, an outcome in which China and Taiwan agree to abandon mutual hostility and form a political union to supplement their economic interdependence. Mutual defection (DD) is the current situation, wherein the two sides get the economic benefits of the relationship but are locked in a stalemate concerning political ties, in part because they mistrust each other. Even though each understands the abstract value of cooperation, each will give into the temptation to defect mainly because it fears that if it takes the initiative to cooperate, the other will exploit its goodwill and secure a political outcome that works to its disadvantage. Sometimes each gives in

Figure 5-2. The Prisoners' Dilemma and Cross-Strait Relations

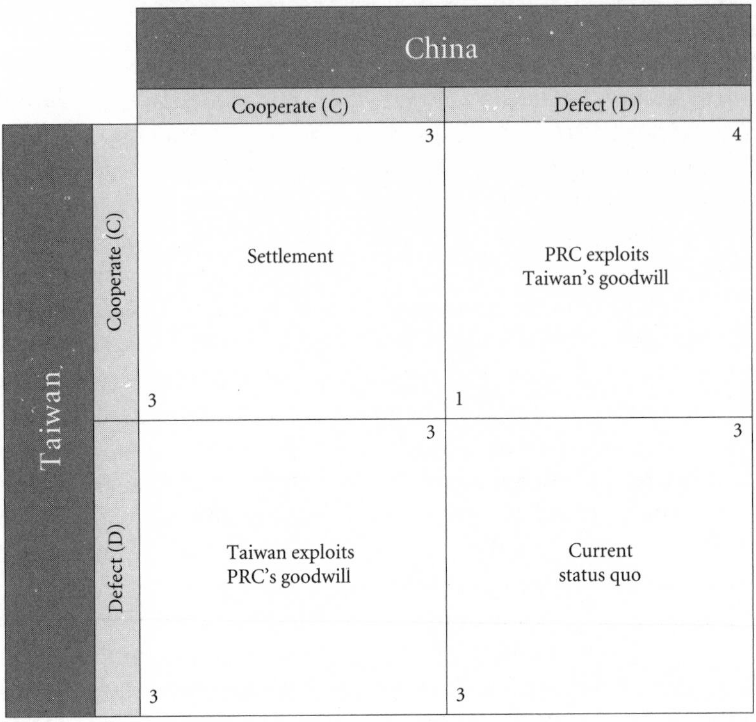

		China	
		Cooperate (C)	Defect (D)
Taiwan — Cooperate (C)		Settlement — 3 / 3	PRC exploits Taiwan's goodwill — 4 / 1
Taiwan — Defect (D)		Taiwan exploits PRC's goodwill — 3 / 3	Current status quo — 3 / 3

Source: Author's illustration.

because the temptation of exploiting the other is difficult to resist. For example, Taiwan fears that the one-China principle is a trap; if it accepts, China will turn the tables and impose a solution that leaves Taiwan in a weak, subordinate position, without U.S. protection. Conversely, China fears that if it makes concessions (such as renouncing force), Taipei will pocket them and so bring about permanent separation, making China look foolish in the bargain. And there are actors on each side who are eager to take advantage of the other. In these two outcomes (CD and DC), it is the fear that each has of being exploited by the other that leads it to prefer the status quo, mutual defection. Taiwan's fear of exploitation and its temptation to defect are magnified by its dependence on the United States. For Taipei, "cooperation" comes with high risk because it means giving up the American ace-in-the-hole in the event that China reneges on its commitments.

In this real-life "game," China and Taiwan both appear to have a compelling incentive to opt for an uneasy status quo instead of a mutually beneficial settlement. When it comes to *solving* the cross-Strait dispute, mutual defection is more attractive than cooperation.[68] Chapter 10 returns to the subject of how the two sides might extricate themselves from this dilemma of mistrust and conflicting interests.

6

Domestic Politics
and Cross-Strait Relations

As if the substantive issues of sovereignty and security were not enough to impede progress on cross-Strait relations, other impediments also are at play. One is domestic politics in Taiwan and China alike. Leaders on both sides who, in the abstract, might see value in resolving the Taiwan Strait issue must take practical account of the internal forces constraining them or they will no longer be leaders. To be sure, the political dynamics differ on the two sides of the Strait. Taiwan is a democracy with a history of conflict between mainlanders and Taiwanese. China is at best an authoritarian regime that is riding the tiger of Chinese nationalism. On Taiwan, voters decide who will be president and who will sit in the legislature. In China, the Communist Party elite selects who will fill leadership positions, through a process that is hardly transparent. Although it goes too far to say, as Steve Tsang does, that "the most important factors that determine whether there is war or peace between the PRC and Taiwan are the domestic politics of the two sides" (sovereignty and security are more important), they do constrain cross-Strait choices.[1]

Taiwan

Politics in Taiwan has affected and continues to affect cross-Strait relations in three ways. First, harsh Nationalist Party repression and the justifications offered for it fostered a distinct Taiwanese identity and perspective on the island's relationship to China and the world, and some fear of outsiders. This consciousness fueled the demand of some Taiwanese for a separate country and animated the political opposition to KMT rule. Second, democratization and the growing economic interaction with the mainland forced the leading opposition force, the Democratic Progressive Party, to moderate its demands regarding the island's political identity in order to gain power. Third, for a variety of constitutional and institutional reasons, that same democratic system is inclined toward demagoguery, fragmentation, and gridlock and resists making tough choices. In short, Taiwanese identity reinforces the substantive objections to China's one-country, two-systems proposal; electoral politics constrains any drive toward de jure independence; and the pathologies of the political system reduce the possibility that Taiwan would approve any good offer the PRC might make.

History and Identity

The mental constructs that people bring to politics can be very powerful, more powerful sometimes than economic interests or observable social and cultural characteristics. If people possess a political identity regarding themselves and where they live, that subjective construct becomes an objective fact. As a corollary, they brand as outsiders or aliens those who they decide do not share their identity. That too becomes an objective political fact. Finally, political identities do not always form naturally. Often they are invented, the result of a political experience that makes adoption of such new mental constructs more likely. Thus the first citizens of the United States defined themselves and their nation in terms of their political and military struggle with Britain. Chinese nationalism became white-hot in the crucible of war with Japan after 1937. And the process of creating a Taiwan political identity—along with the parallel process of defining outsiders—was the product of Chinese rule after 1945.

Strong group identity and fear of "the other" is not a new phenomenon on Taiwan. The three groups of Han Chinese who settled the island early on—from Zhangzhou and Quanzhou in Fujian and from Hakka areas in South China—fought each other and the aboriginal tribes living there. But they set aside their differences when the Japanese army arrived in 1895 to assert imperial control. When officials and soldiers of the Republic of China took over Taiwan in late 1945, the people of Taiwan welcomed their arrival and the opportunity to again be a part of China. There was little immediate regret over the end of Japanese rule and no apparent desire for political independence. The issue was more how Taiwan would fit into the Chinese system, as defined by the ROC. Very quickly, however, the Nationalist Party government alienated the Taiwanese and unintentionally fostered the construction of a Taiwan identity that would be a significant force four decades later.[2]

The speed with which the alienation occurred was remarkable. The first year of Nationalist rule (1946) brought inflation, unemployment, replacement of Taiwanese government employees with mainlanders, food and housing shortages, and the deterioration of public health. The new rulers claimed that Japanese colonialism had weakened Taiwan's roots in Chinese culture and that strong action was necessary to restore them and to free the islanders from their "slavery." Taiwanese hostility grew apace, and some Taiwanese summed up the situation by drawing analogies to two animals unpopular in Chinese culture: "The dogs [the Japanese] had left, but the pigs [mainland Chinese] had come." And dogs, since they did protect property, were ranked more highly. [3]

But it was brutal repression rather than mere incompetence that hastened the Taiwanese shift in consciousness to the idea that they and the mainlanders were really two different peoples. The indiscriminate violence with which the Nationalist government put down the February 28, 1947, incident created a profound bitterness. A Taiwanese offered a keen assessment of the political impact of the crackdown in these remarks to a mainlander in late 1949:

> There were great numbers of people [on both sides] killed. But the troops used machine guns to kill and those who were killed in that way were Taiwanese. I also know that we should not hate the Mainlanders. For instance, we are the brothers and sisters of distant kinspeople from the Mainland. Moreover, you are a Mainlander, and I am Taiwanese. In reality, our ancestors are the same people. Is there any difference between Mainlanders and Taiwanese? But you do not realize that the government has handled the February 28 Incident in such a barbarous way. This has *caused the Taiwanese to turn their hatred of the Kuomintang into hatred of all Mainlanders* [emphasis added]. . . . Although this belief is wrong, the Kuomintang should bear a large part of the responsibility.[4]

By this point, concludes Steven Phillips, the Taiwanese "increasingly saw the mainland government and its representatives on the island as new, yet less competent, *colonial rulers* [emphasis added]." The mental die had been cast.[5]

But worse was to come. Whereas the KMT's response to 2-28 had been rather ad hoc, the "white terror" that began in 1949 was more systematic. The newly reformed Nationalist security services set about with great thoroughness to remove the threat of communist infiltrators and Taiwanese dissidents. Indeed, a retrospective compilation of human rights cases from 1947 to 1991 shows that there were more cases between 1950 and 1954 (184) than for all other years combined (162). Under the provisions of emergency rule, also called martial law, dissent was treated as a criminal offense, to be tried in military courts. The Taiwan Garrison Command deterred any challenge through an oppressive system of surveillance.[6]

The KMT also limited political freedoms and electoral contests for power. The press was subject to censorship. New political parties and opposition activities like demonstrations were banned. Elections were conducted at the lower levels of the political system, ostensibly to train the people for democracy but also as a device to penetrate local society by manipulating rivalries between local factions. Elections for the presidency and for central representative bodies like the legislature and the National Assembly were outlawed. Politics was basically demobilized, and the only Taiwanese whose political participation was tolerated were those who were prepared to play by the KMT's rules. Even public discussion of issues like the February 28 incident was forbidden—with an ironic result. As Robert Edmondson has written, "For most Taiwanese, however, the coercive silencing of [KMT] Chinese nationalism . . . and its obligations to forget [2-28] reinforced its own antithesis, that the KMT was in fact another foreign regime."[7]

The government rationalized its monopoly on power in two ways. With respect to the denial of civil liberties, it asserted that the civil war with the Chinese communists had not ended and that preparations were under way to mount a counterattack to reseize the mainland. In the interests of national security and internal stability, therefore, political freedom was a luxury that Taiwan could not afford. The rationale for deferring elections was that the ROC government was the government of all of China and that its representative institutions had to be elected on a China-wide basis, which was currently impossible because the mainland was still under communist control. In those circumstances, the only elections that could be held were those for seats in the areas under Nationalist control. The claim that the ROC was the government of all of China had another perverse result: the creation of a provincial government for Taiwan, whose territory was almost the same as that under the jurisdiction of the ROC and which had little power. From the KMT's point of view, however, to not have that superfluous level of government would suggest that the ROC was the government of Taiwan only.[8]

This self-serving logic had an insidious effect on politics in Taiwan. The regime's assertion that authoritarian rule was necessary to defend the interests of the ROC state was not lost on its domestic opponents, who had their own vision of Taiwan's identity. As the ROC's claim to be the government of China became increasingly hollow and its hold on power more tenuous, the Taiwanese opposition would combine the two issues, seeking not just popular rule but also a new definition of their homeland.

If the KMT had sought only to restrict overt political activity and competition, with the impact falling just on those who mounted a direct challenge to the regime, the resulting Taiwanese identity might not have been so strong. But the KMT reinforced the effect through a series of policies that affected the broader population. Some were designed to make good Chinese subjects out of Taiwanese who had been "poisoned" by decades of Japanese colonial rule. The educational system was employed to inculcate a Chinese identity, and its first tool was rigid insistence on the use of Mandarin Chinese as the language of school life. Yet that strategy became a source of alienation. As Alan Wachman observes, "Every adult Taiwanese who was educated since the KMT arrived recalls the fines, slaps, and humiliations that were meted out as punishment to students heard speaking Taiwanese at school." Mandatory military service for young Taiwanese men had a similar effect. Designed to build a force for mainland recovery and to impart the KMT's ideology, it served more to intensify the conscripts' awareness of the injustice of alien domination. To this day many Taiwanese men resent their harsh and discriminatory treatment at the hands of mainlander officers during military service.[9]

Social arrangements in the first three decades of KMT rule also reinforced the sense of difference between mainlanders and Taiwanese. In Taiwan cities that distinction dictated where people lived, what language they spoke at home and with close friends, whom they associated with socially, whom they married, and whether they got jobs in the government (mainlanders) or in business (Taiwanese). Whether a person was a mainlander or a Taiwanese correlated strongly with his or her socioeconomic class. Young Taiwanese were particularly conscious of the discrimination that they suffered under this segregated system. The situation in the countryside was different, since it was basically a Taiwanese preserve, but the local policeman—the most tangible symbol of authority—was a mainlander. The social situation would become more complex by the late 1970s, as a growing middle class began to find more diverse educational, economic, and social opportunities. But the political impact of KMT rule was clear. As one American Taiwan specialist summed it up in 1963, "Political domination . . . economic burdens . . . and social discrimination have made the distinction between mainlanders and Formosans apparent in almost every aspect of Formosan life and have kept alive the hatreds and antagonisms that arose from the bloody suppression of the revolt of 1947."[10]

Taiwanese found a variety of ways to passively resist KMT rule. Intellectuals, with their "modern" mentality, had initially shunned the traditional folk religion of the island, but they found it more and more appealing precisely because it was theirs and because the regime sought to limit its spread. Common people put great energy into religious festivals (*baibai*) at which they offered the gods huge, elaborately decorated pigs that had been recently slaughtered. This enabled them "to communicate what might be called an external message about the ethnic identity of Taiwanese and the power of their gods, . . . that people subject to powerful governments sometimes use ritual to talk about politics from their own vantage point."[11]

Some Taiwanese soon translated their harsh experience of KMT rule into the claim that their homeland was a separate country and culture. Take, for example, the view of Su Bing, a nationalist who rejects the idea that Taiwan has anything more in common with China than ethnicity. "At the end of World War II, the Chinese Chiang clique replaced Japanese imperialism to occupy Taiwan and become its new rulers. Like most of the Taiwanese, they also belonged to the Han race, *but there was a difference between the Taiwanese and Chinese nationalities. . . .* The Chinese were newly arrived foreigners from the Chinese mainland, who invaded Taiwan with force. From the standpoint of society, economics, politics, and culture, *they were foreign rulers, just as the Dutch, the Ch'ing Dynasty, and the Japanese had been before them* [emphasis added]."[12] In order to validate that claim, Taiwanese nationalists gathered data that demonstrated, for them, the sharp contrast between their history and culture and that of the Chinese mainland. In fact, Taiwan was quite similar socially and culturally to southeastern China.

Ironically, the Taiwanese designation of the mainlander refugees as outsiders affected the newcomers' political consciousness as well. The Chinese term by which they came to be known —*waishengren* (literally, people from outside the province)—was little used in China, but it became part of the Taiwan vocabulary. Stéphan Corcuffe found through interviews in the 1990s that at least half of the island's *waishengren* regarded themselves as different from Taiwanese.[13]

Yet it is important to understand that this nationalist Taiwanese identity does not have a long history. As Wachman notes, "The cultural identity of Taiwanese appears to have been 'invented' in reaction to the efforts of the mainland elite to make residents of Taiwan cleave to the Chinese motherland, its culture, and its people." The KMT sought to impose a Chinese identity on Taiwanese, belittling their folkways in the process, and brought about the unintended consequence of strengthening the Taiwanese view that their island was a separate nation and that the ROC was an illegitimate regime.[14]

Moreover, Wachman found during the early 1990s that generational differences affected how both mainlanders and Taiwanese characterized their identity. Older mainlanders tended to see all ethnic Chinese (including Taiwanese) as part of one nation. Older Taiwanese agreed that Taiwan was a separate nation but disagreed on whether they were culturally Chinese. Mainlanders who were born on Taiwan found it hard to identify themselves as either Taiwanese or Chinese. They admitted that there was a Taiwanese nation and knew that they were not members of it, but they lacked their parents' strong sense of identification with China. Similarly, Taiwanese who grew up during the latter decades of KMT rule tended to be more confused about their loyalties than their parents. Wachman concluded that "the generation that was adult at the time the KMT came to Taiwan have views of identity that are more easily characterized than the generation raised and socialized since the KMT arrival. The older generation is generally polarized. . . . The generation born since the KMT came to Taiwan are more deeply troubled about their identity." More recent polling has confirmed that finding.[15]

Until the late 1980s, KMT repression prevented the public expression of the Taiwanese identity that it had fostered. Once political liberalization began, this invented mental construct grew to rival Chinese identity. Public interest in Taiwan's past and distinctive cultural character increased. Indeed, as economic ties with and information about the mainland proliferated, Lee Teng-hui saw value in co-opting and strengthening a Taiwan identity to serve as a bulwark against any too-easy accommodation with China. In May 1993, right after the Koo-Wang meeting, he observed: "If the exchanges between the two sides of the Taiwan Straits had not occurred, the question of national identity would not be serious. In the past, the two sides of the Taiwan Straits were totally divided. When we started to make exchanges, the division was blurred and the definition of the two sides of the Taiwan Straits became a big problem."[16] Lee promoted the idea that all people on Taiwan were bound by a common attachment to the island where they lived and by their common yet conflicted experience of the preceding five decades. It was necessary to strengthen, in his terms, this *gemeinschaft* in order to prevent a new tragedy at the hands of the PRC. He therefore ordered the revision of textbooks to end their exclusive attention to China and include more material on Taiwan's history, geography, and so on. At other times, most notably in his inaugural address in May 1996, he promoted Taiwan as the leading edge of Chinese civilization.[17]

In addition to their self-conscious identity and fear of outsiders, Taiwanese also have an anxiety about traitors in their midst, which has manifested itself in different ways. In the years of repression, there was a deep, lingering anxiety that the mainlander rulers of the KMT would cut a deal with Beijing and ignore the wishes of the majority of the population; the PRC magnified those fears when it sometimes called for negotiations between the Chinese Communist Party and the KMT. Who, Taiwanese asked, would represent them? At least some Taiwanese regarded those of their number who decided to join the KMT—such as Lee Teng-hui—as having sold out. Within the *dangwai* (the precursor of the DPP), more radical elements had suspicions about the loyalty of their moderate comrades. In the early 1990s, when the Taiwanese Lee Teng-hui already was president, the DPP played upon fears that his government might strike a deal with Beijing behind the public's back. Among many Taiwanese nationalists, there is a visceral fear of mainlander politicians and what they might do if they come to power, more because they are mainlanders than because of their policy positions. In the current climate of deep division about how to cope with China, each side suspects the other's motives. As one scholar put it, "We have different people fighting for different countries," and each group believes the others to be traitors. Supporters of the current Taiwan administration accuse opposition politicians "who travel to China of conspiring with the enemy to weaken the Chen government's program and compare them to European leaders who collaborated with Nazi Germany in the 1930s."[18]

A November 2003 editorial in a pro-DPP paper brought these various threads together. The author asserted that the mainlanders' control of the mass media was well out of proportion to their numbers (a vestige of KMT rule) and accused some of them of being "fellow travelers of the communists." Moreover, they used their control to shape public opinion and generate support for the KMT and the People First Party by controlling the content of news shows, the selection of guests on talk shows, and so on. To make matters worse, Taiwanese in the KMT (the "localization faction") consciously or unconsciously colluded in this effort. Asked the author, "How will history view these localization activists who have taken to these bandits [mainlanders] as they take to their own fathers, who have been used as tools to play the two sides against each other?"[19]

Since the 1990s there has been extensive polling in Taiwan on the population's level of identification with Taiwan and China and on its preferred outcomes. Three different projects are now under way. The first is a series of polls sponsored by the Mainland Affairs Council, about which methodological concerns exist. More sophisticated are the efforts of the Election Study Center at National Cheng Chi University (NCCU), also sponsored by the MAC, and another project, supported by the National Science Council, that was started by a team at National Taiwan University (NTU) and continued by a joint team of scholars from other institutions. All three surveys found a clear trend toward a stronger and exclusive Taiwan identity, a decline in an exclusively Chinese identity, and variation in whether the exclusive Taiwan identity or a mixed identity was dominant. Figure 6-1 presents the results of the Election Study Center's surveys. A more recent poll conducted by NTU scholars in June 2004 revealed that dual identity had risen to 46.8 percent; exclusive Taiwan identity had fallen to 41.6, and exclusive Chinese identity had slipped to 6.0 percent. A related NCCU study found that this shift had occurred gradually since 1992, as those who began with a solely Chinese identity shifted first to a "double identity" and then perhaps to a Taiwan orientation. Also, it has occurred irrespective of origin (mainlander or Taiwanese), age, educational level, gender, and party affiliation.[20]

To be sure, Taiwan's political leaders have sought to exploit and foster the growing Taiwan identity for political or other purposes. But they could not do so if the phenomenon was not already widespread. Moreover, an important cause of the shift from an exclusively Chinese identity to a more Taiwanese mindset was a series of actions by the PRC. Its recurring efforts to deny Taiwan a wider role in the international system offend the pride of the island's people in their achievements and are seen as a denial of their rights. The missile exercises of March 1996 and the PRC's subsequent military modernization program have made Taiwan more insecure. If KMT outsiders stimulated the formation of a Taiwan identity in the first place, PRC outsiders have intensified it since the early 1990s. Looking forward, Gunter Schubert argues that China's denial that Taiwan possesses sovereignty and its threats to use force "push the so-called status-quo-majority on the island to distance itself even more from a Chinese identity."[21]

That outside influences shape the balance of the identities of Taiwan's people—Chinese, Chinese-Taiwanese, and Taiwanese—suggests that mutually beneficial cross-Strait economic ties may conceivably reverse this trend and strengthen the Chinese identity. Nonetheless, the impact of outside ties on the Taiwan population as a whole can be exaggerated. Polling by Duke scholar Emerson Niou discovered that only 12 percent of the population had

Figure 6-1. Taiwanese–Chinese Identification Trend Distribution in Taiwan 1992–2003

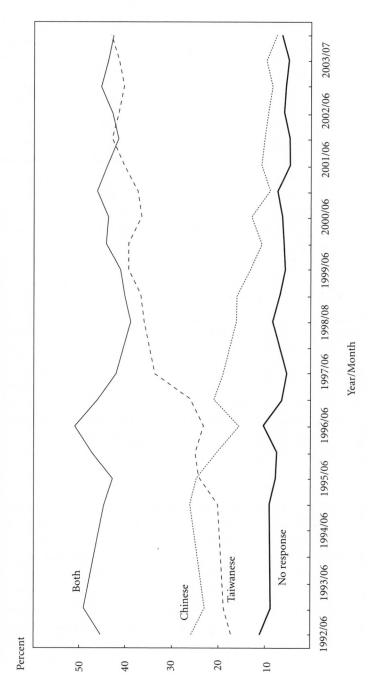

Source: Election Study Center, National Chengchi University (www2.nccu.edu.tw/~s00/eng/data/Political%20Attitude02.htm [August 11, 2004]) (reprinted with permission of the publisher).

made three or more trips to the mainland, 20 percent had made one or two, and 68 percent had made none at all. Niou also found that only 13 percent of Taiwan families had members who had been to the mainland to study, do business, or live or who had plans to do so. The impact of cross-Strait interaction is falling on a narrow share of the Taiwan population.[22]

On the other hand, the consensus of a number of scholars is that the growth—even dominance—of a Taiwan identity does not ipso facto lead to a quest for de jure independence. Robert Marsh found that according to survey data, "although attitudes show a trend toward Taiwan independence and away from unification with China, an even stronger trend supports pragmatism." Rwei-Ren Wu sees this pragmatic nationalism as the product of democratization and characterizes it as "civic, liberal, and above all, pacifist." Gunter Schubert argues, "What is called Taiwanese nationalism today should not . . . be reduced to or falsely equated with a minor political discourse in the island republic claiming that there is a Taiwanese nation fully *distinct* from the Chinese nation." Rigger concludes that there are actually four different kinds of identity: provincial (mainland versus Taiwan origin); nationality (Chinese versus Taiwanese ethnocultural identification); citizenship (ROC or PRC); and policy preference (unification versus independence). Rigger emphasizes that there is more debate on some dimensions (such as nationality) than others (such as citizenship). Nor is there necessarily a correlation between Taiwanese identity and a desire for independence. Moreover, the widely held belief that Taiwan is a state (citizenship identity) does not lead necessarily to a rejection of a policy preference for unification.[23] It could, but the key point here is that Taiwan identity can be shaped, both within Taiwan and through actions of the PRC.

The polls most frequently cited regarding the outcome that Taiwan's residents most desire are those sponsored by the Mainland Affairs Council. They consistently show that around half or more of respondents prefer a continuation of the status quo and express no view on a final outcome. The groups that want the status quo now and either independence or unification later include less than 20 percent each. The share wanting independence immediately is consistently under 10 percent, while the share wanting unification right away is less than 5 percent. While the share of the population that stated a purely Taiwanese identity rose from the mid 20 percent range in the early 1990s to as high as 50 percent in 2000 and to the low 40 percent range in 2004, the percentage that advocated independence rose from the low teens only to the high teens and remained fairly stable. A June 2004 poll found that less than half of those who held an exclusively

Table 6-1. Shifting Political Foundation for Independence versus Unification
Percent

Nine orientations	Year of postelection survey				
	1993 LY	*1996 LY*	*1999 LY*	*2000 LY*	*2002 LY*
Principled believers in independence	9.9	16.8	22.8	24.0	20.3
Lean toward independence	2.3	2.7	2.4	2.5	4.5
Weak opponent to unification	1.6	2.3	2.1	0.6	1.9
Open-minded Rationalists	24.4	26.2	28.8	34.4	22.8
Weak opponent to independence	2.1	1.9	1.8	1.3	3.1
Lean toward unification	4.9	4.8	3.2	2.3	2.8
Principled believer in unification	26.5	23.8	16.4	19.3	18.1
Strong believer in status quo	7.2	7.2	11.0	6.6	11.2
Passivists	21.1	14.2	11.3	9.0	15.3
Total respondents	1,398	1,383	1,357	1,409	2,022

Source: Yun-han Chu, "Taiwan's National Identity Politics and the Prospect of Cross-Strait Relations," *Asian Survey* 44 (July-August 2004): 484–512 (reprinted with permission of the publisher).

Taiwan identity would be prepared to fight to defend a declaration of independence.[24]

More sophisticated survey research, conducted by the team of political scientists funded by the National Science Council, has sought to determine how variables related to PRC behavior affect respondents' preferences for unification and independence. They asked whether Taiwan should become a new independent country, but only if there were no war following a declaration of independence, and whether the two sides should unite, but only in the event that they became compatible economically, socially, and politically. Table 6-1 presents the nine different categories of respondents that this more sophisticated investigation generated. One group is, in the investigators' terms, supremely "rational": it would accept independence with peace or unification with cross-Strait convergence, whichever is possible. Two others are "highly principled": they favor one outcome and would reject the other even under optimal conditions (for example, the principled believers in independence would oppose unification even if there were convergence). Another group truly favors the status quo (for example, it would reject declaring independence even if China did not respond by starting a war). The other five categories are somewhere in between.

The most recent survey, conducted at the beginning of 2002, found that opinion was equally segmented. Table 6-1 reports the distribution of respondents among the nine categories that opinion polling revealed over time. The "open-minded rationalists" (those who agreed with both statements) constituted 22.8 percent of respondents. Among the "principled" respondents, those who favored independence and peace but not unification with a converging China constituted 20.3 percent; those who wanted unification but not independence under those conditions made up 18.1 percent of the sample. Those who were strong believers in the status quo were only 11.2 percent. The rest were more ambiguous in their responses.[25]

The evolution of preferences over time also is interesting. Those who were principled believers in independence and leaned toward independence constituted 12.2 percent of the total in early 1993, rose to 25.2 in early 1999, and fell to 24.8 in early 2002 (more than doubling since 1993). Those who were principled believers in unification or leaned that way constituted 31.4 percent in 1993, fell to 19.6 percent in 1999, and rose to 20.9 in 2002 (declining by a third since 1993). The share of open-minded rationalists fluctuated around 25 percent. Those who were strong believers in the status quo varied from 6 to 11 percent.

Several caveats are in order. For example, with the exception of the last poll cited (see table 6-1), most do not explicitly require respondents to take into account the consequences of their choice. Even when contingencies are introduced, they may not be the right ones. Is economic, social, and political convergence the most important factor to consider in assessing the acceptability of unification? Or might it be Beijing's substantive approach to unification? Similarly, most polls are fuzzy on the definition of the various outcomes. For example, the type of unification is never clarified for respondents. Is it the one-country, two-systems formula or some looser union? Particularly vague is the concept of the status quo, which can mean very different things to different people. Survey results therefore convey only rough general tendencies; they are not a precise barometer of opinion at any point in time. (Techniques like focus groups would be needed to gauge the fine detail of Taiwan opinion.)

Yet these polls and the broader history of the emergence of the Taiwan identity demonstrate that it is both complex and malleable. Whether Taiwan nationalists are correct that their homeland is a separate country is immaterial. What is important is that a significant share of the population believes that Taiwan is an object of identification distinct from—but necessarily exclusive of—China and that the relevant outsider, China, is perceived as a threat to that sense of identity. That past KMT repression was the principal cause of this invented identity remains a point of departure for those Taiwanese who experienced it in some fashion and also an analytic reminder that external forces can shift the balance among identities. Thus Beijing's actions today also can help shift that balance. Taiwan identity is stronger now in spite of growing cross-Strait economic interaction and China's military power. Taiwan's political leaders do exploit these sentiments, for example, by trying to make China an issue during campaigns or accusing those who favor a measure of accommodation with China of being a threat to the island's interests, and they have good, tactical reasons for doing so. But it is only one factor among several that have created the trends concerning identification and preferred outcomes. Finally, Taiwanese identity does not necessarily translate into a drive to legal independence; it does for some people but not others. But it reinforces the more substantive reasons—the belief that Taiwan is a sovereign entity, for example—and so constitutes a powerful bulwark against acceptance of the PRC's one-country, two-systems formula.

The DPP and the Politics of Opposition

The Democratic Progressive Party, which took over the presidency in 2000 and became the leading party in the legislature in 2001, has a unique history that shapes how it tries to rule today. It had its origins in the *dangwai* (literally, "outside the party"), a collection of politicians who opposed the KMT's oppression and its pretensions to being the government of all of China and who, to varying degrees, held to the ultimate goal of a Republic of Taiwan. The *dangwai* politicians were the most visible and articulate representatives of the Taiwan identity that KMT rule had fostered. Beginning in the late 1960s and early 1970s, they sought office at the provincial and local levels of the system. They also competed for the new seats in the Legislative Yuan that were created to take account of the increase in the island's population and to provide the government with a better barometer of its performance (at the time most seats were still reserved for those who had run for election in China in the late 1940s). The deck was still stacked against them in terms of electoral resources, and being an opposition politician still required substantial courage. Yet multimember districts and underlying Taiwanese resentment of the KMT presented opportunities that had not existed before.

The *dangwai* also benefited from a series of blows to the ROC's international position: departure from the United Nations in 1971; the switch in diplomatic relations to the PRC by most of the ROC's diplomatic partners, particularly the United States; and the loss of membership in all international organizations in the UN system. Those events were a boon to the opposition because, as noted above, the regime had justified its denial of democracy and the deferral of new elections to the Legislative Yuan and the National Assembly by its claim that the ROC was the government of all of

China. Because the traditional basis of KMT legitimacy was now in jeopardy, the *dangwai* could challenge both its internally unrepresentative character and its claim that it was something more than Taiwan. The regime became vulnerable because of the Taiwan identity it had created itself, albeit inadvertently.

The *dangwai* also received support from overseas. One way that Taiwanese manifested their alienation from the KMT was to leave the island in large numbers to pursue advanced education, especially in the United States. Most did not return, preferring Western countries to what they saw as colonial rule back home. They secured professional jobs and created social organizations to maintain a sense of community solidarity. These exiles were among the strongest adherents of the idea that Taiwan was and should be a separate country, and they provided the leadership for the second phase of the Taiwan independence movement (the first had been based in Japan and atrophied by the 1960s). For a while, these activists focused on clandestine political action in Taiwan to weaken the KMT regime and gave only secondary emphasis to influencing public opinion abroad. Then in the late 1970s, after the December 1979 Gaoxiong incident, a confrontation that led to the arrest of most opposition leaders, Taiwanese in the United States changed strategy. They sought the assistance of members of the U.S. Congress, such as Stephen Solarz, Jim Leach, and Claiborne Pell, who were not prepared to advocate de jure independence for Taiwan but were more than ready to call for protection of human rights and movement toward a democratic system. Perhaps most important, they gave the *dangwai* moral recognition and a legitimacy that the government sought to deny it at home.[26]

Despite those new advantages, the *dangwai* still faced a strategic and tactical dilemma. Regarding goals, should it focus on democratization or independence? On tactics, should it focus on winning seats in the Legislative Yuan and then criticize the regime from within the system, or should it seek to mobilize a mass movement and challenge the KMT in the streets? Each view had its adherents and its rationale. The parliamentary road, which older leaders favored, would offer some measure of political power but require moderation, the need for which rank-and-file supporters did not always understand. The social movements proposed by younger activists involved a heroic rejection of the KMT regime but entailed greater risks. Multimember districts for legislative elections only reinforced the division, because people on both sides of the issue could run for office.[27]

As a result, the *dangwai*—and the DPP, which was formed from it in September 1986—has always been split into factions that reflect divisions over strategy and tactics. For much of the 1980s and 1990s, the Formosa faction was the leading group in the more moderate camp while the New Tide advocated more radical approaches. To address such differences and to resolve contests over leadership, the *dangwai*–DPP had to develop a decisionmaking structure that could forge consensus or compromise through a complicated process of consultation and bargaining. When the resulting agreements became part of the party platform, the results of subsequent elections usually served as a pragmatic test of whether they should be continued or modified.

The DPP's debate over tactics was resolved in the early 1990s, when Lee Teng-hui pushed through reforms to have full, Taiwan-based elections for the Legislative Yuan and the National Assembly and to elect the president by direct popular vote. The way was now clear, at least theoretically, to gaining power through elections. Social movements and street protests were not abandoned completely, but the party placed increasing emphasis on running for office.

THE DPP AND INDEPENDENCE. Where to position the party concerning Taiwan independence remained a dilemma. That goal, of course, had been part of the defining ethos of the *dangwai*–DPP, and the New Tide at least believed that it could constitute a powerful appeal for votes. The party engaged in a protracted, three-stage debate over how much emphasis to place on the issue. At every stage, ways were found to bridge internal differences.[28]

When the DPP was formed in the mid-1980s, it focused more on process than outcomes. It called for self-determination, for the future of Taiwan to be decided by the people of the island through a democratic process. In the climate of the times, when political liberalization was just beginning, when advocacy of de jure independence was still taboo, and when there was some popular anxiety about the KMT government selling out Taiwan, this was a sensible approach. Yet DPP members who wished to read the term "self-determination" as code for "independence" could do so, as some in the government did. Yet the party's position was still fluid, if only because the division between factions was so deep.

Gradual democratization deprived the DPP of an issue that had served it well and led to greater emphasis on outcomes (independence) than process. In the process, factions like New Tide strengthened their hand. Still, when the party formulated its position before the 1989 legislative elections, it took account of competing internal viewpoints and the larger, not-yet-democratic external reality. Vaguely, its resolution asserted that Taiwan's "international sovereignty was independent" and that it would move to advocating independence if the KMT took steps to sell out Taiwan's interests—a stance that was still conditional, in that responsibility was placed on the shoulders of the KMT. In the end, the New Tide and another like-minded faction did well in the election.

Thereafter, the New Tide continued to move the DPP to the extreme. At the 1991 party congress, before new island-wide elections for the National Assembly, it pushed for a plank that called for an independent Republic of Taiwan. The DPP thus staked out its most radical direction, and the voters registered their verdict. Its candidates won only 24 percent of the vote, a recent record low. Some leaders soon offered more moderate positions, and the party scored better in the 1992 legislative elections. But the debate continued. The poor showing of the DPP's candidate in the 1996 presidential election (Peng Ming-min, who inclined toward independence) and the PRC's missile exercises provided a new incentive for pragmatism and moderation. That summer there was one final clash between the rival viewpoints. In the end the most radical independence elements left to form the Taiwan Independence Party, thus making it easier to explore more centrist positions.

This process, conducted over almost three years, culminated in the adoption in May 1999 of the resolution on cross-Strait relations considered in chapters 3 and 4 ("Taiwan is a sovereign and independent country [or state, the Chinese word is the same]. . . . Taiwan, although named the Republic of China under its current constitution, is not subject to the jurisdiction of the People's Republic of China.") In order to remove the vulnerability that had dogged the DPP for almost a decade—that it could not be trusted with power—the party again emphasized process over ultimate outcomes. As noted above, however, the formulation sought rhetorically to bridge the gap between the so-called fundamentalists and more pragmatic elements.

Behind the scenes, younger thinkers in the party went further. They accepted that independence was a dream that could never be realized and that Taiwan was, at least economically, tied to China. They therefore began to consider models of national union that even the DPP might find consistent with Taiwan's fundamental interests.

The most public example is Wilson Tien, formerly head of the party's international affairs department and since 2003 a member of the Taipei municipal assembly. In a speech delivered to an American foreign policy organization in April 2001, he laid out an approach that sought to reconcile the reality of China with Taiwan's fundamental principles concerning sovereignty. He began by noting the obvious: that Taiwan cannot change its geographical position and that China is "a unified and powerful neighbor."

Given the high priority that Beijing places on unification, "if Taiwan defies its wishes, China will use force to attack Taiwan, forcing Taiwan to become a part of China. . . . [because] Taiwan cannot be moved around, we must face our neighbors." Tien argued that under those circumstances and until China became a democratic state itself, peaceful coexistence was the best that the two sides could expect and that it was an outcome worth pursuing. Negotiations with China would be necessary to establish peaceful coexistence, and sovereignty issues would likely be on the agenda. "We [the DPP] believe that Taiwan might be able to set up a deal in which Taiwan sacrifices part of its sovereignty in exchange for permanent peace across the strait, as long as the proposed political arrangement is reasonable, worthwhile, and acceptable to the Taiwanese people." And Chen Shui-bian had signaled his association with that viewpoint in his statement on New Year's 2001, when he spoke of a process of integration, including political integration (see chapter 3).[29]

The shift in DPP thinking on Taiwan's independence—from the true believers' rigid adherence to principle toward a pragmatic view that would better suit those at the middle of the electoral spectrum—was clearer in retrospect than it was as it was occurring. At every step of the way, DPP "fundamentalists" would engage in rearguard actions, and moderates knew that they could not totally ignore the fervor of their comrades' views even as they continued to adjust the substance of the party's position. That tension would not disappear when the DPP actually became the party in power.

OTHER POLITICAL ISSUES. At the same time that the DPP was wrestling with how to reconcile its historic commitment to an independent Taiwan with existing political and power realities, it also had to confront issues bearing on cross-Strait relations that put the government on the defensive and sometimes provoked a response from Beijing.

The first of these was Taiwan's role in international organizations. After its departure from the United Nations and other institutions in the UN system, the ROC had quietly accepted the reality that it was gone for good. The PRC's presence in those organizations and the consensus under which they operate gave Beijing an effective veto over any effort by Taiwan to return. Moreover, the United States refused to assist Taiwan on this front, partly because it was politically futile and partly because Washington recognized the PRC government as the government of China and "China" was the name on the relevant seat in all of the institutions. Lee Teng-hui had asserted that Taiwan's participation in international organizations would be a key issue in any discussion of unification, but he took no immediate action to promote its reentry. The ROC did seek admission or readmission to international economic organizations such as the Asia-Pacific Economic Cooperation (APEC) forum and the General Administration of Trade and Tariffs (GATT) and its successor, the World Trade Organization (WTO). Here the United States would provide crucial assistance to facilitate Taiwan's inclusion, and the fact that the PRC was not already a member helped.

This equilibrium was upset in 1991, when both North Korea and South Korea became members of the United Nations. Led by Annette Lu Hsiu-lien, a former political prisoner of the KMT, the DPP quickly demanded to know why Taiwan should not benefit from such parallel membership, and Lu Hsiu-lien began a campaign to promote the idea of Taiwan's return to the United Nations. This appeal struck such a chord within the Taiwan public that in 1993 Lee Teng-hui adopted the UN campaign as government policy, despite the reservations of the United States and his own foreign ministry.

Beijing responded quickly and negatively. It had worked for forty years to establish its hegemony in the international system vis-à-vis the ROC, and it was not about to let it make inroads into its preserve. In August 1993, the Taiwan Affairs Office and the Information Office of the PRC's State Council issued a long statement that focused on why there was no justification for Taiwan to join or rejoin international organizations for which statehood was a prerequisite for membership. There then ensued an annual ritual in which Taipei sought to make its case for returning to the United Nations (for example, it published its own manifesto in July 1994) in order to satisfy domestic political sentiment, and the PRC did everything it could to block Taiwan's effort.[30]

The World Health Organization became a new arena for this competition in 1997. Doctors in Taiwan are an important support group for the DPP, so proposing a campaign for Taiwan's reentry into the WHO was an appealing way to respond to one of the party's constituencies that put pressure on the KMT government at the same time. And knowing that full membership was impossible, the party cleverly proposed obtaining observership status, which allows some forms of participation, instead. The KMT government was quick to co-opt the effort, and Beijing was just as quick to mount a defense. Again, politics in Taiwan had intensified PRC-ROC competition in the international arena, thus complicating the efforts at cross-Strait reconciliation.

The DPP also exploited an opportunity to question the government's handling of cross-Strait relations. In the spring of 1993, as preparations were under way for the Koo-Wang talks in Singapore and as the business community pushed for liberalization of economic relations with the mainland, the DPP raised fears that KMT officials might make decisions and agreements that did not properly reflect the popular will. The party used its increased presence in the Legislative Yuan following elections in December 1992 to impose greater supervision of government policy by the legislature, restrict the flexibility of the Singapore negotiators, and strengthen oversight over any agreements reached. As a result, the government limited the scope of the talks to more functional issues and sought to enhance their transparency. (The leader of the DPP effort was the party whip, Chen Shui-bian, who questioned the right of an unelected government to make decisions on behalf of the Taiwan people and asserted the greater legitimacy of a popularly elected legislature to question government policy.)[31]

The DPP was not the only party that sought to build political advantage by taking international initiatives even though they might complicate cross-Strait relations. Indeed, the most significant intersection of domestic politics and external policy was Lee Teng-hui's project to visit the United States, which he undertook because he was facing Taiwan's first direct presidential election and needed to show voters that he could manage the United States. Nor did the DPP rely solely on wedge issues like international organizations and negotiations with Beijing in its campaign for power. The principal focus was on the KMT's domestic vulnerabilities, particularly corruption, or "black gold" (*heijin*).[32] But neither effort would have meant much had the DPP not reduced its key vulnerability in the eyes of the voters—their concern that once in power it might act rashly and provoke military action by the PRC. Yet it balanced its growing moderation on independence by raising issues like membership in international organizations, which forced the KMT to co-opt those issues or risk losing support, and in doing so reshaped the agenda of cross-Strait relations.

MAINLAND TRADE AND INVESTMENT. If the DPP was to win political power, it would also have to address economic issues. It had never displayed much expertise in economics and appeared to favor policies that the business sector disliked, such as enhancing social welfare and environmental protection. But there was the reality of growing economic interaction between the two sides of the Strait, as Taiwan companies facing growing labor costs on the island sought to guarantee their survival by moving production facilities to the mainland. The absence of direct transportation links was becoming a growing impediment to such interaction.[33]

Many in the DPP shared Lee Teng-hui's concerns about Taiwan's growing economic dependence on the mainland and the attendant political vulnerabilities, and they endorsed his policy of limiting investment in the PRC, known by the motto "Avoid haste, be patient" (*jieji yongren*). Others in the party worried that it might lose the election if it did not broaden its base and become more business-friendly. In May 1998, the party debated its approach. Hsu Hsin-liang advocated abandonment of a policy of caution in favor of "boldly advancing to the west" (*dadan xijin*). His colleagues, including Chen Shui-bian, disagreed and reaffirmed the policy of imposing some restraints on the business community. The final position was a compromise of "firming up the base and moving gradually forward [toward China]" (*qiangben jianjin*), but it reflected the DPP's effort to adopt a position that was more favorable to business than Lee Teng-hui's. And as the 2000 election neared, Chen Shui-bian came out in favor of a version of direct transportation links.

The DPP's 1998 dilemma illustrated the cross-cutting nature of the identity and economic issues. Indeed, as Taiwan scholar Wu Yu-shan has demonstrated, two debates have occupied Taiwan's parties and voters. The first was defined by the two polar positions of unification and independence (*tongdu wenti*). The second concerned whether to emphasize security or economic interests in mainland policy (*anquan yu jingji*). Consequently, at least in the abstract, there are four basic policy tendencies that combine the two polar views on each debate, as displayed graphically in figure 6-2. And Wu argues convincingly that it is the working of the democratic system that compelled both the KMT and the DPP to converge during the 1990s: the former became more cautious on unification, and the latter distanced itself somewhat from independence. On economic issues, Lee Teng-hui imposed some restrictions on cross-Strait investment over the course of his presidency, whereas the DPP moved to support transportation links. "Because Taiwan's mainstream public opinion is located in the middle of the identity and interest spectra," Wu wrote, "presidential candidates rushed to the middle ground to capture votes." The majority of voters favored neither unification nor independence (particularly right away) but preferred to preserve the status quo. They wanted the benefits of both security from and economic cooperation with the PRC. The larger political parties pragmatically went where the voters were. Those like the New Party (originally the Chinese New Party) and the Taiwan Independence Party maintained their outside-the-mainstream purity and lost out.[34]

The history of the DPP as Taiwan's opposition party through the elections of 2000 and 2001 revealed the power of public opinion to reshape political programs. True, a segment of the population, the one in which the Taiwanese identity is strongest, does support a Taiwan that is fully independent of China, and that segment has been part of the DPP's support base. Because

Figure 6-2. 2000 Presidential Campaign: Converging on the Center

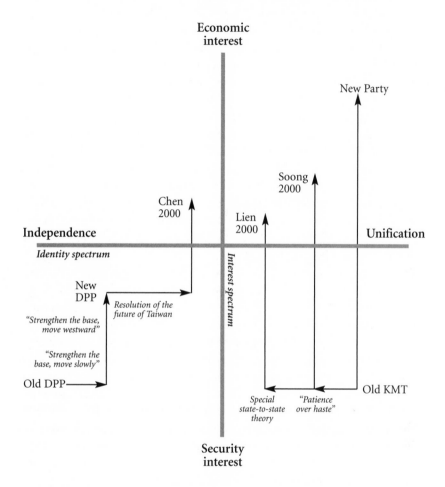

Source: Adapted from Yu-shan Wu, "Taiwan's Domestic Politics and Cross-Strait Relations," *China Journal* 53 (January 2005): 52 (reprinted with permission of the publisher).

of the PRC's policies and the island's electoral system, independence senti-ment will be represented in the legislature and continue to be a force within the DPP. But the party had learned from a decade of experience that if it wished to gain control of Taiwan's presidency and Executive Yuan, even in the context of a KMT split, it would have to moderate its political goals to reassure the public that it would not use power recklessly.

A Dysfunctional Democracy?

Although Taiwan's politics makes it unlikely that Taiwan's people will give the PRC what it wants (one country, two systems), questions remain. How would the island's political system respond if Beijing made an offer that objectively met Taipei's substantive concerns? Is it capable of taking "yes" for an answer? The traditional DPP anxiety was that unrepresentative institutions might approve a "bad" agreement with Beijing. Conversely, one may ask whether the current government system is institutionally incapable of approving any "good" agreement that might be negotiated. Even modest changes in the framework of cross-Strait relations require public support. Existing law requires that the Legislative Yuan approve any agreement with the PRC germane to the execution or enforcement of government or public authority. Any agreement that would require changes in existing laws would, of course, require legislation.[35] Answering these questions requires attention to several features of Taiwan's democracy, how well it reflects the popular will, and how it makes choices.[36]

THE ELECTORAL SYSTEM. Some of the defects of Taiwan's democracy stem from its electoral system. For elections to representative bodies, the KMT borrowed Japan's single-vote, multimember-district (SVMM) model, in which the voter votes for only one of the candidates contending for several available seats. Each party seeks to nominate the number of candidates commensurate with its support and to mobilize and allocate votes among those running by giving cues to its regular supporters. It also has to try to use party discipline to block individuals who have not received an official nomination from running independently. If too many of its adherents run, then its support is scattered too broadly and the number of candidates elected is lower than feasible. If it does not get out the vote on election day, or if too many supporters vote for one of its candidates and neglect others, then the number elected again will be lower than it could be.

This system, as Larry Diamond notes, "has several potentially perverse effects."[37] First of all, it can foster fragmentation of political parties by reinforcing individual ambition among politicians and undermining party cohesion. Both the KMT and the DPP are divided into factions. Each has suffered splintering as individuals unhappy with the direction of the party decide to leave and set up their own operation. Thus members of the KMT, unhappy with Lee Teng-hui's direction, left to form the New Party in 1993. A radical wing of the DPP split off in 1996. For the 2000 election, James Soong left the KMT and Hsu Hsin-liang left the DPP to run independent presidential races. Soong subsequently formed the People First Party, and in

2001, Lee Teng-hui fostered the creation of the Taiwan Solidarity Union, partially made up of people unhappy with the anti-Lee direction of the KMT after his departure.

The KMT itself had fostered a certain level of fragmentation—and corruption—at the grassroots level from the time it began allowing local elections in the early 1950s. In each lower-level jurisdiction, it encouraged at least two factions to contend. In some cases, they were based on clans that had been rivals for generations, and often they were linked to local organized crime groups. Through its county party secretaries, the KMT would use these factional networks of local notables to mobilize the votes at their disposal and in return would reward cooperative individuals with nominations as local government executives and assemblymen. The party would never allow one faction to dominate the local scene; instead it sought to preserve a balance of power to ensure that it could penetrate and control the lowest levels of society. Once democratization occurred, two things happened. First of all, the DPP became in effect another political force at the local level. Second, local faction heads were less willing to accept the KMT's decisions on nominations. If their preferred candidate was not selected, he or she might run anyway, drawing on the faction's built-in support and draining votes from the "official" KMT candidate. (The DPP had similar problems, but it seems to have found ways to ensure party discipline.) This dynamic is more common in elections in which there is only one winner, such as county-level executive or presidential races, than it is for those in which several seats are to be filled and each faction can get its share. But the basic finding is the same: the SVMM system fosters more party factionalism and fragmentation than a single-member district system.[38]

The SVMM system has also encouraged personality-based politics. To be sure, in a multimember district all the candidates of one party run on the party's platform and endorse it, at least rhetorically. Yet because they are to a significant degree competing for some of the same votes, they have to find ways to distinguish themselves. So they emphasize symbolic issues and their personal qualities rather than their policy positions, which presumably are the same, and they may denigrate the character of their rivals. Voters' identification with a particular party tends to be weaker than would be the case in a system in which only one candidate per party runs. Candidates also have to create their own campaign resource base to supplement whatever they get from their party. Once elected on the basis of their own efforts, legislators are not especially beholden to their party leadership and have every incentive to enhance their personal popularity.[39]

The SVMM system also has encouraged some degree of radical politics. Since a legislative seat can be won with a fraction of the votes, candidates have the option of positioning themselves on the end of the political spectrum and appealing to voters with more extreme, ideological views. There is less incentive to move toward the middle. Factionalism and fragmentation occur on issues as well as over the spoils of office.

The frequency of elections also constrains innovative policymaking. For example, legislative elections were held in December 2001, only nineteen months after Chen Shui-bian was inaugurated, giving both the DPP and its opposition reason to delay policy initiatives on cross-Strait relations. Indeed, the gridlock of that period became part of the election campaign, as all sides hoped for and sought a shift in the power balance to strengthen their respective hand. Not long after the election, the campaign for the presidential election of March 2004 effectively began. And after the new president was sworn in, it was only seven months until the next legislative election.[40]

All of these tendencies—fragmentation, politics of personality, and radicalism—obviously are stronger in legislative races in which a larger party will run several candidates than in a contest for an executive position in which it tries to gain support for a single candidate. Yet the SVMM system still has its impact on the latter type of race, exemplified by the defections of those who do not get an official nomination, and on party dynamics in general. Even though Chen Shui-bian's effort to move the DPP to the center for the 2000 presidential race made objective sense, it was not automatic. He was pushing against the tide of radicalism and individualism created in part by the electoral system. As noted below, the SVMM system will likely be replaced in 2008 with a single-member-district system plus a party slate, reducing but not immediately eliminating the pathologies of the current system.

FRUITS OF AUTHORITARIANISM. Both the DPP and the KMT had a hard time adjusting to the reversal of roles following the presidential election of 2000, and policy formation suffered as a result.

Chen Shui-bian faced a series of challenges that are common when an opposition power wins national power for the first time.[41] First of all, having been denied the chance to govern Taiwan for its entire existence, the DPP lacked a pool of leaders who were capable of taking over the many agencies of the central government. Chen and others had served as mayors and county magistrates, but such positions offered only modest experience that was relevant to running all of Taiwan. Chen's initial gambit was to recruit a premier and ministers from business, universities, and even the

KMT, in order to reassure those constituencies and the public as well. But the experiment failed, and he has since relied more on people from within the DPP; however, the party has not overcome the perception that it was not ready for prime time. The fact that a deep economic recession hit Taiwan just when Chen took office only exacerbated that perception.

To make matters worse, the "fundamentalist" faction of the DPP did not give Chen strong support. They resented the fact that he had picked outsiders to fill many ministerial positions instead of giving them to other party leaders. They complained that Chen was not consulting them properly in the formulation of policy but that he then expected all DPP legislators to support his initiatives. And they feared that he would be a trimmer—that he would make unprincipled concessions—on policy toward China. They had tolerated his preelection movement toward the middle because they wanted him to win. When they saw him continue to accommodate Beijing and Washington after winning, they became even more anxious. A key moment came in June 2000, when Chen suggested that in order to resume dialogue he might accept the idea that there was one China but that each side of the Strait had different interpretations of what that one China was. The fundamentalists, who either opposed on principle the idea that Taiwan was a part of China or felt that Chen had already yielded too much, rebelled. Chen therefore backed off. Fundamentalists were also unhappy at the end of 2000, when Chen used the phrase "political integration" when talking about future cross-Strait relations. They worried about both the concept and the fact that they were not consulted.[42]

Similarly, the parties opposing Chen had a hard time adjusting to being out of power. Up until the legislative elections of December 2001, the KMT and the People First Party, led by James Soong, together retained a significant majority in the Legislative Yuan, and they used it to pursue a confrontational approach toward the new administration.[43] (That the KMT took this stance was made easier by the fact that Lee Teng-hui had resigned as chairman right after the March 2000 election.) Among other things, the opposition parties refused to participate in a cross-party task force on cross-Strait relations, an attempt by Chen to forge a broader consensus. Perhaps because they felt that they were Taiwan's rightful rulers, the KMT and the PFP cooperated with Chen only when failure to do so would hurt their standing with the public, as was sometimes the case on economic policy.

PROBLEMS OF GOVERNMENT STRUCTURE. Reinforcing the impact of the electoral system and the KMT-DPP role reversal are more fundamental defects in Taiwan's constitutional and institutional structure. Taiwan's system is rather like the French system, with both a president and a premier. But Taiwan has not yet developed the mechanisms that the French have to mitigate the problems of cohabitation between two power centers. The checks and balances both within the executive branch and between it and the legislature, which were introduced through several constitutional amendments in the 1990s, have created too many checks and too little balance. The president may appoint the premier without securing the Legislative Yuan's approval, but he does not have the power to veto legislation. He may dissolve the legislature only after it exercises its right of taking a vote of no confidence in the premier. The Taiwan system functions at least adequately when the same party controls both the executive branch and the legislature *and* when party discipline can coordinate interbranch relations from behind the scenes. When the government is divided, the checks and balances produce policy gridlock.

The legislature itself has a number of problems. Party discipline has been weak because the electoral system dictates that individual legislators rely on their own efforts to get elected. Once they do, their incentive is to promote their individual popularity rather than public support for the party with which they are affiliated. Corruption and conflicts of interest are common. There is no tradition of party discipline to ensure that individual legislators will vote with their caucus leadership. The institution does not encourage policy specialization and expertise, as do the committee and seniority systems in the U.S. Congress. Instead, Taiwan legislators may regularly shift their committee membership, depending on what they believe will be politically useful in terms of publicity and campaign contributions. Legislation is developed on the basis of coordination among party caucuses and smaller ad hoc groups. As a result, only those bills that command broad consensus secure passage, and no one is accountable for the result. Obstructionism is relatively easy. The alternative would be to subject legislation to votes, in which case the majority must take the blame—or credit—for the outcome. In this sense, the Legislative Yuan is more like the U.S. Senate than the House of Representatives.[44]

The one exception to the gridlock of Chen's presidency proves the rule. The exception was a growing recognition among all political parties that something had to be done about the economic recession that began in mid-2000. The DPP was blamed for doing too little to address the worst economic downturn in the island's history, but the KMT and the PFP also were vulnerable because of the public perception that they were using their parliamentary majority to block Chen's efforts to remedy the situation. The two sides therefore agreed to convene an Economic Development Advisory Conference in August 2001 to push through a variety of changes that had been politically difficult before. Chief among them was a revision of cross-Straits investment policy. The Lee Teng-hui approach of avoiding haste was set aside in favor of a policy of "active opening, effective management" (*jiji kaifang, youxiao guanli*).[45]

THE EMERGENCE OF EQUAL BLOCS. Partly as a reaction to the fissiparous tendencies of Taiwan's democracy and for other reasons, in 2001 two fairly equal political blocs began to emerge. One was made up of the KMT and PFP; it is known as the pan-Blue camp, after the dominant color of the KMT flag. The other was composed of the DPP and TSU, and it is called the pan-Green camp, after the main color in the DPP flag. In the 2001 legislative elections, the Blue camp secured 49.74 percent of the vote, the Greens got 41.14 percent, and the independents and minor parties got 9.1 percent. Of the seats in the Legislative Yuan, the pan-Blue camp had 111 (50 percent); the pan-Green camp had 100 (45 percent), and the independents had 11 (5 percent).

This result probably overstated somewhat the popular support for the DPP and the TSU, since they did a better job than the KMT of picking the right number of candidates, allocating their vote, and campaigning. Yet it is probably not that far off. The DPP's share of the vote (33.38 percent) was consistent with its past performance. The TSU vote came from past Taiwanese supporters of the KMT who were disenchanted with the direction the party took after Lien Chan replaced Lee Teng-hui as chairman. Lee exploited that sense of alienation in order to shore up the forces that opposed a too-easy accommodation of the PRC. Looking toward the presidential election of 2004, the pan-Blue parties came to the obvious conclusion that the only way to defeat Chen Shui-bian was to form a combined ticket.

Although the members of each camp do not take identical positions on all issues (the Green camp is divided most significantly on cross-Strait economic policy), each occupies a fairly well-defined position in Taiwan's political arena regarding the two central issues, unification versus independence and economics versus security. The pan-Green camp is more cautious on unification and economic integration than the Blue camp. This new alignment and power balance reflects more or less accurately the division of public opinion between those who believe that Taiwan's future is tied to that of the mainland and those who see the risks of such entanglement. These two groupings do not necessarily correspond to ethnic divisions on Taiwan, since there are Taiwanese (both Fujianese and Hakka) in the pan-Blue camp. The cleavage is based more on interests, with those who most favor closer economic relations with the mainland tending toward the pan-Blue parties. But it is also geographic. The population of the southern part of the island, which suffered most in the early years of repression, is predominantly ethnic Taiwanese. This area is the DPP stronghold, and it is more suspicious of further integration.

In early 2005, Chen Shui-bian and James Soong forged an alignment that cut across this Blue-Green access. It was a pragmatic adjustment by both men to the division and stalemate of the political system, but it caused some consternation in their respective camps. Whether the arrangement will last and produce results is another question. The most likely scenario for the next few years is that the Blue and Green blocs will remain the primary political actors. The movement toward a single-member-district system for geographic constituencies will increase that probability. As a result, forging consensus on difficult issues will likely persist. Whether division means polarization will depend on the relative salience of the two fundamental issues. If national identity is more prominent, then polarization is more likely; if economic interests are salient, then it is less so. But even economic issues can foster polarization, because of fears that Beijing will use interdependence for political leverage. On both the identity and the economic issue, there remains a hard core on the island that is profoundly suspicious of Beijing and of mainlanders on Taiwan, and it will have to be completely convinced that even the loosest form of association with the mainland is in its interest. Cross-Strait policy is unlikely to stabilize unless it is based on principles that all or most parties support.

CONSTITUTIONAL HURDLES. In addition to the political obstacles to decisive action, there is the fact that if an acceptable proposal to resolve the conflict with the PRC ever were offered, at least some of the actions necessary to approve it would require a constitutional amendment. Pursuant to amendments adopted in April 2000, the ROC constitution had dictated that any amendment first must be proposed by one-fourth of the members of the Legislative Yuan and then passed by three-fourths of the members present, with a required quorum of three-fourths of the members. The amendment would then be referred to the National Assembly, where a simple majority was required for approval. The National Assembly is not a separate standing body; it is called into session only to act on constitutional amendments. Its members are chosen on the basis of proportional representation; voters cast a ballot for the party they prefer, and each party's share of the seats is commensurate with its share of the popular vote. The hurdles that had to be cleared to make any change in "the territory of the Republic of China according to its existing national boundaries"—as might be necessary in a confederal solution to the unification problem—were even more arduous. The requirements in the Legislative Yuan are the same as those for an amendment, but in the National Assembly, a quorum of two-thirds was required and three-quarters of those members present had to vote in the affirmative. (Pursuant to a constitutional amendment passed by the Legislative Yuan in August 2004, the National Assembly was to be abolished in mid-2005; see below.)

Thus, whether under the old system or the new one, passing a constitutional amendment or changing the national territory requires consensus among most of Taiwan's political parties, which then must be able to ensure that their members will vote in favor of it. Given the near parity among the Blue and Green camps, any amendment under the current constitution that a significant element of the population opposed would be unlikely to secure passage.

Taken together, these factors—identity, electoral dynamics, structural problems, political parity, and constitutional requirements—might suggest that the default position of the Taiwan political system on cross-Strait issues will be to do nothing. Even if the pan-Blue forces had won the 2004 presidential election and adopted a conciliatory attitude toward Beijing, they would have been unlikely to go very far before confronting a wall of Green resistance. Under the current structure, the only PRC offer that might win Taiwan's favor would be one that the DPP—pragmatists and fundamentalists alike—found irresistibly attractive.

The Power (and Politics) of Words

Politics on Taiwan (and in China, for that matter) is often obsessed with words. As symbols of reality, they can take on extraordinary importance in political struggles; indeed, they can become the object of struggle themselves. The politics of words are particularly prevalent in political systems in the Chinese world, because of a philosophical clash that goes back to the very origins of the culture: the contest between Confucians and Daoists, who argued, among other things, over the utility of precise terminology. To put it simplistically, Confucians believed that social order was impossible without conceptual clarity and so advocated the "rectification," or "ordering," of "names"—especially terms that refer to human relationships (*zhengming*). Confucius, when asked by the Lord of Wei, a regional ruler around 500 B.C., how to order his state, replied, "Without question, it would be to order names properly." Daoists, on the other hand, held that ambiguity was the essence of things and that words were imperfect tools for conveying that essence ("The Way that can be told of is not the eternal Way. The name that can be named is not the eternal name.").[46] This dynamic is at work in contemporary cross-Strait relations, as each side seeks to maintain a terminological advantage and calculates the relative value of ambiguity and clarity at any point in time. Thus Beijing insists on certain formulations (*tifa*) to describe cross-Strait relations and Taiwan, for example: "There is only one China in the world. Both the mainland and Taiwan belong to one China. China's sovereignty and territorial integrity brook no division." Taiwan's leaders reiterate that theirs is an "independent sovereign state." Lee Teng-hui shifted how he described Taiwan—from a "political entity" in the early 1990s to a "state" in the late 1990s.

This struggle of symbols versus substance and between clarity and ambiguity is particularly common in unequal power relationships. The strong seek to buttress the substance of their power by establishing a terminological monopoly, while the powerless seek to compensate for their actual weakness by gaining some verbal advantage. Each believes that symbols are substance. Thus, as noted in chapter 3, after leaving the presidency Lee Teng-hui advocated using Taiwan as the formal name of his country in order to strengthen Taiwanese identity and so mitigate the vulnerability that he believed flowed from people not being clear about who they were. And, with Lee's support, the Movement to Rectify Names (*zhengming yundong*) sprang up in this period.

Because China's leaders are Chinese and because they suspect that Lee Teng-hui and Chen Shui-bian have a separatist agenda, Beijing is particularly alert to efforts on Taiwan to alter terminology, which they see as important indicators of "incremental independence." The United States, on the other hand, chose to concede victory over words to the PRC at the time of normalization in 1979 and to focus on substance in its relations with Taiwan. For example, Washington has not used the term "Republic of China" since 1979 and tends to use the words "Taiwan authorities" instead of "government" to refer to the government in Taipei. Because Taiwan's leaders and its public are at least culturally Chinese, they resent this diminution of their status.

The desire to "rectify names" and change the symbols of power rather than its substance is particularly strong within the fundamentalist wing of the DPP, Lee Teng-hui's Taiwan Solidarity Union, and politically conscious overseas Taiwanese. And driving them as much as their Confucian cultural heritage is Taiwan's recent history, as they understand it. In their eyes, one element of the suffering that they experienced under the KMT was its effort to impose improper names on the Taiwan reality, such as "the Republic of China." Once the balance of power shifted, they believed that names should change as well.

When Chen Shui-bian was elected, some DPP supporters, particularly those in the fundamentalist camp, sought to capitalize on their new-found power by "rectifying names." Soon after the inauguration, for example, I spoke to a group of Taiwanese Americans in the Dallas area, and one person in the audience asked me whether it would be possible to change the name of the Taiwan representative's office in the United States from "Taipei Economic and Cultural Representative Office" to "Taiwan Economic and Cultural Representative Office," in order to better convey that Taiwan was a separate country. However, in his inaugural address Chen ruled out changing the official name of the country (Republic of China) as long as China did not intend to use force against Taiwan.

Yet there were a variety of proposals from the DPP camp to adjust terminology apart from the national title. One of these involved passports. Printed on the cover of the passport that ROC citizens carry are the words "Republic of China" and "Passport"; in the spring of 2001, proposals surfaced to put the word "Taiwan" on the cover as well. The stated reason for doing so was that Taiwan people traveling overseas were often confused with PRC nationals. The more powerful reason, no doubt, was to assert the island's identity. Indeed, the Taiwan Independence Party was so focused on terminology that it had bogus passports printed with the name "Republic of Taiwan" on the front. The foreign ministry—which was responsible for producing and issuing passports as well as for relations with other countries, some of which might worry about cross-Strait relations—was circumspect about adding the name to the cover. It declared that it was studying the issue but that there was no question of changing the national title. Even the idea of adding "Taiwan" brought charges from conservatives on the island and officials in the PRC that this step was another manifestation of separatist tendencies.[47]

The issue lay publicly dormant until December 2001, when word leaked out that the foreign ministry had decided to print "Taiwan" on the front of the passport. Chen Shui-bian confirmed the report on January 13, 2002, when he announced that he had officially approved the change in a directive to the foreign ministry. The audience that heard his announcement was significant. It was the Formosan Association for Public Affairs (FAPA), the U.S.-based lobby of the Taiwanese American community, whose members— important overseas contributors to the DPP—were in Taiwan to celebrate their twentieth anniversary. The founder and first president of FAPA was none other than Cai Tongrong (Trong Chai), a legislator and key member of the DPP's fundamentalist wing, which along with FAPA placed more emphasis on the power of words. Chen's decision was designed, it seemed, to appeal to the fundamentalist base of his party and its specific priorities; he even referred to his decision as a "birthday gift" to FAPA.[48]

Yet the situation was more complex than it first appeared. Within a day, it was revealed that the recommendation that Chen had approved was to put the words "issued in Taiwan" on the passport, not just "Taiwan." The former formulation was a statement of administrative fact rather than a political claim, which the latter would imply. Foreign Minister Tien Hung-mao stated that his ministry had sought the approach "that would cause the least controversy." In order to stave off more political pressure, Tien said that "issued in Taiwan" was "currently the only proposal as well as the final proposal" and that the measure would be implemented once the cabinet gave its approval. Some in the DPP did not agree. They still favored "Taiwan" only, and they wanted the word to come right after "Republic of China." Not surprisingly, the PRC objected to the whole idea as another step toward Taiwan's independence.[49]

The next stage in this struggle over words came in May, when a group of legislators led by DPP fundamentalist Cai Tongrong passed a resolution on the subject when most of their opposition colleagues were absent. The measure called on the foreign ministry to abandon "issued in Taiwan" and place "Taiwan" right above the word "Passport." The stated rationale was that the ministry's plan would leave the passport looking like the PRC passports issued in Hong Kong, and so (somehow) create equivalence between Hong Kong and Taiwan. The legislators' real reason, no doubt, was that they wanted to make a political statement. Later in the session, the opposition parties passed a similar resolution calling for continuation of the status quo. The foreign ministry stuck to its guns, noting the nonbinding nature of the resolution. Chai's allies in the DPP intensified the pressure in early July, when the central standing committee passed a resolution suggesting that the cabinet abide by his resolution. Later in the month, Chai threatened to amend the Passport Act to require the foreign minister to abide by his wishes, and the ministry quickly announced a delay in the use of the "issued in Taiwan" phrase. When new, machine-readable passports were issued in early October, the cover was the same as before, because, Foreign Minister Eugene Chien said, "No consensus has been reached on this issue."[50]

The standoff continued until June 2003. The next presidential election was about nine months away. Chen Shui-bian and his campaign team were concerned that support among his base voters was weak and that special appeals were necessary to rally them. One of these concerned the passport cover. On June 12, Foreign Minister Chien announced that the word "Taiwan" would appear below "Republic of China" and the national emblem and above the word "Passport," more or less as Cai Tongrong had wished. He asserted that the foreign ministry had the authority to act without legislative approval; that polls had demonstrated that the measure was popular; and that the United States "understood" the change. Opposition politicians were prepared to accommodate the move as long as the national title remained the same, but they also suggested that political motives were at play. A KMT legislator said, "We believe that the DPP will use the measure as a campaign issue to attack any political party who may oppose it."[51]

The 2004 Campaign

As the passport episode illustrated, the stance that Chen Shui-bian adopted for the March 2004 presidential election was very different from the one he had taken in 2000. He appealed more to DPP fundamentalists, Lee Teng-hui's Taiwan Solidarity Union, and overseas Taiwanese contributors than centrist voters. And the core of that appeal focused on the very paralysis of the political system that, as argued previously, aggravates the difficulty of making change in cross-Strait relations and other policy areas. Chen proposed using referenda to decide public policy issues. He called for a new constitution that would remedy the defects of the existing charter. He proposed that this new constitution be approved not by the representative institutions, the Legislative Yuan and the National Assembly, but through the direct democracy of a referendum, and he readily admitted that he offered this new approach precisely because the existing system posed insurmountable barriers.[52] Beijing, of course, feared that Chen sought to remove those barriers in order to prepare the way for independence, and other observers worried that his initiatives would provoke China and increase tensions and instability.[53] And indeed, Chen was trying to make a hostile China an issue in the campaign.

Chen's initiatives also challenged mainstream scholarly views about the island's politics that held that a Taiwanese identity does not translate into a drive for independence and that political parties are compelled to avoid radical platforms in order to compete for the bulky middle of the political spectrum. In Wu Yu-shan's four-cell scheme (see figure 6-3), Chen was moving more into the upper-left cell when he should have stayed in the center. Moreover, unlike in the election of 2000, when Lien and Soong had divided the KMT's supporters between them, Chen would not have the luxury of a divided opposition in 2004. The pan-Blue parties had united behind the ticket of Lien Chan and James Soong. So Chen could secure reelection only by winning more than 50 percent of the vote, which made his tactics all the more puzzling.[54]

There were several explanations of this phenomenon. The first was that Chen believed that his base was insecure and that he had to focus on mobilizing it. The party rank and file were unhappy with his failure to meet their expectations and threatened to sit out the 2004 election. Those expectations were excessive and unrealistic, but that is a common phenomenon in a party that has never been in power. Emblematic of this alienation of the base was party elder Lin Yi-hsiung, who believed that Chen had not worked hard enough to facilitate a referendum to ban future reliance on nuclear power (Lin thus combined two elements of DPP orthodoxy: direct democracy and a "green" approach to energy policy.) During 2002 and 2003, Lin, a noble figure who had sacrificed much for the opposition cause, conducted solitary and silent marches around Taiwan to protest what he saw as his president's weakness. Thus Chen's effort in 1999, 2000, and 2001 to stake out a position that was more centrist than the views of the DPP base came back to haunt him in 2003 and 2004. The danger that he saw was not that DPP supporters would vote for Lien Chan, but that they would not vote at all. Therefore he understandably played up the traditional party themes of a new constitution and the use of referenda, which were part of the "independence plank" of the 1991 party charter, to decide major policy issues. Moreover, this interpretation goes, he sought to use that emphasis to provoke Beijing into a display of anger that would drive wavering voters into his camp.

The second interpretation, which is not inconsistent with the first, was that Chen understood full well that he could not win by appealing to his DPP constituency but would have to turn toward the middle eventually if he wanted to win. Hence which issues he emphasized was a matter of timing. He would appeal to the base for most of 2003 and turn to swing voters in early 2004.

A third explanation is that Chen simply misread the mindset of the electorate. To the extent that polling over the last decade, imperfect as it is,

Figure 6-3. 2004 Election: Moving from the Center to Independence

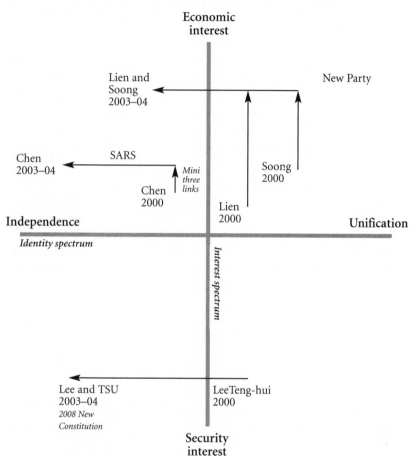

Source: Adapted from Yu-shan Wu, "Taiwan's Domestic Politics and Cross-Strait Relations," *China Journal* 53 (January 2005): 52 (reprinted with permission of the publisher).

reflects at least the general trend, there is little evidence of a change in the fundamental centrism of political opinion, which favors the status quo, or in the more recent balance of political forces.[55] Perhaps Chen miscalculated, as the DPP did in 1991. Alternatively, he may have understood public opinion better than experts thought, but in regard to issues other than any trend toward independence. That is, the Taiwan public was growing frustrated with the operation of the political system, particularly the paralysis in the Legislative Yuan. Chen's call for direct democracy through referenda and a complete overhaul of the governmental structure struck a responsive chord.

All three of these explanations see political tactics as the reason for Chen's return to DPP orthodoxy. The fourth and more worrisome explanation was that the entire Taiwan political spectrum was shifting in the direction of independence and that Chen was exploiting it not only to win electoral victory but also to carry out the core goals of his party in his second term. A variant surmise, common in China, was that popular attitudes had not changed but that Chen, who had been in favor of independence all along, had hit upon a devious way—a new constitution—to declare independence under the guise of improving the political system. He could also hope that his political opposition would fail to expose his agenda or make him pay an electoral price.

Indeed, the pan-Blue parties had a hard time reacting to Chen's proposals. At the outset, they thought that Chen had miscalculated and exposed a vulnerability that they might be able to exploit. Yet their efforts to mobilize opposition were not terribly effective. Then, afraid of losing public support and of being branded as allies of Beijing, the Blue parties adopted the pan-Green goals of referenda and a new constitution. They too were being pulled into the upper-left cell (see figure 6-3). Chen, therefore, did not pay a big price for straying from the old center.

In the end, Chen won by a nose. Far behind in the summer of 2003, he had pulled even by the end of February 2004. The pan-Blue camp was able to rebound and according to some polls was widening the gap again in the week before the election. The day before, however, one or more gunmen shot at Chen and Vice President Lu during a rally in Tainan. Neither was seriously hurt, and the sympathy that they garnered from the attack may have been enough to ensure victory. Chen and Lu beat Lien Chan and James Soong by under 30,000 votes (around two-tenths of 1 percent).

The main reason for the election outcome was that the pan-Green camp fought the campaign better than the pan-Blue camp—even though Chen Shui-bian had few achievements to show for his first term and this time the pan-Blue parties were united. Chen certainly used the advantages of incumbency, and the pan-Blue parties had little experience of being in the opposition. He also controlled the agenda. He used the media to good effect. He kept Lien and Soong on the defensive and blamed them for his administration's lack of success. He played up the Taiwan identity and downplayed his own weaknesses (such as President Bush's criticism in December 2003). He rallied his base through the proposals for referenda and a new constitution and then exploited softness in pan-Blue support. For example, the pan-Green camp got 250,000 more votes than in the 2000 election in the

Hakka areas of Taoyuan, Miaoli, and Hsinchu (a traditional KMT stronghold). The pan-Green camp thus has learned how to conduct modern electoral politics, with all its good and bad features.

The pan-Blue parties, on the other hand, did a fairly bad job in the campaign. For a variety of reasons, they chose not to nominate the candidate who would have been most likely to win, Ma Ying-jeou.[56] Then they had difficulty seizing the initiative and exploiting Chen's vulnerabilities. They did not defend their base very well. They allowed Chen to close the gap in the critical last days of the contest.

The result does indicate that support for the pan-Green camp was growing. In 2000, Chen got 40 percent of the vote. In the 2001 legislative elections, the DPP and TSU got around 45 percent of the votes cast for party candidates. In 2004, Chen and Lu got 50 percent, around 1.5 million more votes that they got in 2000, a remarkable shift. Whether the outcome foreshadowed a continuing surge of sentiment for de jure independence is not so clear. Opinion on the island was pretty evenly balanced: the pan-Blue camp still got around half the votes cast. And because the election reflected the pan-Green camp's skill and the pan-Blue camp's lack thereof, it may actually have overstated the core support for pan-Green objectives. And Taiwan's economic dependence on the mainland placed limits to the further growth of Green sentiment.

The results of the referenda that Chen had sponsored were not valid, because fewer than 50 percent of eligible voters cast ballots. The likely explanation is that most pan-Blue supporters accepted their leaders' argument that Chen exceeded his authority in calling for the referenda—in that he exaggerated the extent of the external threat, the relevant criterion. Thus whether voters accepted a ballot for the referenda, in addition to one for the presidential race, was by and large determined by whom they supported for president: those who supported Chen did so; around five out of six of those who voted for Lien did not. Thus the failure of the referenda does not reflect rejection of referenda per se.

The rules of the political game changed significantly in August 2004, when the Legislative Yuan (LY) passed amendments to the constitution. The key ones affected the LY electoral system and the means of ratifying constitutional or territorial changes. One amendment abandons the SVMM system and shifts to single-member districts and a second vote. In addition, it reduces the number of LY members from 225 to 113. Effective with the Legislative Yuan that will convene in 2008, seventy-three members will be elected from geographic districts, six will be elected by aboriginal Taiwanese, and thirty-four will be drawn from party lists. Voters will cast one vote for a legislator to represent the geographic district in which they live and a second one for the party with which they identify. The number of legislators appointed from each party list will be proportionate to the party's share of the second vote. In addition, the length of a legislator's term was increased from three years to four, the same as the president's term. Because the first election to which this amendment applies will occur around the same time as the next presidential election, there is the possibility that the two elections will take place on the same day, thus reducing the degree to which electoral politics complicates governing.

In a second amendment, the procedures in the Legislative Yuan to ratify constitutional amendments and territorial changes will remain the same but the National Assembly is to be abolished. In its place, amendments will be ratified by popular referendum, with the support of at least half of the eligible voters required for passage. In effect, a supermajority of indeterminate size will be required for ratification, because the number of actual voters will be less than the number of total eligible voters.[57]

An ad hoc session of the National Assembly to be held by mid-2005 will consider these significant amendments, but their impact on the operation of the Taiwan political system remains to be seen. The electoral changes should reduce the tendency toward fragmentation and radicalization, since political forces that represent fractional segments of the political spectrum will no longer have the opportunities to gain power that they did in the past. Over time, therefore, there should be a trend toward a two-party system and a convergence of political views around two basic alternatives—accommodation of and resistance to China, perhaps. Even so, the long-entrenched culture of personality politics will likely continue, and the electoral system will not, on its own, dictate the contours of the struggle for power. As for the shift to a referendum for final ratification, the key hurdle remains the Legislative Yuan. Only proposals that enjoy broad party and public consensus are likely to be passed.

The PRC

Clearly, the PRC lacks the open, lively, competitive character of Taiwan's democratic system. But one of the more important political developments in China over the last twenty-five years has been the gradual emergence of what can legitimately be called public opinion. Individuals and groups outside the communist regime have some degree of freedom to voice their views on a variety of policy issues. That is not to say that there are no taboo areas or that the links between the people and government leaders are as developed as in democratic systems. Forbidden zones remain, and the links are still being formed. Yet there are issues on which the Chinese leadership believes that it cannot ignore the public's views.

Not only has the circle of politics in China expanded, the Taiwan Strait issue has simultaneously become more salient in political debate, whether within the leadership or between it and the public. That is because it is wrapped up in the very ethos of Chinese Communist Party (CCP) rule. From the beginning of the communist period, securing Taiwan's "return to the motherland" was a staple of regime propaganda and a goal that was not subject to question. Taiwan was one of the Chinese territories lost to foreign countries in the nineteenth century and therefore emblematic of the humiliation that a weak China had suffered at the hands of "imperialism." Japan, which was the CCP's adversary from the 1930s until the end of World War II and the object of chauvinistic diatribes ever since, also had held the island and allegedly "brainwashed" its people. And it was to Taiwan that Chiang Kai-shek—Mao's opponent in the civil war—had retreated and continued low-level harassment against the PRC. Sticking in the communist craw was the fact that until the early 1970s Chiang's ROC regime continued to be the government of China in the eyes of much of the world. That the United States—the leading postwar imperialist country and Taiwan's protector—has been in Chinese eyes the key obstacle to fulfilling the national mission of unification has added another layer of grievance. For more than five decades, the only message that the Chinese public has heard is that Taiwan is an issue of national destiny and a litmus test of regime credibility. No conflicting point of view has been allowed. By virtue of history, nationalism, and foreign policy, a leader who is perceived to have mismanaged the matter and to have been duped by the United States is a leader who is vulnerable to criticism from his colleagues, from foreign policy experts, and even from the public. The danger for the party was that its already weak legitimacy would be further undermined. Regaining the island is the brass ring of Chinese politics; to somehow "lose" Taiwan can be the kiss of death for party leaders.

The Taiwan Issue within the Chinese Communist Leadership

Mao Zedong dominated Chinese politics and policy toward Taiwan from 1949 until his death in 1976. Deng Xiaoping did the same from 1978 until the early 1990s, when his health began to fail. Until that time, Taiwan was neither an issue in conflicts among the elite nor a subject of informed public debate on the limited occasions when it was allowed.

That situation changed in the 1990s. Jiang Zemin, who came to fill Deng's role as the PRC's paramount leader, did not have either Mao's or Deng's prestige within the communist elite and so was more open to challenge. Policy came to be refracted through a personalized and collective leadership system in which the incumbents of principal offices had to build consensus for their initiatives. There was some open discussion of policy issues among scholars, think tanks, and the mass media. Periodic crises in cross-Strait relations during the 1990s evoked flurries of Chinese commentaries and proposals with the recurring theme that Beijing needed to be more resolute in coping with Taiwan (and American) perfidy. Leaders' freedom of action varied by issue and over time. The consensus nature of leadership fostered a certain aversion to creativity.

Jiang did hold the top position in each of the three major hierarchies, all of which are relevant to Taiwan: state president of the PRC (government); general secretary of the Chinese Communist Party; and chairman of the central military commissions in both the party and state structures (the party structure is far more important). He also has held the chairmanship of two significant "leaders' small groups"—one on Taiwan and the other on foreign affairs—in which individuals who formulate policy, like Jiang, meet with representatives of the key implementing agencies.

The only major exception to Jiang's dominance on Taiwan came in 1995 when some of his colleagues opportunistically criticized him for allowing the Lee Teng-hui visit to the United States. Even in that case, information was limited, and Western scholars disagree to some extent on the degree of elite conflict. Robert Suettinger, who was in the U.S. government at the time, concludes that during the 1995–96 crisis "there can be little doubt that leadership frictions and competition for power continued throughout the period, and may have intensified, given the high tension of the situation." At least two of Jiang's civilian political rivals—Qiao Shi and Li Ruihuan—used the Taiwan crisis to put Jiang on the defensive. What is less clear is whether there was a split between the military and the rest of the leadership on how to respond to the Lee visit. One school of thought, represented by Suettinger, John Garver, and Tai-ming Cheung, concludes that military leaders, along with some civilians, had opposed civilian policies for some time and used events like the Lee visit to impose their views on Jiang, constraining his options and forcing a tougher policy that employed military training exercises as tools for intimidation. Others, particularly Michael Swaine and You

Ji, tend to dismiss the idea of a deep division over Taiwan. They see a consultative policy process, not a factional one, in which the leadership altered its policy consensus to respond to changing circumstances. Both civilian and military leaders agreed that a tough response to Lee's visit was required. The military, which has a relatively significant impact when national security issues are on the agenda, was one participant in that process. Actors differed on the timing and nature of the response. Civilians stressed diplomatic and political measures while military officers favored military ones. Andrew Scobell splits the difference. He confirms that the PLA led the charge in advocating a hard-line response to the Lee visit but also finds that by October 1995, civilian and military leaders had reached a consensus on a tougher approach.[58]

For most of his tenure, however, Jiang was fairly free to call the tune, and his approach to Taiwan was remarkably consistent—and conventional: he called for unification under the one-country, two-systems formula; preferred a peaceful resolution but built up China's military capabilities to at least deter any provocative action by Taiwan; blocked Taiwan's participation in the international system wherever possible; and pursued a positive relationship with the United States.

One potential source of policy change in China is the leadership turnover that occurs every five years, in conjunction with the selection and convocation of a new Communist Party Congress and a new National People's Congress (on the government side). Moreover, transition occurs from one leadership generation to another. The latest transition began, at least in a formal sense, with the meeting of the Sixteenth Party Congress in September 2002 and the transfer of positions from the so-called third generation to the fourth. The political maneuvering began long before that, of course, but the key questions concerned who would fill the top positions in the government, party, and military hierarchies and what changes in policy would result. The answers were not immediately clear.

Studies of the fourth generation of Chinese leaders offer some clues and guesses about what to expect from them on the question of policy changes. Cheng Li tells us that the Cultural Revolution was the defining political experience for the fourth generation, which left them ideologically less dogmatic, intellectually more sophisticated, and more down-to-earth and politically astute than their predecessors. Most of the members of the fourth generation have pursued a higher education, including postgraduate studies; their professional training is concentrated in the fields of engineering and natural sciences, although some are economists and lawyers. They complete the transition, begun in the third generation, from a leadership of veterans of the revolution to a leadership of technocrats, people whom Li defines as possessing expertise, practical experience, and leadership positions. They are, to be sure, as elitist as the revolutionary generation, but their right to rule has a very different basis.[59]

Concerning general policy predilections, Li suggests that individuals in the fourth generation tend to be techno-nationalists, people who want to build the state and national power through technology. They are probably more aware of the need for political reforms than their predecessors, but they want to bring about political change in a managed and controlled way. Yet this mindset is balanced somewhat by an awareness of the imperatives of a globalized economy.

Li observes that just because fourth-generation leaders have had more exposure to the West, they are not necessarily pro-Western. The string of negative events in U.S.-China relations in the late 1990s left them "cynical about the moral superiority of the West, resentful of Western arrogance, and doubtful about the total adoption of a Western economic and political system. Yet, even in the face of a crisis such as the tragic incident in Belgrade, they understand the need for cooperation instead of confrontation.... Their policies toward the United States will be firm but not aggressive." Concerning Taiwan, Li suggests, "Taiwan's growing demand for independence and the mainland's uncompromising sovereignty claim on the island have placed fourth-generation leaders in a very difficult situation. Any major policy mistake from either side of the Taiwan Strait may profoundly jeopardize the course of China's modernization."

Another window on the new leaders' views are the revelations found in the volumes *Disidai* by Zong Hairen and its English-language counterpart, *China's New Rulers*, by Andrew Nathan and Bruce Gilley. During vetting prior to their selection as the successor cohort, the men of the fourth generation offered opinions on Taiwan that were fairly conventional. Hu Jintao, for example, expressed confidence that the proliferating web of economic and social ties will inevitably lead to a mutually satisfactory solution. He regarded Chen Shui-bian and the forces he represented as a temporary phenomenon. The key to progress was Taiwan's acceptance of the one-China principle and the 1992 consensus. "Taiwan independence" was a problem that deserved serious attention, and "the choice between war and peace was Taiwan's to make." It was to prevent independence that China would not and could not renounce the use of force. And although China would allow Taiwan's people to manage their own affairs after unification, "that did not mean that they could declare independence through a referendum." Finally, Hu alleged that U.S. interference was the reason that the Taiwan issue had been unresolved for so long.[60] Zeng Qinghong placed a similar emphasis on the one-China principle and the need to reserve the option of using force. If the former were abandoned, he said, cross-Strait relations would be between two countries (*guo*). If the latter were dropped, there would be no deterrent against separatism, Taiwan would seize the opportunity to become independent, China would have to use force to reverse that decision, and unification would not occur peacefully. He also highlighted the generosity of the one-country, two-systems offer to Taiwan, particularly how it was better than the deal that Hong Kong got. He dwelt on U.S. responsibility for blocking unification. But he, like Hu, expressed confidence that Chen's influence over the Taiwan public would wane.[61]

Both Hu and Zeng were reading from Jiang Zemin's script. That was to be expected, of course, since their statements were part of their "job interview" for higher office. And it is no accident that Zeng's positions reflected Jiang's, since Zeng had advised Jiang on Taiwan strategy and had served as his secret emissary in the early 1990s. If anyone in the fourth generation will work to protect Jiang's legacy, it will be Zeng. Whether Hu Jintao's approach is any more creative is impossible to say. His strategy for winning the top positions was to not challenge the orthodoxy of the 1990s.

A final yet inconclusive set of clues is found in the annual speeches, drafted by the Taiwan Affairs Office, that PRC leaders give every January to mark the anniversary of Jiang Zemin's 1995 "eight-points" speech on Taiwan policy. Zhou Mingwei, who is certainly a member of the fourth generation, if not the fifth, became deputy director of the Taiwan Affairs Office in 2000, after the anniversary speech for that year. Presumably he was involved in drafting subsequent speeches. Qian Qichen, then the vice premier, gave the address for several years before 2004. Did the speeches that Qian Qichen gave after Zhou moved to Beijing include new ideas that would indicate the thinking of China's rising leaders about the Taiwan Strait issue?

There are interesting new elements in the addresses for 2001, 2002, and 2003. The 2001 speech was the first in which Qian offered the formulation that Taiwan and the mainland both belonged to one China. It expressed sympathy for "the sufferings of the Taiwan compatriots in having endured a long period of colonial rule and despotic oppression" and understanding of "the strong aspirations of the Taiwan compatriots to be masters in their own house." The 2002 speech expanded on that latter point and welcomed DPP members who were not "stubborn Taiwan independence elements" to visit China as long as they agreed to travel under what China considered an appropriate status. Gone were the harsh warnings in the 2000 speech that "Taiwan independence can only mean war."[62]

It is very hard to say whether the more moderate formulations of the latter speeches reflect the influence of a member of a new leadership generation. They do suggest that PRC officials have a better understanding of Taiwan ways of thinking and seek rhetorical ways of appealing to the island's public, something that has been missing for a long time. Yet they may simply reflect changes in the broader context that might have dictated greater PRC rhetorical moderation: Chen Shui-bian's pledge not to take certain steps; the emergence of forces in Taiwan that could constrain and undermine him; and the Taiwan recession. Nor did this series of statements signal a change in fundamental PRC policy. So it is difficult to ascribe any special influence to Vice Minister Zhou and thereby a different outlook on the part of fourth-generation leaders. Moreover, that Zhou did not get a seat on the Central Committee at the time of the Sixteenth Party Congress (November 2002) may indicate that he has less influence on Taiwan policy than people thought. Then, in January 2004, he was relieved of his position, but probably for reasons unrelated to Taiwan policy.

If the fourth generation's views on Taiwan were unclear, the pace of their assumption of power was measured. In November 2002, at the Sixteenth Party Congress, Hu Jintao became general secretary of the Chinese Communist Party and state president, and Wen Jiabao was named premier of the state council, with line authority over government ministries. Tang Jiaxuan succeeded Qian Qichen as the senior cabinet official in charge of external policy, and Li Zhaoxing replaced Tang as foreign minister.

But to the surprise of some, Jiang Zemin, the leader of the third generation, continued as chairman of the party and state military commissions. And he retained influence in another way. Jiang's protégés gained a majority on the politburo of the Chinese Communist Party and its standing committee, the key policymaking bodies. The most important of those protégés was Zeng Qinghong, who was Jiang's right-hand man when he was general secretary and for a time in the 1990s was his representative in secret talks with Taiwan. There was no evidence that Taiwan was an issue in this stage of the succession.[63]

It is a reasonable working hypothesis that because Jiang maintained influence in the wake of the Sixteenth Party Congress by retaining some of his positions and by placing his protégés in others, policy continuity regarding Taiwan was greater. Leadership transition in China is a more seamless and gradual process than in the United States, and at least on this issue, Jiang had guaranteed that it would be. Moreover, Hu Jintao and the rest of his cohort have learned from history that the way to get to the top of the leadership ladder is to be very quiet about their policy preferences while climbing the rungs. They have been very skillful about masking their views, leaving outsiders—and probably most Chinese—ignorant about how they would handle this key issue of China's external policy.[64]

Although Jiang retained the Central Military Commission (CMC) chairmanships in late 2002 and early 2003, it was unclear how long he would do so, and there was some speculation at the time that he might give them up after a couple of years. The length of his tenure resurfaced as an issue in the summer and fall of 2004, in the run-up to the third plenary session of the Sixteenth Central Committee. Following the reelection of Chen Shui-bian, Jiang apparently sought to use the Taiwan Strait issue, among others, to create support for the idea that he should stay on. There was no real disagreement on fundamental policy. Rather, Jiang or people acting on his behalf tried to create a climate of uncertainty to justify his remaining in office. In the end, Jiang gave up the chairmanships.[65]

With Jiang's retirement, Hu Jintao occupied all the offices associated with the status of paramount leader. Still, it may take him time to accumulate the power and flexibility needed to initiate any new departures in PRC policy—assuming that he is inclined to do so. He understands that the CCP's legitimacy is, in part, a function of how it handles the Taiwan Strait issue. In addition, even if Jiang does not retain positions, as a CCP elder he has some right to be consulted on issues in which he takes an interest. And there is no real evidence that Hu and the rest of the fourth generation of leaders think any differently than the cohort led by Jiang Zemin. That may not be good news. To be sure, China's approach on Taiwan from 2000 to late 2003 was more moderate than before, in part because China calculated that its growing economic interaction with Taiwan put time on its side and in part because it recognized that past intimidation had been counterproductive. Yet Jiang consistently misread Taiwan's position on fundamental issues, in effect regarding Taipei's substantive opposition to the one-country, two-systems approach as tantamount to the pursuit of Taiwan independence. It was he who raised the salience of the "one-China principle" as a basis for reconciliation, which only increased Taiwan's leaders' fear that affirming the PRC's principles meant falling into a negotiating trap. Beijing continues to accumulate military power in order to some day have the capacity at least to deter Taiwan and perhaps to coerce the island into submission. Moreover, if

Cheng Li is correct that the Hu Jintao generation possesses an elitist outlook, they are unlikely to have a proper appreciation of the very populist consciousness that shapes Taiwan's approach to cross-Strait relations.

Thus the recent changes in the PRC's leadership probably portend continuity in PRC policy toward Taiwan, with all the risks and opportunities that continuity entails. Reinforcing the dynamics of elite politics is the substantive nature of the Taiwan Strait issue itself, elaborated in previous chapters, and how Beijing has seen fit to address it.

Public Opinion and Nationalism

Charles Tilley distinguished two types of nationalism in the history of Europe: one was "the mobilization of populations that do not have their own state around a claim to political independence"; the other was "the mobilization of the population of an existing state around a strong identification with that state." The first type was an age-old phenomenon that occurred whenever rulers of one religion or language conquered people of another religion or language. The second type was uncommon before the nineteenth century, and then it existed "chiefly in the heat of war."[66]

With some qualification, the distinction that Tilley observed applies well to the two sides of the Taiwan Strait. Taiwanese nationalism, or sense of identity, has been the response of the island's people to KMT repression and later to the PRC's opposition to the idea that they should have their own state. Conversely, the Chinese state exists, and historically Chinese nationalism has been a response both to the state's domestic and international weakness and to the continued division of the country. Indeed, as John Fitzgerald points out, the history of the twentieth century reveals contending efforts (Confucian, republican, KMT, and CCP) to reconstitute a Chinese state from the ashes of the imperial system, each of which "advocated a distinctive and mutually exclusive definition of the national self."[67] Taiwan spurs Chinese nationalist sentiment today because it stands as evidence of the weakness of the state. To the extent that identification with the nation-state and its fate is the lens through which policy choices are viewed—as it often is with regard to Taiwan, in apocalyptic terms—it creates pressure on government policy.

There are several layers to Chinese nationalism. There is a racial and ethnic dimension, a belief that the Chinese nation is best equated with the Han Chinese people and that they are superior to any other racial or ethnic group. A more benign expression of this perspective was the Confucian claim that traditional China was the acme of civilization, to which other, bar-

barian people should show deference and from which they should learn—the belief that China was the original source of much that is good in the world. A harder edge was displayed during the late nineteenth and early twentieth centuries, when the political challenge that the Chinese mounted to the Manchu Qing dynasty and to foreign "imperialism" took on a strong ethnic and even xenophobic strain. It was in this period that Chinese intellectuals adopted racial categories to conceptualize the world. And some Chinese historians acknowledge today that the Confucian world was in fact extremely Sinocentric, characterized by "a fierce racism, rejection of other cultures, . . . and cultural superiority." In the 1909 Nationality Law, Chinese anywhere were deemed to be citizens of China.[68]

A century later, ethnocentrism remains strong. The PRC continues to suggest that ethnic Chinese the world over have a special bond or obligation to the "motherland." In the 1980s attacks by Chinese students on Africans studying in China exposed the racial dimension of Chinese identity, and limited survey research gives some indication of the degree to which Chinese regard themselves as different from other peoples. In surveys of political attitudes in 2000, 2001, and 2002, Beijing residents were asked to assess on a scale of one to seven how peaceful and moral Chinese, Americans, and Japanese were. In this measure of ethnocentrism, they placed Chinese between 1.61 and 1.78 on the scale in the three successive surveys—that is, relatively peaceful and moral. They scored Americans between 3.42 and 3.60 and Japanese between 3.90 and 3.96. Since Beijing residents are relatively cosmopolitan, the contrast would likely be stronger among Chinese in other parts of country. And during the 2004 Olympics, *Renmin Ribao*, the Chinese Communist Party newspaper, suggested that although Chinese were at a genetic disadvantage vis-à-vis black athletes when it came to track and field, they were suited to sports that required agility and technique, such as gymnastics.[69]

One expression of ethnocentrism that is relevant to Taiwan is the idea that if Chinese people must live under foreign rule, their Chinese cultural essence will be leached out of them. That is one explanation for why both the KMT and the CCP in the 1930s did not advocate the return of Taiwan to China—Japanese colonialism had made the people of the island less Chinese. Once the KMT took over the island, however, it embarked on a deliberate effort to restore the "Chineseness" of the population. As late as March 2001, Vice-Premier Qian Qichen, speaking to the National People's Congress, remarked on the lingering impact of Japanese rule: "The shade of 'awareness as the emperor's people' [that is, being Japanese] has still not dispersed among certain people."[70]

One of the ways that the PRC government and Chinese in general justify their mistrust of Lee and Chen Shui-bian is to suggest that they are somehow not Chinese. In 1994, after Lee gave an interview to Japanese journalist Ryotaro Shiba in which he portrayed himself as Taiwan's Moses, mainland critics explained his purported perfidy by pointing to his Japanese background. As one author wrote, "He [Lee Teng-hui] also repeatedly claimed that before he reached the age of 22 (that is, in 1945, before the retrocession of Taiwan to China) he had been a Japanese. If one understands that he is not ashamed of, but even proud of his country being conquered by Japan, then it will be easy to understand on what kind of ideological basis he has based his various fallacies of today."[71] Edward Friedman writes: "Lee Teng-hui was interpreted in super-patriotic China as the carrier, if not the embodiment, of pro-Japanese tendencies (an immorality akin to being pro-Nazi), which in the PRC felt like treason, insanity, or worse."[72] One test that Beijing set for Chen Shui-bian was whether he would admit that he was Chinese, probably knowing full well that an unqualified admission would create problems for him with his DPP base. The furthest that Chen was willing to go—in his inaugural address, for example—was to say that "the people on the two sides of the Taiwan Strait share the same ancestral, cultural, and historical background."

Equating Chinese national identity with the Han ethnic identity has a corollary: that good Chinese should not rely on outsiders to achieve their political goals and that to do so is a form of treason. At times of tension, Chinese commentators have used such rhetoric to explain setbacks in the journey toward unification, and Lee Teng-hui became their favorite whipping boy. One observer accused him of plotting with foreigners to further separatist objectives: "If the person in power resorts to the former colonialist and foreign forces in trying to split the country, he will drag Taiwan into an abyss and stand condemned through the ages. People on both sides of the Taiwan Straits must maintain high vigilance." Another author referred to him a "marionette and pawn" of the United States, "a stick which foreigners use to stir up troubled waters in China."[73]

A second layer of contemporary Chinese nationalism is the history of China's encounter with the West and Japan, at least up to the victory of the CCP in 1949. In this narrative, a great and virtuous civilization experienced "one hundred and fifty years of humiliation" at the hands of barbaric and rapacious foreigners. Relying on their superior power and taking advantage of the weakness and stupidity of China's prior leaders, foreign imperialists were able to impose their exploitive and unjust dominance, bringing shame to the Chinese people. Worse yet, foreign armed forces took advantage of China's weakness to defeat it in wars and lesser military actions, commit horrible abuses against a defenseless people, and acquire some of the country's sacred territory (including Taiwan). This history of victimization represents, in the Chinese nationalist consciousness, a stain that must be washed clean, a blood debt that must be paid. Geremie Barmé writes: "As the children of the Cultural Revolution and the reform era come into power, they are finding a new sense of importance and self-worth. They are resentful of the real and imagined slights that they and their nation have suffered in the past, and their desire for strength and revenge is increasingly reflected in contemporary Chinese culture."[74]

In this discourse, traitors have a special, negative place. It is bad enough that evil foreigners render China weak and powerless, but it is even worse if the country and its cause are betrayed from within. Accusations of treason remain hardy perennials in contemporary Chinese nationalism, and Lee Teng-hui, to take a contemporary example, has not been spared. For example, after his 1995 visit to the United States, an authoritative commentary in *People's Daily* (*Renmin Ribao*) and the Xinhua news service accused him of treason: "Lee Teng-hui joined the Chinese Communist Party in his early years, which he later betrayed. He had for many years followed Chiang Ching-kuo, who did not favor 'Taiwan independence' but has now betrayed him. Having now embarked on the road of 'Taiwan independence,' he has betrayed the great reunification cause of the Chinese people, including the Taiwan compatriots. For their part, the 1.2 billion Chinese people have long made up their minds never to allow the plot of 'the independence of Taiwan' in any form to succeed. Should Li Teng-hui continue to go down along that dangerous road in defiance of the will of the people, he would certainly be utterly discredited and stand condemned by the Chinese nation through the ages."[75]

China's sense of victimization manifested itself in a new and special way in the 1990s. A significant body of Chinese opinion concluded that the United States had adopted a policy of trying to block China's emergence as a great power, an effort that was all the more galling in the PRC because the country was successfully building its economic, military, and diplomatic power. This perception of a U.S. policy of containment is the third layer of contemporary Chinese nationalism, and Chinese analysts assemble an array of evidence to justify it:

—deploying U.S. military forces in East Asia

—strengthening the U.S. alliance with Japan, which may remilitarize itself

—maintaining alliances and security relations with other Asian powers

—viewing China's military modernization as a threat

—obstructing China's quest for symbolically important roles in the international community, such as serving as host for the 2000 Olympic games

—undermining China's political system through the advocacy of democracy and human rights

—pursuing trade policies, such as protection of intellectual property rights, that impede China's economic growth

—encouraging Tibetan separatism

—supporting Taiwan's separatism and opposing China's reunification.[76]

These three sources of current Chinese nationalism are not without some ironies. First of all, the current focus on victimization is of recent vintage. In the Mao period, Marxism-Leninism transmuted nationalism into anti-imperialism, and accounts of China's past emphasized the Chinese people's victory over foreign aggression and exploitation. Victimization became the dominant narrative in the 1990s, as China was growing stronger. (Note also that both China and Taiwan have their respective victimization narratives. For China, the victimizers were and are the West and Japan; for Taiwan, they were the post-1945 Chinese rulers.) Second, equating the Chinese nation with the Han ethnic group ignores the fact that China is actually a multi-ethnic state. Indeed, the strongest display of nationalism in China today may be among some of the minority nationalities, particularly Tibetans. Similarly, the idea of a unified Chinese identity overlooks the strength of regional identities that have emerged over the last quarter-century. Edward Friedman in particular has explicated the sharp differences in perspective on a range of social and political issues between North and South China. And David Goodman has shown in China, as in Taiwan, the operation of multiple identities whose relative salience varies with the circumstances.[77] Third, the Chinese nationalistic approach to Taiwan emphasizes ethnic uniformity and the history of division and frustrated unification under a unitary state. Although some in Taiwan pursue a nationalist agenda in the service of a new and separate state, the mainstream view has focused in effect on the shape of the Chinese state, whether it might accommodate a Taiwan that possesses sovereignty.

The greatest irony of all is the PRC government's ambivalent approach to rising nationalistic sentiment. To be sure, it has used nationalism to bolster its legitimacy in light of the bankruptcy of communist ideology. On the other hand, it seeks to contain "patriotic" pressures, on Taiwan or the United States for example, that threaten the regime's control or that conflict with the country's interests as the CCP defines them. Although the regime certainly fosters nationalism through the educational and propaganda systems, popular sentiments have a reality that is independent of, and sometimes poses a challenge to, the government.[78]

One explanation for the dilemma that the regime faces is that Chinese nationalism today is not a single, unified force. Scholars distinguish different streams, identified by the stance that its adherents think China should take toward the advanced world. Joseph Fewsmith and Stanley Rosen identify three basic outlooks: cosmopolitanism, which is prepared to embrace the capitalist and democratic West; nativism, which proposes to reject it; and the intermediate, mainstream stance of self-strengthening, the desire to build up China's power so that it can meet the West more on the basis of parity and without jettisoning Chinese values. Suisheng Zhao devises a similar trichotomy. For him, nativism advocates a return to traditional Chinese values and confrontational vigilance against foreign insults and pressure. Antitraditionalism blames China's past for its failures and calls for adoption of Western models. Pragmatism sees both internal and external causes for problems and argues for selective borrowing from abroad for the purpose of making China strong again, plus an assertive foreign policy.[79]

Nationalistic attitudes appear to vary by social class. Johnston's research on political attitudes found that Beijing residents who were wealthier, better educated, more traveled, and more opposed to military spending perceived *less* difference between Chinese and Americans than other Beijing residents. Those same respondents tended to express their feelings of nationalism in terms of pride in being a citizen of China rather than in terms of the kind of xenophobic, narrowly nativistic beliefs depicted, for example, by the phrase "My country, right or wrong."[80]

Attitudes also vary according to the individual's place in the political system. Fewsmith and Rosen specify three levels at play in the politics of Chinese foreign policy.[81] The first is the level of the elite, high-level officials in the government, the Chinese Communist Party, and the military who debate foreign policy issues and sometimes seek to use those issues in their struggles over power. The elite has grown in size and complexity as China's foreign policy has had to address more and more issues (see chapter 7).

The second level is what Fewsmith and Rosen term sub-elites: "'public intellectuals' . . . who take part in public discourse and try to influence informed public opinion and government policy on a range of issues." Sub-elites include both intellectuals who work for government think tanks and those who do not and individuals who write for the government, for each other, or for the broader public. Sub-elites are made up not only of individuals but also institutions, particularly economic ones.

The third level is the general public, which has minimal knowledge of the world at large and no direct impact on external policy but which is still relevant to government decisionmaking. The leadership keeps an eye on mass opinion, through polling and other means, because it worries about political stability and because it knows that both elites and sub-elites may seek to mobilize the public to support their policy preferences.

The three analytic categories of cosmopolitanism, self-strengthening, and nativism are expressed in different ways at different times at the three different levels outlined above. Self-strengtheners are most prevalent in the foreign policy establishment, which dominates the elite level, but they are challenged by some elements of the government that are more willing to integrate with international regimes and by "old left" Maoists. The populist level ranges from nativists, who applaud anti-Western polemics, to cosmopolitans who find meaning in global pop culture; the midstream finds the more Chinese-style entertainment of capitalist Hong Kong and Taiwan more appealing. Over the past fifteen years, nativist modes of thought have increased at all levels. Among the intellectuals of the sub-elite, cosmopolitanism is in decline, replaced by competing intellectual traditions, most with nationalistic content.[82]

Public Opinion and the Policy Process

How does public opinion affect the conduct of Chinese foreign policy? Specifically, how do nationalistic sentiments affect controversial issues like Taiwan, which conflate concerns about ethnic solidarity and treason, the historical stain of national division, and contemporary U.S. containment of China?[83]

The most sophisticated recent case study of the politics of foreign policy is David Finklestein's analysis of the "peace and development" debate of 1999, which occurred in the aftermath of the accidental NATO bombing of the Chinese embassy in Belgrade. The bombing, in which three people died, magnified the themes of victimization and American containment to a peak of intensity, and righteous indignation and moral grievance combined to fuel the most serious demonstrations in China since Tiananmen.[84]

At the outset of the crisis, Jiang Zemin and his colleagues reacted on two levels. On one hand, they did not try right away to suppress the uproar that the incident had provoked; instead they permitted somewhat violent demonstrations at the U.S. embassy in Beijing and did not restrict discussion on call-in shows, thus allowing the public to vent its anger for a while.

On the other hand, they fostered a debate on foreign and security policy among intellectuals (Fewsmith's and Rosen's sub-elite), perhaps the first in the history of the PRC. Both university professors and analysts at government think tanks participated, offering their views at public and closed-door conferences and to the mass media. There was something of a synergistic interaction between the media and intellectuals. Government analysts offered their views to the media and fed media coverage of issues, and the coverage enhanced their prestige. Generally, that was an unusual opportunity, for the normal constraints on free thought had been purposefully relaxed.

The "official debate" on peace and development—the one that occurred among government intellectuals as opposed to academics and the public—unfolded over time. The opening came when Jiang Zemin gave a speech in which he offered some of his own views on the crisis and posed some questions about the world situation. The foreign affairs office of the Central Committee then asked analysts to address what Jiang had said, offering their views on whether "peace and development" was still the major global trend, as Deng Xiaoping had declared in the 1980s; whether the United States was becoming more interventionist; and whether China's security environment had deteriorated.[85]

Discussion on these issues among members of the leadership and government intellectuals occurred from May to August 1999. There were, of course, those who took the hitherto orthodox viewpoint, arguing that Kosovo did not represent a significant change in the geopolitical equation, the intentions of the United States, or China's security. They argued that for a relatively weak China to confront the United States would be too dangerous. Others had a darker interpretation. They asserted that the United States was "bent on maintaining its global hegemony by military means," including through intervention in the civil wars of sovereign states. Kosovo was only the latest in a series of U.S. interventions that indicated a new trend and also raised the possibility of American intervention in Taiwan, the South China Sea, the Korean peninsula, and even Tibet, Xinjiang, and Inner Mongolia. Hence China's security was in greater jeopardy. People in this camp argued that China should thus take the lead in organizing a coalition against U.S. hegemonism.[86]

In the middle of the official debate, beginning in late July, the media began asking government analysts and academics to express their views on the Kosovo conflict; again, that energized the broader public's engagement. Then in August, the leadership met for its annual retreat at Beidaihe, where it arrived at a new consensus that emphasized continuity ("peace and development" was still the dominant trend) but which bowed toward the more negative view in admitting that "hegemonism and power politics" was on the rise. Thereafter, government intellectuals no longer offered opinions in the public media, and academics did so only until the end of the year. Jiang Zemin had managed the politics of foreign policy by permitting the controlled expression of conflicting views, some of them implicitly critical of his leadership.[87]

A dynamic similar to the response to the Belgrade bombing can be seen in some Taiwan episodes. In the case of Lee Teng-hui's visit to the United States, Jiang came under some pressure from within and without the immediate leadership circle and sparked a firestorm of nationalistic attacks on Lee and the United States. This was, for example, the period when the nativist tract *China Can Say No* (to foreign attempts to dictate to China) was published. Moreover, elements of the party and the government criticized the Ministry of Foreign Affairs for its weakness regarding U.S.-China relations. Under that pressure, "those with more moderate views on Sino-U.S. relations found it difficult to express their opinions." Jiang had to bide his time before fighting back.[88]

Lee's "special state-to-state" announcement happened to come in the summer of 1999, in the midst of the debate about the Belgrade bombing. There was again an outburst of nationalistic fervor that overlay the stronger reaction to the bombing and lasted for about a month. When the leadership met at Beidaihe for its summer conclave, Taiwan was discussed at length, and the critics said their piece. Jiang likely reminded them that relations were on the mend after the damage caused by Belgrade and that China lacked the ability to respond militarily to Lee's remarks. Ultimately, however, the meeting "agreed on a nuanced but only slightly less militant approach to the Taiwan issue. Qian announced . . . essentially a reiteration of existing policy." And Jiang secured a symbolic victory at his September meeting with President Clinton at the Asia Pacific Economic Cooperation forum, when Clinton acknowledged that Lee's remarks had created trouble.[89]

Jiang's handling of these incidents is consistent with the results of scholarly analysis of the CCP leadership's handling of nationalistic political forces. Suisheng Zhao concludes that its pragmatic approach treats nationalism in an instrumental, reactive, and state-centered way: "Being instrumental and state-led, nationalism may be used to flex China's muscles in international affairs if it is deemed desirable by Chinese leaders to enhance their political power. But being reactive to international currents, nationalist sentiments may decrease if perceived external pressure diminishes and if China's confidence in international affairs increases."[90] Yongnian Zheng reports a mainstream consensus that China needs to avoid both conflict and isolation in the international environment, resist the temptation to overturn the existing order, and use its access to the global system to build China's power. "Therefore, if China wants to be a great power, nationalism must be contained. . . . Nationalism and rational choices are not necessarily contradictory to each other. . . . The aim of China's nationalism is to pursue national power and wealth through domestic development. As long as the leadership pursues its 'interest,' its nationalistic 'passion' can be constrained and remain rational."[91] Fewsmith and Rosen argue, however, that the leadership's ability to manage nationalistic politics declines when it is divided; when U.S.-China relations are tense; and when the mobilization of general opinion is high. Thus 1995–96 was a period where high elite conflict joined with bilateral tensions to unleash popular nationalism. 1997-98 was a more relaxed phase all round. Then in 1999, U.S.-China tensions, greatly exacerbated by the bombing of the Chinese embassy in Belgrade, stoked nationalist fires in China and divided the leadership.[92]

Conclusion

In sum, politics in both Taiwan and the PRC complicate cross-Strait relations, but in different ways. In the authoritarian PRC, competition and debate among the leadership is the political factor that is most important in shaping cross-Strait politics. Even in China, however, public opinion matters. A coalition of leadership opponents of central policy and like-minded intellectuals can constrain flexibility in developing cross-Strait policy; a burst of nationalistic opinion—fueled by a sense of victimization and fears of treason—can constrain it even more. The Chinese leadership may be ambivalent and cautious in manipulating nationalism, yet it is one of several forces that make it difficult for China to formulate a Taiwan policy that might elicit a positive response from the island's people. The idea, which the regime itself has promoted, that Lee Teng-hui and Chen Shui-bian are somehow traitors to the Chinese race makes it hard to contemplate other explanations for their resistance to unification, such as uncertainty over how the Taiwan government would fit in the Chinese state. A leadership transition that temporarily left Jiang Zemin as head of the Central Military Commission and many of his associates on the politburo standing committee has slowed the emergence of new policy ideas, if any exist. Some Western observers have suggested that when it comes to Taiwan, the transition from Deng Xiaoping has not ended and that the current leadership is pursuing a "dead man's policy." Historical baggage, a new nationalism, and contemporary politics all constrain the creativity in developing cross-Strait policy that is so badly needed.

On Taiwan, the history of KMT repression fostered in Taiwan's people an intense fear of outsiders and of traitors in their midst, plus a separate Taiwanese national identity that has increased in relative salience over time. The electoral system for filling legislative seats further encourages some politicians to stake out radical positions. Yet Taiwanese identity, fear of outsiders, and democracy do not spell an inevitable drive for full independence. Over the course of the 1990s, Taiwanese nationalists became increasingly pragmatic and began to see the political value of moderation, as Chen Shui-bian's 2000 electoral strategy made clear. But historical consciousness and the dynamics of the political system do impose limits on how far the leaders and the public might be willing to go in reaching a modus vivendi with the PRC. Chen must ensure that he has the support of his base, as his tactics in 2003 and 2004 suggest. The pan-Blue camp, had it come to power, would have faced a real challenge in reassuring those who fear a sell-out to China. After all, if Taiwan's leaders—Blue or Green—ever enter into negotiations with Beijing, they will be bargaining over the ultimate future of 23 million people. However, more than half of those people vote. Complicating matters even further is the Taiwan political system's tendency to gridlock and paralysis in the absence of broad consensus.

Politics therefore reinforces a status quo that is defined by political deadlock and national insecurity. True, cross-Strait economic relations are mutually beneficial. But if there is to be an improvement in this mix of effects, coping with political dynamics will have to be part of the approach.

7

Decisionmaking Systems

The decisionmaking systems in place in both China and Taiwan contribute to their reciprocal security dilemma. Decisionmaking on each side is quite centralized, especially in times of crisis, and each is prone to misread the other's intentions and then to overreact. Misperceptions and miscalculations therefore reinforce the security dilemma.

China

To even offer the hypothesis that the PRC's decisionmaking system is somehow dysfunctional may be somewhat surprising because Western students of Chinese foreign policy are in general agreement that Beijing is more or less a rational actor. This consensus, as summarized by Iain Johnston, is that "China has been relatively successful . . . in using limited amounts of force, in coordination with diplomatic tools, to pursue clearly defined, limited political aims." As one analysis of the 1995–96 crisis concluded, "from China's perspective, coercive diplomacy did not hurt the prospects of unification, but it did reduce the momentum toward independence." China had skillfully applied force to alter the intentions of its adversaries and so protect its own political objectives.[1]

However, there are several problems with the conventional wisdom. The first is the historical record itself. Johnston, for example, found that during the cold war "China was more dispute-prone than most other major powers except for the United States." When China resorted to violence, it tended to do so at higher levels than did the other major powers and India. Chen Jian and Shu Guang Zhang drew on materials released since the death of

Mao that reveal crisis decisionmaking that was erratic and prone to miscalculation, thus belying the conventional picture of a cold war China that was deliberate and controlled in its threats and use of force. The other problem is more conceptual, focusing on the role of misperceptions in China's shaping of its security policy. An actor that misunderstands the intentions of its adversary is more prone to bad decisions.[2]

Decisionmaking Structure and Process

The PRC decisionmaking structure for Taiwan policy in the late 1990s, as described by Michael Swaine, included the following elements:[3]

—The paramount leader, who retains ultimate decisionmaking power.

—A small, informal nuclear circle of senior leaders who supplement the paramount leader in his role.

—The Politburo Standing Committee (PBSC), one member of which takes charge of Taiwan policy.

—The Politburo, which often deliberates important external policy decisions but tends more to build consensus for and confer legitimacy on the decisions of the paramount leader and the PBSC.

—The Taiwan Affairs Leaders' Small Group (TALSG), which supervises policy implementation and coordination. The TALSG is the forum in which decisionmakers interact with senior officials from the implementing organs in the party, government, and military systems. It has no permanent staff.

—The ministerial-level Taiwan Affairs Office (TAO) of the Central Committee of the Communist Party and the State Council. The TAO serves as a general office for the TALSG, preparing agendas for its meetings, coordinating paper flows and interaction among relevant agencies, submitting analysis and policy recommendations to TALSG members, and supervising the work of the Taiwan affairs offices at the provincial and lower levels. (The general office of the Central Committee plays a policy coordination function similar to that of the TAO, reviewing and distributing policy reports to senior leaders and drafting speeches.)

—The Ministry of Foreign Affairs and the Ministry of State Security, under the State Council, and the General Staff Department, under the Central Military Commission, are responsible for Taiwan issues in their area of competence. In addition, the party's United Front Work Department has responsibility for developing party-to-party and people-to-people contacts between the two sides of the Strait.

—The Association for Relations across the Taiwan Strait (ARATS), under the jurisdiction of the TAO, is a semiofficial body created in 1991 to conduct political contacts and address routine functional problems with Taiwan through its Taiwan counterpart, the Straits Exchange Foundation.

Connected in one way or another with most of these agencies are a variety of information collection and analysis organizations. The TAO has a research bureau that collects information, conducts policy research, and makes policy proposals. Its sources include the Taiwan media, intelligence information, and first-hand contacts. The Ministry of Foreign Affairs has a Taiwan affairs office that produces analytic reports for senior officials based on reporting from PRC embassies and Xinhua news agency offices. The Second Directorate of the General Staff Department of the People's Liberation Army collects intelligence relevant to the PLA's mission, while a variety of institutes produce analysis for the military. The Ministry of State Security directs the work not only of the China Institute for Contemporary International Relations, which provides analysis on the external dimension of the Taiwan Strait issue, but also of the Taiwan Studies Institute of the Chinese Academy of Social Sciences.

In addition to these Beijing organizations, Wang Daohan, Jiang Zemin's mentor, set up several research organizations in Shanghai to provide an alternative stream of analysis. These include the Institute of International Studies of the Shanghai municipal government, the Taiwan Research Institute of the Shanghai Academy of Social Sciences, the Shanghai Municipal Taiwan Research Institute, and the Shanghai Institute of International Strategic Studies. In addition, Xiamen University has its Institute for Taiwan Studies.

The TALSG was reconstituted in the first half of 2003, after a Communist Party turnover in state and party positions in late 2002 and 2003. Hu Jintao became the TALSG head, and Jia Qinglin, chairman of the Chinese People's Political Consultative Conference (a united front body), became deputy head, but there was some early confusion about the other members. A Hong Kong communist media outlet in December 2003 reported that the other members were Tang Jiaxuan, a state councilor and former foreign minister; Wang Gang, director of the CCP Central Committee's general office; Liu Yandong, head of the CCP's United Front Work Department; Wang Daohan, head of ARATS; Chen Yunlin, head of the TAO; Xu Yongyue, minister of state security; and Xiong Guangkai, deputy chief of staff for intelligence. An earlier report by a Taiwan newspaper omitted Wang Gang but included Guo Boxiong, vice chairman of the Central Military Commission. If a person of Guo's seniority represented the PLA on the TALSG, it would indicate the growing influence of the military on Taiwan policy.[4]

Also unclear for a while was the precise role of Jiang Zemin. He had been paramount leader with respect to Taiwan policy until the leadership transition, and for good reason. He held the top positions in the party, state, and military hierarchies. He understood that the Taiwan Strait issue was the third rail of Chinese communist politics, and because he would get the blame if there were a policy failure, he could not afford to delegate it to someone else. He also had the conceit to believe that he could make progress where others had failed and so gain the credit for completing the mission of national unification. In the 2002–03 leadership transition, Jiang gave up all of his positions but one, the chairmanship of the Central Military Commission. That and the PLA's stake in the issue of defending China's territorial integrity and national sovereignty would give him a basis for intervening on Taiwan if he chose to do so.

Under political pressure, Jiang resigned from his CMC position in September 2004, a change that will certainly reduce his role in decisionmaking but not necessarily eliminate it. His status as a former party general secretary and state president—plus a personal tendency to vanity—would lead him to expect to be consulted on Taiwan policy, an expectation that the cautious Hu Jintao can be expected to satisfy. Because during his time in office Jiang showed no inclination to deviate from the fundamentals of Deng's one-country, two-systems formula, he may constrain any temptations that Hu might have to explore more creative approaches. However, there is no evidence so far that Hu has been tempted by any such alternatives.

Swaine concludes that during routine periods the policy process on Taiwan has become "highly regularized, bureaucratic, and consensus oriented." As the issue has become more complex and its salience for senior leaders increased, so too has the number of actors and their responsibilities. Decisionmaking is characterized by "extensive horizontal and vertical consultation, deliberation, and coordination." Units in each institutional hierarchy send analysis and proposals to the leadership bodies—the TALSG, the CMC executive committee, and the top echelon of the State Council—which then are processed for consideration by the senior leadership of the general office of the Central Committee. "At the uppermost level of the policy-making process differing party, government, and military views are resolved or muted through a process of informal deliberation among the senior leadership."[5]

Yet even so Swaine's information indicates a policymaking process that remains fairly centralized. Jiang Zemin dominated Taiwan policy. The consensus norms of the PBSC constrained him somewhat, but it was not an absolute constraint. Line agencies provide information, make recommendations, and carry out instructions but appear to have no role in the making of decisions. This is consistent with the making of Chinese foreign policy as a whole, regarding which Ning Lu concludes: "The most important characteristics . . . are that it is highly centralized and that in terms of key decisions it is very much personalized."[6] And Swaine suggests that in a crisis, centralization will become even more pronounced. The Politburo Standing Committee tends to intervene without waiting for the TALSG to develop coordinated policy recommendations. Senior military leaders and the CMC will participate in decisionmaking that has a military dimension.[7]

Misperceptions

Centralization can foster misperceptions about an adversary's intentions, as can political orthodoxy that excludes certain lines of analysis. Both are at work in how Beijing leaders view Taiwan.

HISTORY. One clue to Chinese leaders' thinking about Taiwan—and an important example of misperceptions at work—is Su Ge's *Meiguo duihua zhengce yu Taiwan wenti* (*The China Policy of the United States and the Taiwan Question*), published in 1998.[8] This was a major event in the history of PRC scholarship, for Su, one of China's true experts on the United States, sought to conduct an objective, nonideological, scholarly study on one of the most sensitive political issues in China. He drew extensively from previously classified U.S. documents—but not, unfortunately, from Chinese government archives. This was probably the fairest treatment of the subject that a politically constrained PRC scholar could present. Moreover, Su received high-level endorsement of his work. The book won a presidential citation from Jiang Zemin, who, according to a copy of a newspaper article inserted into the book, "personally recommended that the book be read by all Chinese officials."

Su's book therefore provides a good window on how the Chinese leadership, to say nothing of lower-level officials, thinks about the history of the Taiwan Strait issue. Su's conclusions about the history of the U.S. role in the Taiwan question are probably their conclusions, and to the extent that Su ignores competing interpretations, his readers are unlikely to know that they exist. To be sure, a reader who tested Su's assessments against the evidence that he provided for them might come to different conclusions. Given the high-level endorsement, however, it is safe to assume that Su's readers accept his judgments at face value.

Those judgments present a story that is at significant variance with those that an American official or scholar might reach. Su overstates the desire of the United States to deny the island to China in 1949–50 and the scope of Washington's "two-China" policy, and whereas the thrust of American scholarship describes U.S. foreign policy during the cold war as a response to the initiatives of China and its allies, Su places the blame on the United States. For him, the North Korean invasion in June 1950, which "caused a delay in the timetable for China's unification for an unlimited period," was merely the pretext that Washington used to neutralize the Taiwan Strait rather than an understandable attempt to block the conflict on the Korean peninsula from spreading to Taiwan. The Eisenhower administration, Su claims, moved ahead with the U.S.-ROC defense treaty because of pro-Taiwan pressure from within and the need to get Nationalist support for a UN resolution to freeze the status quo in the Taiwan Strait, not because of the PRC's effort to change that status quo by shelling the offshore islands in September 1954. The shelling in 1958 was for him another result of the U.S. effort to create two Chinas rather than of Mao's effort to get Washington and Taipei to sacrifice the islands. Of course, Su is honest enough to provide sufficient evidence for the careful reader to infer China's true role. Yet this failure to assign at least some responsibility explicitly to China for causing crises reflects Beijing's tendency to assign blame to the United States and others in general.[9]

Again, the purpose here is not to refute Su's study, which, read as a whole and considering the constraints under which he worked, is a remarkable piece of scholarship. It is to suggest that what a Chinese reader would regard as the key points (the executive summary, so to speak) would convey a rather skewed view of the U.S. role in the Taiwan Strait issue. Chinese officials today persist in their belief that the United States blocked unification in 1950 when in fact the responsibility should be laid at North Korea's door— and at Mao's for approving the attack on South Korea. Zeng Qinghong, one of Jiang Zemin's key subordinates and now number five on the Politburo Standing Committee, offered this version of history during vetting prior to his 2002 elevation to that body. "The United States bears a big responsibility for the fact that the Taiwan issue is still unresolved. As you know, the United States sheltered the Taiwan authorities continuously for over twenty years after ordering the seventh fleet into the Taiwan Strait. For many years it has never stopped selling advanced arms to Taiwan, . . . which in fact helps the 'Taiwan independence' forces."[10]

LEE TENG-HUI AND CHEN SHUI-BIAN. Chapter 3 details how Beijing misunderstood the position of Taiwan's leaders on unification and concluded from their statements and actions that their goal is to permanently separate Taiwan from China and to rule out unification. To be sure, Lee and Chen said and did things that Beijing found offensive. Yet in his authoritative policy statements, Lee Teng-hui did not oppose unification in principle but took a firm and consistent stand on the terms and conditions that would define Taiwan's status in a unification agreement. Although Chen led a traditionally pro-independence party, his formal statements clearly preserve the option of certain kinds of unification. For both, however, the one-country, two-systems approach simply was not an acceptable basis for discussion. For Beijing, on the other hand, it was the only basis. China's interpretation of Chen's and Lee's statements is a function of its politically orthodox point of departure, from which it derived the conclusion that Lee and Chen were separatists. A less narrow approach to the question of national unions would yield a very different conclusion. A different approach to how Taiwan might be part of China would produce a more positive answer on the part of Taiwan to the question of whether it should be a part of China.

Moreover, Beijing tended to ignore the impact of its own actions on Lee's and Chen's behavior. Its failure to engage Lee Teng-hui in the early 1990s and Chen Shui-bian in 2000, when they were open to engagement, on anything approaching their terms only created a sense of frustration on their part, which in turn led them to adopt more inflexible positions. China sometimes does conclude after the fact that its own policies have made matters worse (acknowledging, for example, that the March 1996 missile exercises contributed to Lee Teng-hui's election victory that month), but it has never fundamentally revised policy based on those conclusions. In addition, it appears that Beijing's assessment of the formal positions that Lee and Chen took during their presidencies was shaped by prior judgment of their intentions, which were sometimes based on extraneous factors. The evidence here is not extensive, but it is interesting nevertheless. With respect to Lee Teng-hui, it is useful to consider when it was that Beijing decided that he was a separatist. The 2000 white paper concluded that "since the early 1990s" Lee had "gradually deviated from the One-China Principle."[11] That judgment is consistent with the argument in chapter 3 that Lee hardened his position from around 1993 in response to politics within Taiwan and to the continuing rigidity of the PRC.

Yet there seems to have been a competing judgment about his alleged separatist intentions that formed at the very beginning of his presidency, in 1988. According to that view, Lee was a separatist all along. Illuminating in this regard is the memoir of Xu Jiatun, who was the PRC's representative in

Hong Kong in the late 1980s but escaped to the United States in April 1990 because his views on the Tiananmen incident were at odds with Deng Xiaoping's. Xu reports that as early as 1989, he sent an assessment to Beijing that a shift in the balance of power was occurring in Taiwan from mainlanders to Taiwanese. The projected milestones would be Lee's reelection as president in 1990 and the emergence of ethnic Taiwanese majorities in both the National Assembly and the Legislative Yuan following the elections of 1991 and 1992. For Xu, Lee's separatism was not as extreme as that of the more radical factions of the DPP, but it was still separatism, and the trend would only grow. He concluded that "the probability of peaceful unification would decline and the chance of a military solution would grow." And according to him, Beijing shared that view.[12]

What is most interesting about Xu's assessment of Lee Teng-hui as a separatist was that he based it on Lee's ethnicity, not on his views. That is, Lee must have been in favor of some degree of independence simply because he was Taiwanese. Contributing to a negative Chinese judgment at this time were warnings about Lee that "disgruntled and defeated" mainlanders on Taiwan conveyed to the PRC leadership no later than late 1990. Those individuals would have enjoyed some credibility simply because they were mainlanders and supposedly as opposed to separatism as Beijing was. Lee heard about the warnings and in December of 1990 had his secret emissary urge his PRC interlocutors to ignore them. At least at that meeting, the PRC representative said it regarded Lee as an acceptable negotiating partner.[13]

It is difficult to sort out the relative weights of competing Chinese views of Lee Teng-hui. The early assessment that he was a separatist, as reported by Xu Jiatun, was made when the institutions for decisionmaking on Taiwan were still developing and may have been superseded by other more nuanced ones as those institutions matured, at least temporarily. On balance it may be that Lee's approach in the early 1990s was reassuring. On the other hand, it is also plausible that the negative judgment of the late 1980s colored the PRC's reaction to his later policy proposals, however positive. If so, it would regard with suspicion any claims by Lee that he favored unification and discount his substantive objections to the one-country, two-systems proposal.

When did the PRC decide that Chen Shui-bian was similarly beyond the pale? That is harder to judge, for lack of evidence. What is clear from public sources is that Beijing has consistently regarded Taiwan independence to be the goal of the Democratic Progressive Party, in part because of the independence clause in its platform. In his report to the CCP's Fifteenth Party Congress, in a coded reference to the DPP, Jiang said, "Except for a handful of people who stubbornly cling to the position of independence of Taiwan, all parties and personages of all circles in Taiwan are welcome to exchange views with us on relations between the two sides and on peaceful reunification."[14] And once Chen became the party's presidential candidate, it linked him to that objective in spite of his effort to moderate the DPP position and move toward the center.

For example, when in November 1997 DPP candidates won more magistrate and mayor positions than expected, Beijing expressed a willingness to consult with people in the party, on the condition that the talks occur under the one-China principle. But it also said that if the DPP persisted in 'Taiwan independence,' there would be no consultations.[15] During the campaign for the 2000 presidential election, a Hong Kong communist paper editorialized that Chen was an advocate of Taiwan independence just like Lee Teng-hui. It noted his efforts to project a less confrontational position to win votes and to "fade out the color of his 'Taiwan independence' stance and dispel the worries of the voters on his 'Taiwan independence' project."[16] Once Chen won the contest, various PRC media reiterated that separation was his goal as well as that of his party. The director of the Taiwan Studies Institute of the Chinese Academy of Social Sciences made this categorical judgment soon after the election: "Chen Shui-bian's mounting the stage and the DPP's becoming the ruling party will cause the development of future cross-Strait relations to enter an extremely uncertain situation. . . . The DPP's 'independence' charter and Chen Shui-bian's 'Taiwan independence' idea conflicts fundamentally with the mainland's basic policy for handling the Taiwan question."[17] Some observers may have held out the hope that he was opportunistic enough to pursue some kind of agreement, but the view of his core beliefs was negative—and skewed. When in August 2002 Chen stated that there was "one country on each side," even the optimistic minority adopted the mainstream position. In the view of PRC commentators, Chen had reneged on the pledges of restraint he had made in his inaugural address and revealed his true intentions: "This shows that Chen Shui-bian has gone back on his own words and cannot keep his promise and reflects his incorrigible nature as a 'Taiwan independence' advocate, . . . turning from a recessive 'Taiwan independence' advocate into a dominant 'Taiwan independence' advocate."[18]

Such misperceptions are particularly pernicious because they are very difficult to correct once they receive official imprimatur. Su Ge's "executive summary" reflects a historical orthodoxy within which all analysis must be done. Once senior leaders judge that Lee Teng-hui and Chen Shui-bian are separatists, offering an alternative view or policy is difficult at best. Even when Taiwan leaders project a flexibility that Beijing perceives as incompatible with its basic judgment, a response in kind is unlikely.

TAIWAN POLITICS. PRC leaders and analysts also have skewed views of Taiwan's political dynamics. Zeng Qinghong, Jiang Zemin's principal protégé, offered this view of Chen Shui-bian: "He has power but no idea of how to use it; he is not a skillful politician. The Taiwanese support him for the time being only out of a certain emotionality, but emotion has to be sustained for a long time [to have any impact]. . . . The Taiwan people's emotions toward him cannot be sustained for long."[19] The 2004 elections proved Zeng wrong: Chen showed, in the context of Taiwan's democratic system, that he was a skillful politician and that he could sustain "the emotions" of the electorate.

The PRC's Taiwan analysts are quite thorough and on target when it comes to the main actors in the political system and trends that can be accurately measured by open-source quantitative data. Yet there are gaps on intangible issues, where judgments must be based on a good feel for the dynamics of Taiwan politics, such as the sources of Taiwan identity, the personalities of Taiwan leaders, and dynamics of electoral politics. On these, China's Taiwan analysts suffer from conceptual blind spots and a lack of reliable information. And they are severely constrained when it comes to Beijing's own policies and actions as a causal factor in Taiwan outcomes.

One example is Chinese analysis of Taiwan's identity. As described in chapter 6, the consensus of Western and Taiwan scholarship is that it was KMT authoritarian rule that fostered the belief among Taiwanese that they had a unique identity and that mainlanders were outsiders. This subtle and well-developed picture of Taiwan identity as invented, complicated, and malleable contrasts sharply with the limited and fairly primitive picture seen in the PRC. Chinese scholars devote very little attention to the Western and Taiwan view of identity as an explanatory variable and are in error when they do. One example is a discussion by Hu Lingwei, a younger scholar at the Shanghai Institute of East Asian Studies.

In a July 2003 article on political instability in Taiwan, he correctly notes the importance of "national identity." As he put it, "During the [current] transitional process of Taiwan society, the Taiwan public has slipped into a crisis of national identity because there is no way to create a national identity that is clear and consistent." For Hu, the story of the last fifty years is one of moving from clarity to ambiguity, to the point of confused complexity.[20]

Yet the details of that process that Hu offers only reinforce mainland stereotypes of Taiwan politics. The point of departure was a strong Chinese identity within the Taiwan populace. "Aside from the penetration of alien culture during the Japanese period, Taiwan society historically was grounded in Chinese culture—in the Ming and Qing dynasties *and* during the rule of the two Chiangs." The Taiwanese identification with the "ROC" was strengthened during the early decades of KMT rule, Hu says, because of the policy focus on retaking the mainland and propaganda supporting that goal. The mainland was demonized in the process.

There was something of a shift during Chiang Ching-kuo's time, as he brought Taiwanese into the KMT, fostered economic prosperity, and allowed more political participation. And Jiang legitimized the idea of being both Chinese and Taiwanese. This was the time that, Hu claims, the consensus on national identity within the Taiwan public was the strongest. And reinforcing this sense was Taiwan's superior position vis-à-vis the PRC—economically, culturally, and diplomatically. During this period, the Taiwan public "highly identified with the 'ROC' and through the form of the ROC, recognized they were Chinese and believed that although Taiwan was small, it could still represent China."

In Hu's view, it was China's growing power and international stature under the post-1978 policy of reform and opening up that caused a loss of confidence on Taiwan and a crisis of identity. "The idea on Taiwan that one China was the ROC [and the object of identity] was exposed as completely weak." Under these circumstances, politicians [Lee Teng-hui] could manipulate a historical sense of "victimization" and encourage a search for "self-identification." The population was then used by "Taiwan independence forces" to create a base in public opinion for their project.

Hu's correlation between the relative growth of the PRC's power and the growing ambiguity and crisis of identity on Taiwan is probably true of mainlanders on the island, since they had the strongest association with the Republic of China. Yet it misreads the mindset of most Taiwanese. For them, harsh KMT rule fashioned the belief that they were a separate people. The growth of the PRC's power created not a crisis of confidence but an opportunity to challenge the KMT's self-serving rationale for repression. It is true that political leaders promoted a Taiwan identity once democratization occurred, but they were by and large responding to sentiments that already existed. Moreover, this sort of analysis ignores the phenomenon of dual identity. And negative PRC actions—such as the missile tests of March 1996 and opposition to Taiwan observership in the WHO—have themselves strengthened Taiwanese identity—something that neither Hu nor any other PRC scholar can acknowledge publicly.[21]

THE 1995–96 STRAIT CRISIS. Moving from perceptions to how specific decisions are made, even Swaine's excellent study does not provide much detail. The best research available is his and other scholars' examination of the Taiwan Strait crisis of 1995–96.[22] The consensus of those accounts is as follows:

—The PRC leadership believed that Lee's actions to expand Taiwan's international space reflected his intent to ensure Taiwan's independence.

—It regarded Lee's activities and U.S. complicity in them as a threat to China's vital interests.

—It chose to employ coercive diplomacy to demonstrate China's serious resolve, to compel Taiwan and the United States to reverse course, and to deter other countries from following the U.S. lead.

—It concluded after the crisis that the benefits of the action had outweighed the liabilities.[23]

In evaluating the quality of Chinese decisionmaking during this episode, there are several questions that must be addressed. First of all, was this simply a case of a PRC reaction to a Lee Teng-hui action? That is the conventional wisdom, and it is a staple of PRC foreign policy rhetoric that others always bear the responsibility for creating problems. Yet efforts by Lee to expand Taiwan's international space by traveling and seeking membership in the United Nations can be read as his reaction to Beijing's rejection of his view that Taiwan deserved an international role. Moreover, it was consistent with his view that the ROC, as a sovereign state, deserved to participate in the international system. That Lee would make that kind of overt response is consistent with his political style, and in his mind it was probably a way to enhance his leverage vis-à-vis the PRC.

Second, did Beijing accurately perceive Lee Teng-hui's intentions when it concluded that he was pursuing an independent Taiwan? By and large, the scholars cited here tend to accept the PRC's assessment.[24] Only one, Edward Friedman, arrives at a conclusion similar to the analysis in chapter 3. He asserts that Beijing badly misperceived what Lee was up to. "Beijing dismisses the rhetoric of Taiwan President Lee Teng-hui as a thinly veiled language of splittism. . . . President Lee's language holds the promise of a democratic and confederationist China, which is the region's best hope for prolonged peace and prosperity. . . . It is dangerous when Beijing's chauvinists experience President Lee's discourse on democracy, peace, and prosperity through broad engagement as a threat to Chinese strength and unity, a threat which must be met by Chinese military force."[25]

Third, did the PRC accurately judge U.S. intentions? It appears that Beijing believed what it wanted to believe: that Washington would not allow Lee Teng-hui to visit the United States. But Warren Christopher clearly tried in late April 1995 to signal Vice Premier Qian Qichen that Congress might well take the decision out of the administration's hands. The mixed signals may have continued, but China can be faulted for not taking the warnings seriously. It is also worth noting that if Lee was not pursuing a secessionist agenda, then the United States could not have been supporting such an agenda either, as Beijing claimed. Indeed, the Clinton administration was the victim of domestic political pressure to treat Lee well, pressure that Lee himself had stimulated.[26] A more controversial question concerns the PLA's summer 1995 exercises, which it conducted to show China's displeasure and resolve concerning Lee's trip. Did Beijing interpret a relatively mild U.S. rhetorical response as an invitation to act more aggressively later on? On this question, for which there will be no answer until PRC archives are opened (if ever), there is obvious disagreement. It does seem, however, that the dispatch of the two carrier groups in March 1996 caught Beijing by surprise.

Fourth, was coercive diplomacy the appropriate way to deal with the challenge that Lee represented? Again, if the definition of the problem and the assessment of the affected interests were flawed, then the action taken could well be flawed too. In a way, PRC leaders were attacking symptoms of the problem and not addressing the cause of the problem itself. Their response to Lee Teng-hui's high-profile travel (and U.S. cooperation) succeeded in discouraging subsequent trips. But if the underlying problem was a rather fundamental difference of opinion on *how* Taiwan might be a part of China, then perhaps coercive diplomacy only exacerbated the problem.

Fifth, did Beijing misread the results of the December 1995 Legislative Yuan elections? American scholars conclude that the decline in KMT seats and the increase in New Party seats confirmed Beijing's view that coercive diplomacy was effective. That may have been Beijing's view, and it may have encouraged a similar effort before the March presidential election. But it also demonstrates a PRC tendency to overinterpret Taiwan politics. As discussed in chapter 6, Taiwan legislative elections are contests of personalities and symbols, not struggles over policy lines. Smaller parties have an easy time carving out a niche of the political spectrum. That the New Party, splintered from the KMT, increased its share of seats was to be expected. Voters' views on cross-Strait relations and Lee Teng-hui's policies no doubt were one reason that the New Party did relatively well, but it was not the only reason.

Its anticorruption stance and the dynamics of the electoral system itself were probably more important.

Sixth, how should the balance of costs and benefits be assessed? Chinese spokesmen admit that coercion had its costs. Beijing has been more cautious in later elections about taking even low-level military steps because it has gradually realized that its actions in 1996 (and statements in 2000) were counterproductive, in that they probably strengthened political positions that they opposed. On the other hand, Robert Ross reports that the conclusion of the leadership was that the benefits outweighed the costs.[27] Yet if one looks again at the two sides of the ledger above and does so more objectively, it is difficult to avoid the conclusion that China's course of action was a failure. That Beijing sees it as a relative success should itself be a cause for concern.

To be sure, the PRC succeeded in reminding all involved that the Taiwan issue was important, but Taiwan, Japan, the United States, and others knew that. It is true that Lee Teng-hui sought no more high-profile overseas trips and that the United States and Japan were unlikely to grant them anyway. Perhaps some had doubted Beijing's willingness to use or threaten the use of force, and their doubts were negated. Perhaps the PRC missile exercises, by causing a drop in the Taiwan stock market and in the value of the new Taiwan dollar, demonstrated the vulnerability of Taiwan's economy and civilian psyche. Yet those were mere tactical achievements; the setbacks, on the other hand, were strategic in scope. Lee Teng-hui did better in the election than expected prior to the missile tests, and for Beijing to claim that the tests were successful because the DPP did worse is disingenuous in the extreme, since it regarded Lee as the leader of the independence forces. The alienation of Taiwan's populace at Beijing's attempted intimidation seriously undermined its political goal of promoting reunification. The United States did not change its fundamental approach to the Taiwan Strait issue in China's favor and felt compelled to reinforce its own credibility by sending carriers. Lee Teng-hui refused to accept Beijing's one-China principle as a condition for resuming dialogue. And other actors in East Asia, Japan, and the United States in particular had to conclude that under certain circumstances China's need to constrain Taiwan might outweigh its commitment to peaceful reunification.

Centralization and Misperception

But the argument here is not just that the PRC misperceives the intentions of Taiwan leaders and the dynamics of the island's politics. All states, Taiwan included, misread the actions of their adversaries to some extent. It is also that centralized decisionmaking leads to bad decisions. And the best examples here are Beijing's immediate responses to the bombing of the PRC's embassy in Belgrade in May 1999 and the April 2001 EP-3 incident involving a U.S. reconnaissance aircraft and a PLA naval air force fighter.[28]

BELGRADE. The attack on the embassy, which caused the death of three people, occurred before midnight local time on the evening of May 7, when it was almost 7:00 a.m. in Beijing on Saturday, May 8. It may be speculated that the Foreign Ministry received only fragmentary information at first because of damage to the embassy's communications system but that early on, Jiang Zemin, Qian Qichen, and other senior decisionmakers were contacted. Perhaps the Foreign Affairs Leading Small Group (FALSG) was assembled on Saturday. Or perhaps there was a decision early on to short-circuit the decisionmaking process and convene a meeting of the Politburo Standing Committee, rather than wait for the FALSG. If so, it was probably an enlarged meeting that brought in others who had either institutional or substantive reasons for attending, particularly military and intelligence officers.

By noon on May 8, however, the leadership had already formulated an initial response to the attack, in the form of a government statement that condemned it as a violation of Chinese sovereignty and international law. But the key issue was whether the United States had intended to target the Chinese embassy because it was the Chinese embassy. On Saturday (U.S. time) President Clinton offered his view that the attack was a "tragic mistake" and "tragic accident." He also expressed his regrets and condolences to the leaders and people of China. (It would take the U.S. government several days to realize that NATO had intended to bomb that particular building, in the belief that it was a Serbian government structure.)[29]

The issue of intentionality was important because of the policy implications. If China reserved judgment until more information became available, then it might have greater flexibility in resolving the conflict. If it decided quickly that the attack was intentional, then it would be locked into a tougher course of action. The available open-source information indicates that the leadership decided early on that the attack was intentional.

The first sign of that conclusion came on Sunday, in editorials issued by *People's Daily* (*Renmin Ribao*) and the Xinhua news agency, whose timing indicates that the leadership had either made up its mind on intentionality in its meetings during the day on Saturday (in China) or during the night as the articles were being readied for publication. The *People's Daily* article charged that "NATO's subsequent chicanery, which claims that it did 'not intentionally target the Chinese embassy,' cannot cover up the bloody fact.

The fact that three missiles blasted the embassy from different angles completely exposed the aggressors' evil intentions." Two Xinhua articles the same day assumed an intentional attack.[30] In Xinhua articles on Monday, May 10, which must have been prepared over the weekend, missile experts from the China Aerospace Industry Corporation offered technical evidence to reject DOD's initial explanation of collateral damage and to assert that the attack was "absolutely premeditated no matter how it is analyzed."[31]

Also on Sunday, the leadership decided what the United States would have to do to correct the situation. For on Monday afternoon, Beijing time, Foreign Minister Tang Jiaxuan asked that the "U.S.-led NATO" take four steps: make an "open and official" apology; carry out a "complete and thorough" investigation of the attack; promptly publicize the details of the investigation; and severely punish those responsible. The Foreign Ministry also announced that it was "postponing" bilateral dialogue with the United States on human rights and proliferation of weapons of mass destruction and suspending exchanges between the two military establishments.[32]

Authoritative press commentary on Monday reiterated the prior points and also introduced the four demands (indicating that the decision on the demands came on Sunday). Hyperbole and morale outrage became the order of the day.

Open-source material permits several inferences about how the policy process operated in the critical forty-eight hours after the Belgrade bombing. The leadership rushed to judgment on the threshold question: whether the bombing was intentional. That verdict was rendered, it appears, on the evening of Saturday, May 8, at the latest, just as President Clinton was making his first statement and long before the U.S. government itself had a chance to figure out definitively what had happened. Based on the judgment that the attack was deliberately aimed at China, Beijing then made demands on the United States. There was no way of knowing in advance whether one of the demands, that those responsible for the attack be severely punished, could be met. In the case of the bombing, excessive demands were not really dangerous, for this was a *political* dispute, not a military one. If Jiang found it harder to resolve the crisis because he had created expectations that were unachievable, that would be a problem between him and his domestic critics. But in a crisis that was more military than political, this tendency to rush to judgment could aggravate the difficulties of effective crisis management.[33]

THE EP-3 INCIDENT. On the morning of Sunday, April 1, 2001, a U.S. reconnaissance plane was flying along the South China coast in international air space near Hainan Island. Two PLA navy F-8 jets flew up to intercept it and monitor its movements, and consistent with a recent pattern, one of the Chinese pilots brought his plane dangerously close to the EP-3. Too close, in fact. The Chinese plane collided with the U.S. plane at around 9:15 a.m. The F-8 broke up in flight, and the pilot bailed out but did not survive. The pilot of the EP-3 barely regained control but was able to fly it to Lingshui airfield on Hainan. He tried to notify the tower that he was in distress and sought permission to make an emergency landing. There was no reply, and the pilot landed anyway. The U.S. crew was taken into custody, and a tense stand-off between the United States and the PRC ensued. This crisis was different from the embassy bombing in one important respect. In the bombing, there was no doubt as to what happened: NATO planes had bombed the PRC's diplomatic mission. The issue was to determine why the attack had occurred (was it intentional?) and what to do about it. In the EP-3 case, the facts were not as clear, and each side scrambled to find out what had happened. As of late morning local time, the U.S. embassy in Beijing knew of the intercept, the collision, and the emergency landing but not how the collision had occurred. In part because of concern over the status of the twenty-four-person crew of the EP-3, American diplomats sought to contact their counterparts in the Chinese government. For the rest of the day, their phone calls produced either no response at all or no useful information. That lack of responsiveness did not affect the ultimate outcome of the incident, but it did aggravate the concern and feelings of mistrust on the American side. While it was still daylight, Beijing time, the U.S. Pacific Command in Hawaii issued a press release stating the basic facts of the incident. While it did not assign blame for the "contact," it did state U.S. expectations regarding the treatment of the crew.[34]

The Ministry of Foreign Affairs and the Ministry of National Defense were likely reluctant to return phone calls because they were having a difficult time getting information from PLA naval air force units on Hainan. In the end, someone in the communications chain apparently chose to accept the information received without subjecting it to the appropriate scrutiny, for by the evening of April 1, the leadership had decided what had happened and how the United States should respond. At around 9:30 p.m., Beijing time, a Chinese official, Assistant Foreign Minister Zhou Wenzhong, finally met with Ambassador Joseph Prueher. He presented the Chinese government's view of the incident, which was identical to a Ministry of Foreign Affairs statement that would be released about 10:30 p.m., while the meeting was taking place.[35] Zhou told Prueher that the EP-3 and the F-8 had been flying on parallel courses approximately 400 feet apart. The EP-3, Zhou charged, banked sharply to the left and hit the F-8. The United States was to blame and should take full responsibility for the incident.

Prueher was a retired naval aviator, and he noted a fundamental problem with the Chinese version of events, one that Chinese officials either did not realize or understood but failed to mention. That was that if the EP-3 had banked hard left and traveled a distance of 400 meters, the faster-moving F-8 would have flown more than 400 meters forward, thus making a collision impossible. But even if Assistant Minister Zhou now appreciated the problem, it was too late to stop the public statement being released simultaneously, too late to stop the media attack on "American perfidy," and too late to back out of an embarrassing position. Diplomats on both sides were ultimately able to resolve the matter so that the crew was released several days later and the plane returned (in pieces) later still. But the Chinese government's quick and faulty decisions made that process harder and left more ill will on both sides than was objectively necessary.

The danger, therefore, is that senior individuals responsible for making foreign policy will, based on their own faulty perception of other actors' intentions, "highjack" the policy response. Because those leaders are senior, they are unlikely to be challenged by their subordinates, whose understanding is more nuanced than theirs but who feel obliged to defer to them. Bonnie Glaser and Phillip Saunders observed that specialists in civilian foreign policy research institutes are reluctant during a period of crisis or leadership conflict "to put controversial analysis forward in a nationalistic policy environment."[36] It is true that as a result of the 1995–96 crisis and the 1999 and 2001 episodes, the PRC has sought to remedy the defects in its decisionmaking process concerning Taiwan. For example, the agencies responsible for interpreting developments on the island are probably more accurate in their analysis of events and their significance. The temptation to overreact has been resisted. Beijing showed greater restraint as the campaign for the March 2004 Taiwan presidential election unfolded.[37] Yet the tendency for top-down analysis continues, as does the likelihood of misperception. Moreover, the "regularized, bureaucratic, and consensus-oriented" policy process that Swaine describes prevails during routine periods. Periods of crisis, in which senior leaders whose view of Taiwan is not especially sophisticated take over the conduct of policy, are another matter. Robert Suettinger's judgment on how the new Chinese leadership would cope in a future crisis is telling: "At some point, . . . Hu [Jintao] and Wen [Jiabao] may find themselves in a situation in which they need reliable information, short time-frame decisions, and sound judgment on a foreign policy issue. It is fair to wonder whether the decision-making system currently in place in China—opaque, non-communicative, distrustful, rigidly bureaucratic, inclined to deliver what they think the leaders want to hear, strategically dogmatic, yet susceptible to political manipulation for personal gain—will be up to the task of giving good advice."[38]

Taiwan

Curiously, outsiders know less about Taiwan's decisionmaking process for external policy than they do about China's, in spite of the fact that Taiwan's is by now a far more open political system. What is known is that Taiwan's system has more actors than the PRC system, because the legislature and the media are active; that its various agencies are similarly "stove-piped," lacking sufficient horizontal coordination; and that its organization is fairly disjointed, in that different elements do not form a coherent whole. At the top levels, Taiwan's system is as personalized as the PRC system, if not more so. Senior officials' access to the president and the extent of their power have been a function of their personal relationship with him. The key elements within Taiwan's executive branch, again as outlined by Michael Swaine, are the following:[39]

—The president of the ROC, who constitutionally is the commander-in-chief of the armed forces, has ultimate power over defense, foreign, and mainland policy and has line authority over key senior civilian and military officials. Within the Office of the President (OOP) are advisers who support the president, particularly the deputy secretary general for external relations.

—The premier (the president of the Executive Yuan), nominates and has line authority over the ministerial-level agencies, including the Ministry of Foreign Affairs, the Ministry of National Defense, and the Mainland Affairs Council. The premier supervises a rather ad hoc policy formulation process within the Executive Yuan. The premier is also a member of the National Security Council.

—The National Security Council, an advisory body to the president, is responsible for setting national security policy and planning security strategy over a wide range of issues. It may be expanding, but in the past it has had a small staff that, while it has exercised some supervision over other national security agencies, has had no decisionmaking power or responsibility for interagency coordination. Chaired by the president, its membership includes two vice chairmen (the vice president and premier), plus the ministers of foreign affairs, national defense, and economic affairs; the secretaries-general of the NSC and the OOP; and the director of the National Security Bureau (Taiwan's lead intelligence agency).

—The Ministry of Foreign Affairs, the Ministry of National Defense, and the Mainland Affairs Council. The latter deserves special mention. It is responsible for research, planning, review, and coordination of mainland policy plus implementation of cross-Strait programs in which multiple agencies are involved.

—The General Staff Headquarters (GSH) of the Taiwan armed forces, under the leadership of the chief of the general staff. Previously, the GSH was the key policymaking body concerning military matters, under the direct authority of the president (the Ministry of National Defense was more of an administrative body). Legislation passed in 2001 sought to streamline the hierarchy, placing the minister of national defense between the president and the GSH and its chief.

—The National Security Bureau, which is the principal agency for collecting and analyzing external intelligence.

Swaine emphasizes that the power of various high-level positions is a function not so much of their authority as vested in law but of the personal relationships between the incumbents and the president. If, for example, the chairman of the Mainland Affairs Council is a close confidante of the president, that person and the MAC itself will have more influence in the policymaking process, even though it has the status of a ministry.

The policy process that results from this structure is "concentrated in the hands of a few senior civilian and military leaders, and [is] strongly influenced at times by the views and personality of the president." There is poor interagency coordination at both higher and lower levels. Under Lee Teng-hui, the formal process was fragmentary, and he tended to supplant it with ad hoc, separate, private meetings with individual subordinates and advisers. He did not always trust the advice of foreign policy professionals and enjoyed mulling policy ideas with scholars outside of the formal system. Chen Shui-bian toyed with adopting a more consultative process, but the temptation to make decisions without consulting the relevant agencies persisted.[40] Like Beijing, Taipei is capable of misperceptions. An account of U.S.-Taiwan relations during the presidency of Lee Teng-hui, for which Lee provided information, reveals a pattern of reading the worst into Washington's actions.[41]

A good case study of the Taiwan policy formulation in action is the process that culminated in Lee Teng-hui's statement in July 1999 that cross-

Strait relations was a "special state-to-state relationship." As the end of his presidency approached, he worried more and more about Taiwan's existence and the integrity of the state (*guojia zhutixing*). He was increasingly frustrated by Taiwan's treatment in the global community, which he felt was manifestly unfair, and he feared that the island's international identity would soon be lost. At some point, he sought the views of specialists on international law on whether the ROC was a state and was chagrined to learn that they believed that it was not.[42] He charged Yin Zongwen, then director of the National Security Bureau, with finding foreign legal specialists who could prove that Taiwan was not a part of the PRC. Yin recommended instead that experts be recruited in Taiwan to prepare the full background and then ask foreign scholars how much they could help Taiwan. One of Lee's aides proceeded to recruit Tsai Ying-wen, a lawyer who was not a government official, to lead the effort; a small group to "strengthen the position of the ROC's sovereignty" was then inaugurated in August 1998. Tsai in turn enlisted a number of young legal scholars to conduct research. Serving as advisers to the small group were two staff members from the National Security Council, Chang Jung-feng and Peter Chen Bi-chao, and Lin Bih-jaw, deputy secretary-general of the Office of the President and an international relations scholar. The responsible government agencies did not participate in this effort and were unaware of it, as was the United States government.[43]

Another reason for Lee's effort was to prepare for cross-Strait political talks. Taipei knew that it could not avoid discussing political issues and that they would come up when Wang Daohan visited Taiwan on a visit scheduled for the fall. But the PRC's one-China principle and its one-country, two-systems model put Taiwan at a disadvantage. Consequently, it "must first of all secure an equal status during negotiations . . . [and] break the framework set up by the Chinese communist authorities." Taiwan had previously used the ambiguous term "political entity" to assert in an elliptical manner, without complicating cross-Strait exchanges, that its governing authority possessed sovereignty. But, as a senior official of the National Security Council asserted several days after Lee's statement, "the Chinese Communist authorities have repeatedly ignored our goodwill. Instead, [they] have utilized this kind of ambiguous term to suppress us internationally. *Therefore, the president has to make it clear in our statement* [emphasis added]."[44]

In February 1999 the group gave its initial briefing to Yin Tsung-wen, who had just become secretary-general of the National Security Council, and in May sent him a "research report." Thereafter the report was sent to Lee. In its introductory section, it defined cross-Strait relations as special state-to-state relations and based that assertion on the revisions to the constitution that had occurred since 1991. It was this section of the report that Lee used in his interview with the German news organization Deutsche Welle. The report also suggested that the constitution and Taiwan's laws be amended through a staged process to make them consistent with the new formulation on Taiwan's status. It also recommended revision and ultimate abolition of the National Unification Guidelines. The group urged avoiding a number of formulations that had been part of Taiwan's lexicon: "one China"; "One China is the ROC"; "one China under divided rule" (*yige fenzhi de Zhongguo*); "one country, two governments"; "one China, each with its own interpretation" (*yige Zhongguo gezi biaoshu* or *yizhong gebiao*); and "Taiwan is part of China, and the mainland is a part of China." Moreover, it stated, the ROC did not possess sovereignty over the mainland and the PRC's sovereignty did not extend to Taiwan.[45]

Lee reviewed the document in detail and decided to implement it over a defined period of time. In late May Lee reviewed the work of the small group with Vice President Lien Chan, including the possibility of constitutional amendments, and somewhat to Lee's surprise, Lien offered his support. Soon after, Tsai sent Lee a memorandum on amending the constitution that recommended that the amendments be pursued in the current session of the National Assembly. Lee approved the memo. Within a few weeks, Tsai and Chang Jung-feng briefed Su Chi, chairman of the Mainland Affairs Council, on the new initiative and Lin Bih-jaw brought Foreign Minister Jason Hu into the loop.[46]

At that point, obviously, some of the appropriate officials were aware of the initiative. Plans were made to have an interagency discussion in mid-July. There was no sense that announcement of the formulation was imminent. Lee apparently had thought about timing and judged that it was inappropriate to act either during the UN General Assembly, which began in September, or during the campaign for the March 2000 presidential election. Then Lee received a report that, about the time of the PRC's national day, Beijing would announce the visit to Taiwan of Wang Daohan, the head of ARATS, and that it would use the occasion to stress that the cross-Strait relationship was an internal manner in which it, the central government, would treat Taiwan as a local government. Lee thus decided that he needed to preempt Beijing's statement and do so quickly. He apparently told few people of his decision.[47]

Early July and an upcoming interview by Deutsche Welle provided what Lee regarded as an ideal opportunity to present his views (particularly because Germany had been divided into two states for four decades before it was reunified). The Government Information Office (GIO) sent him the questions that Deutsche Welle would pose during the interview and some draft answers. To a question that referred to Taiwan as a renegade province, the GIO draft response read, "The Republic of China is a state with independent sovereignty and not a renegade province as the Chinese Communists say." If Lee had reiterated this standard formulation, there would have been no crisis. (As discussed in chapter 6, because words are so important in this issue, any change in a verbal formula is taken very seriously, and a new formula may be read as a radical change.) But he rejected the GIO draft because it was too weak. "If even I don't speak clearly [on this issue] how can we expect foreigners to not be confused? And how can we expect international society to speak in accordance with justice and focus on Taiwan's difficult situation?" Lee retrieved the research report of the small group, which had been laying idle for two months, and decided to draw on it in answering the "renegade province" question. On the morning of July 8, he reportedly said, "When I raise this, I'll be criticized. If so, let them criticize." Then on July 9, Huang K'un-hui, secretary-general of the Office of the President, learned of the new formulation and notified Lin Bih-jaw and Chang Jung-feng. The two advisers of the small group felt that this was the wrong time for Lee to make such as statement; a better occasion would be after the adjournment of the National Assembly and while Wang Daohan was in Taiwan. But Lee insisted on going forward.[48]

Chen Shui-bian has displayed a similar tendency to restrict participation in decisionmaking and exclude those officials who, by virtue of their positions, should have the opportunity to comment on the consequences of different choices for the mission of their agencies. In the spring of 2004, as the presidential campaign was coming to an end, a panel of Taiwan national security experts recommended that "the president should regularly convene formal meetings of the National Security Council in order to consolidate and coordinate policy directions between various Cabinet agencies and important principal officers," suggesting that such contact and coordination was not occurring.[49] And during Chen's reelection campaign, he made four controversial announcements that had an impact on Taiwan's national security and foreign policy:

—the August 3, 2002, proclamation that there was "one country on each side" and his call for referendum legislation

—the May 20, 2003, declaration that there should be a referendum on Taiwan's participation in the World Health Organization

—the September 28, 2003, call for making a new constitution and approving it through a referendum

—his November 29, 2003, decision to hold "defensive referenda" (see below).

Press reporting on those episodes indicates a clear pattern in Chen's decisionmaking style. The August 3, 2002, statement was made by video transmission to a meeting of overseas Taiwanese supporters, who tend to be more radical in their support of Taiwan independence and on whom the DPP relies for campaign contributions. Chen therefore had an incentive to tailor his message to his audience. But it also reflected Chen's frustration at Beijing's treatment of him, most recently its success in getting the South Pacific country of Nauru to switch diplomatic relations to the PRC just as Chen was becoming chairman of the DPP. It was consistent with a tougher policy toward China that Chen had discussed with his national security advisers and with Lee Teng-hui as early as late June and approved in mid-July. Yet the "one country on each side" statement was not in the prepared text of his August 3 address. Chen's own National Security Council aides were taken aback. One admitted to the *Taipei Times* that the formula was not expected. "The influence of those words," he said, "is obviously too intense and the government and the whole national security system need to reevaluate the possible side effects." Another noted that given the prevailing uncertainties about the leadership transition in China, "it does not do Taiwan any good to make waves in the cross-strait situation right now. . . . The president may perhaps be trying to break the impasse . . . but an even more important priority is to ask 'what is the goal of opening up the impasse?'" An official in the Office of the President also revealed that the statements had "damaged the mutual trust" between Taiwan and the United States and led Washington "to cast doubts on President Chen's personality and leadership."[50]

The WHO referendum announcement was one of a series of steps that Chen took in the spring of 2003 that the media interpreted as unexpected encroachment on the power of the Executive Yuan and the premier. The referendum announcement was termed a "surprising move." Again, it raised concern in the United States because of its "political sensitivity."[51]

Chen announced the new constitution/referendum plan at a celebration of the twentieth anniversary of the DPP. It was similar to a proposal that Lee Teng-hui had made a few weeks before, and it was a long-standing goal of the fundamentalist wing of the party. The process proposed could be interpreted as the creation of a new state and so a fundamental challenge to the PRC, and certainly Beijing interpreted it that way. And yet reportedly, Chiou I-jen, the secretary-general of the Office of the President, and Lee Ying-yuan, a high-level party official and former diplomat in the United States, became aware of the proposal only one day before the announcement. The announcement was of serious concern to Washington, and it happened that Foreign Minister Eugene Chien was visiting the United States at the time. I attended a luncheon in Chien's honor on that day, hours after Chen's speech, and Chien was clearly caught off guard.[52]

Chen's November 2003 announcement of a "defensive referendum" came after the Legislative Yuan, which was controlled by the pan-Blue camp, severely restricted the president's authority to call referenda, keeping most of the power to itself. The only exception concerned national security, if Taiwan was subject to an external threat that could interfere with its national sovereignty. Having been bested by the opposition on the legislation, Chen chose to exercise the only authority that was available to him by calling for "defensive referenda," citing Beijing's buildup of ballistic missiles targeting Taiwan. But although sovereignty and China were involved, reportedly the primary stimulus for his initiative was unhappiness among fundamentalists in the DPP, for whom a referendum with a broader, more provocative scope was a high priority. He acted "largely because of the enormous pressure from our traditional supporters, who were very discontented with the DPP's withdrawal of a clause in the law which would have allowed for votes to change the country's name, flag and territory," said one Chen aide. An important issue here was timing. Chen had planned to call for the defensive referendum in mid-December, but under fundamentalist pressure, he decided to advance the announcement by two weeks. Consequently, it happened to come before the rumored visit to Taiwan of a high-level U.S. official and the visit to Washington of Chinese Premier Wen Jiabao.[53]

Lee's "state-to-state" episode and Chen's four initiatives display a policy process in which Taiwan's president sometimes formulates policy ideas through channels that are separate from regular government agencies; those agencies do not get adequate opportunity to scrutinize those ideas; and the president makes decisions on his own. It confirms a picture of a structure that is institutionally weak and that lacks adequate coordination, in which misperception of other actors' intentions is fairly common. It is not a system that is likely to generate sound responses to the political and military threat that Taiwan faces, and indeed it aggravates Taiwan's sense of insecurity.

Moreover, failure to consult in advance with the United States on decisions that bear on its role as the guarantor of Taiwan's security only increases Washington's fear that it may be drawn into conflicts that either are unnecessary or undermine U.S. interests. That only aggravates Taiwan's situation.

8

The Leverage Game

In May 2001, scientists in Taiwan announced the results of research on the genetic origins of the island's *Minnan* (southern Fujian) majority. This is the part of the population known as Taiwanese, as opposed to mainlanders, Hakkas, and aborigines. The researchers found that they were in fact descended from the Yueh people, who were scattered along the southeastern coast of China during the later Zhou dynasty (770–221 B.C.). The political implication: Taiwanese were not ethnically Chinese. Not to be outdone, PRC researchers announced in December 2001 that four aboriginal groups in Taiwan exhibited a specific chromosomal pattern characteristic of the Li ethnic group on Hainan Island and that all five groups were descended from the Baiyue people of eastern China. The Baiyue were said to have migrated to both Hainan and Taiwan, where they maintained the same lifestyle and customs. The Chinese message: even Taiwan's aborigines had a connection with the mainland.[1]

These dueling conclusions illustrate one small episode in the constant battle by each side of the Strait to gain political advantage over the other. Each sees this struggle, in which even prehistory is fair game, as a zero-sum contest, in which the gains of one are the losses of the other. The rivalry only deepens their mutual mistrust. Like domestic politics on both sides of the Strait, it exacerbates the difficulties of untying the knots posed by the sovereignty and security issues. If there is to be mutual engagement on the substantive issues, the poisonous effects of the leverage game—as it is played out in the international community, in Taiwan itself, and in cross-Strait relations—cannot be ignored.

The International System

After the fall of the mainland to the Chinese communists in 1949 and the beginning of the Korean War, the ROC maintained diplomatic relations with a majority of countries and retained China's seat in the United Nations and other international organizations. But once decolonization began in earnest in the late 1950s, most new states established diplomatic relations with Beijing. The ROC's response was both rigid and short-sighted. Chiang Kai-shek maintained that the ROC was the legitimate government and the Beijing regime was composed of traitors; therefore no coexistence or compromise between the two was possible (in Chinese, *hanzei buliangli*). He believed that allowing the PRC into the United Nations on an equal basis or other countries to have diplomatic relations with both Taipei and Beijing was morally wrong; it also was a big blow both to his own legitimacy and his rationale for denying political freedom to the people of Taiwan. The United States tried to convince him that the only way to preserve the ROC's international position was to be pragmatic, but Chiang preferred, Canute-like, to stand on principle.[2] As a result the ROC left the United Nations in October 1971, right before it was about to be expelled.

Today, the ROC maintains diplomatic relations with about twenty-six countries and the Holy See. Its diplomatic partners are the Central American countries, plus a few in the Caribbean and Africa. From time to time, Beijing tries to cut into those numbers while Taipei tries to pick off smaller nations that have diplomatic relations with Beijing. The main incentive that each offers to third countries is foreign assistance, and they long ago created a bidding war between themselves. Moreover, every time Taipei loses a diplomatic partner, it sets off a mini-crisis in Taipei. For example, the tiny Pacific nation of Nauru announced that it was transferring recognition from the ROC to the PRC in July 2002. The transfer occurred right before Chen Shui-bian was to take the position of chairman of the Democratic Progressive Party, and he took it as a personal insult. If Beijing ever uses its growing budgetary resources to mount major defections, it would likely create a loss of confidence in Taiwan. While Taipei regards recognition by as few as twenty-plus countries as evidence that the ROC is a sovereign state, what would recognition by only ten countries imply?

As noted in the previous chapter, the DPP in the early 1990s began pushing the KMT government to try to reenter international organizations, an endeavor that was both popular and consistent with Taipei's demand that it be allowed to have an international role as a precondition for unification. So

Lee Teng-hui co-opted the opposition's issue. The first target was the United Nations. In 1993, Taipei officially began to lobby for reconsideration of its representation. Then in 1997, doctors in Taiwan, who are strong supporters of the DPP, advocated an effort to make Taiwan an observer within the World Health Organization. Again, the KMT government agreed.

In each case, Beijing, which was not going to give up easily the gains it achieved over decades of struggle, successfully opposed the initiatives. The PRC government has claimed a monopoly on membership in state-based international organizations, labeling Taipei's effort to break that monopoly as splittism, and its presence in these organizations and its leverage over many of their important members gives it a great advantage in fending off Taipei's campaigns. Yet Taiwan has refused to abandon its efforts, and the UN and WHO campaigns, which have taken on a rather ritualistic character, continue. They do offer a certain utility for each side. For the PRC foreign ministry, blocking Taipei's efforts is a way of proving patriotism. For Taipei, striving for membership satisfies a public demand and puts Beijing on the spot. And Taiwan can hold on to the hope that it will make progress over time, just as the PRC did decades before.

Taiwan has a greater advantage when it comes to joining organizations for which statehood is not an absolute prerequisite for membership *and* in which the PRC is not a member. Thus Beijing and Taipei simultaneously joined the forum for Asia-Pacific Economic Cooperation in 1991, the World Semiconductor Council in 1999, and the World Trade Organization in 2001. Even these outcomes required behind-the-scenes activity by the United States to prevent membership being restricted to states and to control the PRC's terms of entry in order to afford access for Taipei simultaneously and on reasonable terms. Moreover, there were intense negotiations over terminology and status, which the two sides take very seriously. For example, Taiwan entered the WTO under the name of the "separate customs territory of Taiwan, Penghu, Jinmen, and Mazu," but Beijing moved unsuccessfully to add the words "of China" or "of the People's Republic of China" and thus downgrade Taiwan's status to the level of Hong Kong and Macau. Similarly, Taipei was able to secure the title of permanent mission for its lead official at WTO headquarters in Geneva. Beijing tried and failed in 2003 to get that designation changed to "economic and trade office," the same as that for Hong Kong and Macau. Taiwan's accession to the Government Procurement Agreement has also been held up because of wrangling over terminology; Beijing tries to limit intimations of sovereignty and Taiwan tries to create them. For example, Taiwan was encouraged to contribute to the new Global Fund—a partnership of governments, civil society, the private sector, and affected communities created by the G-8 nations and the UN General Assembly to combat HIV/AIDS, tuberculosis, and malaria. Although it was willing do so, in the amount of $1 million, it was temporarily frustrated by how the funds should be channeled. The U.S. government apparently preferred that the contribution go through a private organization, but Taiwan insisted that it be made under the name Taiwan. The Bush administration ultimately relented.[3]

Since China and Taiwan have joined these organizations, there has been a struggle over how Taiwan should participate and what kind of contact the two sides should have with each other. Taipei seeks to elevate its participation and encourage contact with the PRC in order to reinforce its position that it is a state with equal status; Beijing seeks to restrict participation and contact to minimize any such suggestion. A small example concerns the Office International des Epizooties, an intergovernmental organization that focuses on animal health. In early 2004, the PRC, which entered as a member long after Taiwan, sought to have Taiwan's name changed from "Taipei China" to "the separate quarantine area of Taiwan, Penghu, Kinmen and Matsu." Similarly, Beijing has consistently opposed attendance by Taiwan's president—or any other Taiwan official with a political position—at the leaders' meeting held in conjunction with the annual APEC ministers' meeting. And it has been able to use the consensus norms of APEC and its political leverage to limit Taiwan's participation to that of an entity whose status is clearly economic. In 2001, the conflict over Taipei's representative to the leaders' meeting resulted in Taipei's sending no one. However, the PRC cannot block attendance by Taiwan's minister of economic affairs at the ministerial meeting. Nor can it really refuse a meeting between that official and its own minister, but it refuses to discuss bilateral issues and restricts the agenda to APEC matters. Finally, Taiwan had hoped that the WTO would provide a channel for interaction to substitute for the suspended dialogue between the Straits Exchange Foundation (SEF) and the Association of Relations across the Taiwan Strait (ARATS). But Beijing rejected discussing bilateral issues, such as the three links, under the WTO rubric. It even tried to avoid dealing with the Taiwan representative to the WTO on trade disputes, preferring to communicate its concerns to the business association involved. But ultimately it accepted that its membership obligations required it to communicate directly on those narrow issues.[4]

Once in the WTO, Taiwan began aggressively exploring the establishment of free trade areas with friendly countries, which, as a member of the WTO, it had the right to do. But PRC trade minister Shi Guangsheng warned that "countries which have established diplomatic ties with China must observe the one-China principle while developing economic and trade relations with Taiwan." If they did not, they would find themselves in "political trouble."[5]

It is not only in large governmental organizations that pressure is exerted. Whenever China seeks to join international organizations of which Taiwan is already a member, such as the World Veterinarian Association or the Lions Club, it insists that the name used by Taiwan be changed to something that China finds acceptable.[6]

The leverage game is also played in East Asia. By virtue of its political influence with the countries of Southeast Asia, China was able to exclude Taiwan from the meetings of the ASEAN Regional Forum, the principal multilateral security organization in the region. And as the countries of the region have explored free-trade arrangements on either a bilateral or regional basis, Beijing has used its economic clout to exclude Taiwan from them. For example, it is unlikely that Taiwan will be able to join the projected free-trade area among China and the countries of ASEAN. Whereas Taiwan's exclusion from regional security meetings is by and large a symbolic setback, isolation from multilateral tariff-cutting agreements can put it at a serious competitive disadvantage.

This thrust and counter-thrust might have only modest relevance to cross-Strait relations if it were not related to core issues and did not affect the political climate in Taiwan regarding the PRC. Yet Taiwan's role in the international community goes to the heart of the disagreement over whether it is a sovereign government. Although Taiwan's struggle to get back into the United Nations or become an observer at the WHO may seem like a fool's errand and although it has an obvious political motivation—responding to domestic constituencies and raising the salience of China in Taiwan politics—it is consistent with a long-held position. In addition, Beijing's diplomatic quarantine has the counterproductive effect of alienating the very constituency that it should be trying to cultivate: Taiwan's people. Beijing may take delight in playing hardball with Taipei and believe that intimidation will work in the long term, but its tactics more likely betray a fundamental misreading of the Taiwan psychology.[7]

The United Front

Soon after the election of Chen Shui-bian, Chinese vice premier Qian Qichen told a conference of officials from various agencies who worked on some aspect of the Taiwan issue that "we should increase contacts with all the political parties and all the figures from various circles in Taiwan who support the one-China principle, who oppose 'Taiwan independence,' and who advocate enhancing cross-strait ties. Compatriots on both sides of the strait and all those who support China's reunification should be united, and make joint efforts to strive to develop cross-strait ties and to advance the process of peacefully reunifying the motherland." Two months later Qian told an audience at the Foreign Affairs College that "as long as Chen Shui-bian refuses to accept the 'one China' principle, we will continue to exercise pressure on him. At the same time we will act even more actively to win the support of the world media and the people in Taiwan." Qian was advocating another way of exerting Chinese leverage on the Taiwan government, the united front strategy, which it has also pursued in Hong Kong to protect its interests under the one-country, two-systems formula. His pronouncements only heightened the mistrust of those people on Taiwan who believe that Beijing is undertaking such a strategy.[8]

Hong Kong Revisited

Beijing has not relied on formal institutions alone to secure its position in Hong Kong (see chapter 4); it also has pursued an aggressive strategy of building up bases of power within Hong Kong society that would help it better preserve stability, control, and political dominance. A "united front from below" has helped bias the results of a semidemocratic competition for power in its favor.

The PRC had long worked to build underground political influence in Hong Kong. Its original base was the workers who were members of communist unions, and the Chinese Communist Party had a clandestine branch in the colony that directed the activities of those and other supporters. Communist papers disseminated Beijing's views for those who were curious. As reversion became a real possibility, Beijing acted to broaden its social base in the territory by adapting the approach that the CCP had used when took over major Chinese cities at the end of the civil war: systematically co-opting the leading businessmen into a united front that would share power with the executive branch of the Hong Kong government and deny it to anyone else. The Tiananmen Square incident and the British effort in 1992–93 to democratize the political system, which exceeded the degree of democracy that the PRC could tolerate, only increased the appeal of this strategy. "Patriotic" corporate figures dominated the Hong Kong delegation on the Basic Law drafting committee, and China's original candidate for the first Hong Kong chief executive—Anson Chan, chief secretary of the civil service—was set aside in favor of a businessman after she supported the British reforms. [9]

Hong Kong's business elite had reasons to be drawn into a mutually supportive relationship with Beijing. They had a fundamental interest in the preservation of stability and prosperity in Hong Kong and feared, rightly or wrongly, that a democratic system would lead ultimately to higher government expenditures for social welfare, thus undercutting economic growth. More important, they wanted to continue to benefit from the burgeoning Chinese economy. Since the late 1970s, manufacturing companies had moved their production facilities to South China in order to cope with rising labor costs in Hong Kong and take advantage of low costs on the mainland. Low-end services like product testing had followed in the 1990s, and large-scale investment projects beckoned for those with access and resources. Many Hong Kong businessmen therefore made a pragmatic bargain with the new sovereign: they would support China politically in Hong Kong (which was in their interest anyway) in order to secure economic opportunities on the mainland. Beijing drew on this pool of willing partners to fill out the political bodies in Hong Kong and the PRC (such as the Hong Kong Special Autonomous Region election committee) and to stand for office in various legislative constituencies.[10]

Business was important in another way: reshaping the tone of the mass media. The media, of course, are a crucial institution in a democratic system, one that can work as an efficient check on government abuse of power. And despite laws that permitted press restrictions, Hong Kong media were free under the British, and by and large they remained so after reversion. During late 2002 and early 2003, for example, newspapers, radio, and television were a principal source of criticism of the national security legislation proposed pursuant to Article 23 of the Basic Law. Moreover, any heavy-handed effort to control the media would be met with widespread public opposition. The only exceptions to the general pattern have been the pro-PRC media: *Wenhuibao*, *Dagongbao*, and *Commercial Daily*, which since 1997 have been strong supporters of the SAR government. On the other hand, there is evidence that more subtle means have been employed to limit the independence of the media and their potential as a source of political opposition. Lo Shui-hing concludes that "although the mass media remain critical of government policies and officials, a silent revolution has begun in the media industry where critics of the HKSAR government are increasingly marginalized and balanced. . . . It will be difficult for [it] to shape public opinion in such a way as to make all the Hong Kong people totally uncritical patriots. Yet it is possible to bend public opinion toward the political stance of both the HKSAR government and Beijing."[11]

As part of the united front strategy, Beijing has chosen to contend with the opposition on the battlefield of direct elections. In the Democratic Alliance for a Better Hong Kong (DAB), which was founded in 1992, the PRC is developing a party to compete with the Democratic Party and its allies for the votes of middle- and lower-class citizens of Hong Kong. For example, the DAB is gradually creating a presence in the housing estates that are the homes of lower-class voters, with paid organizers in each district. It seeks to provide services to residents and takes positions on grass-roots management committees, and it runs candidates for office. Much of this is funded by contributions from the pro-PRC business community.[12]

In promoting the DAB, Beijing can rely on allied organizations that have a long-time presence at the grass roots of Hong Kong society. Chief among these are the communist Federation of Trade Unions (FTU), the New Territories Association of Societies (NTAS), and the Kowloon Federation of Associations (KFA). These organizations, which were the core of the PRC's united front effort before the business community assumed its primary position, support "patriotic" candidates in elections and work to mobilize their staff and members during campaigns.[13]

There is little question that the united front strategy is a coordinated effort directed from Beijing and implemented in Hong Kong. The public agent is the PRC's Liaison Office (prior to reversion it was the Hong Kong branch of the New China News Agency). Behind the scenes is the Hong Kong branch of the Chinese Communist Party. The liaison office, concludes Lo Shui-hing, "is playing a crucial role in local politics." It coordinates the nomination and campaigns of friendly candidates in Legislative Council (LegCo) and local elections, often as part of a party list but sometimes as "independents."[14]

Another time-tested feature of the PRC's united front strategy is the practice of stigmatizing the opposition. For Mao and his heirs, the united front always had a specific, instrumental purpose. It "isolates the enemy by winning the vast majority to the side of the revolution; then, through struggle, the isolated and now vulnerable enemy is destroyed." In Hong Kong, the adversary and object of struggle is the Democratic Party and its allies. Beijing is not out to destroy Martin Lee and others like him because the political costs of doing so would be too high, but it does seek to keep them weak and thereby nonthreatening. One way it does so is to foster the impression that they are not legitimate members of the political community, just as it asserted that Taiwan's Lee Teng-hui was a traitor. The test of political correctness is whether one is "patriotic" as Beijing defines it. Supportive members of the business community and of the DAB are patriotic by definition; members of the opposition who constitute too great a challenge are not. Indeed, one of Deng Xiaoping's rationales for limiting the scope of direct elections was that it would give too much power for those who he thought did not love China enough. As he said in April 1987, even before Tiananmen, "We say that Hong Kong's administrators should be people of Hong Kong who love the motherland and Hong Kong, but will a general election necessarily bring out people like that?"[15]

The purpose of this political loyalty test is to signal to the people that they should deny support to opposition politicians. "By declaring them its enemies, Beijing also wishes to weaken their mass base by scaring away would-be supporters and persuading Hongkongers that the parties would not be able to help them with their interests in the mainland." The main way of sending this signal is to deny the opposition access, either to Chinese officials in Hong Kong or to the mainland itself. Another is to take ordinary measures to block opposition members from winning seats that are reserved exclusively for "patriotic" Hong Kong people, such as seats in the National People's Congress. There is some modulation in the degree of stigmatization: opponents of the HKSAR who are moderate in their behavior are treated better than those who are consistently provocative. To be sure, most supporters of the opposition are inured to the denigration of their leaders, but it does create a political hurdle for those at the margin.[16]

The patriotism litmus test reared its ugly head again in early 2004, as pressure built in Hong Kong for constitutional reform to institute universal suffrage and more representative democracy. Beijing gave increasingly strident reminders that only individuals it deemed patriotic could govern Hong Kong and warned that it would intervene if a majority in favor of greater democracy won a majority of the seats in the Legislative Council in the September 2004 elections. This blunt articulation of what the one-country, two-systems approach meant in practice did not go unnoticed in Taiwan.[17]

Cultivating Taiwan's Blue Parties

One target of the PRC's united-front strategy in Taiwan was Chen's strongest opponents, the KMT, the People First Party, and the New Party. Clearly, if those forces remained divided, as they were in the 2000 election, Chen Shui-bian would easily win reelection. If they could unite first to obstruct his initiatives and then compete effectively against him in the 2004 election, then Beijing's nemesis would be removed from power. There were reports, for example, that the PRC had provided funds to friendly politicians on the island, and some individuals connected with the DPP have claimed that Beijing is using the "pro-unification" media, such as *United Daily News* (*Lianhebao*), to project its message to the Taiwan public. The head of the government information office even charged that China was trying to buy up radio stations on the island through a front company in order to broaden its effort. Beijing reportedly has sought to facilitate KMT support and assistance for Taiwan companies on the mainland by asking the KMT to establish a "service center" in China to assist in business exchanges.[18]

That China placed great hopes on the Blue parties can be seen in a commentary in a Hong Kong communist paper about the 2001 Legislative Yuan elections, in which the KMT did worse than expected. The author explicitly criticized the KMT for its shortcomings and advised it on how to revive its fortunes. The first problem was Lee Teng-hui, who had used the party for his own ends and, by implication, had been allowed to get away with it. Second, the KMT was unable to cooperate with others, particularly James Soong, and so had lost public support. Third, the KMT did not take a clear-cut stand on Beijing and unification and so could not win popular support. And fourth, it allowed Lee Teng-hui to brand the KMT as a "foreign regime" and a party of "traitors." To address those problems, the author called for bringing in new blood at the top, such as Ma Ying-jeou, the mayor of Taipei. The author also advised the KMT to focus on planning for the 2004 presidential election, create a new tone for its publicity, and adopt a systematic mainland policy.[19]

Beijing also worked to ensure cooperation among the KMT and the other components of the Blue coalition. Chen Yunlin, director of the Taiwan Affairs Office, stated in January 2001: "We have come into extensive contacts and carried out extensive exchanges with the Kuomintang, the People First Party, the New Party, and other social organizations and well-known public figures who visited the mainland successively; and have reached consensus of opinion to a different degree with the visitors on upholding the one China principle, maintaining the consensus reached by the ARATS and the SEF in 1992, opposing division, and realizing cross-strait 'three links' as soon as possible."[20]

However, it appears not only that Beijing was trying to manipulate the KMT but also that the KMT was seeking Beijing's help. PRC analysts told an American researcher in 2001 that KMT officials visiting the mainland had urged the PRC to not open a dialogue with Chen Shui-bian, which would boost his popularity, and instead wait until the KMT returned to power, at which point it would pursue a cross-Strait policy more to Beijing's liking. According to the analysts, some KMT officials suggested that the PRC try to weaken Chen domestically by attacking him for pursuing independence. The KMT quickly denied the allegations.[21]

Stigmatizing the Green Parties

Consistent with its approach in Hong Kong, Beijing imposes political loyalty tests on various Taiwan organizations. For example, NGOs on the island that wish to have exchange agreements with their mainland counterparts have been required to include adherence to the one-China principle in those accords. More significant, Beijing has stigmatized the DPP and the Taiwan Solidarity Union, which emerged under Lee Teng-hui's leadership in 2001, on the grounds—correct or incorrect—that they are pursuing Taiwan's independence. Jiang Zemin occasionally used the loaded word "patriotic" in referring to political groups in Taiwan.[22] As with Hong Kong, Beijing has manipulated the Green parties' access to China in order to undermine their position in Taiwan politics.

When Chen Shui-bian became Taiwan's president, Beijing's official attitude toward him initially was reserved. It claimed that it would listen to his words and watch his deeds (*ting qi yen, guan qi xing*). Soon, however, it saw an interest in blaming him for all of Taiwan's woes and, by implication, promoting the political fortunes of his opponents. Thus in July 2001, Qian said the following to a delegation of members of the pro-unification New Party (the audience was significant):

> The rejection of the one-China principle by the leader of the Taiwan authorities [Chen] has hampered the improvement of cross-strait relations as well as aggravated Taiwan's political turmoil and economic difficulties and harmed the Taiwan compatriots' interests. If the leader of the Taiwan authorities truly cared for the Taiwan people's personal interests and Taiwan's social stability and economic development, he should show his sincerity for improving cross-strait relations, recognize that the mainland and Taiwan belong to one China, and accept the consensus on upholding the one-China principle reached by the Association for Relations Across the Taiwan Strait and the Strait Exchange Foundation in 1992 to meet Taiwan compatriots' wish for stability, peace, and development.... The "Taiwan independence" splittist forces are trying to create rivalry among the Taiwan people by inciting contradictions among people of different origins. This will only worsen

the political, economic, and social chaos in Taiwan. This is unpopular and not in line with the mainstream feelings in Taiwan. The Taiwan authorities should consider Taiwan's economic development and Taiwan compatriots' interests and allow cross-strait "direct three links" as soon as possible.[23]

Beijing has manipulated access to China to make its point about who should be in power and who should not. It has welcomed delegations from the DPP's various opposition parties and met with them at a high level; its initial position regarding the DPP, however, was that it would have no contact with its members until it renounced the goal of independence, which was still in the party charter. Then on January 24, 2002, Qian Qichen announced an end to the total quarantine of the DPP. He called on the party to discard its Taiwan independence party platform but also said that the PRC was "convinced that the broad masses of DPP members are different from the small number of stubborn 'Taiwan independence' elements. We welcome them to come for sightseeing and visit in an appropriate status and increase their understanding." Drawing a line between most DPP members and the few diehards seemed to open the prospect for more interaction. Almost immediately, however, the gesture turned sour. The Taiwan Affairs Office spokesman included Chen Shui-bian and Annette Lu among the "stubborn elements," although Chen was later moved to an ambiguous category. Moreover, the term "appropriate capacity" was defined to mean that DPP members could come only as scholars or in some other private capacity, not as party members, and "their visits must not contradict the 'one-China' principle." Clearly, the PRC was exercising its right to decide who was an acceptable interlocutor and who was not. As with Hong Kong individuals of questionable "patriotism," Beijing decided at its sole discretion which associates of the DPP would have access to China and Chinese officials.[24]

Although generally cultivating Taiwan's business sector was a key element of the PRC's political strategy, entrepreneurs who supported the DPP got a different treatment. There were reports, not always verified, that those individuals would not be welcome in China. Xu Wenlong, the head of the petrochemical group Chi Mei, was attacked personally by the PRC's trade minister, Shi Guangsheng: "There is no way we will allow anyone to engage in such activities, fishing for political benefit on Taiwan island and fishing for economic benefit on the mainland." The Beijing book fair in August 2000 banned the works of one Hong Kong author favorably disposed to Taiwan, and the authorities required participating Taiwan publishers to insert in nearly 50,000 books a statement that said "We do not recognize any contents and expressions in this book that violate the stand of Taiwan being part of the PRC territory."[25]

The Taiwan Business Community

There has long been concern on Taiwan that the island's growing economic dependence on the mainland will give Beijing greater leverage in Taiwan politics. T. J. Cheng has noted the fifth column effect on interdependence—that is, that Taiwan business people with a presence in China might promote their interests in ways that are biased in favor of Beijing and in the process evoke fears among other Taiwan residents of "traitors" in their midst.[26]

That Beijing has seen the business sector as an instrument of leverage, as it has done in Hong Kong, is indisputable. In 1990, then-president Yang Shangkun stated the goal of using economics to promote China's political agenda (*yi jingji zu zhengzhi*) in Taiwan and using the private sector to pressure officials (*yi min bi guan*).[27] To facilitate its influence over Taiwan business people on the mainland, Beijing has sought to incorporate them into its Leninist network of organizations. Taiwan business associations began forming in 1990, and within six years there were thirty-two. These associations have links with the Taiwan Affairs Office and its subordinate offices, the security services, and local party and government units, and the secretariats of the associations are drawn from those Chinese organizations. The existence of this network does not ipso facto make Taiwan business people an instrument of the PRC's will. Not all companies—perhaps only a third—are members. Moreover, Taiwan companies sometimes urge Beijing to soften its policies toward Taiwan instead of using its influence the other way. Yet the effect is not trivial, and it aggravates Taiwan concerns about "traitors" (see chapter 6).[28]

Cheng is correct in his assessment that the mere fact that Taiwan business people have operations on the mainland does not make them advocates of unification. On this fundamental matter, they prefer to continue the status quo. And some businessmen believe that a cross-Strait political stalemate gives them leverage with Beijing that they would not otherwise have. Yet Taiwan executives do seek to exert influence on Taipei on lesser policy issues in ways that not only promote the economic interests of their companies but also further, perhaps unintentionally, Beijing's political objectives.

The most obvious example concerns the three direct links, particularly transportation links. Taiwan companies with affiliates on the mainland have a clear interest in ending their government's policy of requiring an intermediate stop between a Taiwan port and a PRC port, because that requirement adds to the cost of doing business. In a very competitive global economy, even a small increase in costs can have a significant impact. The absence of direct transportation has led some Taiwanese subcontractors to move to the mainland to be near their customers.

The issue here is not whether direct transportation is a good idea. Chen Shui-bian favored it during his campaign, in part because he wanted to secure business support for the DPP. The obstacle has been the basis on which the two sides of the Strait would discuss the matter. The Chen administration preferred government-to-government talks, because transportation was within the jurisdiction of governments. The PRC rejected that idea and offered Taipei a choice between two alternatives: it could either accept the one-China principle, in which case SEF and ARATS would conduct the negotiations, or it could authorize private business associations to meet with their mainland counterparts. This put the Taiwan government on the horns of a dilemma. It believed that accepting the one-China principle as Beijing defined it would deny Taiwan's sovereign status and place it in a subordinate position, thereby establishing unfavorable terms and conditions for later political talks—the same reason that it opposed the acceptance the of one-China principle more generally. If, on the other hand, it allowed business associations to conduct the talks, it would also be reducing the government's status. Moreover, most of the relevant associations in Taiwan are truly private, while those in China are tied to the regime. However, not to talk with Beijing would expose the Chen administration to criticism from the business community. Whichever choice Taiwan made, its interests would be hurt. As a way out, Taipei proposed a hybrid approach, in which the talks would be held under the nominal aegis of business associations but government officials from each side would actually conduct the negotiations. (Early in 2005, the two sides used just such a mechanism to arrange direct charter flights for Taiwan business people returning home for the lunar new year.)

The Taiwan business community has understandably not taken a position on these issues of political principle. Its main interest, reducing the costs of production, is eminently practical. Beijing could have compromised on how to discuss the three links and thereby brought about talks sooner rather than later. But it preferred to maintain business pressure on Chen rather than give him a policy success that would aid his reelection, consistent with its tactic of roiling Taiwan politics from time to time to keep Chen on the defensive.

Cases: Direct Links and SARS

The contest to see which side could best exercise political leverage over the other was on display in two episodes. The first, in October 2001, concerned how China characterized the three direct links—trade, communication, and transportation—which it had advocated since 1979 and which the Taiwan business community supported. The other was the outbreak of severe acute respiratory syndrome (SARS) in both China and Taiwan.

Characterizing Direct Links

For a number of years, Beijing officials had referred to the three links as "domestic" or "special domestic" links, entirely consistent with its view that the cross-Strait dispute was an internal one. Taipei had resisted that characterization because it feared that accepting the "domestic" characterization would constitute its at least implicit acknowledgment that Beijing was the central government and that it was a subordinate government, lacking in sovereignty. That acceptance, in turn, would weaken Taipei's position in political negotiations, whenever they might begin.

On October 16, 2002, Qian Qichen was interviewed by reporters from *Lianhebao* (*United Daily News*), the Taiwan newspaper that was perhaps the most critical of Chen Shui-bian's cross-Strait policies. It is often described as "prounification," and it was an outlet that Chinese leaders were comfortable using to air their views. The reporters knew that the term "domestic" had become an obstacle to progress on the three links and asked Qian how to remove the obstacle. Qian replied that the links were termed "special domestic" because China thought that foreign carriers should be excluded (appealing thereby to the profit motive of Taiwan carriers) but said that if Taiwan did not like the term it did not have to use it. When the reporters pursued the issue, Qian said, "Let's call them cross-strait air and shipping routes."[29]

Like corn thrown into a flock of chickens, the remark set off a flurry of commentary and counter-commentary in Taipei. KMT legislators such as Chiang Ping-kun, vice president of the Legislative Yuan, raised it during the interpellation of Premier Yu Shyi-kun. Journalists sought the views of other officials. The *China Times* (*Zhongguo Shibao*), the other anti-Chen paper, immediately carried out an opinion poll that found 61 percent of those polled favored the three links. The *Lianhebao* warned that "the current opportunity [to establish direct links] will never come back if missed." A PRC newspaper proclaimed that this was a strategic goodwill gesture designed to depoliticize the dispute and reported that Taiwan companies were pressuring the government to establish the links. The Taiwan government responded to this clamor by welcoming the remarks as an important gesture but pointed out that the three links would be achieved only through negotiation, which Beijing opposed, and that Taiwan had to be wary of being marginalized. The thrust-and-parry demonstrated the concerted effort of the PRC government, the Blue parties, the conservative media, and the business community to exert pressure on Chen Shui-bian.[30]

SARS

The Chen administration had the advantage in the case of SARS, and it sought to put China on the defensive in both the international and domestic arenas. In the end, China won in the international arena, blocking Taiwan's effort to use the epidemic to secure observership in the World Health Organization, but it hurt its image in Taiwan. And Taiwan overplayed its hand somewhat, undermining its relations with the United States.[31]

Early on, SARS seemed to have a very small health impact on Taiwan, and the Taipei government took credit for a more effective response to the disease. In late March, it also sought to put Beijing in a bad light for its failure to inform the international community of the extent of the spread of SARS in China. Moreover, the Mainland Affairs Council criticized Beijing for not responding to its requests for information: "Because the mainland is not sharing information, the source of the contagion has not been clear and the period of risk for the outbreak has been lengthened. This hasn't helped us protect ourselves from an epidemic." A day later, Chen Shui-bian blamed China for accelerating the spread of SARS by its silence.[32]

Scoring points aside, Taipei did have a case to make. The best way to contain the epidemic would be for the quarantine authorities on the two sides of the Strait to collaborate and share information. That there were hundreds of thousands of Taiwan people on the mainland only made such cooperation more compelling. For Beijing to do so, however, would constitute a modest recognition that the government in Taipei was a sovereign and equal entity, which it did not wish to grant, particularly since the Chen administration was unwilling to accept the one-China principle. There was an attempt early on to make contact through the private sector. In early April, a three-person Taiwan delegation that included a researcher from Academia Sinica's Institute of Biomedical Sciences and a senior figure in the Tzu Chi charitable organization visited China for discussions with counterparts. Yet even private sector cooperation was limited.[33]

Once SARS spread, it had a major impact on economic and social interaction between the two sides of the Strait. Travel plummeted and a wide variety of cultural, educational, and religious exchanges were delayed or cancelled. Business travel became complicated as the Taiwan government placed executives returning from the mainland in ten days' quarantine at a military base. Some Taiwan nationalist groups called for a suspension of cross-Strait exchanges in order to contain the disease. Discussions began on the island on whether, in light of the epidemic and the PRC's initial lack of transparency, Taiwan's companies should rethink their investment decisions. New investment projects slowed once the seriousness of the epidemic became apparent. The Mainland Affairs Council appealed to Taiwan businesses to shift investment back to the island, and the Ministry of Economic Affairs began work on a package of incentives to encourage them to do so. Some expressed the hope that the risks of SARS from China might attenuate the differences over mainland policy between the KMT and PFP on the one hand and the DPP and TSU on the other. Others were optimistic that the shared consequences of disease might actually facilitate better cross-Strait relations.[34]

But the major reason that conflict prevailed over cooperation was the international dimension of SARS, at two different levels. On the operational level, the World Health Organization had a compelling reason to include Taiwan in its investigation and countermeasures. Given Taiwan's broad exposure to China and its extensive practical role in global affairs, how the Taipei government handled the epidemic would have important consequences for the WHO's overall effort to contain it. Yet China posed political obstacles to the organization's efforts to carry out its medical mission, seeking to limit its contact with the island in the early stages and insisting on use of politically correct terminology. In at least one case, an officer of the WHO referred to Taiwan as a province of China. As the disease spread on the island, however, the organization decided that it needed to send its personnel there regardless of the PRC's views on the matter. Beijing preserved its view of itself as the sovereign by announcing that it had agreed to the WHO's sending experts to Taiwan. Even so, the experts chose not to meet with officials at or above the ministerial level or to meet with reporters. Still, on the operational level, SARS had a minimally satisfactory outcome for all sides. The WHO could do its job. Taiwan had more contact with the organization than it ever had. And China preserved its principles.[35]

On a broader political level, the outcome was not as favorable. Taiwan quickly saw in SARS an opportunity to leverage its long-term goal of securing observer status in the World Health Assembly, the WHO's plenary body. This project had begun in 1997, promoted by Taiwan's doctors, who by and large support the DPP. But it had gone nowhere because the PRC was able to use its influence with the organization and its member states to block Taiwan. SARS raised new hopes. As early as mid-March, Taiwan officials began to argue that Taiwan's exclusion from the WHO posed a serious danger to global health. Thereafter, government officials, politicians, and the media all offered variations on that theme. It was argued, for example, that if China had not blocked the WHO from assisting Taiwan early in the epidemic, there would not have been so many cases or deaths. And SARS presented a timely debating point for arguing that Taiwan should have observer status at the WHA session that would begin in mid-May.[36]

The PRC mounted a strong defense, using its political muscle to block Taiwan's attempts, but the price of victory was deeper alienation of Taiwan's public. Beijing's main rhetorical argument, that it was trying to help Taiwan cope with the SARS crisis, was deemed insulting. (When on May 23 ARATS contacted SEF to offer assistance—the first communication in many months—SEF sent a chilly reply that China should use the assistance at home and stop offending Taiwan's sensibilities.) After the World Health Assembly had decided not to take up the issue of Taiwan's observership, the PRC ambassador to the WHO, Sha Zukang, imperiously remarked to Taiwan reporters, "Who cares about you?" ("*Shei li nimen?*"). That provoked intense anger in Taiwan, anger that was only exacerbated as the island's television stations played the interview over and over again. On Taiwan, SARS had turned into a public relations disaster for the PRC.[37]

In response, Chen Shui-bian immediately called for a referendum on Taiwan's joining the WHO, which would allow him to kill two birds with one stone. On one hand, he could tap into the genuine popular bitterness over SARS (its Chinese origin, the WHO issue, and so forth), using it in the campaign for the March 2004 presidential election while positioning himself as the defender of Taiwan's interests. On the other hand, by promoting a referendum he could accomplish a long-term objective of the DPP. The KMT-PFP opposition could neither oppose the WHO bid nor condone the PRC's behavior (it did urge Beijing to demonstrate "new thinking"), but it did accuse Chen of using the issue to promote his electoral advantage.[38]

The United States was the other object of leverage, and here the outcome was a draw. Early in the epidemic, Washington sent personnel from the Centers for Disease Control and Prevention to Taiwan as a way of compensating for the WHO's reluctance to go, a gesture that was appreciated on the island

and reinforced Taiwan's image of the United States as an alternative source of the practical services that international organizations like the WHO provide. At the World Health Assembly, Secretary of Health and Human Services Tommy Thompson expressed unprecedentedly strong support for Taiwan's observership. However, the Bush administration did not appreciate Chen's call for a referendum on the WHO because of concern that it would complicate relations with Beijing at a time when China's cooperation on North Korea was vital. Public allegations that Douglas Paal, director of the American Institute in Taiwan, was pressuring the Taiwan government to be more restrained only made matters worse.[39]

Beijing and Taipei would no doubt assert that most or all of their initiatives on SARS were undertaken for the most serious and noble of reasons. But it is hard to deny that each also sought to gain a political advantage from the crisis or to prevent the other from doing so. For both sides, this was just another round in a zero-sum struggle for political advantage that was very difficult—perhaps impossible—to resist. Exercising restraint to maintain the goodwill of the other, to limit the scope of the problem, or even to find ways to cooperate also was unlikely. Linked to the political competition were the other issues that form the strands of the cross-Strait knot. The risk and inconvenience that SARS posed forced Taiwanese business executives to reconsider their investment strategies and so the future degree of economic interdependence between Taiwan and China. Conflicts over whether the Taipei government possessed sovereignty dictated that Beijing would reject any contact between quarantine authorities and Taiwan would seek to use the SARS controversy in its WHO campaign, which Beijing redoubled its efforts to oppose. Electoral imperatives would lead Chen Shui-bian to use the episode to strengthen his political position by exacerbating animosity toward China. And the reluctance of the two sides to find ways to cooperate was another manifestation of the underlying security dilemma and their mutual lack of trust.[40]

Conclusion

In January 2003, Chen Shui-bian summed up the leverage game from his point of view:

Despite frequent economic, trade, and cultural exchanges, as well as the large number of people traveling between the two sides, considerable differences and some prejudice still exist between Taiwan and China. The People's Republic of China continues to be Taiwan's greatest political oppressor and the most serious military threat to our national security. China's primary goal is to "marginalize" and "downgrade" Taiwan to the status of a local government by isolating us politically while trying to involve us economically. At the same time, Beijing is stonewalling our attempts to resume talks and normalize Taiwan-China relations.[41]

That is not to say that the PRC is always successful in its efforts. Public disclosure of its efforts—such as tolerance of the Blue coalition's fundraising parties on the mainland during the 2004 election campaign—provide the DPP with a weapon to suggest that the Blue camp is somehow not "patriotic."[42] And Chen Shui-bian was playing the leverage game as well, trying to expand Taiwan's international space and, as the next chapter describes, maximize Taiwan's benefits from its U.S. relationship. Neither side can resist the temptation to undermine the other's position. Each will respond when challenged. And each draws from these skirmishes the conclusion that the other cannot be trusted. Beijing interprets Taipei's actions as evidence that it intends to permanently separate Taiwan from China and to use the United States to pursue that goal. The Taipei government and parts of the Taiwan public read a variety of worrisome messages in Beijing's activities: China's international quarantine is further proof that it will not acknowledge that Taiwan is a sovereign entity, and its multifaceted manipulation of Taiwan's politics through its united front strategy demonstrates a cynical disrespect for Taiwan's democracy, belying any promises about the island enjoying a "high degree of autonomy" under the one-country, two-systems framework.

There is, moreover, a fundamental asymmetry at work here. Because Taiwan has a far more open political system than the PRC, it is vulnerable to Beijing's "interference in its internal affairs." Taipei lacks a similar level of access to the mainland. To be sure, Beijing's leverage game alienates a significant element of the Taiwan public, thereby undermining its own objectives. And Taipei gains some international leverage by contrasting the island's democratic character with the mainland's authoritarianism. Still, it is an uneven contest and so fosters a sense of insecurity on the island.

Indeed, the leverage game is the political version of the security dilemma described in chapter 5. It has the potential both to exacerbate current cross-Strait tensions and complicate any effort to either ameliorate or resolve the dispute. If there is to be an improvement in the uneasy status quo, the two sides will have to abandon or suspend the game.[43]

9

The U.S. Factor

The United States has been at the center of the cross-Strait dispute since it began. PRC spokesmen are fond of saying that unification already would have occurred if it were not for U.S. intervention, although in fact it was North Korea's invasion of South Korea, to which Mao Zedong gave his consent, that blocked an early takeover. Ever since, both Beijing and Taipei have sought to obtain Washington's help for themselves and deny it to the other. In response, the United States has pursued a policy designed to protect its global and regional interests and avoid becoming captive of either side.

Dual Leverage

As related in chapter 2, the ROC preserved American support through the 1950s and 1960s. It had diplomatic relations, a defense treaty, and U.S. backing for its claim that it was the government of China. That Washington regarded China as a threat to stability in East Asia facilitated that support. But Beijing got the upper hand in the 1970s, when the Nixon and Carter administrations concluded that it would be an effective make-weight in containing the Soviet Union. When the United States recognized Beijing as the government of China and terminated its defense treaty and diplomatic relations with the ROC, the PRC expected the blow to give Taipei little choice but to negotiate on its terms. That did not happen right away, however, and passage of the Taiwan Relations Act gave Taipei something of a boost. Beijing sought to create new leverage on Taiwan by restricting U.S. arms sales, which it succeeded in doing through the August 1982 communiqué. Soon thereafter, however, the Reagan administration solidified relations with Taipei, and the democratization of Taiwan that began in the late 1980s gave Americans new reasons to support Taiwan. Then, as Beijing acquired advanced weapons systems from Russia after the fall of the Soviet Union, the arms sales communiqué increasingly became a dead letter.

In this struggle, the traditional mainstays of Taiwan's support were the U.S. Congress and the Republican Party. Congress could be counted on to act as a check on the executive branch, deterring initiatives that were harmful to Taiwan's or, more precisely, to the KMT's interests. Republicans were more reliably anticommunist than Democrats, and they made China the most partisan foreign policy issue. A number of conservative Democrats were recruited as well. Although there is little or no evidence, it is almost certain that Taipei did not count on sentiment alone to ensure its support but supplemented it with more material inducements.

In the late 1970s and early 1980s, as Congress focused more attention on human rights around the world, the KMT's policy of internal repression became a liability. But the island's democratization in the late 1980s and early 1990s closed the gap between congressional liberals and conservatives over the island's political system and thus created a broad and sympathetic coalition. American advocacy organizations are active on both the left and the right. The Taipei Economic and Cultural Representative office—Taiwan's de facto embassy in Washington—has at its disposal a stable of lobbying and public relations firms, many of which focus on Congress. Because Republicans are probably still Taiwan's strongest supporters, Republican administrations are better able to work out differences on Taiwan policy quietly. But all administrations formulate policy with the potential congressional reaction in mind. Taiwan can still depend on Capitol Hill for bedrock support.

Nonetheless, Congress is usually more effective in stopping or reacting to administration actions (when it knows about them) than it is in taking its own initiatives. That is partly a function of the general limits on Congress's ability to influence foreign policy but also of the dearth of tools that directly relate to Taiwan policy. Congress, for example, cannot dictate the level of U.S. support for Taiwan's bid to be an observer at the WHO. What it can do—and does—is require reports on administration plans and actions.[1]

An exception to this general rule was the effort in late 1994 and the first half of 1995 to secure executive branch approval for Lee Teng-hui's request to visit the United States. Lee sought the visit for a variety of reasons: to ensure a balance between developments in cross-Strait relations and in Taiwan's foreign relations; to give himself negotiating leverage vis-à-vis Beijing; and to improve his chances of winning Taiwan's first direct presidential election in March 1996. It also was consistent with his belief that Taiwan should have a full role in the international community. He had telegraphed his desire for a visit in early 1994, and although the Clinton administration refused to grant him an extended transit in April of that year, he became even more determined to push forward. He met resistance from his own foreign ministry, which feared that such an initiative would alienate the U.S. executive branch. So Lee bypassed his diplomats, and in the summer of 1994, working through the Taiwan Research Institute, he employed Cassidy and Associates, an influential Washington lobbying firm, to help him. Cassidy mounted a broad and sophisticated campaign to pressure the Clinton administration to grant a visit. All points of leverage were energized—the media, governors, campaign contributors—but Congress was the focus. The central objective was to pass legislation—nonbinding if that was sufficient and binding if not—requiring that Lee be issued a visa. After nearly unanimous votes on sense-of-Congress resolutions and additional lobbying by Democratic senators, Clinton gave in.[2]

Lee's victory was secured at some cost. Beijing suspended non-economic cross-Strait relations and engaged in coercive diplomacy toward Taiwan. It caused a deterioration in U.S.-China relations that took two years to repair. When the PRC began retaliatory missile exercises in March 1996, Washington, in order to demonstrate its resolve and to prevent an accidental conflict, sent two carrier battle groups to the Taiwan area, an action that cheered people on Taiwan. But the Clinton administration remained resentful of Lee's manipulation of the U.S. political system, which had created the crisis in the first place. It kept Taipei somewhat at arm's length, urged resumption of cross-Strait dialogue (urging that some in Taiwan saw as pressure), and focused on repairing U.S.-PRC relations. Among the steps taken was Clinton's reaffirmation of past principles of U.S. policy, expressed in a place, Shanghai, that made Taiwan uneasy. These were the "three nos": the United States does not support two Chinas or one-China, one-Taiwan; it does not support Taiwan independence; and it does not support Taiwan's membership in international organizations for which statehood is a prerequisite.[3]

Taiwan, of course, does not rely on Congress alone. On a variety of issues it must rely on the administration in office if it is to protect and promote its fundamental interests. The United States is Taiwan's primary source of advanced weaponry—on which Taiwan relies to deter the PRC and maintain public confidence on the island—and it is the executive branch that makes the final decision. Congressional pressure can have an impact, but it is mainly at the margin. Similarly, it was the executive branch that ensured that Taiwan got into APEC and the WTO on reasonable terms. As noted above, Congress cannot dictate the precise U.S. approach taken on Taiwan's annual WHO campaign. The executive branch decides the terms and conditions of Taiwan's leaders' transits through the United States, which facilitate the ROC's broader diplomacy by making it easier to get to Latin America and the Caribbean, where most of Taiwan's diplomatic partners are. And most important, it is the administration that decides how to strike the balance between Taipei and Beijing. If it appears to tilt too far in the PRC direction, it creates great anxiety on the island.

Taiwan's leverage over the United States improved with the arrival of the George W. Bush administration in January 2001. Bush's foreign policy team had criticized the Clinton administration's treatment of Taiwan's leaders and view of Taiwan's democracy. In addition, its members share the concern that an increasingly strong China might challenge U.S. dominance in East Asia and the view that Taiwan might become a battleground between a revisionist China and a status quo United States. So the new administration moved quickly to improve the relationship, particularly in the security field. Ironically, Taiwan opponents of the Chen administration, who had previously emphasized the importance of preserving good relations with the United States, criticized it for relying too much on the United States and warned that too close an alignment could bring about undesirable conflict.[4]

Then the wheel turned. The Bush administration soon recognized the dangers of too much confrontation with China, and following the September 11 attacks and growing tensions on the Korean peninsula, it saw China not as an inevitable adversary but as significant partner in the struggle against terrorism and rogue states. As Secretary of State Colin Powell said in November 2003, "It is upon such concrete forms of cooperation on issues of regional and global importance that a 21st century U.S.-China relationship will be built, issue by issue, experience by experience, challenge by challenge, initiative by initiative, program by program. . . . Building and sustaining a healthy overall relationship is good for America, it is good for China, it is good for the region, and good for the international community."[5] The Chen government took steps to maintain alignment with the Bush administration's global priorities by providing significant assistance for relief and reconstruction in Afghanistan and Iraq, but it no longer had the luxury of a conflicted U.S.-PRC relationship.

Taipei's goal is to strengthen its relationship with the United States however it can, and Beijing's, of course, is to weaken that relationship. It sees those ties in strategic terms. In January 2001, Qian Qichen offered a telling—and probably exaggerated—commentary on China's view of the impact of the United States:

> If foreign countries [the United States] interfere in the Taiwan issue, the local Taiwan Independence factions will rely on this kind of foreign interference to stir up splittism, and cause the Taiwan problem to drag on forever. That is just not possible. The question of national reunification must be decided. If the American Government takes a stance of supporting peaceful reunification, then it will be of very great use. If it says to Taiwan "do not be afraid, we will protect you and we will sell you arms, we will stand behind you, we can act behind the scenes for you," then the situation is quite different. Consequently, if the US wants to play a role here, first they must not support Taiwan independence, and they must not support Taiwan splitting away. They must not support any type of splittist activities by Taiwan on the international stage. [If they do not,] I do not see where Taiwan has any power, nor any reason to refuse reunification.[6]

That is, Beijing sees U.S. support of Taiwan as the only obstacle to the success of China's application of pressure on and intimidation of Taiwan.

China, of course, lacks Taipei's resources when it comes to influencing Capitol Hill and the American public and so focuses on the executive branch. It mounts pressure when it believes that U.S. policy is shifting too far in Taipei's direction, to the point of restricting relations if that seems to be necessary to get Washington's attention, as with the Lee Teng-hui visit. In another example, Beijing stepped up the pressure in early 2002, when George Bush's rhetoric was favorable to Taiwan and his administration permitted a visit by the island's defense minister, Tang Yaoming, to attend a defense forum of the U.S.-Taiwan Business Council. Foreign Minister Li Zhaoxing called in Ambassador Clark Randt and, displaying a time-tested repertoire of rhetorical flourishes, berated the Bush administration for its recent actions and its "trampling" of the principles of the three U.S.-PRC communiqués of 1972, 1978, and 1982. "Pampering and supporting 'Taiwan Independence' can only meet with the resolute opposition of all the Chinese people and will be doomed to failure," Li said. An article in *Jiefang Junbao*, the military paper, made similar criticisms and warned that "if the 'Taiwan Independence' forces and foreign forces dare move the situation in the Taiwan Strait to military conflict, the Chinese People's Liberation Army has the confidence, determination, and capability to go all out to support the scenario that our motherland has made to resolve the motherland unification issue." When Bush inadvertently used the phrase "Republic of Taiwan," a Hong Kong communist paper warned that the statement "could reveal that, at the bottom of his heart, Bush entertains the absurd thought of Taiwan being a country; and that the U.S. government is attempting to promote a strategy of 'playing off Taiwan against China,' and to re-play the 'Taiwan card.'"[7] In response to all that invective, the administration used the April visit of Vice President Hu Jintao to reassure the Chinese leadership that U.S. policy had not changed.

Although Beijing occasionally chooses to exert political pressure on Washington, it prefers not to draw the United States into the dispute unless absolutely necessary, partly because it views the Taiwan Strait issue as an internal affair but also because it understands that heavy-handed use of its leverage can be counterproductive. But it does seek to use high-level contact between U.S. and PRC officials—the sort of contact that Taiwan does not get—to suggest that U.S. support for Taiwan is waning. It also seeks to change the verbal formulations that Washington uses in ways that it believes are favorable to its unification campaign and then tries to use them to constrain future U.S. behavior. A key example is its effort to manipulate the American rhetorical stance on Taiwan independence. The public position of the U.S. government had been—and still is—that it "does not support" Taiwan independence. The PRC would prefer to have Washington say that it "opposes" that objective. Thus in the wake of Lee Teng-hui's visit, President Clinton sent a letter to Jiang Zemin restating the U.S. position. Beijing soon leaked information that Clinton had used the word "opposed." In Robert Suettinger's account, however, "The Chinese either missed or ignored the difference between 'does not support' and 'opposes' . . . . Jiang and others were overstating the congruence between the U.S. position and their own, perhaps for domestic political reasons, perhaps to increase the pressure on Taiwan."[8] More recently, Beijing exploited a comment that George W. Bush reportedly made in private to Jiang Zemin during their summit at Crawford, Texas, in October 2002 stating that he was "against" Taiwan independence. Beijing made the statement public and proceeded over the months that followed to portray it as a major U.S. commitment.[9]

The high point of the Chinese campaign to use the U.S. position as leverage in the contest with Taipei came in late 2003. As Chen Shui-bian's campaign proposals made China more and more nervous about an independence breakout, Beijing pushed the Bush administration to rein in Chen. It took some comfort in President Bush's December statement that "the comments and actions made by the leader of Taiwan indicate that he may be willing to make decisions unilaterally to change the status quo, which we oppose."

Yet the United States never moves completely into China's camp. Because of Taiwan's political influence in the United States and U.S. uncertainty about the PRC's intentions, it seeks to limit the leverage that Beijing applies. That was clear in the late-2003 episode, when Washington was concerned about Chen Shui-bian's goals. In the same address in which Secretary Powell applauded cooperation with the PRC on foreign policy, he also cautioned: "We have to take note of the military build-up opposite Taiwan on the Mainland because that sends a very different kind of signal. Whether China chooses peace or coercion to resolve its differences with Taiwan will tell us a great deal about the kind of role China seeks with its neighbors and seeks with us."[10] And there were reports in the fall of 2004 that, consistent with tradition, the Taiwan government preferred the reelection of Republican George W. Bush, whom it expected to be more favorable to Taiwan, to the victory of his Democratic challenger, John Kerry.[11]

The leverage game that Beijing and Taipei play against the United States has an important consequence: when either thinks that it has gained an advantage in Washington, it often exaggerates the significance of that gain. Reality then intervenes and there is a sense of disappointment, even betrayal, because the United States has not acted according to its expectations. More seriously, the side that believes incorrectly that its exercise of leverage has been successful then acts on that assumption, only to have the United States bring it up short. The emphasis in Chinese culture on trust and dependability only magnifies the disillusionment that accompanies a perceived treachery.

Taiwan's sense of betrayal at the hands of the United States has a long history. The Truman administration was prepared to abandon the island and the ROC government to the communists in early 1950, only to reinstate its protective shield after the beginning of the Korean War. The Nixon administration's shift on China policy in 1971 and 1972 came as a rude shock to the KMT government. Nixon had been a staunch anticommunist and friend of Taiwan, but he pursued the opening to Beijing even as he promised Chiang Ching-kuo that he would not sell Taiwan down the river. Jimmy Carter brought off normalization in secret negotiations, and the repair of the damage to Taiwan that the Congress attempted by passing the Taiwan Relations Act was more apparent than real. Ronald Reagan, another anticommunist and friend of Taiwan, agreed to reduce arms sales to Taiwan. The joint communiqués of 1972, 1978, and 1982 were negotiated without consulting Taipei.[12]

More recently, any improvement in U.S.-PRC relations fosters fears in Taiwan that Washington might sacrifice the island's interests in order to secure China's cooperation on U.S. goals. As Chen Shui-bian wrote in early 2004, "Beijing-Washington relations have improved a lot. Moreover, Beijing's tactic of using Washington to pressure Taiwan is more and more evident."[13] And any U.S. criticism of Taiwan is read there as a hypocritical violation of fundamental U.S. principles. When President Bush in December 2003 publicly objected to Chen's proposal to conduct a referendum opposing China's missile buildup, Chen's sense of betrayal was obvious. "It is not right that while almost all people in the world can enjoy the freedom from fear, only the people of Taiwan are denied this basic right. According to the U.S.'s founding spirit, the resolution and efforts of the 23 million people in Taiwan to seek peace and democracy should not be regarded as acts of provocation." A few days later, Chen said, "The U.S. waged a war in Iraq in order to give the Iraqi people democracy. Why can't the Taiwanese people vote to ask China to dismantle its missiles aimed at Taiwan and renounce the use of force against our country in a referendum? . . . Why does the U.S. restrict our rights to pursue democracy?"[14]

Beijing's belief in U.S. duplicity is no less profound. When Beijing objects to U.S. policies toward Taiwan, it often does so by asserting that Washington has violated its commitments in the 1972, 1978, and 1982 communiqués. Some in China understand that the U.S. commitments in those documents were more nuanced than Beijing asserts, but for most Chinese the claim that the United States has broken its word and victimized China rings true. For example, China had been pleased with President Bush's criticism of Chen Shui-bian, cited previously. But its response to the Bush administration's positive assessment of Chen Shui-bian's May 2004 inaugural address was anything but pleased. Washington, it felt, had misread Chen's intentions and was encouraging his separatist agenda. It registered its displeasure through a commentary disseminated by the Xinhua News Agency that harshly criticized the congressional testimony of James Kelly, assistant secretary of state for East Asia, which had been delivered in April, before Chen's speech. Although Kelly's testimony was the most negative statement of U.S. policy on Taiwan ever delivered publicly, China ignored the parts that were positive from China's point of view and focused instead on the parts that suggested that China's intentions were not completely pacific and on those that China thought represented excessive U.S. intrusion into the issue. Moreover, China's objections were not kept at the policy level: "These remarks not only seriously violate the one China principle and the three Sino-U.S. joint communiqués, but also interfere in China's internal affairs; they cannot but arouse a high degree of attention." Although moralistic rhetoric, the comment revealed the real PRC concern: that the Bush administration was again encouraging, in the author's words, "the arrogance of the Chen Shui-bian Taiwan authorities in pursuing their 'Taiwan independence' separatist activities."[15]

Analysts working at Chinese research institutes that focus on Taiwan urged Washington to reinforce its rhetoric with concrete deeds, such as recalling the U.S. representative in Taipei or suspending arms sales. Chinese officials more realistically refrained from asking the Bush administration to do more and instead implored the United States to scrupulously abide by the position articulated by President Bush on December 9—that is, to stick to a one-China policy and oppose any unilateral change in the status quo. In addition, the Chinese hope to build on what they see as greater convergence between Washington and Beijing in their assessments of Chen and the dangers posed by his policies. They seek greater cooperation, including a bilateral crisis management mechanism, to prevent the unwanted escalation of cross-Strait differences into open conflict.

U.S. Leverage

The United States is not merely the passive object of PRC and ROC attempts to shape its actions. Because Washington desires good relations with the two sides of the Taiwan Strait and has a profound stake in preventing conflict between them, it seeks to shape their interaction to reduce the possibility of conflict through both policy rhetoric and, more important, the conduct of policy. Whether the critical U.S. role in preventing conflict implies an active role in resolving the dispute is another question.

The "One-China Policy"

The U.S. "one-China policy" is one of the least understood aspects of U.S. foreign policy. Many regard it as a set of rigid principles from which more detailed policies are derived, and analysts pour over the "sacred texts" of U.S.-PRC-Taiwan relations trying to figure out what those policies are, spending much time and ink in the process. Beijing and Taipei, of course, argue from their preferred texts what U.S. policy should be. The PRC would like Washington to base its policy on the communiqués of 1972, 1978, and 1982, as it interprets them. Taiwan grounds its expectations in the Taiwan Relations Act and other U.S. commitments. Both Beijing and Taipei emphasize the principles that accord with their respective interests and try to bind Washington to them. Simultaneously, each tries to de-emphasize and divert the United States from those principles that undermine its goals.[16]

This view of the U.S. one-China policy as a set of rigid principles is correct, but only to a certain extent. In normalizing relations with Beijing, the Carter administration recognized the government of the PRC as the sole legal government of China. That commitment has dictated the U.S. approach to the PRC's membership in international organizations in which membership requires statehood; that is, the PRC is the only representative of the state called China. The Carter administration also pledged to conduct relations with Taiwan on an unofficial basis, thereby determining the legal form of the institutions and the practice of the bilateral relationship. For example, for many years U.S. officials who wished to serve in Taipei had to separate from their home agencies and become employees of the legally private American Institute in Taiwan (AIT), whose office in Taipei fulfills almost all the functions of an embassy. When that period of service ended, they had the right to return to their agency, with their time in federal service magically increased by the amount of time that they worked for AIT. Congressional legislation in 2002 permitted more flexibility in the mechanics of personnel administration, but the principle of unofficial relations remained.

In short, the word "one" in the "one-China policy" indicates that Washington does not have a two-China policy, at least for purposes of international organizations and formal bilateral relations. Yet it has not taken a position on what "one" means substantively for a possible unification between Taiwan and China, and it has generally remained agnostic on the key question of whether the Taiwan government possesses sovereignty.[17] That is one reason that the U.S. government has never taken a position on the one-country, two-systems formula. But its legal commitments have not stopped the United States from maintaining a substantive relationship with Taipei that is more robust than its ties with many countries with which it has formal diplomatic relations, nor have they deterred the Bush administration from supporting Taiwan's proposal that it be an observer at the World Health Assembly. If Beijing relaxed its rigid approach to these issues and accommodated Taipei's position, Washington would easily adjust.

For the most part, however, the U.S. one-China policy is not a tight lin-ear argument that starts from first principles and follows a deductive logic. It is also a set of verbal formulas that must be read together but that vary in their relative emphasis over time. These include the affirmation of the one-China policy itself; the three U.S.-PRC communiqués; the Taiwan Relations Act; insistence on peaceful resolution of the cross-Strait issue; continued arms sales to Taiwan; nonsupport for "two Chinas" or "one China, one Tai-wan"; nonsupport for Taiwan independence; nonsupport for Taiwan's membership in state-based international organizations; the so-called "six assurances"; recognition of the need of the assent of the people of Taiwan for any cross-Strait solution; and so on.[18]

It is worth noting that these elements are not necessarily mutually com-patible. The 1982 communiqué is arguably inconsistent with the Taiwan Relations Act; Beijing certainly thinks so. Moreover, Washington combines these elements flexibly in various permutations and combinations to accord with its assessment of the circumstances. For example, when, as AIT chair-man, I went to Taiwan in July 1998 to report on Bill Clinton's just-concluded visit to China and to make the case that U.S. policy had not changed, I asserted that all elements continued to guide U.S. policy. In July 1999, after Lee Teng-hui's "state-to-state" announcement, the Clinton administration enunciated its "three pillars": the one-China principle; peaceful resolution; and the need for dialogue. In June 2003, George Bush reportedly pointed to five elements: the three communiqués; the Taiwan Relations Act; no support for Taiwan independence; helping Taiwan defend itself to the extent possi-ble; and providing defensive weapons.

More significant, however, is that the one-China policy is a set of unstated operational guidelines that have governed the conduct of U.S. policy for decades. All stem from the fundamental U.S. policy objective of preserving peace and stability in Asia and from its long-standing role as guarantor of that objective. In order to prevent war and instability and to preserve peace in the Strait, successive administrations have exerted influence on Beijing or Taipei or both. These unstated guidelines promote the goals of preventing a military imbalance between China and Taiwan; discouraging provocation by either side; discouraging both overconfidence and a lack of confidence; maintaining public support in the United States for U.S. policies; and main-taining some degree of ambiguity on the U.S. use of force.

A special word is required on the last of these guidelines, what is usually referred to as "strategic ambiguity." The essence of this concept is that the United States does not state explicitly whether it will come to Taiwan's defense in the event of an attack by the PRC. The resulting uncertainty about U.S. intentions, it is argued, shapes the intentions of the other two actors. Neither believes that it has a blank check. It constrains China from making an unprovoked attack on Taiwan by raising at least the possibility that the United States will intervene, and it constrains Taiwan from taking steps that Beijing would find intolerably provocative by suggesting that Washington would not intervene or would otherwise punish Taiwan.

Many have argued that for the United States to declare in advance what it would do in a variety of circumstances is unwise, for a variety of reasons. First, it is impossible to predict all contingencies. Second, specifying the circumstances under which the United States would act would not eliminate probing by either Beijing or Taipei and might increase it. Third, the U.S. response will be guided as much by American domestic politics as by how conflict began. Fourth, strategic clarity reduces U.S. flexibility and increases U.S. obligations. Fifth, ambiguity is useful to those countries that might contribute to the defense of Taiwan (most particularly Japan) but whose governments are unwilling to face a public discussion of that possibility. Thus a blanket commitment to defend Taiwan would likely release it from any responsibility that it has to help maintain the peace and render Washington a hostage to Taipei's actions—the entrapment problem.[19]

All of this is true, and it helps illuminate the pitfalls of proposals that the United States should defend Taiwan merely because it is a democracy.[20] The advocates of strategic ambiguity would ask what aspect of Taiwan's democracy is worthy of a U.S. security commitment. Is it all of the initiatives taken in the name of Taiwan's democracy?

Yet most discussions of strategic ambiguity only scratch the surface of U.S. policy. On one hand, public statements are not accurate measures of the actual degree of ambiguity. If, hypothetically speaking, Washington informs Beijing privately that it will defend Taiwan under any circumstances, China has no illusions about U.S. intentions; if, again hypothetically, Taipei is informed of or learns about this statement, then there is no ambiguity whatsoever. Moreover, it is the task of U.S. diplomacy to interpret how past public statements apply in any new set of circumstances. Finally, to the extent that U.S. statements about the use of force shape Beijing's and Taipei's intentions, what is important is not what Washington says but how others interpret its statements. If the United States is publicly vague about its intentions but Beijing nevertheless concludes that it will defend Taiwan under any circumstances and becomes more prudent as a result, then stability is strengthened. If Taipei is aware that Beijing has adopted that interpretation of Washington's statement, it may become less prudent and so undermine stability.

This wheels-within-wheels phenomenon illustrates that the supposed value of strategic ambiguity is also a liability: that a lack of clarity about U.S. intentions will lead one or both of the parties to take risks rather than exercise caution. Indeed, it was the Bush foreign policy team's grave concern about the danger that Beijing would miscalculate American resolve that led them to adopt a policy of greater clarity in the spring of 2001.

In the real world, U.S. policymakers position themselves somewhere along a continuum between clarity and ambiguity. Neither complete clarity nor complete ambiguity is ever possible. Whether to emphasize ambiguity or clarity depends on whether it serves U.S. interests in the circumstances at hand. Until the mid-1990s, ambiguity was preferred. Then in March 1996 and April 2001, Washington determined that its interests demanded greater clarity about U.S. intentions, in part to show U.S. resolve and in part to reduce the possibility of miscalculation. And, as noted, the United States complements its overt statements and actions with private communications. What Beijing and Taipei believe that Washington and the other will do is more important than public statements.

U.S. policy therefore has placed its emphasis on process rather than substance. Washington has long declared an "abiding interest" in the peaceful resolution of the dispute, but it has avoided saying anything on how it is to be resolved. As a corollary, the United States has placed a premium on retaining flexibility in order to pursue its fundamental policy objectives in the face of changing circumstances. It has sought, by and large, to avoid being tied down by the principles of the various "sacred texts" if those principles run contrary to its fundamental objectives.

There is another, historical factor at play in any discussion of U.S. policy. At various times since World War II, the United States has made decisions affecting the future of the people of Taiwan under circumstances in which it was impossible to solicit their wishes or in which Washington assumed that it knew best. This practice began with Franklin Roosevelt's decision to return the island to China after the defeat of Japan, and it was at its most obvious in the decisions of Richard Nixon and Jimmy Carter to normalize relations with the PRC. There were, of course, strategic reasons to make those choices, and until the early 1990s, there was no way to consult the island's population because of the KMT's repression.[21] Yet in those instances Washington arguably ignored a moral responsibility to act—or not act—on behalf of a people who had been denied a voice. Now that Taiwan is a democracy, even an imperfect one, the bias of American policy has been to eschew going in a direction that would put it at odds with the Taiwan people. Accordingly, over the past decade it has adopted the practical position that any cross-Strait solution must have the Taiwan public's support.

Washington's Policy Approaches

How the United States has sought to preserve peace and stability in the Taiwan Strait has evolved over time and in accordance with shifting circumstances. Several different approaches are hypothetically acceptable. These are—in increasing order of activity—opting out, context creation, deterrence, and intermediation.

—Opting out is a decision by the United States to wash its hands of the dispute because U.S. interests do not justify the commitment of time or resources necessary to shape its resolution.

—Context creation means shaping the environment in which both China and Taiwan operate. The premise here is that the two sides can mitigate their differences on their own through greater interaction and that direct U.S. involvement is unnecessary. Context creation can be either one-sided or two-sided, depending on whom it objectively benefits. In some cases, it benefits one side of the Strait; in others it benefits both.

—Deterrence involves warning an actor not to take actions that would create unwanted instability, with the implication (clear or ambiguous) that the United States will respond if the warning is not heeded. Yet as Tom Christensen points out, deterrence must not rely on threats alone if it is to be successful. Warnings are more likely to induce restraint when they are softened by reassurances. If the threatened actor believes that the party issuing the threat is ignoring its legitimate interests, it is liable to become more reckless and engage in threatening behavior itself.[22] In a situation in which Washington is trying to shape the actions of two actors that are at odds, as in the Taiwan Strait case, deterrence can be dual or asymmetric. In dual deterrence, Washington directs both warnings and reassurances toward both Beijing and Taipei, and the mix designed for each varies with the circumstances. In asymmetric deterrence, the United States tends to convey most of the warnings to one party and most of the reassurances to the other.

—Intermediation involves some level of U.S. activity as a go-between in order to reduce the possibility of conflict or to improve the prospect of peace and cooperation.

These approaches are analytic constructs rather than mutually exclusive policy options. When one approach is dominant, others may supplement it, but the history of U.S. involvement can be traced as alternation among them. The two principal approaches employed have been deterrence and context creation, each with its own variants.

The one time that Washington aggressively pursued intermediation was in the late 1940s, when the Nationalists and the Communists were on the brink of resuming their military conflict, which they had suspended to fight Japan after it invaded China in 1937. President Truman sent General George Marshall to mediate the dispute in the hope of preserving peace. The effort failed, fundamentally because the two sides had contradictory goals and mistrusted each other and the United States. That experience produced a U.S. allergy to later efforts to intermediate between Taipei and Beijing. And in 1982, at the time that it issued a communiqué to Beijing on reducing arms sales, Washington pledged to Taipei that it would not mediate the dispute.

The closest that the United States came to opting out was in late 1949 and early 1950. The Truman administration decided that although the fall of Taiwan to the Communists would set back U.S. interests in the near term, saving it required military resources that did not exist and would make it harder to persuade China to end its alignment with the Soviet Union on defense and foreign policy over the long term.

Asymmetric deterrence was the order of the day in the 1950s and 1960s, when Washington saw a danger that China might attack Taiwan. As part of its larger strategy to contain communism, it took significant steps to warn Beijing from that course. The United States concluded a mutual defense treaty with the ROC in 1954–55 and deployed significant military assets to the island to support and collaborate with the Nationalist military. It took a variety of other steps to sustain ROC "morale." When Beijing attacked Jinmen and Mazu in 1958 to probe for weakness in ROC and U.S. resolve, the Eisenhower administration worked aggressively to aid in the islands' defense. On balance, that was asymmetric deterrence, with most of the threats directed at Beijing and most of the reassurances toward Taiwan.

Yet the approach was not totally one-sided. Washington worried that Chiang Kai-shek, under his policy of mainland counterattack, might provoke open conflict, drawing the United States into an unnecessary war with the PRC. So Washington secured his commitment that he would not undertake significant offensive action without first consulting the United States. Moreover, the United States occasionally sought to signal reassurance to Beijing that its goals were not the same as Chiang's. In 1958, the Eisenhower administration sought Chiang's public commitment to emphasizing political over military means of settling the dispute. And in 1962, the Kennedy administration dissociated itself from an ROC effort to take advantage of the unsettled situation on the mainland created by the Great Leap Forward. By and large, however, the United States pursued a policy of asymmetric deterrence directed at China.

The United States shifted to context creation in the early 1970s. This approach took one form as the Nixon and Carter administrations sought to normalize relations with the PRC, clarifying Taiwan's status and the U.S. commitment regarding its future relations with Taiwan. That tipped the balance of power in the PRC's direction, to the point that both the ROC and its friends in Congress regarded the Nixon and Carter initiatives as serious betrayals.[23] That is what might be called negative context creation. But even here, Washington did not seek to accelerate the trend that it had created.

A more positive variation occurred in the late 1980s and early 1990s, when social and economic cooperation between the two sides of the Strait was growing. There were expectations that proliferating economic ties might create the basis for a political reconciliation, but Washington did not seek to intensify the movement that was occurring here either. As Secretary of State George Shultz put it in February 1987, "We have welcomed developments, including indirect trade and increasing human interchange, which have contributed to a relaxation of tensions in the Taiwan Strait. Our steadfast policy seeks to foster an environment within which such developments can continue to take place." Among the ways in which Washington fostered that environment were forward deployment of U.S. forces in the Western Pacific; trade liberalization; good relations with both the PRC and Taiwan; insistence on peace; and arms sales to Taiwan.

Taiwan's democratization complicated Washington's effort to preserve stability. An open and competitive system permitted the public expression of hitherto repressed ideas (Taiwan independence), new political forces (the Democratic Progressive Party), new policy proposals (promoting Taiwan's international participation), and the need for politicians to appeal to the electorate. All of those developments have aggravated Beijing's suspicions that the island's leaders have a separatist agenda and sometimes have led it to undertake coercive diplomacy to impose restraint. That in turn has drawn in the United States, in its self-appointed role as guarantor of the peace. It was those vectors that created the crisis of 1995 and 1996.

The Clinton administration thus moved to dual deterrence after Lee Teng-hui's visit to the United States. On one hand, Washington sought to restrain Taipei from pursuing policies that the PRC might regard as provocative; on the other, it acted to restrain Beijing from using or threatening force against Taiwan. Thus when the PRC fired missiles close to Taiwan before the March 1996 election, two U.S. aircraft carrier battle groups sailed into the vicinity of Taiwan to ensure that those displays of force did not escalate through accident or miscalculation. In addition, there were efforts to improve high-level communication with Taipei.[24]

Yet warnings were not enough. Washington thought that it would be more effective to allay Beijing's fears that the United States actually supported Taiwan separatism and to calm Taipei's anxiety that it was going to sell out the island's interests in order to secure Beijing's goodwill. Reassurance in either direction was unlikely to completely eliminate the misperceptions of U.S. policy, yet it was important for its own sake and to increase the effectiveness of U.S. warnings. The Clinton administration sought to reassure Beijing primarily through a series of statements in the late 1990s that reaffirmed and made more explicit the commitments made at the time of normalization, the most famous of which were the "three nos" of June 1998. In that context, my role as AIT chairman increasingly was to be the leading "reassurer" of Taiwan and its leaders.[25] The fact that I had the flexibility to speak for the U.S. government at greater length than other U.S. officials facilitated that role. Thus, right after the Clinton statement, I said in Taipei that all the elements of U.S. policy toward Taiwan remained in effect. During the same period, when the United States was urging the resumption of dialogue, I was authorized to say that resumption should occur on a mutually acceptable basis—by implication, not on Beijing's terms.

Unlike Beijing, the Clinton administration did not regard Taiwan's democratization itself as the cause of tensions. Instead, it approved and sought to make a virtue out of the new political reality on the island. As AIT chairman, I began in the fall of 1998 to address, with State Department approval, the implications of those developments. I expressed the administration's confidence that Taiwan's democracy contributed to peace and stability and that the island's people were "wise and prudent enough to support responsible approaches regarding Taiwan's future." Moreover, I stressed that "the results of cross-Strait dialogue must meet with the Taiwan public's approval" but that "any result that enjoys broad support will be more lasting as a result."

Democracy presented a new challenge as the 2000 Taiwan presidential election loomed and with it the possibility that the DPP might win and replace the KMT. As much as Beijing disliked Lee Teng-hui, it feared the DPP and its pro-independence history even more. By the late 1990s, U.S. policymakers anticipated that Chen Shui-bian, the likely candidate of the

DPP, might well become Taiwan's next president and began an effort to hedge against that scenario. The U.S. government stepped up its communications with Chen in Taipei and encouraged him to visit Washington so that he could have low-key conversations with policymakers. From those encounters, Chen gained a better understanding of how the United States viewed the election—that it was the political initiatives of Taiwan's leaders that mattered, not who the leader was. That clarification both reinforced the moderate approach that Chen was already taking on cross-Straits issues during the campaign and permitted productive interactions after he was elected. Beijing was less prepared, and once it realized the likelihood of Chen's victory, it responded with threatening statements. Washington took steps to prevent the situation from getting out of control, among them a statement by Clinton that reiterated the U.S. emphasis on process, but with a new twist. He said that the United States expected the Taiwan Strait issue to be resolved not only peacefully, but also with "the assent of the people of Taiwan."[26] The Clinton administration was pursuing dual deterrence in a new context.

As described in chapter 5, the early Bush administration believed that its predecessor had been insufficiently firm with China and had provided too little support for Taiwan. It therefore took steps to rectify the situation. It warned China not to miscalculate U.S. resolve to defend Taiwan, and it took a variety of steps to strengthen the island's defenses. This shift to a more asymmetric deterrence—warning Beijing and reassuring Taipei—was done very deliberately.

Subsequently, the Bush administration shifted back toward dual deterrence. The growing gap between China's military assets and Taiwan's raised concerns that Beijing might actually try to coerce Taiwan into negotiating on its terms. But the larger strategic context had changed significantly. The Bush administration no longer regarded China as a certain adversary of the United States in East Asia. Although that possibility was not totally dismissed, for the near and medium term, Beijing became a partner in the effort to battle terrorism and contain the threats to peace and stability posed by rogue states. That China assumed a central role in 2003 by creating a forum for negotiations on the North Korea issue was particularly significant.

At the same time, Washington became increasingly concerned about political initiatives from Taipei to which the PRC might decide it had to respond, such as a new constitution to be ratified by referendum. Washington was concerned about a Chinese overreaction, and by December 2003 was expressing its frustrations with Chen in public.

One approach that the United States has not taken on the Taiwan Strait issue is to become an intermediary between Beijing and Taipei, although proposals to that effect have been made. For example, David Shambaugh in early 2001 suggested that Washington try to "jump-start" negotiations and use its "considerable influence and leverage" to bring the two sides to the table.[27] But the closest that the United States government has come to serving as an intermediary was in the late 1990s, when the Clinton administration urged the two sides rhetorically to resume the discussions between the semiofficial Straits Exchange Foundation and the Association for Relations across the Taiwan Strait that had begun earlier in the decade. Yet this was part of the larger approach of dual deterrence, part of an effort to reduce tensions and the possibility of miscalculations. Washington was careful to confine itself to rhetorical exhortations and to emphasize that any dialogue that occurred must be on a mutually acceptable basis. The United States stood on the outermost margins of an intermediary role.

The other approach that the United States does not consider an option is opting out. The U.S. stake in peace and security in the Taiwan Strait is so great and the need to preserve its credibility among all regional actors so profound that it cannot simply wash its hands of the issue. And Taiwan has sufficient leverage over U.S. policy to ensure that no administration would follow that path.

The U.S. approach to the Taiwan Strait issue since 1995 has been dual deterrence, with one short exception. It works to shape the intentions of both Beijing and Taipei so that neither acts in a way that is provocative to the other. Yet, as noted above, these policy approaches are more analytic constructs than mutually exclusive policy options. Although one may be dominant in a particular period, the others are not completely absent. Some level of deterrence has always existed. Thus, amid positive context creation in the early 1990s, the Bush administration provided Taiwan with advanced systems like F-16s to compensate for the PRC's military modernization and so strengthen deterrence. The second Clinton administration supplemented dual deterrence with calls for dialogue—a restrained type of intermediation.

Moreover, which approach Washington emphasizes and its precise implementation is a reaction to shifting circumstances in an increasingly dynamic environment. If a broad majority on Taiwan was to conclude that economic interdependence was far more important than the issues of sovereignty and security, then context creation might again be an appropriate approach for the United States. Within the approach of dual deterrence, Washington must decide how to balance its mix of warnings and reassurances vis-à-vis Beijing and Taipei. If the PRC's military modernization is a growing concern or if Taipei's political initiatives seem too provocative, warnings take precedence over reassurances for both sides.

To shift from dual deterrence to asymmetric deterrence, as the Bush administration did when it came into office in 2001, carries risks. An actor who believes that it is no longer the object of restraint may feel free to act as it wishes toward a party that is restrained. That was Taipei's response to the initial Bush policy, based on the belief that it had received a blank check from the United States. Timothy Crawford uses the term "pivotal deterrence," in which one actor—the pivot—is engaged in dual deterrence vis-à-vis two others. He writes, "As with all types of deterrence, therefore, the point is to prevent war by making the potential belligerents fear the costs. . . . A key to pivotal deterrence is that the pivot avoid firm commitments. These will embolden the beneficiary; so the pivot maximizes its leverage over both adversaries by keeping its freedom of action."[28] If either Beijing or Taipei believes that the United States is no longer restraining it, the U.S. effort to preserve peace and stability is undermined.

If effective deterrence in the Taiwan Strait requires both threats and reassurances, then dual deterrence is tantamount to making a conditional commitment to each side. In effect, Washington's message to both Beijing and Taipei is that it will defend Taiwan under some circumstances and not others. That is why the United States tells China that it insists on peaceful resolution and does not support Taiwan independence and why it urges Taipei not to unilaterally change the status quo while denying any U.S. intention to sell out Taiwan. In April 2004, in response to Chen Shui-bian's proposal for major constitutional change, James Kelly, assistant secretary of state for East Asian and Pacific affairs, declared both that the United States would fulfill its obligations to help Taiwan defend itself and that "there are limitations with respect to what the United States will support as Taiwan considers possible changes to its constitution."[29]

How does strategic ambiguity relate to dual deterrence? If the former concept simply means that the United States will not say what it will do if a conflict occurs, then that meaning has been transcended. The 1995–96 crisis showed Washington that in a new era defined by democracy in Taiwan and military modernization in China, silence about its probable response was not sufficient to prevent conflict. Instead, it would have to be clearer about what actions on either side it considered destabilizing in order to ensure that they did not occur—hence the replacement of a more passive approach with dual deterrence and a more active effort to encourage restraint. Ambiguity remained, of course, regarding what actions were considered destabilizing. A competition emerged among Beijing, Taipei, and Washington over who had the right to so define any particular action. Ambiguity was also manifested in the difficult search for the proper balance of warnings and threats. Ambiguity, therefore, was sometimes a tool for ensuring dual deterrence and sometimes an obstacle.[30]

Conclusion

In order to protect its fundamental interest in peace and security in East Asia, the United States has played a critical role in managing the Taiwan Strait issue. Although the object of leverage by both Taipei and Beijing, it has exerted its own leverage on each to prevent the dispute from spinning out of control. It has emphasized process (peaceful resolution) over substance. Its default approach has been one of dual deterrence, combining warnings and reassurances. It has avoided intermediation, preferring to let circumstances emerge that allow Beijing and Taipei to find a way to solve the dispute themselves. Opting out, however, is not an option.

10

Muting Pressures,
Reconciling Differences

To summarize the discussion thus far, the following can be said: Relations between China and Taiwan are potentially dangerous as well as mutually beneficial. There is extensive economic and social interaction across the Strait. Taiwan and the mainland are collaborating with each other to compete in the global economy in an array of products and services. Taiwan's young people see the PRC as a place of employment opportunity. Taiwan universities, museums, sports organizations, and charities have mainland programs. All such interaction is a basis for broader cooperation between the two sides of the Strait. At the same time, each side is increasing its military power, the PRC decidedly so. The cross-Strait dispute could, through design, accident, or miscalculation, erupt in war. It would be a war that the United States would probably end up fighting.

Preventing the outbreak of war is an important policy objective of all three sides—the United States, Taiwan, and China—because each has a lot to lose. Mutual deterrence is one way to achieve that goal, and deterrence has been effective over the last five decades. Yet deterrence is a complicated undertaking, and changing circumstances over the last decade have made it more complicated. There is always the danger that each side will misperceive the intentions of the other and overreact to actions that are objectively non-threatening, as the crisis of 1995–96 demonstrated. At that time and at other times of rising tensions, the United States was compelled to intervene at least diplomatically to prevent further escalation of the conflict or the eruption of war through accident or miscalculation. Complicating matters even further is not only China's growing military power, which gives it options it lacked before, but also a fundamental asymmetry in the dangers that each side fears. Taiwan fears a military attack by China, as it always has. What China fears of Taiwan is not the use of force but political initiatives—steps such as a declaration of independence—that would permanently sever the island from China. Since "separatist" actions are in the eye of the victim of separation, the danger increases that China will act on the basis of a flawed misperception of Taipei's motives.

An alternative to war or deterrence would be a negotiated solution to the conflict. There was some hope in the early 1990s that such a resolution might be possible, but it soon vanished. Ever since, the cross-Strait story has alternated between periodic tensions and uneasy stalemate.

There are two core issues that are obstacles to any negotiated solution. The first is a fundamental disagreement over the legal identity of the Taipei government. Does it possess sovereignty now and would it also do so within the context of any unification arrangement? Taiwan has consistently answered those questions in the affirmative and argued, in effect, that it should and does have the absolute right to rule within the territory under its jurisdiction (minus any powers it might voluntarily choose to cede) and to participate in the international community as a full member. It believes that it should not be subordinate to the PRC government. Beijing, on the other hand, has consistently promoted the one-country, two-systems formula for unification, under which Taiwan would be a special administrative region subordinate to the central government, which would be the exclusive sovereign. Any participation by Taiwan in the international system would be under Beijing's aegis and at its discretion. Taiwan would enjoy home rule but not sovereignty. And Beijing's redesign of the Hong Kong political system strongly suggests that it would seek to ensure that only forces with which it was comfortable would "rule at home."

In this regard, Beijing misunderstood and misrepresented the intentions of Lee Teng-hui and Chen Shui-bian. It regarded their opposition to the one-country, two-systems formula as opposition to unification itself. In the PRC's eyes, they were separatists, promoting either two Chinas or Taiwan's independence. A disagreement over *how* Taiwan might be a part of China was translated, in Beijing's mindset, into a dispute over *whether* Taiwan saw itself as a part of China. The PRC missed opportunities to engage both Lee and Chen early in their tenures. That it did not frustrated the two presidents and gave them less incentive to compromise. In each case, a spiral of mistrust and political confrontation ensued.

The second core issue is the security dilemma that exists between the two sides. Each mistrusts the intentions of the other and so seeks security in new weapons systems that only foster the adversary's anxiety. China has refused to renounce the use of force because it sees the threat of attack as its principal deterrent against a political breakout by Taiwan. Taiwan regards Beijing's refusal as a sign of bad faith. Taiwan relies on its alliance with the United States as its ultimate deterrent against PRC aggression, which China sees as proof of malevolent intentions on the part of Washington *and* Taipei. Having secured U.S. backing, Taiwan would be very reluctant to give it up unless it had a high degree of confidence that it was no longer necessary, and so far China has not offered that kind of reassurance. Indeed, it is not clear that China sees any value in making Taiwan feel more secure.

These two issues form a two-stranded conceptual knot that has to be untied if there is to be a negotiated settlement. Moreover, the strands that form the knot are twisted—that is, sovereignty and security are linked. Taiwan fears that if it gave up its claim to sovereignty, it would have little basis to ask for security assistance from other countries.

Aggravating matters—tightening the knot—are three other factors. The first is the impact of domestic politics in each country. In Taiwan, decades of repression fostered a significant fear of outsiders, a strong Taiwanese identity, and, in some quarters, the ambition to make the island a separate country. The Democratic Progressive Party became the primary vessel of the Taiwan sense of identity, and it entertained the idea of promoting independence as a goal. It backed away from that objective in a pragmatic bid for political power because the island was at least economically dependent on the mainland and because it had to convince voters that it would not act in a reckless manner. Yet the combination of separate identity and fear of outsiders constrains many Taiwanese from accommodating China too easily. On the PRC side, Taiwan can become an issue in elite conflict, as some leaders occasionally see political advantage in attacking others for their conduct of Taiwan policy. When public opinion, well informed or not, sees both reason and opportunity to criticize the leadership, that criticism creates constraints as well. Thus it appears that Hu Jintao will defer any major initiatives on Taiwan policy for the short term.

Politics has another impact. If there should be a negotiated settlement, it would have to be ratified within Taiwan's political process. Given the fundamental nature of the issues, that would probably require amending the constitution, which in turn requires the support of most of the island's political parties. Otherwise securing the requisite supermajorities would be impossible. Without that sort of broad consensus, it would be difficult to ensure that an agreement would endure and not provoke chronic partisan bickering, instability, and polarization. Even if Beijing offered an arrangement that was optimal from Taiwan's perspective, securing approval would not be automatic. The second aggravating factor is the decisionmaking system on each side. In both Beijing and Taipei, policy formulation on this issue is centralized and personalized. Each side is prone to misperception and miscalculation.

The third aggravating factor is the zero-sum leverage game that each side plays against each other. Taipei seeks to break Beijing's monopoly in the international community, and Beijing works hard to preserve it. China mounted a united front campaign focused on the island's business community and pan-Blue political parties to undermine the Chen administration and to ensure that Chen was not reelected. (Because the PRC is a relatively closed system, Taiwan cannot be an actor in Chinese politics.) The leverage game exacerbates mutual mistrust.

Part of this game is the role of the United States. Taiwan seeks to solidify and strengthen its ties with the United States, even to the point of manipulating the U.S. political system; Beijing seeks to weaken that material and psychological support. The United States cannot afford to opt out of the Taiwan Strait issue in spite of these conflicting pressures; its stake in peace and security is too great. It has provided security support to Taiwan, which Beijing regards as the key obstacle to resolving the dispute on its own terms. The default U.S. approach has been dual deterrence: restraining Beijing from using force against Taiwan but refusing support for any separatist aims in Taiwan and constraining Taiwan from taking provocative political initiatives while calming the island's periodic fears of abandonment.

Can this twisted, tightened knot ever be untied? Obviously, it could if either side would concede on fundamentals. Beijing could abandon the goal of unification and permit the emergence of a totally independent Taiwan. Taipei could renounce its claim of sovereignty, accept the one-country, two-systems proposal, and trust China enough to give up U.S. security assistance. One cannot rule out the possibility that China's strategy of using economic attraction and united front tactics to weaken Taiwan's position will ultimately work, producing the latter scenario. But the differences over principles and the dynamics of Taiwan domestic politics suggest that such outcomes are highly unlikely. Just as obviously, it may be that this knot can never be untied and that all parties concerned will have to live and cope with a conflict that cannot be resolved (see chapter 11). Nonetheless, it is still worth exploring the possibility of a negotiated settlement. Are there ways of bridging the gaps in the two parties' conceptual views of sovereignty and security? Are there ways of reducing the impact of the aggravating factors—domestic politics, the leverage game, and decisionmaking systems? If the answer is yes on both counts, how might the two sides return to the negotiating table?

Is There Substantive Common Ground?

Because there are real substantive issues that divide Beijing and Taipei, some way must be found to bridge the gaps if there is ever to be a settlement of the dispute. That is, even if aggravating factors were mitigated, disagreements over sovereignty and security would still remain. This section explores the ideas that have been floated so far and how each side has responded to them.

The Sovereignty Dispute

The sovereignty dispute raises the question of whether there are forms of political union that encompass sovereign entities. If there are, hypothetically Beijing could get what it wants (unification) without Taipei giving up what it wishes to preserve (sovereignty). Of course, a number of arrangements seek to preserve some authority and independence for political units within the context of a larger union, among them the following:

—a conventional unitary nation-state, in which political subdivisions enjoy some delegated powers

—"special autonomy" regimes, in which the delegation of power to subunits is especially extensive and entrenched

—federalism, in which the component entities in theory retain some sovereignty in their own hands although not always with any practical consequence

—suzerainty, protectorate status, or mandate or trust territories, in which the lesser entity in principle could retain the full attributes of sovereignty but has ceded, at least temporarily, many elements of sovereignty to a foreign entity

—commonwealth structures, in which most of the attributes of sovereignty in principle and in practice and in the eyes of the world rest with political entities within a larger state or superstate conglomerate that retains a thin residuum of sovereignty (such as the British Commonwealth)

—a confederation, in which separate sovereign states reassign some limited sovereign powers to a collectivity to be exercised by a supranational institution (such as the EU)

—divided states, in which a people (such as the Germans or Koreans) is at least temporarily split into two or more states.[1]

The United States began as a confederation and then evolved into a federal system. Even after the shift, in 1787, the term most commonly used to refer to the country was "these United States," a reflection of the individual states' belief in their respective sovereignty. It was only after the Civil War that the current name, the United States, with its stronger implication of a unitary system, became common.

As deLisle points out, the various models of complex or intermediate sovereignty are complicated by first principles about the initial locus of sovereignty. "In some of the models, sovereignty initially resides in separate components that transfer sovereign rights to another entity or partially merge their sovereign powers in a larger entity. In other models, a single unitary state delegates—ultimately as an internal, discretionary and revocable matter—to a subordinate entity some of the sovereign authority that the state alone possesses."[2] Taiwan's stance on the initial locus of sovereignty, particularly in Chen Shui-bian's eyes, would be consistent with the former approach, not the latter. The sovereign status of the ROC or Taiwan is a fact, not something that Beijing would grant.

A related issue is Taiwan's consistent insistence that its government is in a fundamental sense equal to that in Beijing. That principle underlay Lee Teng-hui's ambiguous formulation of "political entities" and his later, more explicit assertion that the ROC was a state, just like the PRC. Chen Shui-bian has reiterated the idea of parity between the two sides. Taiwan's opposition to the one-country, two-systems formula stems from its (correct) belief that the arrangement would result in its subordination to Beijing. The closest that Beijing has come to addressing Taiwan's concern is to promise "consultations on an equal footing." Yet this clearly relates to the form of the negotiations, not the legal status of the parties to the negotiations. It refers to the process by which reconciliation would occur but not to the ultimate outcome.[3]

At least in the abstract, the approach that constitutes the middle ground between the two sides is a confederation, in which the ROC and PRC would be equal, constituent parts of a larger China. And on Taiwan, the concept has increasing appeal as a formula for addressing its political relationship with China, precisely because the units that form a confederation retain sovereignty in a meaningful way. Moreover, there have been cases of confederations in which the individual units of the state retain some ability to conduct external relations.[4]

In a systematic review of the Taiwan Strait issue, the International Crisis Group (ICG) comes to a similar, though not identical conclusion. It considers four possible options, two of which have little or no appeal to Taiwan and one of which would be hard for Beijing to swallow. The first option is the one-country, two-systems option. ICG regards that as a federal model but observes that "the degree of subservience to central authority still implied continues to have no attraction for Taiwan." The second is what it calls an "asymmetric 'federacy' linking an autonomous entity to a larger state, offering Taiwan a stronger separate identity and more actual autonomy, as well as demilitarization and international security guarantees." That would be hard for Taiwan to accept; securing demilitarization and security guarantees would be difficult. The third option is a confederation, which, ICG believes, "has lingering support in Taiwan but not in Beijing, which continues to find antithetical any notion of sovereign equality."

ICG's fourth option is a Greater Chinese Union, which conceptually is between a confederation and the "thinnest" possible federation. Under this rubric, both sides would accept a larger common identity, and Taiwan would maintain its current political system and gain membership in many international organizations.[5]

It was in the direction of confederation that the DPP began to move as it accepted the reality of the magnetic force of the PRC economy and recognized that full independence was an illusion. Younger DPP thinkers had begun to consider approaches to peaceful coexistence and national unification that might entail diminution of Taiwan's sovereignty (see chapter 6). And, as noted previously, at the very end of 2000 Chen Shui-bian said: "We appeal to the government and leaders on the other side to gradually build trust between the two sides, starting from the integration of cross-strait economic, trade, and cultural affairs and then jointly searching for new framework of lasting peace and political integration between the two sides, thereby working together to explore the space of unlimited possibilities in the utmost interests of the people on the two sides of the Strait."[6]

There were some in Chen's own party, particularly in the fundamentalist faction, who objected to his new formulation precisely because it charted a path toward political union with China.[7] But scholars sympathetic to Chen endorsed the move as a pragmatic way to preserve Taiwan's interests, pointing to the European Union as a good model. Byron S. J. Weng of Chi-nan University commented that "political confederation ... is not hard to create but difficult to maintain ... the EU has achieved a great deal without threatening the political sovereignty of its member states. The member states still have the veto power over any policy that they chose not to accept [that is not completely true]. Perhaps it is the premise that political sovereignty will not be taken away that makes the economic integration successful." David Huang of Academia Sinica saw integration along the lines of European integration as a long-term process and so a win-win option for both sides. It was good for China because, although the final outcome is not certain, unacceptable outcomes (Taiwan's independence) become much less likely. Huang argues that if Beijing were to offer the integration approach, Taiwan should accept it because it would bring economic benefits and constitute Chinese recognition that Taiwan possesses sovereignty. "Once the integration process kicks off, China will in fact have admitted that Taiwan has a certain form of sovereignty or autonomy." The PRC's reaction, Huang predicted, would spell the fate of the proposal. "Now that Chen has given away the 'certainty' of direction toward cross-strait integration, is Beijing willing to accept the uncertain outcome of such integration?"[8]

Not to be outdone, the KMT quickly entered the lists a few days later. Chairman Lien Chan specifically offered confederation as his formula for "political integration." His aides asserted that his was much clearer than Chen's proposal and that "while it is too early to consider unification, the confederation idea is worthy for consideration." As they later elaborated, confederation would be a "roof" built by both sides but preserving the principles of equality, separate government, peace, and gradualism. Confederation was an appropriate middle ground between a commonwealth or a federation. The former was "a loose organization without any goal of unification while in a federation, all the member states enjoy no rights of autonomy." Interestingly, the examples that the KMT cited were historical (Switzerland from 1291 to 1796, the United States from 1778 to 1787, and Germany from 1815 to 1866). Perhaps to maintain some distinction between the KMT and Chen and the DPP, the European Union was left unmentioned.[9]

Beijing rejected the integration/confederation proposals. The first signal came on March 4, 2001, from a spokesman of the National People's Congress, who said that the PRC "disagree[d] to the mode of the 'confederation system.'" Later in the month, in an interview with the *Washington Post*, Jiang Zemin offered his view: "Federation or confederation, both an organizational form of the state, is not to be copied everywhere. Their existence and adoption are based on the specific historical background and distinct national conditions. Confederation involves the union of two or more sovereign states. In essence, it does not imply a unified state. Federation does not conform with the historical tradition and national conditions of China." He argued that some of the features of the one-country, two-systems approach, such as Taiwan keeping its military forces, "have gone beyond what members of a federation may enjoy. The United States is a federation. Its states do not have what Taiwan may enjoy under the 'one country, two systems' formula." Chinese officials then had to scramble to resolve the inconsistency between Jiang's oft-stated pledge that "anything can be discussed" and his apparent rejection of the confederation formula. An unnamed PRC official said that "Taiwan may put forward its proposals, such as confederation or federation, and the two sides may eventually reach a certain compromise in their political negotiations." Of course, Beijing insists that those discussions must occur under the one-China principle, which, based on its own definition, is probably inconsistent with a confederal solution.[10]

The answer to Chen's integration proposal came in an article in *Liaowang*. The author offered a long analysis that dismissed the seriousness of the idea, questioned Chen's intentions, and came to this conclusion:

> It is lamentable that as a lawyer, the leader of the Taiwanese authorities has wasted all of this ingenuity; his clever words are all for naught, his "'Integration Theory" largely discusses "reunification and amalgamation." But not only has he not discussed clearly whether there ultimately will be "reunification" or not, he has been unclear as well, even more than speaking unclearly, he has purposely let everyone interpret him as they will, so that he can have it any way he wishes, and from this "peacefully move toward splittism." Blinded by greed, he deceives himself and others. The concept of "Integration Theory" is an excuse that is ambiguous while it obfuscates; but it cannot conceal the obvious scheme of splittism that is hidden behind it.[11]

Guo Zhenyuan, a researcher at the China International Affairs Institute, drew out some important practical implications of the confederation model, which he termed "not a truly unified country but an aggregate of sovereign states." He noted: "Given that there are many differences and contradictions between the two sides of the strait, even if a confederation system is established, it will certainly be difficult to consolidate it amid the continual intensification of conflicts of interest." He asserted that a one-country, two-systems approach would allow the two sides to take advantage of each other's strong points. Why that was not true of confederation and why conflicts would not occur under the one-country, two-systems model were not explained.[12]

A later analysis by the Institute of Strategic Studies at Tsinghua University in Beijing focused more on the practical difficulties. It acknowledged that a U.S.-style confederation should not be rejected out of hand conceptually; the operational question was the power of the central government and whether it would be able to achieve its goals. A federation "as a unified country" was also conceptually acceptable, although how to divide powers between the highest level of government and the subordinate states "may prove to be the Achilles' heel in this model."[13]

These points are well taken. Confederations of various forms are political unions that are prone to conflict. Recall Weng's statement that "political confederation . . . is not hard to create but difficult to maintain." Or, to put it differently, if a confederation is not created well it is likely to be unsustainable. The negotiation process that brings it about must be comprehensive in scope. Witness the difficulties that undermined the U.S. confederation and the irreparable harm done to the federation of 1787 because the issue of slavery was not addressed up front. In the case of Taiwan and China, resolving the issues of national defense and foreign policy would be particularly tough.

But practical difficulty is one thing; blindness to opportunity is another. If Beijing refuses to show flexibility on Taipei's claim that its government possesses sovereignty, then there will never be an opportunity to address the difficulties in working out a confederal arrangement that meets the minimum needs of each side. The DPP government has been willing to at least entertain the idea of a national union as long as it is one that accommodates its legal identity. That some PRC scholars do not as a matter of principle rule out models of union other than one-country, two-systems model is a positive sign. Yet the government's apparent rejection of these approaches has become a central obstacle to progress.

There probably are other reasons that PRC leaders find confederation so unappealing that they reject it on principle rather than on the level of practicality. One reason, which was offered right after Lien Chan made his proposal public, was the slippery-slope problem. An anonymous PRC official told a Taiwan newspaper that "if Taiwan tries to establish a 'confederation,' many autonomous regions inhabited by the minority ethnic groups in China, such as Xinjiang, Tibet, and Inner Mongolia will follow its example, and China will then deviate from the direction of reunification and will be split up even before a 'confederation' can be established."[14]

That observation may offer a clue to Beijing's fundamental resistance to Taipei's approach to unification. PRC leaders may believe that to pursue a political union in which Taiwan would possess sovereignty—a confederation perhaps—would undermine their fundamental authority over the territory under their jurisdiction. For them to accept the idea that there would be another and equal sovereign unit within that union, particularly when the other unit is organized democratically, would undermine the PRC govern-ment's position as the exclusive sovereign and the vanguard role of the Communist Party. Beijing thus may see no choice but to offer only home rule to Taiwan under the one-country, two-systems model because it is inex-tricably linked with how Beijing views its rule at home.

Security

Creating a zone of convergence on security issues and the joint political will to move there is not as easy as dealing with the sovereignty question, on which there is a conceptual common ground and at least one side has shown interest. Some ideas have emerged, but they all have drawbacks.

IDEAS ON THE TWO SIDES OF THE STRAIT. As noted in chapter 5, since 1979 the two sides have taken steps or floated ideas on how to address mil-itary issues, but all of them raise as many questions as they answer. To reiterate and expand that discussion:

—Beijing has promised that Taiwan could keep its armed forces after unification, with the proviso that they be of a certain size, have the mission of maintaining national defense and security, and not threaten China.

—The PRC has suggested occasionally that it would continue to allow Taiwan to purchase "necessary weapons from third parties as long as they shall not harm the interests of the country."[15] But it seems reasonable that the PRC would retain final say over such acquisitions, because it would be the sovereign.

—Taipei has renounced the use of force, which is something of a symbolic gesture since it really does not pose a threat to the mainland. It has urged Beijing to do the same, but China has refused, on the grounds that such a concession would only encourage "separatism."

—Both sides have discussed reaching some kind of agreement on ending the state of hostilities, but nothing has happened because of the overriding sovereignty issue.

—Jiang Zemin tentatively explored an arms control mechanism, wherein China would reduce its missiles if U.S. arms sales diminished, but he did so in a way that made Taipei feel more insecure, not less.

Neither together nor separately do these steps seem to create enough common ground to mitigate the mistrust that the two sides feel toward each other. Statements of intentions are not trivial, but in a climate of mutual mistrust they are not sufficiently reassuring. The PRC's military power will continue to grow. Ending the state of hostilities might be a useful step toward developing a more comprehensive solution to Taipei's security problem, but it would not in and of itself solve the problem. And none of the PRC's offers amount to the sort of incentives that Taipei would likely need to give up U.S. support, as Beijing would probably ask it to do.

CONFIDENCE-BUILDING MEASURES. Another potential source of common ground is the extensive repertoire of confidence-building measures (CBMs) that have been developed, particularly in Europe, over a number of decades. Their purpose is to reduce uncertainty between armed adversaries and to limit the possibility of military conflict occurring by accident or miscalculation, particularly when opposing forces operate in close proximity to each other. These take a variety of forms:

—declarations, such as renunciations of the use of force
—communications measures, such as hotlines, ship visits, and functional exchanges
—maritime safety measures, to limit accidents between ships patrolling the same area
—constraint measures, such as thinning out forces near borders
—transparency measures, such as notification of exercises and troop movements, data exchange, exchange of military attachés, and publication of defense white papers
—verification measures, to ensure compliance with agreements and understandings.[16]

There has been some discussion, mainly by Western analysts, about using CBMs in the current cross-Strait context. The principal focus has been how they might prevent crises like those of 1995–96 and early 2000 from escalating through accident or miscalculation, but there is no reason why CBMs could not be used as a device to help resolve the dispute. Military CBMs might be very useful in ameliorating and attenuating the sense of insecurity that Taiwan would continue to feel even in the context of some sort of settlement.

Taiwan has expressed an interest in pursuing CBMs. Chen Shui-bian advocated them during his election campaign, and they are one element of Taiwan's national defense policy, as described in the current defense white paper: "Through dialogue and exchange of security issues between two sides of the Taiwan Strait, we hope to promote transparency in military affairs on both sides to increase mutual understanding so as to maintain stability and security in this region."[17]

Traditionally, Beijing has been unwilling to discuss CBMs, for a couple of stated reasons. One is its blanket refusal to talk with Taipei because the latter has not accepted the one-China principle. Second, the PRC has opposed using CBMs for the cross-Strait situation because of how it defines Taiwan. China has developed a variety of interstate CBMs with Russia and Central Asian countries, but Beijing argues that CBMs should be undertaken only between states, and, according to its definition, Taiwan is not a state. This in spite of the fact that CBMs have also been established between states and nonstate actors: the United Kingdom and the IRA; Israel and the PLO. The unstated reason, probably, is that the PRC believes that its interests are better served by destroying Taiwan's confidence rather than building it.[18]

Beijing's position began to shift in October 2002 when Jiang Zemin, in a meeting with President Bush, suggested that if the United States addressed China's concerns on arms sales to Taiwan, it would consider redeploying missiles that targeted the island. As noted previously, there were several problems with this proposal, the most significant being that Jiang suggested that Washington and Beijing should negotiate over Taiwan's security. But it had the positive virtue of admitting that there was a link between PRC deployments on one hand and Taiwan's perception of threat and arms acquisitions on the other, and it recognized that fostering confidence might have value. Then, in May 2004, China stated that CBMs could be on the agenda of cross-Strait interaction—but only if Taipei accepted the one-China principle and abandoned any claims to independence.[19]

ARMS CONTROL. Confidence-building measures seek to manage and constrain the *use* of military capabilities; they do not speak to the existence and extent of military assets and so provide only a partial answer to the question of insecurity. Arms control would limit capabilities themselves, but there has been little or no discussion of it in the cross-Strait context, although Jiang Zemin's missile-redeployment proposal might be seen a start in that direction. To the extent that the Chinese military buildup reduces Taiwan's incentives to enter into a settlement, particularly one that entails an end to its U.S. security relationship, an arms control regime that placed limits on that buildup theoretically could improve the incentive structure. For arms control to work, however, credible verification is essential. However, there is nothing in past Chinese behavior to suggest that it would be prepared to accept intrusive verification.

The ideas floated so far do little to address the special, asymmetric security dilemma that exists between China and Taiwan and the significant overhanging issue of mutual mistrust. But any solution to the Taiwan Strait dispute will have to address the fears that each has about the other. For example, Taiwan's anxiety about the PRC's capabilities and intentions is so ingrained that even an agreement to terminate hostilities or China's formal renunciation of the use of force would not allay its mistrust. Taipei would be concerned about postsettlement PRC efforts to manipulate Taiwan's political system.

In order to reduce the cross-Strait security dilemma, some Western specialists have proposed an agreement based on pledges by each side not to do what the other most fears.[20] Thus Beijing would renounce the use of force regarding Taiwan and Taipei would pledge not to declare independence. Such an approach is similar to Beijing's approach to an agreement to end the state of hostilities, under which it would be giving at least a limited pledge not to use force (since hostilities would no longer exist) and Taipei would accept the one-China principle (an implicit commitment not to declare independence).

This proposal is initially appealing because it takes seriously each side's mistrust and perceptions of threat, yet it falters when it comes down to operationalizing the trade-off. How would the terms "use of force" and "declare independence" be defined? Each side would seek to define its obligation as narrowly as possible and the other's commitment as broadly as possible. Indeed, China is now concerned not about a Taiwan declaration of independence, which Taiwan leaders know would provoke a strong PRC response, but about other steps that have the same substantive effect. Moreover, even if definitional issues could be resolved, neither side would trust the other not to renege on its commitment. And if one side or both claimed that the other had reneged—if Beijing, for example, charged that activities in or by Taiwan were inconsistent with a no-independence pledge—who would judge the validity of the claim and decide what to do next?

This example indicates the complexity of ameliorating or resolving the security dilemma. It is not enough to find a way to reconcile the substantive differences between the two sides. Any solution must also address the fears that each has that the other will cheat on its obligations and place it in a more disadvantageous position. Beijing and Taipei were willing to give each other some benefit of the doubt in the early 1990s, but they gave less thereafter, as each took steps that caused the other to question its fundamental assumptions. It may be that some mix of political declarations, military CBMs, and arms control would appear to be enough to ameliorate the cross-Strait security dilemma, if each side could be assumed to keep its obligations. Unless the corrosive effect of mistrust is neutralized, the two sides are unlikely to step onto common ground, even though it objectively exists. Taiwan, of course, will be more reluctant to do so because it sees U.S. support as a better guarantee of its security than the PRC's promises.

There are several ways out of this conundrum.[21] The first is to rectify perceptions. Because each side to some degree misperceived the intentions of the other, neither could take seriously any gestures of reassurance that were inconsistent with its misperceptions. The second way out, one related to the first, is to talk. Since 1995, there has been very little direct contact between authorized representatives of the two governments. The "communication" that has occurred has been in the media, often for propaganda purposes. The absence of direct contact—and with it the lack of opportunity to correct misperceptions—only exacerbates the mistrust. Yet Beijing has sought to withhold dialogue unless Taipei gives some signal in advance that it does not have a separatist agenda.

The third way is to sweeten the pot, to increase the incentives for a settlement. If, for example, Beijing were to concede on the sovereignty question, Taipei would likely come to a more relaxed view of its vulnerability. Not only would such a concession create a very different assessment of Chinese intentions, it would also bring with it substantive safeguards. Beijing, of course, would be reluctant to make such concessions because other subordinate units might seek the same treatment, making demands that might be interpreted as a threat to China's security.

The fourth way of ameliorating the cross-Strait security dilemma is to use process to facilitate substantive progress. Here the issue is whether it is better to seek a solution more or less all at once or to break it into steps. "Grand bargains" are intellectually appealing but often politically impractical, precisely because they do not take account of the mistrust factor. Indeed, any effort to "solve" all or most of the issues at one time will magnify the parties' suspicions because the risk of being left with nothing more than broken promises is so great. The alternative is to segment the process so that concluding and implementing an agreement on one issue builds confidence for tackling the next issue. Resolving relatively simple problems makes it easier to address harder ones. A process of conditional and reciprocal action (otherwise known as "tit for tat"), wherein one side's move at round X is rewarded or punished in the other side's move at round $X + 1$, will increase the likelihood that both will cooperate and not renege. (In game theory terminology, this is a shift from a one-round game to a multiround, or iterative, game.)

One suggested solution to the problem of how to phase negotiations in an environment of mistrust is an interim agreement. The premise of such an approach is that there is simply insufficient political will on each side to resolve all the issues and that there is potential danger in the status quo. Bounding the disagreement for an agreed-upon period and creating some measure of political confidence would, it is argued, reduce the chance of conflict and improve the prospects for full resolution. One example of such an approach, as first offered by Kenneth Lieberthal in the late 1990s, called for an arrangement that would last for several decades. The keys to that arrangement would be the trade-off cited above: Taiwan would explicitly commit to not pursuing de jure independence; the PRC would explicitly commit to not using force.[22]

Generally, Taiwan has tended to prefer an incremental process of addressing technical issues first as a way of building confidence and then moving to political matters. China has tended to want to accelerate the process and move faster to political issues. The interim agreement idea illustrates the problem of trying to resolve too much, too soon. Negotiating the no-independence and no-force commitments at the heart of the approach might undermine the whole effort. During the interim period, Taiwan would no doubt seek to protect its sovereignty claim and prevent Beijing from taking coercive actions that fell short of the use of force. China would likely try to get Taipei to refrain from actions that fell within its broad definition of asserting independence and to obtain some assurance that unification would come after the interim agreement expired. Negotiations would founder on the problems that are at the core of the dispute. Such efforts at equity protection illustrate a larger point: in incremental processes each side would need some degree of confidence that the overall direction of the process was one that it could accept—that is, negotiations would have to occur within the context of some shared sense of goals.

Aggravating Factors

Even if the two governments could broaden the common ground on sovereignty and security, they would still have to lessen the aggravating impact of their respective efforts to exert leverage on the other and the constraints imposed by domestic politics. Those are factors that can be managed but not neutralized.

Leverage Game

If there is to be progress, it is essential that China forswear any intention to meddle in Taiwan's politics through united front activities, before or after any settlement. That Beijing even has the option of shaping Taiwan policy from within creates an unfair advantage, since China has a closed political system. It also creates profound anxiety among those in Taiwan whom Beijing should be trying to attract: the people who most suspect its motives. To give up this advantage would be a trust-building act of good faith. And in a way, this issue is a practical corollary of the sovereignty issue. If Beijing is prepared to accept that the Taipei government is a sovereign entity with the right to rule in the territory under its jurisdiction—acceptance that, for Taiwan, appears to be the sine qua non of any settlement—then it should not take actions to manipulate politics on the island. United front activities by definition presume that Taipei does not possess sovereignty. It is not always easy, of course, to determine whether Beijing is conducting such activities, and it would never admit to doing so. Some on Taiwan will never be convinced that the PRC is not meddling. But an effort to make a significant improvement in the current situation would likely be noticed by most and build confidence.

On the international front, what is necessary is a diplomatic truce. Under such an arrangement, perhaps, Taipei and Beijing would not seek to steal each other's diplomatic partners. Neither would they seek to fortify their respective positions by trying to secure inappropriate support from the United States. Taiwan's efforts to gain some status in the United Nations and the World Health Organization would continue but on a more restrained basis, so that Beijing would not have to respond with a full-court press. In return, Beijing would not seek to limit Taiwan's participation in those organizations in which it is already a member, like the World Trade Organization. And it might even end its opposition to Taiwan's observership in organizations where statehood is a prerequisite for membership. Mutual restraint in the international sphere will create a better atmosphere for cross-Strait dialogue. In June 2000, Taiwan's foreign minister floated the idea of a diplomatic truce. Although at the time it met with some objection from legislators and although the competition continued unabated thereafter, a truce remains the best way of enhancing the prospects for cross-Strait negotiations.[23]

Domestic Politics

Political scientists often use the "two-level game" to understand the impact of domestic politics on intergovernmental negotiations. That is, a government's negotiators must "play" at two different "tables" at the same time. At one table are the representatives of the other government; at the other are domestic constituencies that have a stake in the discussions. A successful negotiation requires satisfying those at both tables. If domestic interests are ignored, then an agreement may not receive approval back home and domestic opposition may increase. On the other hand, if domestic constituencies demand too much or prefer no agreement to one that is deemed a bad agreement, then the negotiations will deadlock.[24]

In the case of cross-Strait negotiations, the difference between the two political systems creates significant but cross-cutting asymmetries. On one hand, although each set of negotiators would be subject to some constraint from domestic constituencies, the constraint is far greater on the Taiwan side. Both the island's media and its legislature would demand a high degree of accountability from those bargaining on Taiwan's behalf. Any settlement arrived at would be subject at least to the approval of the Legislative Yuan and probably would require amending the constitution. Under current arrangements, that would require passage by three-fourths of the Legislative Yuan members present (with a quorum of three-fourths of its members) and then by three-fourths of the National Assembly members present (with a quorum of two-thirds) for territorial issues and by a majority vote for non-territorial ones. Pursuant to amendments that are likely to be passed in summer 2005, the second stage will become a popular referendum in which approval requires a majority of *eligible* voters, effectively a supermajority since voting is voluntary.

The PRC negotiators, on the other hand, would be responsible only to the leadership of the Chinese Communist Party, which would decide whether to ratify any agreement. Public opinion is not a trivial factor on the mainland, but the government has more scope for shaping it. In an ironic way, that would strengthen the hand of the Taiwan negotiators, who could make a credible argument that they have very little discretion and could secure ratification of an agreement only if it met the fundamental concerns of the broad majority of the population. The only circumstances under which the PRC would find its efforts rejected at home would be if it reached an agreement for which key policymakers had failed to prepare their colleagues in the leadership and the public. That is not out of the question, but less likely than a public revolt on Taiwan.

On the other hand, the same asymmetry might give the PRC side an advantage. There is a significant element of the Taiwan population that favors some accommodation of the PRC for economic and other reasons, and it has significant influence in the political system. It is, in effect, Beijing's silent ally. The Taiwan side lacks such an asset within the PRC system. There are local constituencies in China that have a stake in good economic relations with Taiwan and that would oppose higher cross-Strait tensions. But they have no reason to support the Taiwan government's views on political issues, and they have little or no influence on China's decisions in any case.

How might the impact of politics be mitigated? One way, of course, is for Beijing to wait for—and even promote—a shift in the balance of power in Taiwan. And that indeed is China's strategy: to facilitate cross-Strait economic relations and subtly encourage those political forces whose views are compatible with its own. That strategy may work over the long term, but the probability is not great. Such an approach ignores the part of the population that is most afraid of China, represented by the Democratic Progressive Party and the Taiwan Solidarity Union, and the fact that China's own actions often alienate those groups. And because any fundamental decisions about Taiwan's future will require the support of the DPP, ignoring and alienating it will be counter-productive. Moreover, because of that same political resistance, there is no certainty that the leaders of the KMT and the PFP would, if elected, make the sort of concessions that Beijing would probably want.

The alternative is for Beijing to accept that the political and substantive center of gravity in Taiwan is unlikely to shift in the direction of the one-country, two-systems model and to adjust its expectations accordingly. That would entail significant concessions on the issues of sovereignty, international space, and security and a corollary pledge to end any attempt to play some of the island's political groups off against others. Such accommodations would appeal to the broad majority of the island's people and ameliorate the fear of outsiders in Taiwan political culture, disarming the residual power of DPP fundamentalists and the Taiwan Solidarity Union.

The PRC's accommodation on core issues would also address to some extent the difficulty under Taiwan's political system of making decisions on controversial issues. Because the Legislative Yuan gives power to minorities to obstruct and reject proposals, it is necessary to mobilize broad majorities on even those issues that do not require constitutional amendments. Moreover, although the DPP often is divided on mainland policy, it will arguably be harder for a KMT-dominated government to mobilize such a majority because the DPP, as the opposition, will be tempted for partisan reasons to oppose any initiative (which makes Beijing's refusal to deal with Chen Shui-bian all the more shortsighted). In this case, substance can be used to overcome the problems of process.

It is unclear, however, what domestic price the Chinese leadership would pay for accommodation. Nationalistic opinion on the mainland—opinion that the regime has done a lot to shape—of course opposes the separation of Taiwan from China. Whether well-informed Chinese believe that the one-country, two-systems model is the only acceptable one for resolving the dispute is another question. At a minimum, Beijing might foster more open discussion of Taiwan policy and new concepts of unification—new interpretations of the one-country, two-systems formula, perhaps—in order to prepare the public. If there was to be a challenge to a new Taiwan policy, it would be more likely to come from within the leadership than from without. Rivals might seek to use the shift as a weapon to attack those in charge. The leadership as a whole might conclude that a creative approach to Taiwan might undermine the Chinese Communist Party's right to rule.

What is clear is that little is likely to happen until there is a broader consensus on Taiwan concerning the mainland. A relatively pragmatic leader like Chen Shui-bian cannot get the fundamentalist wing of the DPP to support moderate policies if he is simultaneously being attacked by the Blue parties and ignored by Beijing. (As described in chapter 3, Chen did try to foster consensus on mainland policy in 2000 through an extragovernmental task force, but the effort failed because it was too public and because the KMT and PFP refused to participate.) Similarly, a government led by the Blue parties will be unable to make progress with the mainland if its efforts are not tolerated by the DPP and TSU.

Finally, domestic politics have a bearing on the timing of an initiative. Even a strategy that addresses the substantive concerns of each side and mitigates the effect of aggravating factors is likely to fail if it is executed when domestic politics are unfavorable. Windows of opportunity open after new leaders on both sides have been installed but well before the next competition for power (election time in Taiwan and during the leadership transition that occurs in China every five years). A window opened right after Chen took office in May 2000, nineteen months before legislative elections and almost three years before the Chinese leadership transition that would occur in the fall 2002 and the spring 2003. But Beijing chose not to respond to Chen's overtures. By the time the PRC leadership shifts had occurred, the Taiwan presidential campaign had already begun. To complicate matters even further, Hu Jintao's assumption of the top positions in the party and government hierarchies did not mean that he had become the leading figure on Taiwan policy. But with Jiang Zemin's retirement from the chairmanship of the party and state Central Military Commissions in September 2004 and March 2005 respectively, Hu is now clearly in charge. And with Taiwan's December 2004 legislative elections out of the way, a new window for negotiations has opened. Whether the two sides have the political will to seize the opportunity is another question.

Decisionmaking Systems

Taiwan and China are not unique in their tendency to misread the intentions of the other and then respond in ways that exacerbate the situation. But they are exceptional in the absence of direct authoritative contacts that might have a corrective effect. As a result, each bases its assessments largely on what the other does in the public domain. The best way to ameliorate this problem is through communications to mitigate at least some mutual misunderstandings.

Returning to the Negotiating Table

The potential for finding common ground on the issues of sovereignty and security and for containing the impact of politics, the leverage game, and decisionmaking systems on both sides is hypothetical. None can be realized without a process through which the two sides can talk to each other. If each side is to reassure the other about its intentions, there has to be a venue in which to do that. If they are to take preliminary steps, such as establishing a diplomatic truce, some communication is needed to work out the details in advance to ensure a clear understanding of reciprocal obligations and adequate compliance. Yet there has been no dialogue since 1999, for a variety of reasons that need to be addressed if Beijing and Taipei are to return to the negotiating table.

Principles as Preconditions

The first obstacle to dialogue is the precondition that Beijing has set on resumption of talks. Specifically, it has insisted that the Chen administration accept the one-China principle or the 1992 consensus or both. Generally, imposing preconditions for negotiations denies the side that is asked to accept them enough information about what the end of the process will be to make beginning talks worthwhile. With specific reference to the demand that Taiwan accept the one-China principle, as explained in chapter 4, Taipei has been unwilling to accept it for fear of making concessions up front that would sacrifice its fundamental interests.

As for the 1992 "consensus," the two sides never agreed on the substantive meaning of "one China" and Taiwan's relationship to it, which is the heart of the dispute. In theory, that ambiguity could be a basis for the two sides to return to dialogue. If, for pragmatic reasons, Beijing needs a symbolic fig leaf to justify resuming dialogue—and if Taipei is willing to take a chance on offering one—then the 1992 consensus would be the best option. Each could emphasize what it chose to from its own statement and ignore unfavorable elements in the other's. But such a face-saving exercise is far more likely under a KMT government than a DPP one. Ma Ying-jeou, the KMT mayor of Taipei, has said that he would be willing to reaffirm the 1992 consensus. But it is hard to see how even that would mollify Beijing, since Ma's definition of each formulation contradicts the PRC's.[25] The Chen government has been more cautious, fearing that accepting the 1992 consensus as a precondition for negotiations would end up being a back-door acceptance of the one-China principle as Beijing defines it. A *Taipei Times* editorial laid out the logic. It distinguished between the PRC's international and cross-Strait or domestic definitions of the one-China principle and then warned: "There is no doubt that as soon as Taiwan signed up for the 'domestic' version, this would be portrayed by China internationally as agreeing that it [Taiwan] was part of the PRC. For any Taiwanese government to consider any concession or agreement on the 1992 consensus would be diplomatic suicide."[26]

The "consensus" may have outlasted its value as a means to bridge differences. Chen's reluctance to meet the PRC's preconditions for dialogue makes sense. There is no way of knowing in advance what Beijing is offering in terms of either substance or process in return for such a concession. And there is fear that if Taiwan's core interest—sovereignty—is not protected at the outset, it will be impossible to protect it later on.

It is worth noting that this is not the first time that Beijing has imposed preconditions for dialogue, and the ultimate outcome of that exercise is instructive. After Lee Teng-hui's 1995 visit to the United States, it demanded that he "return to the one-China principle" and renounce actions it believed contravened the principle, such as the UN campaign and presidential travel. Taipei demurred on the grounds that accepting the principle would be to submit to "verbal annexation."[27] Then in the fall of 1997, Beijing shifted course. Jiang Zemin called for talks to end the state of hostilities and for political negotiations, all on the premise of the one-China principle. The principle was later elaborated in a relatively mild form that indicated that "China" did not necessarily mean the PRC. In February 1998, Taipei responded and for the first time expressed a willingness to move toward political negotiations. The two sides then began a process of mutual signaling in which each accepted the positive elements of the other's signal and ignored the negative elements. The PRC stopped setting its preconditions for the resumption of contacts. This process culminated in the visit of Koo Chen-fu to Shanghai and Beijing in October. At least for those meetings, the one-China principle was not an obstacle.[28]

To be sure, Beijing has concerns about Taiwan's intentions; that is why it imposes preconditions in the first place. It wants some reassurance that what it considers its goodwill will not be exploited. Yet its desire for reassurance is unnecessarily magnified by its misperception of what Taiwan wants, and its way of securing reassurance has the result of making Taipei even more insecure. That Beijing sets the bar so high creates the impression that it does not want Taipei to clear it. That is, China prefers to delay negotiations until it feels it is in a stronger position.

The best way for China to reduce tensions and secure clarity on Taiwan's goals is to resume dialogue. And the most sensible way to do so is for Beijing to employ the precedent of 1998: setting aside its preconditions. Its definition of the one-China principle is too freighted with negative implications and Taiwan politics are too radioactive on the issue to expect that any government on the island would endorse it without some advance understanding of what it means. And too much has happened since 1992 for Beijing to expect that Taipei's reaffirmation of the "consensus" arrived at then can be a substantive basis for talks now.

Private Channels

One reason that it is so difficult for the two sides to return to and stay at the negotiating table is that they conduct their dispute totally in public, hence the impact of domestic politics is too constraining. Taiwan is a democracy, and the public will have to ratify the results of any negotiation through some democratic mechanism. Yet there are unlikely to be any results if private channels do not complement public discussion.

There are any number of individuals—business people, scholars, and so on—who act as self-appointed vehicles of private communication, and there are times when one side or the other at least gives the impression that these go-betweens operate with its blessing. All too often, however, this mechanism fails because the intermediaries do not really speak for the leaders they claim to represent. As a result, confidence in this channel of communication has declined over time.

But there was also at least one instance—in the early 1990s—when the authorized representatives of the senior Beijing and Taipei leaderships met regularly over a period of four and a half years. Lee Teng-hui had received and spurned offers for secret channels before his reelection as president in 1990. Thereafter, he decided that a secret channel would facilitate the progress that he needed to make on cross-Strait relations in order to create a climate for democratization in Taiwan. He therefore authorized his chief personal aide, Su Chih-cheng, to explore an offer that came from Nan Huajin, a Hong Kong figure with good mainland connections. That resulted in a meeting in Hong Kong around January 1, 1991, between Su and Yang Side, who was the representative of Yang Shangkun, then the PRC state president and the key figure on Taiwan policy. Su used the meetings to urge Beijing to ignore charges that Lee favored Taiwan independence, explained Taiwan's new institutional structure for cross-Strait relations, and revealed that Lee would soon announce that he did not regard the PRC as a hostile adversary. When Su complained about warnings that "disgruntled and defeated" mainlanders on Taiwan were passing to the PRC, Yang reassured Su that Beijing saw Lee as an acceptable interlocutor and would not help his domestic opponents. (Whether that reflected a shift from Beijing's earlier negative assessment of Lee is unclear; see chapter 7.)[29]

There then ensued at least four more meetings in 1991 that reduced the sense of hostility and increased goodwill, but no progress occurred on substantive issues, such as ending the state of hostilities. In June 1992, however, there was at least a procedural breakthrough because Wang Daohan, the foreign policy mentor of Jiang Zemin and head of the recently established Association for Relations across the Taiwan Strait, participated. As in the December meeting, Su explained the underlying political realities on Taiwan. Wang raised concern about direct popular elections of the president; Su responded that Lee was promoting this reform to respond to public opinion. Wang suggested party-to-party talks; Su replied that they were a nonstarter "because Taiwan already had a government." Su also suggested that a face-to-face meeting between senior leaders, with careful preparation in advance, was the only way to break the cross-Strait logjam. Su's candidates for the meeting were Wang and his Taiwan counterpart, Koo Chen-fu, chairman of the Straits Exchange Foundation. Wang agreed, and there ensued a process that culminated in the Koo-Wang meeting in Singapore in April 1993.[30]

The next meeting on which there are any details occurred in November 1994. By then, the PRC representative was Zeng Qinghong, one of Jiang's key aides. There was an exchange of proposals on transportation links and on a meeting between the two presidents. Although late 1994 was a time of growing tensions between the two sides, the atmosphere of this meeting was good, and it was agreed that continued communications would reduce misunderstandings. Subsequent contacts sought to facilitate a positive Taiwan reaction to Jiang's January 1995 speech and a good Chinese reaction to Lee's April response. Then in March 1995, a Taiwan politician from the New Party exposed the channel, and Beijing decided to terminate it.[31]

What is known of the operation of this channel suggests that a similar private exercise would help create a favorable environment for cross-Strait negotiations today. Because the key interlocutors were clearly speaking for their principals, all could have confidence in what was said. Each side could explain the dynamics of its domestic political environment and how they would—or would not—affect negotiations. Each could test its ideas for removing substantive and procedural obstacles. Each could preview upcoming actions and statements, place them in an objective context, and attempt to influence the other's reaction.

A DPP government in particular would need a setting in which it could present a clear and authoritative statement of the goals of its mainland policy and respond to PRC perceptions (and misperceptions). The Chinese side might elaborate on what the one-country, two-systems model would really mean for Taiwan. For example, would the political system foreclose certain outcomes, as in Hong Kong? Might the formula be modified to accommodate something like a confederation? The two sides might use such private discussions to determine whether there is any basis for at least a symbolic common understanding of the one-China principle and the 1992 consensus, which might afford a face-saving means of resuming dialogue. They could discuss a diplomatic truce and a PRC commitment to not meddle in Taiwan politics. They might discuss military confidence building and arms control measures in order to alter Taiwan's threat perception. More ambitiously, they might begin to chart areas of substantive common ground and a process by which they would move toward it. As noted above, the Taiwan government will be more likely to enter into negotiations if it has a clear sense of what will happen if it does so. But all of this is best done out of the public eye. A private channel would not negate the need to gain political approval for whatever agreement might be reached, but without such a channel, there may never be an agreement.

Principles as a Limiting Framework

The mutual mistrust that exists between Beijing and Taipei probably makes a grand bargain, in which all issues are resolved all at once, impracticable. It complicates the option of an immediate interim agreement, which seeks to create boundaries around the dispute. At the same time, even if some sort of communication resumes, that mistrust dictates the need for some type of formal understanding that provides initial mutual reassurance and creates a process for moving forward.

The Middle East peace process that began in 1993 provides an example of how two parties can create a staged course of action to work their way out of a security dilemma and move toward a mutually acceptable settlement. That process began with secret but authorized talks between representatives of Israel and the PLO in Norway. Through those talks, each side gained an appreciation of how the other viewed the conflict and of how its own actions, taken to protect its own security, stimulated reactions by the other that only made it more insecure. The goal that emerged was a declaration of principles on Palestinian self-government that was signed at the White House in September 1993. The method, as described by Yossi Bellin, was to try to "locate the limits beyond which the other side could not go, to understand what our own limits were, and to strive towards the construction of broader options in which both sides would have room to manoeuvre." Once the process became public in 1993, it was subject to the political dynamics in both Israel and the Palestinian territories and to events (such as terrorist acts) that called into question both sides' commitment to the process.

The next stage involved a series of issue-specific agreements, such as one to regulate traffic across the Allenby Bridge, in which the issues of Israeli and Palestinian sovereignty were made very concrete. It culminated in the signing in August 1995 of an interim agreement that governed the withdrawal of Israeli forces from Gaza and the West Bank, the Palestinian takeover of security responsibilities in the wake of the Israeli withdrawal, Palestinian renunciation of the goal of destroying Israel, and a mandate for negotiations on a permanent settlement. The final stage was talks on a permanent settlement, which foundered only at the last minute.[32]

It may seem odd to recommend a mechanism—the declaration of principles—that began a process that ultimately ended in failure. True, the document created boundaries around the dispute and identified, in at least general terms, the ultimate objective of the process. Its very negotiation fostered mutual understanding and reduced mistrust. The statement of a series of goals to be met sequentially fostered confidence as negotiations on specific issues ensued. In the end, however, the process aborted before the final goal was reached.

Yet a close examination of the Middle East peace process that began with the Oslo declaration of principles suggests that at least some of the factors that fostered failure do not exist in the cross-Straits case; the mechanism therefore might have a greater chance of success in the latter circumstance.[33] First of all, Israeli authorities in the occupied territories did not share the vision of the peace process and so were slow to implement the Oslo roadmap. Their reluctance to abandon their hedge against Palestinian violence only revived Palestinian suspicions that the occupation would never end. But neither China's nor Taiwan's hedging techniques have the impact that the Israeli occupation does. Second, violence is a regular tool of political combat between Israel and some Palestinian groups, with a corrosive effect on the peace process. The Taiwan Strait is militarized and creates a sense of insecurity, but there has been no use of force or loss of human life. Third, the economic cooperation and people-to-people interaction between Israelis and Palestinians that were to be a product of successive negotiations and were to reduce tensions and mistrust already exist to a significant extent between China and Taiwan. Fourth, the political environment in which the leadership in Beijing and Taipei must operate does not encourage creativity and concessions, but it surely is not as poisonous as that in Israeli and Palestinian communities; in addition, the elements that reject any form of modus vivendi are much smaller. Finally, as problematic as decisionmaking is in both China and Taiwan, it does not compare with the problems posed by the mercurial Yassir Arafat, the only person in the PLO who counted. Moreover, whereas it was Arafat's unwillingness to make the conceptual leap necessary for a reconciliation with Israel that, as much as anything, doomed the effort, the premise of a cross-Strait peace process is that China *does* make the conceptual leap required to meet Taiwan's needs.

Still, the failure of Oslo is an important reminder that reciprocal actions do have to be meaningful and credible to sustain each side's confidence and allay concerns that the other will renege. Leaders on both sides need to mitigate negative attitudes about the other and to prepare their publics for new approaches and tough concessions, even if it requires setting aside nationalistic myths and narratives of victimization. Some level of dialogue is always useful because it creates a bond between negotiators that becomes a permanent asset even when setbacks occur. A "code of conduct" that imposes consequences for nonperformance and counterproductive behavior will discourage competition for leverage and China's temptation to meddle in Taiwan's politics. And a successful negotiation must have a conceptual foundation whereby each side recognizes and accommodates the needs of the other.

A declaration of principles between Beijing and Taipei would have three major purposes. First of all, it would state what the two sides agree on. For example, they could commit to a diplomatic truce. More important, they could agree to explore the formation of a political union whose constituent units possessed sovereignty, whereby Beijing would fulfill its historic goal of unification and Taiwan would preserve its political status. Each might promise to show restraint in its acquisition and deployment of advanced military systems. Second, a declaration of principles would allow each side to state what it will not do in order to reassure the other. For example, Taipei could make commitments similar to those that Chen Shui-bian made at the time of his inauguration to signal that he was not going to take radical actions. Beijing could pledge not to interfere in Taiwan's politics. Third, a declaration would also lay out a plan of action for subsequent unilateral steps and bilateral negotiations on a variety of issues, sequenced in a way that ensured that the steps were conditional and reciprocal in order to build mutual confidence.

Beyond a Declaration of Principles

Of course, a declaration of principles would not in and of itself resolve the cross-Strait conflict or eliminate the security dilemma, even though it would provide a framework for doing so. It only creates a process. To be successful, that process should maximize incentives for cooperation while minimizing the mutual mistrust that will understandably persist. It should also foster sufficient momentum to give both sides the confidence that it will not stall and that ultimately a mutually satisfactory outcome can be achieved. And it must take account of the need to secure, on a periodic basis, the endorsement of Taiwan's competitive political system.

One area where confidence can be built is in the increasingly complex cross-Strait economic relationship. The absence of meaningful interaction between Taiwan's Straits Exchange Foundation (SEF) and the PRC's Association for Relations across the Taiwan Strait (ARATS) has only intensified the need to address it. A couple of examples will illustrate potential opportunities. First of all, Taiwan companies with a significant presence in China depend somewhat on Taiwan banks for capital, and those banks have sought to expand their role in servicing their clients. Yet banking regulators and supervisors in Taiwan's Ministry of Finance need to be able to monitor the mainland affiliates of the island's banks in order to ensure the financial health of the institutions as a whole. To do so requires the concurrence and cooperation of PRC authorities, which the political dispute between Beijing and Taipei prohibits. Second, the SARS epidemic in the spring of 2003 brought home the ease with which infectious diseases can spread when the people of two jurisdictions are regularly moving from one to the other. Cooperation among health officials of various jurisdictions helps to limit the spread of disease across borders, and failure to cooperate can accelerate infection, feed a sense of panic, and aggravate political problems. Third, accession to the WTO requires both China and Taiwan to open up their markets for agricultural goods. Yet cross-Strait trade in farm products cannot really begin until sanitary and phytosanitary issues are addressed, which requires interaction between the quarantine agencies of the two governments.

In all three cases, the political gridlock that prevents contact between the relevant officials through SEF and ARATS also prevents cooperation in these areas. Once the gridlock is dissolved, as it would be through the establishment of a broader framework of interaction, there would be an extensive agenda of issues to be addressed. Not all would be quickly resolved. Because the Taiwan farm sector would be vulnerable to PRC imports, there would be pressures to maintain barriers to trade. But in most cases, the two sides share sufficient interests to create new mechanisms for cooperation. Every success would enhance their mutual confidence.

The most delicate area, of course, concerns security. If the security dilemma is to be ameliorated, it will have to occur between the military establishments of the two sides; if it is not ameliorated, then it will be difficult to sustain momentum for political and economic cooperation.

One arena concerns the political dimensions of the security dilemma. That can be addressed through a consensus that the two sides would reach in the declaration of principles *if* Beijing was willing to concede on the sovereignty issue (and so change its own threat perception about Taipei's stance) and pledge not to interfere in the island's domestic politics (which would alleviate Taiwan's fear of a fifth column).

A second arena involves military intentions and capabilities. The first step here would be an agreement to end the state of hostilities. That idea, of course, was first proposed more than two decades ago, but no progress was made because the PRC linked it to the one-China principle. But the declaration of principles presumably would sever that link and open the way to formally ending the conflict, which began in the late 1940s.

A second step would be confidence-building measures, of the sort discussed above. A necessary precondition for these would be the PRC's decision that it is in its larger interests to use such measures to reduce Taiwan's sense of insecurity. Once that happened, then the two militaries could begin discussions on concrete measures to reduce tensions and foster a greater sense of predictability about their respective intentions.

A third step might be discussions of new arms acquisitions. Again, a necessary conceptual breakthrough would be the clear realization on the part of the PLA that its systematic buildup is driving Taiwan to seek defensive systems—and the United States to provide them. Obviously, any arms control arrangements would be linked with broader understandings about the future of the U.S. security relationship with Taiwan.

On balance, negotiations on various functional matters and on sensitive security issues would provide more benefit to Taiwan than to the PRC. The former facilitates Taiwan's economic development and the latter would reduce its sense of insecurity. Beijing's concession of sovereignty would be a victory for Taipei. The danger, from Beijing's point of view, would be that Taiwan would exploit its goodwill by not moving forward on its highest priority (the security dilemma again). To allay those concerns and to reassure Beijing that an incremental process would have a satisfactory outcome, the two sides should probably conduct political discussions, in parallel with functional and political talks, on how to actualize a new Chinese union. As suggested in chapter 8, designing confederations and similar structures so that they can be sustained over a long period of time is very difficult. In this case, the two parties would have to address which sovereign powers the Taipei government would retain; which powers, if any, it and Beijing would cede to the new central government; which political rights, if any, Taiwan's people would cede or limit in return for the benefits of a larger union and in order to reassure Beijing; what role the Taiwan part of the new political union would play in the international system; and the implications of the new union for Taiwan's security relationship with the United States. The more these issues are fully discussed, the more likely the resulting institutions will work to the benefit of both sides.

In any arrangement like this, there is always potential for cheating by one side, the other, or both. The temptation to exploit the goodwill of one's adversary does not disappear with the drawing of a roadmap. If obligations are to be honored on a reciprocal and conditional basis, the failure to meet an obligation (or the appearance of failure) can bring the process to a halt and even reverse it. To the extent that deadlines are set for honoring an agreement, missing deadlines for whatever reason can create doubts about a party's good faith. Loss of momentum can be the death of a sequenced arrangement, as was the case in the Middle East peace process.

To cope with this inevitable problem, there would need to be a joint monitoring and coordinating mechanism, empowered by the political leadership of both sides, to supervise the various negotiations, watch for emerging problems, energize discussions when they start to flag, determine responsibility when apparent episodes of cheating occur, and revise prior arrangements when it becomes clear that they are not working. Coordinating mechanisms will be necessary not only between the two capitals but also within them. Even if top leaders on both sides concluded that a negotiated agreement was in their interests, some domestic actors would have a more negative assessment. Skeptical bureaucratic agencies and political forces could try to use what influence they had to stall implementation and undermine what had been achieved.

This latter problem is much more severe on the Taiwan side than the PRC side. As noted earlier, Beijing may be the bigger obstacle to reaching an agreement, but Taiwan's political system is the greater impediment to carrying it out. If there is to be a cross-Strait accord, Taiwan's leaders will have to create better mechanisms to forge a consensus on what best meets Taiwan's fundamental interests—before negotiations begin, while they are going on, and during implementation. The stronger the consensus at every stage of the process, the more likely it is to endure. Effective coordination will be required within and among political parties, within the executive branch, between the executive branch and the legislature, between the government and the political parties, and between the government and the business community. Taiwan does not currently have those mechanisms, and China's united front tactics discourage consensus building on Taiwan. Beginning negotiations with the PRC before they are created almost guarantees that such a process will fail.

An additional way to contain any cheating problem is to enlist international guarantors for the agreement. If difficulties arise, they can intercede to identify the obstacle and restore momentum. The issue of guarantors raises the much larger question: the role of the United States.

An Intermediary Role for the United States?

Hitherto the United States has chosen to preserve peace and stability in the Taiwan Strait by moving flexibly among various policy approaches—context creation, dual deterrence, single deterrence. But, as noted above, at no time has it ever determined that the best way to promote its fundamental interests is to serve in some manner as an intermediary between Taipei and Beijing. For decades, Washington has taken the position that the dispute should be settled by the two parties themselves. In 1982, moreover, the Reagan administration pledged to Taipei that it would neither pressure Taiwan to negotiate with Beijing nor seek to play the role of mediator itself. And the U.S. government has never expressed—certainly not publicly and probably not privately—an opinion on the substance of a possible solution.

Yet a case might be made that the obstacles to resolving the Taiwan Strait dispute are so daunting that the only way that they will be removed is if the United States helps to remove them—and that doing so would in fact promote U.S. interests because of the danger of allowing the situation to fester. An enduring peace in the Taiwan Strait would eliminate both the modest possibility that the United States might be drawn into a war between Taiwan and China and, even in the absence of conflict, the time-consuming need to manage a fractious problem that has bedeviled U.S. diplomacy in different ways for more than fifty years. In theory, therefore, a greater U.S. role makes sense. The question is how to do it. What are the downside risks?

Intermediation could take several forms. The first is to serve simply as a messenger. That is, U.S. officials would only pass messages between Beijing and Taipei. The second form is what might be called intellectual facilitation. Here, the United States would transmit the views of one capital to the other and in addition offer its analysis of what those views meant in order to elicit a fuller response. It would not, however, offer any views of its own. The third form is process facilitation, whereby Washington would provide a venue in which the two sides might talk with each other, as Norway did in 1993 for Israel and the Palestinians. A fourth approach would be mediation between the two parties on the substance of the dispute, the role that the United States assumed in the Middle East peace process during the second Clinton administration. These four are basically mutually exclusive, for they entail different modes of facilitating communication. A fifth, which could supplement any one of the four, is to serve as a guarantor for whatever settlement the two sides concluded.

Each of these approaches to intermediation has advantages and disadvantages. Serving as a simple messenger is useful only if the messages contribute to better understanding between the two sides; to transmit restatements of public propaganda would be a waste of time. Similarly, intellectual facilitation—supplementing one side's statement with U.S. analysis—is productive only if the other side is prepared to listen seriously and respond in kind. Moreover, such a role would inevitably drag the United States into debates with one party about the substantive views of the other, which could result in perceptions of U.S. bias or irresolvable disagreements. Also, both message-carrying and intellectual facilitation are poor alternatives to dialogue between the two sides themselves. The best way to clarify positions and intentions is for them to enter into private bilateral discussions of the sort that occurred in the early 1990s. If there is an initial need for an intermediary, there are others who could serve these roles just as well as the United States but who would not carry its considerable political baggage.

Process and substance facilitation entail even greater problems. Washington would become inextricably enmeshed in the details of the issues and become an object of manipulation by Beijing or Taipei or both. It would become the umpire of disputes that occurred as the process proceeded—for example, over whether each side was abiding by a diplomatic truce. It would become responsible for the outcome of the negotiations and so be blamed for any breakdown.

Aside from these pros and cons on modalities, there are several more fundamental issues that the United States would have to address before it embarked on some sort of intermediation effort. The first is whether it could get the support of both parties for assuming that role. The part of "honest broker" is impossible to perform unless each side believes that the broker will deal honestly, from beginning to end. Here, Washington would carry a historical handicap. In 1946, General George Marshall conducted a mediation effort between the ROC government under Chiang Kai-shek and the Chinese Communist Party under Mao Zedong in order to try to avert a war between them. The effort failed because the two sides preferred to try to vanquish the other rather than share power. Both ended up mistrusting the United States, which itself developed an allergy to mediating between the two. Subsequently, at various times and in various ways, Beijing and Taipei both have concluded that Washington has acted in ways that favor the other. Consequently, each would be reluctant to accept a U.S. role in resolving the dispute.

Beijing would be happy, of course, if the United States simply ended its security relationship with Taiwan, and it sometimes seeks Washington's help in restraining what it regards as Taipei's provocative actions. But it has always asserted that the dispute is a Chinese internal affair, and so it is unlikely to internationalize it by accepting U.S. diplomatic involvement. For decades, Taipei feared U.S. intermediation because it believed that Washington had betrayed its interests on a number of occasions and was neither willing nor able to be an honest broker. It was in response to those concerns that the Reagan administration, at the time of the 1982 communiqué, pledged that it would neither seek to be a mediator nor pressure Taiwan to negotiate.

More recently, Taiwan has looked on a U.S. role more favorably. In July 2000, two months after his inauguration, Chen Shui-bian called the United States to play "a more active and constructive role as a stabilizer and balancer to maintain peace in cross-Strait relations," even if it would not be a mediator. In January 2003, he said, "We hope that the United States will continue to play the role of stabilizer, balancer, and facilitator in the Taiwan Strait."[34] Although the United States pledged that it would not serve as a mediator in 1982, when ROC confidence in U.S. commitments was at a low ebb, today Taipei might see it in its interest to release Washington from that commitment.

It is not the 1982 pledge per se that constrains the United States. It is the knowledge that Taipei might change its mind. Even if Taiwan believed sincerely at the outset that Washington should play an intermediation role, it might get cold feet part way through a negotiating process because it disliked its likely direction. It might also conclude that the United States was selling it out again, on this most fundamental of issues. It is Washington's knowledge of Taiwan's not-so-latent fear of abandonment that restrains it from assuming a role that might confirm that fear. Close bilateral communication could mitigate these dangers to some degree, but it would never eliminate them. And if Taipei became truly desperate, it would likely mobilize its friends in Congress to protect its interests.

A similar logic might apply to congressional support for a U.S. effort. There might be a consensus at the outset that U.S. intermediation was consistent with U.S. interests and would not undermine Taiwan's interests. Yet there would be no guarantee that such a consensus would hold as the negotiations proceeded and concessions were required from Taipei. No administration could be certain that congressional support could be sustained for the duration of the process, no matter how much consultation there was. And if Taiwan changed its mind about Washington's role, it would likely use Congress to check the executive branch.

A related, second point is that it is necessary to make absolutely certain that any intermediation would be consistent with fundamental U.S. interests in East Asian peace and security. One of the reasons that the past U.S. approach toward the Taiwan Strait issue has worked is that it has not usually interfered with the U.S. interest in cooperating with the PRC on other matters. To raise a recent example, during 2003 and 2004 China played an important role in creating a multilateral process by which to address the crisis on the Korean peninsula. That process was favorable to the United States, because it provided a venue in which North Korean intentions could be ascertained; because it included America's allies, Japan and South Korea; and because it would create either momentum for a diplomatic solution or justification for increased international pressure on Pyongyang. Managing that process, in which China was at the center, was complicated enough. To try to manage it while simultaneously trying to facilitate a resolution of the

Taiwan Strait issue would create a manifold increase in its complexity. In effect, China would be intermediating a U.S.-North Korea dispute while Washington would be intermediating a China-Taiwan dispute. In the past, Beijing has sometimes made Taiwan an obstacle to cooperating with the United States, as is its prerogative. Yet deeper U.S. involvement regarding Taiwan would put other equities at risk *and* place them in greater jeopardy should Beijing choose to create a link between Taiwan and those other issues—for example, by seeking to extract payments on the side with respect to Taiwan for its contribution to diplomatic efforts regarding North Korea.

Third, an intermediation role for Washington is problematic because in a profound way it is a party to the dispute. The United States is the sole external source of Taiwan's security and as such alleviates some of its sense of insecurity. That role would quickly be on the table in any negotiations that sought to address the problem of the security dilemma. Reducing Taiwan's dependence on the United States while simultaneously building up its confidence that the PRC would not exploit any concessions it made would be one of the trickiest parts of breaking the stalemate. To be sure, if the two sides were to make progress on that issue, Taipei would no doubt hold bilateral discussions with Washington. Beijing might or might not understand how such discussions would be essential to a solution.

Similarly, the United States made commitments at the time of normalization of its relations with the PRC that bear on the international dimension of the question of whether the Taiwan government possesses sovereignty. That would likely affect its ability to be even-handed on other dimensions (for example, the status of the Taiwan government within a Chinese union), if only because Beijing would oppose a U.S. stance that was inconsistent with its definition of those commitments.

Fourth, there is the difficulty that the United States would face in limiting its role to what it believed was an appropriate scope. Wherever Washington drew the line, either Beijing or Taipei, or both, would seek to pull it over the line in ways that transformed the U.S. role. That is, the old leverage game would continue in a new form. The depths of the U.S. involvement in the Middle East peace process present a cautionary tale. As Ross writes about the point in 1996 when the United States moved from the role of facilitator to that of mediator: "No longer would we be in the business of helping the parties, easing their efforts, reassuring them at critical moments, bringing them together at times, and pressuring when necessary to get them to cross thresholds and make decisions. I was about to become a broker, negotiating with each, finding out what they could do, drafting for them, and brokering the compromises." Yet note that even the facilitation elements—helping, easing, reassuring, reconciling, pressuring—were considerable, entangling Washington in the tiniest details and on a nearly full-time basis. Ross concludes that the more appropriate role is to shape the strategic context in which the actors with the most at stake operate. "Ultimately, the United States may make its greatest contribution to peace by standing against efforts to impose solutions and standing for the principle that regional leaders must finally exercise their responsibilities to confront history and mythology. Only when they are prepared to do that will the peace agreements endure." If there is ever to be an agreement between Taiwan and China, it will be more enduring if it is their creation and its implementation is their responsibility.[35]

Finally, before the United States entered into an intermediation role, it would be important to assess the nature of the negotiating problem. What are the obstacles—both substantive and procedural—to reaching an agreement? The kind of intermediation role required—if one is appropriate at all—will hinge on that. To put it one way, because mistrust between Beijing and Taipei is the key impediment to resolution of this dispute, it is not clear how much Washington can contribute to its removal. If the two sides had the mutual trust and political will to resolve this, they would not need Washington's aid. To put it another way, if both Beijing and Taipei are more or less equally responsible for the current impasse, then perhaps a neutral role for the United States would be appropriate. If, on the other hand, one party is more responsible, then perhaps intermediation—or at least neutrality—is not fitting.

The thrust of the preceding analysis is that although Taipei is not completely blameless, Beijing bears more of the onus for the current deadlock. It has misperceived the fundamental views of Taiwan's leaders, particularly regarding the sovereignty issue, while Taipei has understood fairly clearly what the one-country, two-systems formula means. Each engages in tactics that create a spiral of mutual mistrust. And China has gradually yet systematically been increasing its military power, thus rendering Taiwan more insecure. Both sides play the leverage game, but it is only Beijing that has the option of playing in the more open Taiwan system. Beijing has set unreasonable preconditions for resuming dialogue. On the other hand, Taiwan's political dynamics create problems. Taiwan's very fractious and open democracy limits its government's ability to formulate a negotiating position. And even if negotiations were successful and Beijing made an offer that was responsive to Taiwan concerns, small minorities on the island might use their extraordinary veto power to block adoption.

The dual reality is that the PRC would be the main obstacle to getting to an agreement that makes substantive sense and that, if such an agreement was reached, the Taiwan political system would be the main obstacle to getting it adopted. That in turn would complicate any effort of the United States to play a significant intermediation role. It would likely have to side with Taipei to facilitate the beginning of negotiations and a substantively satisfactory outcome, a stance that Beijing would likely resist. Then it would have to take the side of those on Taiwan favoring adoption, which might be perceived as exerting pressure and would be inconsistent with U.S. democratic values as well.

So does the U.S. interest in peace and stability in East Asia require it to undertake some kind of intermediation effort concerning the Taiwan Strait issue and so reduce significantly the possibility of conflict by helping resolve the underlying dispute? To put it more precisely, is the danger of conflict high enough and the chance of success great enough to risk failing at the effort and so undermining U.S. objectives (to say nothing of the political position of any administration that undertook such a task)?

The analysis in this chapter strongly suggests that under current conditions there are too many factors constraining the United States to justify a major intermediation role such as process or substantive facilitation. Even if Washington itself were not a party, neither Beijing nor Taipei has sufficient confidence in U.S. intentions to accept its playing a central role. Even if Taiwan was comfortable with U.S. intermediation at the beginning of the process, it could mobilize U.S. public opposition to the administration if it ever got cold feet. And the contribution that China makes to other U.S. foreign policy objectives is significant enough that failure would have serious ramifications. Intellectual facilitation and relaying messages entail fewer risks and could alleviate the impact of cross-Strait mistrust and defective decisionmaking systems. But they should be designed to bring about a better mode of communication—direct dialogue—between Beijing and Taipei, so that they themselves remove the obstacles dividing them. These conclusions about the U.S. role may be related to the underlying structure of the Taiwan dispute. The United States has always been agnostic on the question of whether the Taiwan government is a sovereign entity for purposes of unification. If Washington was to take a position on the matter or even get drawn very deeply into a discussion of it, either Beijing or Taipei would believe it was taking sides. This either-or question is one that the two sides must answer for themselves. On the security question, the United States is inextricably involved as the guarantor of Taiwan's safety and of regional stability generally. It therefore cannot take on the additional—and contradictory—role of honest broker. Again, either Taipei or Beijing—or both—would likely end up concluding that the United States was taking sides. Regarding the factors that aggravate the dispute, Washington can play a modest role in ameliorating the tendency of each party to misperceive the intentions of the other. Because of Taiwan's dependence on the United States, there may be room for Washington to enhance other aspects of decisionmaking within Taipei's executive branch, but there is little that it can do to fix the dysfunctional features of the broader political system. And the United States will remain an issue in the domestic politics in both China and Taiwan. Both on substantive issues and exacerbating factors, the United States can make only a modest contribution to untying the cross-Strait knot.

Transition

The discussion thus far has sought to explicate why the Taiwan Strait dispute is so difficult to solve and what would have to happen if a fundamental solution was to be found. In conclusion, what is needed is for the two sides to summon a multifaceted creativity designed to address issues of substance, political competition (both internal and external), and negotiating process. In an optimal world, the governments in Taiwan and China would summon that creativity, plus a good measure of skill and restraint, to make process and substance mutually reinforcing and so resolve their dispute in a way that meets their respective objectives and protects their interests. Neither side could get all that it wanted, but the benefits of reconciliation would outweigh the costs of living with the status quo or facing the specter of conflict. Political hostility and military threats would become a thing of the past, and the people on both sides could capitalize on what they have in common economically, socially, and culturally.[36] In that happy context, the United States, which has been a party to this conflict since it began more than fifty years ago, would be relieved of one burden of international leadership.

Yet perhaps the knot cannot be untied. Perhaps the gaps concerning the issues of sovereignty and security are too broad to be bridged. Perhaps the tremors caused by politics, leverage games, and decisionmaking systems undermine any effort at bridge building. The thrust of the analysis so far has exposed the many obstacles to resolution, in part to dispel any illusions about the nature of the problem. If Beijing is unwilling to concede on the legal character of the Taipei government and reduce the sense of insecurity of the island's population and if the Taiwan political system is too fragmented and polarized to take "yes" for an answer, what then? The PRC's leaders will continue to hope that the strength of economic imperatives will wear down the resistance of what they regard as the Taiwan independence forces. But the resilience of the Taiwan identity plus ninety miles of water and U.S. support are likely to frustrate Beijing's strategy of attrition. The danger, of course, is that the status quo is not sustainable and that the elements of Chinese nationalism, Taiwan nationalism, growing militarization, tendencies to misperception and miscalculation, and the ambivalent role of the United States will combine to form an explosive reaction. I therefore change the subject: from how the two sides of the Taiwan Strait issue might break the stalemate between them to how to preserve and manage a cold peace so that it does not dissolve into conflict and war.

11

If a Settlement
Is Not Possible?

If some sort of stalemate is more likely than resolution of the Taiwan Strait issue, then the parties will have to manage it skillfully to prevent it from spinning out of control. The costs of conflict would be horrendous, certainly for the people of Taiwan and probably for the population of China's east coast. Because both Taiwan and China are links in a number of the same international supply chains, even an increase in tensions—to say nothing of outright war—would be likely to affect the global economy. The turmoil created in the information technology sector after the September 1999 earthquake on Taiwan, when for a short period the price of semiconductors rose sharply, provides some indication of how global markets would be shaken by military conflict. Understanding the nature of the underlying reasons for the dispute will be as important to managing a stalemate as it is to securing a solution. This chapter examines the old challenge of bounding and stabilizing the dispute and preventing conflict in view of the more recent growth of the PRC's military power and Taiwan's intensified nationalism.

The Worst Case

How might such a conflict occur? There are two obvious triggers. One is that the PRC would simply lose patience with Taiwan's recalcitrance and decide that it had no choice but to use force to achieve unification. China's March 2005 antisecession law indeed identified three conditions under which Beijing might use "non-peaceful means": "In the event that the separatist forces of Taiwan independence should act under any name or by any means to cause the fact of Taiwan's secession from China, or that major incidents entailing Taiwan's secession from China should occur, or that the possibilities for a peaceful reunification should be completely exhausted."[1]

Moreover, as the PRC acquires offensive military capabilities—faster than Taiwan secures defensive systems—it will gain confidence that it can win a conflict militarily and therefore see less reason to exercise forbearance. Michael Swaine estimates that within the 2007–2010 time frame, China could attack a wide range of civilian and military targets on Taiwan with ballistic missiles, medium-range bombers, and cruise missiles; transport one to two divisions by sea and air; and conduct limited air and sea denial operations up to 250 miles from China's continental coastline. By 2020, the People's Liberation Army (PLA) is likely to have acquired sufficient military capabilities to

—patrol a single, noncarrier surface and subsurface battle group within 1,000 nautical miles of China's continental coastline

—conduct both sea and air denial operations within 500 nautical miles of China's continental coastline

—undertake a sizable naval blockade, with air support, of islands within 200 nautical miles of China's continental coastline

—deploy three to four divisions (that is, approximately 45,000 to 60,000 fully equipped soldiers) within 200 miles of China's continental borders by land, sea, and air transport.[2]

Yet China's leaders have over the years consistently found reasons to remain patient, among them the Marxist belief (or illusion) that economic forces will ultimately trump the Taiwanese identity and China's deep aversion to fighting the United States. The premise for patience in Beijing's eyes is that unification is still possible. So although a "bolt from the red" (an attack from communist China) cannot be ruled out, as long as Beijing thinks that the door is not closed or about to close, it can afford to play a waiting game.

The second of the two triggers is that Taiwan will take actions that the PRC believes close the door on unification. What would be critical would be Beijing's *perceptions* of the impact of Taiwan's actions, whether that perception is objectively accurate or not. And, as previous chapters have suggested, Beijing's record is not good on that score. China has misread the views and actions of Lee Teng-hui and Chen Shui-bian, seeing in their opposition to the one-country, two-systems model and their desire to expand Taiwan's international space a rejection of unification per se.

Complicating matters would be potential miscalculations on Taiwan's part. If Taipei assumed both that the PRC had too much to lose (economic growth, international prestige) by responding militarily to its political initiatives and that the United States would come to the island's defense under any circumstances, then it would be more likely to take risks. Taiwan is more inclined to be cautious when it takes seriously China's threats to use force and has doubts about U.S. intervention. If, on the other hand, Taipei assumes that Beijing is a paper tiger and that Washington has issued Taiwan a blank check, it could lose twice: the PRC could attack and the United States could remain neutral.

How Taipei assesses potential risks creates a dilemma for Beijing as it seeks to shape the calculus of the island's leaders. If China is vague about what it will tolerate, then Taiwan will see little danger from taking steps that are arguably provocative and may in fact take them. On the other hand, if Beijing is explicit about what it will abide and if Taipei doubts China's resolve, then Taiwan might be tempted to take those actions precisely to show that China is a paper tiger.

How would Beijing act on its assessment that Taipei had created a *casus belli*, given the economic costs that conflict would entail and assuming that the United States would be likely to help defend Taiwan under any circumstances? The most likely strategy would be coercion: destroying both the nervous system of Taiwan's military resistance and the island's will to fight, thus inducing it to agree to negotiations on China's terms. Indeed, Taiwan's greatest point of vulnerability is probably psychological.[3] China could employ a variety of means to carry out *suzhan sujue* (quick war, quick resolution):

—attacks on the island's command and control systems in order to paralyze the national command authority and the armed forces' ability to organize a defense

—missile attacks on airfields, missile batteries, and radar to undermine the Taiwan air force's ability to secure control of the airspace[4]

—missile attacks on population centers to create panic

—information warfare attacks on the cyber-infrastructure

—a blockade of the ports of Keelung and Kaohsiung (to include the sowing of mines) to drive up insurance rates on shipping, the island's economic lifeline

—special operations activities to incapacitate key infrastructure facilities.

One reason to achieve a rapid victory would be to reduce damage to the island's physical plant. Another would be to limit U.S. involvement. If civilian morale on Taiwan collapsed within a couple of weeks and the leadership sued for peace, U.S. intervention would be less likely. Beijing would also count on its diplomats to convince Washington that it had acted in response to an unacceptable provocation from Taipei and rely on its missile, air, and naval forces to discourage the United States from entering the combat area.

That, to be sure, would be a high-risk strategy on Beijing's part. It rests on the twin assumptions that Beijing would regard the Taiwan challenge as so egregious that a coercive response was necessary whatever the cost and that the island's morale was so fragile that it would collapse after a few early shocks. There is no certainty that U.S. forces could be deterred or denied. But most of the steps in this blitzkrieg strategy could be undertaken with little or no warning.

Such a campaign, which would maximize the PRC's strengths and exploit Taiwan's weaknesses, would pose a grave challenge to the United States. Unless it was absolutely clear that Taiwan alone had behaved in a totally reckless manner, which is unlikely, a Chinese resort to force would challenge the credibility of the U.S. security commitments on which peace and stability in East Asia have rested. Accepting a quick PRC victory would transform the strategic situation in Asia, establish Beijing as the primary power in East Asia, and incline other actors to defer to China on political and security issues. China's economic clout would reduce any temptation—even in the United States—to try to isolate or punish China for its past aggression. And even if Taiwan were clearly to blame, its supporters in the U.S. Congress and the American public might still press the administration in power to come to its defense.

Assuming that Taiwan had not clearly provoked the conflict and that it could hold out psychologically and militarily until U.S. forces could be deployed in strength, the result would be a major war. For the first time since World War II, the United States would be fighting a major industrial power, a power that also is a permanent member of the UN Security Council. And for the first time ever, it would be at war with a nuclear power. Preventing escalation would be very difficult. Some in Taiwan—mainly civilian defense specialists and legislators—would like to acquire the offensive missile capability needed to take a war to the mainland. The United States, in order to protect its own forces from interdiction by Chinese missiles and submarines and to relieve the pressure on Taiwan, would likely attack Chinese targets (horizontal escalation). Because U.S. conventional capabilities far outstrip those of the People's Liberation Army, leaders in Beijing would at least consider the option of using China's strategic nuclear forces (vertical escalation) before they accepted the humiliation of defeat and surrender.

That is only a scenario, and a worst-case one at that. The likelihood of occurrence is rather low, but China's ability to project military power and use it in new ways will only increase. And the consequences of any major conflict would be great. The physical damage on both Taiwan and the mainland could be serious, but even more significant would be the political and economic costs. China might win the battle to limit Taiwan's options, but it would lose the "war" to secure the Taiwan people's voluntary acceptance of unification with China. Beijing and its allies on the island would face a sullen population at best. In addition, China would have lost the struggle to reassure its neighbors that its growing power is not a threat to the East Asian region. Relations with the United States would deteriorate sharply once the long-standing American expectation of a peaceful resolution was dashed, and Washington would likely impose economic sanctions on China. The benefits of growth and social stability that China gains from its participation in the global economy would be put at risk. All of these potential outcomes make it imperative to ensure that the probability of conflict remains low.

Recent events have indicated that "thinking the unthinkable" is not merely an academic exercise. Chen Shui-bian's proposal for a new constitution during the campaign for the March 2004 Taiwan presidential election raised concerns in both Beijing and Washington that the situation was about to spin out of control, and that proposal remains the most likely cause of conflict during Chen's second term.

Managing Constitutional Revision

Previous chapters have described the initiatives that Chen Shui-bian proposed during the 2004 election campaign and the Chinese and U.S. responses. To briefly recap the story, in the fall of 2003 Chen Shui-bian sought to rally his political base by proposing a new constitution for Taiwan, to be approved by popular referendum. He also authorized two advisory referenda to be held on the day of the election. China interpreted any new constitution, particularly one approved by a referendum, as the functional equivalent of a declaration of independence. Although it had hitherto sought to avoid becoming an issue in the election, it concluded that it had to show its resolve to deter a Chen challenge to its interests. Abandoning restraint, it issued warnings that China would sacrifice the 2008 Olympics and its economic development to forcibly prevent the permanent separation of Taiwan from China. Beijing also pressured the United States to restrain Chen, and in December 2003 President Bush publicly expressed his administration's concern about a "unilateral change in the status quo." Chen moderated the language of the election-day referenda, but his narrow victory on March 20,

2004, left both China and the United States worried about what he would do next and whether a train wreck was imminent between Chen's constitution proposal and China's sense that a red line was about to be crossed.

A New Constitution: Ipso Facto Independence?

Why would China consider a new Taiwan constitution and its approval by referendum to constitute, ipso facto, the permanent separation of Taiwan from China, or, as one Chinese official warned, a "juridical declaration of independence"? Why, for example, did the Taiwan Affairs Office say in April 2004 that Chen's proposed process for constitutional change was "a time-table to stride towards Taiwan independence that will inexorably cause tension and danger in the Taiwan Strait?"[5]

First of all, no doubt, there was the 1991 DPP charter and its rhetorical link (described above) between a new constitution and a new country (a Republic of Taiwan). As Jacques deLisle notes, "one of the things that new states routinely do is make new constitutions."[6] Zhang Nianchi, a scholar and head of the Shanghai Institute of East Asian Studies, made a similar observation: "It is incorrect [for the PRC] to mention simply 'opposing referendum' or 'opposing constitutional reform.' What is to be opposed is 'the making of a new constitution through referendum.' . . . If Taiwan has the 'right of referendum' and it is stated in the 'constitution' then it would mean that 'cross-Strait relations' has become 'relations between two countries.' If 'referendum is written into the constitution,' then it is tantamount to 'Taiwan independence,' whether the citizens exercise this right or not." Elsewhere, Zhang wrote, "No matter whether Taiwan actually carries out a referendum on independence and unification, as long as Taiwan has the legal authority for such a referendum, Taiwan has really reached the point of throwing off the ROC constitutional framework whose sovereignty includes the mainland. When that time comes the ROC will no longer be the central authority [that claims to represent China] and will not be the residual part [of China] to which the prior central authorities retreated in 1949 in the civil war. It will be an independent country that is not subordinate (*lishu*) to PRC sovereignty. This country would be Taiwan and cross-Strait relations would become the relations between two countries." A military scholar, Luo Yuan, argued that the ROC constitution "already exists in name only, except some vestiges of China in Section 4" (which requires that any change in the "traditional territory" be done by the National Assembly).[7]

Michael Swaine portrayed PRC views on why a new constitution approved by a referendum would be so provocative. First of all, "such a move would sever any legal or procedural continuity with Taiwan's existing political system." Second and more important, Swaine wrote, is that Chinese observers argue that a new constitution approved through a referendum would "negate the past source of Taiwanese sovereignty, which, according to the existing constitution, resides with the people of 'China.' . . . Redefining the source of state legitimacy as belonging to the citizens of Taiwan alone would almost certainly persuade a large number of Taiwanese that 'one China' no longer exists and that Taiwan is a separate sovereign state." Implicit in this argument is that the 1947 constitution was approved by the National Assembly of the time, which nominally represented the people of China.[8]

Yet such Chinese arguments are excessively formalistic and conflate issues of territory, government, and constitution.[9] It is true that Chen Shui-bian proposed to create a new constitution in a manner that was inconsistent with past procedures and to that extent would have broken continuity.[10] That was a serious matter, in part because it might have deprived the new charter of legitimacy in the eyes of some of Taiwan's people. But since the PRC government since its founding has rejected the mere existence of the ROC constitution, it is unclear why it should be concerned about such continuity. Second, the 1947 constitution is vaguer than PRC observers suggest. It says that "the sovereignty of the Republic of China shall reside in the whole body of its citizens." That statement could be understood pragmatically to refer to those citizens who are most relevant to the ROC government, those who are under its jurisdiction. And Lee Teng-hui and others have made the argument that the people of Taiwan, through free elections, already have established the popular sovereignty basis of their government. To suggest, on the other hand, that the process of approving the 1947 ROC constitution was somehow a sovereign act of the people of China is ludicrous, since it was created and ratified through a completely undemocratic process.[11] (Moreover, for an authoritarian government like the PRC to stress popular sovereignty is ironic.) Zhang Nianchi's objection to the right of referendum in the constitution is odd, since that right, along with the right of initiative, is already there; what he objects to, no doubt, is the purposes for which the DPP might exercise that right. Moreover, the people of Taiwan do not need to approve a new constitution to believe that the ROC is a sovereign state. They already do. Nor would that act affect their view of whether "one China" exists.[12]

The issue has always been whether Beijing would, as a basis for unification, acknowledge that the Taiwan government possessed sovereignty. In and of itself, a new constitution approved through a referendum would not foreclose the possibility of some form of unification that the people of Taiwan might accept; Beijing, however, has effectively foreclosed it by insisting on the one-country, two-systems model. As noted previously, Chen tried, in a *Time* magazine interview in mid-February 2003, to signal that the door to a union of some kind was not closing by acknowledging that although "currently, there are two separate, independent countries across the Taiwan Strait. . . . who knows if these two separate countries might become one over time?"[13]

The PRC views cited above may have been the reason that Beijing believed that a referendum-approved constitution for Taiwan represented a fundamental challenge. If they were, Beijing's belief would constitute a reality that might have to be addressed. Yet these explanations may also be a rationalization by lower-level experts for a simpler assessment by senior leaders: that Chen has always been in favor of independence; his reassuring words about ultimate unification could not be trusted; the timetable clarified his direction toward his goal; and a trend toward de jure independence was gaining momentum. That being the case, the only questions were who would stop the trend (the United States or China?); when the trend should be stopped (sooner or later?); and how it should be stopped (with political pressure or military force?).

Again, this Chinese assessment of Chen's goals might have been correct. There are forces within the pan-Green camp who certainly do wish to create a separate Republic of Taiwan, and it is conceivable that they might have tried to highjack the constitution-writing process to achieve their goals. But Beijing has made similar dire assessments in the past that turned out on examination to be a flawed perception of Taiwan's leaders' intentions. In the early 1990s, it judged that Lee Teng-hui's claim that the ROC was a sovereign entity and his quest for international space were part of a Taiwan independence agenda—in my view, a misjudgment. It used coercive diplomacy and pressure on the United States to reverse the trend— in my view, an overreaction. Although Beijing understands that the firing of missiles at that time was counterproductive—in that it increased electoral support for Lee and U.S. support for Taiwan—and although it certainly does not want to be drawn into a conflict, the PRC decisionmaking system is capable, through misperception and miscalculation, to make conflict more likely.

A New Constitution: Content

Another way to judge the impact of any new constitution is to evaluate its content. Would it focus solely on the structure and operation of domestic institutions, or would it include attention to the matter of sovereignty?

Would it preserve some link between Taiwan and the ROC on one hand and the state called China on the other? In that regard, two issues would likely be crucial for Beijing. One is whether the title Republic of China would be changed. Even though the PRC has hitherto held that the ROC government ceased to exist in 1949, it would likely value preservation of that term as a symbolic link to a competing representative of China. Another is whether the national boundaries will somehow be altered. The ROC constitution does not specify what the boundaries are, but traditionally the Taipei government has claimed that it possessed sovereignty over the territory controlled by the PRC, Taiwan and its associated islands, and Mongolia (and the constitution refers to Mongolia). Post-1991 amendments to the constitution identify the "free areas" of the ROC as those in which elections for president, vice president, and members of the Legislative Yuan will be held and contrast those with the "Chinese mainland area." Finally, one of those amendments requires that "the territory of the Republic of China, defined by its existing national boundaries," may be changed only through a process similar to that for a constitutional amendment. If a new constitution was to retain the existing, vague language on this matter, Beijing could see it as a reassuring link between Taiwan and China. If, on the other hand, it confined the sovereign territory of the ROC as Taiwan, Penghu, Jinmen, and Mazu, Beijing would probably feel compelled to act.

The predictions coming out of Taipei in early 2004, before the election, were that a new constitution would not change the name Republic of China. On the issue of boundaries and territorial scope, however, Chen Shui-bian was less clear-cut and not always reassuring. In a February 6, 2004, interview with the *Los Angeles Times*, Chen said that Taiwan would make a fool of itself internationally if it persisted in the traditional ROC claim that "our state" included Mongolia and the PRC.[14] After the election, he softened that position somewhat in an interview with the *Washington Post*: "I have said before that in our future efforts in re-engineering the constitution, we will only do so based upon the principle of maintaining the status quo and not changing the status quo. I believe those articles relating to the territory in our constitution will not be the core of emphasis in our constitutional reform project. *I think there is no problem with the content of Article 4 in our constitution. The question lies in how to define it and interpret it* [emphasis added]."[15] Chen also signaled that constitutional revision would focus on reform of Taiwan's domestic political institutions, not issues bearing on sovereignty.[16]

The content of a new Taiwan constitution is relevant to the discussion of sovereignty in chapter 4. Four types were distinguished: domestic sovereignty (how public authority is organized within the state); Westphalian sovereignty (independence or nonsubordination vis-à-vis outside parties); international legal sovereignty (possession of formal juridical independence and the right to participate in the international system); and interdependence sovereignty (the ability of public authorities to regulate the flow of information, goods, people, and so on across borders). A new constitution for Taiwan could address one or more of these areas, and some would be more controversial than others. Less problematic—or not problematic at all—would be changes in domestic and interdependence sovereignty. In Chen Shui-bian's statements, his focus *appears* to be on domestic sovereignty: reforming how political authority is organized and distributed (government institutions, election system, and so forth). Interdependence issues are not really constitutional in character. More controversial are the areas of international and Westphalian sovereignty. Taiwan has already made political claims in those areas: that it is an "independent sovereign state," not subordinate to the PRC, as Hong Kong is; and that as such it deserves to participate in the international system. As I have argued, these claims do not negate the possibility of certain kinds of national unification.

Thus in the spring of 2004 Beijing had concerns about the content and process of a new or revised Taiwan constitution. Sovereignty issues like territory might be addressed, and approval by referendum in itself raised sovereignty concerns. The danger was that Beijing would perceive a challenge to its fundamental interests and the closing of the door on any kind of unification. Those concerns and Chen's victory strengthened the voices of those in China who argued for coercive action to blunt what was deemed a separatist trend. The United States had little choice but to step in.

The Washington Factor

As related above, during the Taiwan presidential campaign the Bush administration grew increasingly concerned about Chen's intentions and his failure to consult his only ally about his initiatives. When Chen won a second term, the administration sought to influence his future course by shaping his inaugural address through discussions with his advisers.

There were conflicting American views of how to manage what many thought was a volatile and dangerous situation. Some argued that it was Taiwan that was fostering instability and had to be pressured to stop. Around the time of Chen's election, some had concluded that a new constitution would formalize Taiwan's "separate sovereign status" even if it did not declare independence; that Beijing would regard that as a *casus belli*; and that Chen had calculated, incorrectly, that "President Bush's commitment to Taiwan will deter China regardless of what Taiwan does" and that China was "unwilling to pay the price of conflict." Therefore, this view held, Washington should convince Taipei that its assumptions were wrong, define clearly and credibly the limits of U.S. commitment, and get Chen to back down.[17] China, certainly, wanted Washington to restrain Chen. As the PRC foreign minister put it in coded terms to Secretary of State Colin Powell the day after the election, "The U.S. side [should] abide by the one-China policy and do more to benefit the peace and stability across the Taiwan Straits as well as the development of relations between the Chinese mainland and Taiwan."[18]

Others held that China, not Chen, was the source of the tension, and that the way out was for Beijing to relax its preconditions for dialogue. As one observer put it, the PRC should "accept serious high-level discussions between the two sides to reduce tensions and devise a roadmap for increased economic, social, and perhaps eventual political ties across the Strait." The Bush administration itself called for dialogue without preconditions, a rejection of Beijing's view. By inference at least, advocates of this viewpoint would not regard a new Taiwan constitution as provocative in and of itself, certainly not provocative enough to justify a Chinese military response. Again by inference, they would urge the United States to focus on deterring any threat to Taiwan.[19]

The Bush administration continued to pursue the U.S. default approach of dual deterrence: warning Taipei against taking provocative political initiatives and Beijing against using force, while reassuring each that Washington was not acting contrary to its fundamental interests. Although Washington did not ignore the PRC military buildup and its destabilizing effects, it directed more of its attention toward Chen's political initiatives. In not so coded terms, James Kelly, assistant secretary of state for East Asia, warned Taiwan in late April to avoid any actions that Beijing would see as justifying the use of military force. In particular, he stressed that Beijing might overreact, that Taiwan should not regard China as a paper tiger, and that Taiwan was obligated to take U.S. security interests into account:

> We have very real concerns that our efforts at deterring Chinese coercion might fail if Beijing ever becomes convinced Taiwan is embarked on a course toward independence and permanent separation from China, and concludes that Taiwan must be stopped in these efforts. . . . A unilateral move toward independence . . . carr[ies] the potential for a response from the P.R.C.—a dangerous, objectionable, and foolish response—that could destroy much of what Taiwan has built and crush

its hopes for the future. It would damage China, too. We, in the United States, see these risks clearly and trust they are well understood by President Chen Shui-bian and others in Taiwan. . . . While we strongly disagree with the P.R.C.'s approach, and see military coercion as counterproductive to China's stated intent to seek a peaceful outcome, it would be irresponsible of us and of Taiwan's leaders to treat [Beijing's] statements as empty threats. . . . As Taiwan proceeds with efforts to deepen democracy, we will speak clearly and bluntly if we feel as though those efforts carry the potential to adversely impact U.S. security interests or have the potential to undermine Taiwan's own security.[20]

Kelly also voiced continuing concern about Chen's constitutional project, with specific attention to issues of process: "There are limitations with respect to what the United States will support as Taiwan considers possible changes to its constitution. We are uncertain about the means being discussed for changing the constitution [that is, use of a referendum]. We do no one any favors if we are unclear in our expectations."[21]

In addition to process concerns, the administration opposed any changes that touched on Taiwan's sovereignty. But it did not altogether oppose Chen's desire to revise the constitution, even as it took seriously the PRC's anxiety. It was prepared to accept revision *if* it was restricted to the reform of Taiwan's domestic political institutions *and* if it followed the established process. It therefore urged Taipei to stay within those substantive and procedural limits and refrain from changing the articles that touched on the island's relationship with China. It would then press the PRC to show restraint. Constitutional revision aside, Washington also hoped that Chen would take a reassuring and constructive approach to cross-Strait relations. It pressed its case in meetings with senior Taiwan officials in the weeks before the May 20 inauguration.

Chen's Second Inaugural Address: Retreat

The Bush administration succeeded in shaping Chen Shui-bian's inaugural address so that Beijing would not, at least in the U.S. view, have reason for conflict. The speech had three major, interrelated themes: cross-Strait relations, constitutional revision, and island-wide unity.[22]

On cross-Strait relations, President Chen sought to do three things. First, he tried rhetorically to reassure the PRC and the United States about his intentions. He reaffirmed by reference the promises and principles of his first inaugural address, including the so-called "five nos" (*sibu yimeiyou*): that as long as China did not intend to use force he would not declare independence, not change the national title, not insert the two-state theory into the constitution, not promote a referendum to change the status quo regarding independence or unification, and not abolish the National Unification Guidelines and the National Unification Council.

There were other rhetorical reassurances. The people on the two sides of the Strait, Chen said, shared a common heritage. Economic and other types of interaction between Taiwan and China were important. Any unilateral change in the Taiwan Strait status quo should be avoided. Chen did not rule out "any" future cross-Strait outcome for Taiwan as long as it had the Taiwan people's approval, and he made particular reference to the European model of integration. And finally he stated that he appreciated that the PRC could not relinquish its insistence on the one-China principle.

Having offered those reassurances, Chen also restated a number of long-standing elements of Taiwan policy. The Republic of China was a fact, and he was obligated to defend its sovereignty. Taiwan's membership in international society was a fact, and he would continue to seek international space. A peaceful process free of threats was essential. Any cross-Strait outcome had to be acceptable to the people of Taiwan. Chen also qualified his positive statements somewhat. In his mind, his reaffirmation-by-reference of the "five nos" no doubt included the condition that he stated in his first inaugural address: that he would stay his course "as long as the CCP regime has no intention to use military force." Chen did not say "one country on each side," but he equated China and Taiwan to the PRC and the ROC. He stressed that if there was to be no unilateral change in the status quo, both sides needed to work together to guarantee it.

Chen then offered a proposal for improving cross-Strait relations. First, he would establish a committee on which various political parties and social sectors would be represented in order to draft consensus guidelines for promoting cross-Strait peace and development. He urged Beijing to foster an environment of peace, development, and freedom of choice and to create channels to resume cross-Strait dialogue and communication, specifically on creating a "peace and stability framework." He proposed the expansion and liberalization of nongovernment interaction so that Taiwan and China together could meet the challenge of globalization. He called for the opening of the three links. Those ideas were consistent with Chen's preelection proposal for a peace and stability framework, which included the idea of military confidence-building measures.

On the second issue, constitutional revision, President Chen reaffirmed his objective to reengineer Taiwan's constitution so that it accorded better with contemporary needs. The goal, he said, was to enhance good governance and administrative efficiency and to ensure a solid foundation for democratic rule of law. He reiterated the specific issues of the DPP's revision agenda: whether to have five yuan or three; whether to have a presidential or parliamentary system; whether to elect the president by relative or absolute majority; how to change the Legislative Yuan; and whether to retain the National Assembly, whose sole power is to ratify constitutional amendments. On the last point he signaled his strong preference for abolishing the National Assembly and approving subsequent revisions by referendum. On the other hand, he proposed explicitly that issues related to national sovereignty, territory, and the subject of unification and independence be excluded from this exercise because "consensus has yet to be reached" on those matters.

Concerning process, Chen said that there would be a constitutional reform commission—including members of the ruling and opposition parties, legal experts, scholars, and representatives of various walks of life—that would forge "the highest level of social consensus on the scope and procedure of constitutional reform." Thereafter, the rules in the current constitution would be followed. That is, the Legislative Yuan would have to assemble a quorum of at least three-fourths of its members and then three-fourths of the legislators assembled would have to approve the proposed amendments. A new National Assembly would then be elected to vote on the new charter. That process would be completed by the time Chen left office.

Clearly, this proposal represented a shift from Chen's ideas during the campaign, when he had proposed changing the referendum law so it could be used to approve this round of constitutional revision. And he had forecast no role for the Legislative Yuan or National Assembly, because, he charged, the existing process unjustly frustrated the popular will. Now, he was prepared to use the existing process; the thrust of his proposal was that referendum would be used in future exercises. Then, Chen had suggested that a new constitution would address the territorial scope of the Republic of China and would explicitly exclude the Chinese mainland. Now that issue would not be addressed—which is not to say it could not be addressed in future revisions.

Chen's third theme was island-wide unity and strengthening. As he put it: "We must seek to establish a civil society . . . to create an identity with this land and a common memory if we are to transcend the limitation of ethnicity, lineage, language and culture, and to build a new and unified sense of shared destiny." Taiwan, he said, was a multiethnic society, and members of all ethnic groups had been victims in the past. But now all residents were part of the "new Taiwan family," however short or long their connection with Taiwan. All, he claimed, had a "shared sense of belonging" and all possessed a sense of shared destiny.[23]

With respect to both constitutional revision and cross-Strait relations, Chen managed to skillfully put the ball in Beijing's court and make a tough response more difficult. The PRC had regarded Chen's campaign proposal for approving a new constitution by referendum as the functional equivalent of declaring independence. Now he advocated following the existing process and fencing off sovereignty issues. Even so, he promised the most significant overhaul of the ROC structure since 1928, and he indicated that future revisions would be approved by referendum and could, by implication, include sovereignty issues. Concerning cross-Strait relations, Chen did implicitly reaffirm the National Unification Council and National Unification Guidelines, but he also proposed a cross-Strait peace and development committee and guidelines. Again, this posed a challenge to Beijing. If it saw in these proposals an emerging negative trend, when and how should it respond? So Chen effectively moved the debate and did so with U.S. concurrence. For the previous year, he had carried the burden of proving that he was not the one unilaterally changing the status quo. Now he had shifted that burden to Beijing.

There were a variety of responses to Chen's address. Some in the pan-Green camp believed that Chen had given nothing away. DPP elder Yao Chia-wen focused in particular on the fact that the president had not made an explicit pledge not to change the national designation; he had done so by generally reaffirming the commitments of his first inaugural address. Others felt betrayed. "What kind of goodwill did he receive from China? He fooled Taiwan's voters," remarked a legislator of Lee Teng-hui's Taiwan Solidarity Union. Chen himself had to calm overseas supporters who had come for the inauguration. He said to one group: "As I pursue my ideals, I must be creative and wise as I consider the practical obstacles. I must display a responsible and principled approach. But I most sincerely assure you that I will gain the affirmation of the U.S." And Chen did receive affirmation from Washington. On June 3, 2004, Deputy Assistant Secretary of State Randall Schriver remarked that "the Administration welcomed the responsible and constructive tone struck by President Chen Shui-bian in his May 20 inaugural address" and expressed the hope that, with a positive response from Beijing, cross-Strait relations might improve.[24]

China's response was anything but positive. Indeed, on May 17 Beijing preempted the inaugural address with a statement of its own, released by the

Taiwan Affairs Office (TAO). The point of departure was that Chen Shui-bian could not be trusted. His actions over the previous four years, the statement said, essentially violated each of the five pledges that he had made in his first inaugural address, thus giving Beijing no reason to take seriously any reaffirmation of those pledges. He was engaged in "frenzied provocation" of the status quo, which, in the TAO's definition, was that "the mainland and Taiwan belong to one and the same China." Cross-Strait relations were "at the brink of danger" because he had established a "timetable to move the island to independence through the making of a new constitution."

The statement did have some interesting, positive elements. It did not mention the phrase "one country, two systems." It laid out a series of areas in which progress could be achieved (resumption of dialogue, ending the state of hostility, military confidence-building measures, the three links, and so on). But the precondition for pursuing this agenda was that whoever held power in Taiwan would have to "recognize that there is only one China in the world and both the mainland and Taiwan belong to that one and same China, abandon the 'Taiwan Independence' stance, and stop separatist activities." Given China's expansive definitions of independence and separatism, there was virtually no prospect that Chen would accept those terms.[25]

The PRC media commentary that followed the speech reflected the tone and content of the May 17 statement. One observer stated, "However 'beautifully' Chen Shui-bian packaged his speech and however experienced he is at playing with words, his 'Taiwan-independence' separatist nature could not be disguised." Another wrote, "Chen Shui-bian was obviously playing some tricks. The 'peace' he wanted was 'peace for Taiwan independence' and 'peace for separation.' However, this is a dead alley that leads nowhere."[26] China fired other rhetorical shots. Scholars, including some in government think tanks, urged preparations on political, military, and economic fronts. Officials warned that "pro-independence" Taiwan business people would not be welcome on the mainland. The need to reestablish China's credibility and deterrence against Taiwan was deemed a high priority. And Beijing was not pleased that Washington had responded so positively to Chen's inaugural address. In its view, he had not changed his separatist objectives and U.S. praise only encouraged him to move in a dangerous direction.[27]

On the other hand, there were signs of some rethinking of China's policy. The leading advocate was Zhang Nianchi. Right after the March election he argued that "instead of asking heaven to protect the Chinese nation, we had better thoroughly reexamine and adjust our thinking and policy," which, he said, could "no longer cater to the dramatic changes in Taiwan that have significantly impacted the basis on which these policies have been implemented." Instead, "our most urgent task is to formulate a new Taiwan policy and a new Taiwan line that keeps abreast of the times, addressees the needs, and represents the pragmatism and truthfulness of the [new generation of leaders]; and to guide cross-strait relations with our policy advantage." Another Shanghai scholar, Zhuang Jianzhong of the Center for RimPac Strategic and International Studies, offered suggestions to both Taipei and Beijing. If Chen Shui-bian could state that he would observe the one-China idea that Zhuang felt was the basis of the ROC constitution, that statement could be regarded by Beijing as a return to the one-China position. If, in addition, Chen did not restate the two-state or one-country- on-each-side formulations, Beijing should resume dialogue and negotiations. It should also reduce Taiwan's sense of insecurity, "consider how to solve the international space problem of Taiwan," and act in ways to undermine "the separatists' slander that the mainland persistently squeezes and presses Taiwan." Finally, Wang Zizhou, a scholar at a think tank under the Academy of Social Scientists, predicted at a seminar in Singapore that China "would definitely have a new concept to resolve the Taiwan issue" within the next two decades. The one-country, two-systems model would "probably be insufficient to resolve the Taiwan issue" and it needed to be supplemented or reinterpreted "with more intelligent formats."[28]

Some of these proposals included conditions that might be difficult for Taiwan to meet because of mistrust or domestic politics. And there was no certainty whatsoever that they reflected anything more than a decision by the PRC leadership to permit scholars to consider more creative approaches—as opposed to a decision to adopt them. But if there is to be a conceptual alternative to the one-country, two-systems approach, it is likely to begin through exercises like this one.

Domestic and External Constraints

After the very different line he took during the campaign, Chen Shui-bian's reversal was significant. But questions remained, and the answers would govern the prospects for peace and stability in his second term.

The first question was the firmness of his commitment to his inaugural pledges. Might he reverse course again under pressure from elements in his own camp that were unhappy with his May 20 speech? These "dark Green" forces apparently believed that they could get Chen to abandon his pledges concerning substance and process. Lee Teng-hui continued to advocate enacting a new constitution rather than revising the old one and changing the national title to Taiwan. He urged public support for that effort, asserting that "the public was stronger than the government"—that is, that Chen's mind could be changed. Lee Hung-hsi, a constitutional lawyer and Chen's former professor, advocated abrogating the current charter and said that "sticky topics of national boundaries, symbols and the national title would have to be negotiated by political parties"—that is, that such topics were not out of bounds. Lee also said that Chen would have to listen to public opinion and that if Lee Teng-hui was able to generate a lot of support for a new constitution in the future, Chen's position might change by then. An editorial in the pro-DPP *Taipei Times* described the Republic of China as an "ancestral tablet before which . . . the Taiwanese people have been forced to pray" and noted that in geography textbooks the ROC is defined to include mainland China and Mongolia: "What kind of super-imperialistic Constitution is this, including the lands of other countries in its territory?"[29]

Chen himself hinted that he was open to pressure in remarks to the pro-independence Formosan Association for Public Affairs. Drawing an analogy to his pet dog, he said: "He did not run in a straight line when he was running after me, but he was right there before me when I reached my destination. As long as you have confidence in me, our dream will definitely come true."[30] Then, in his National Day speech on October 10, 2004, Chen appeared to push the envelope. He did reiterate many of the conciliatory themes on cross-Strait relations that he had expressed in his inaugural speech, but he also equated the Republic of China with Taiwan more explicitly than he had then, saying that the sovereignty of the ROC was vested in the 23 million people of Taiwan and referring to Taiwan as a country of 36,000 square kilometers—that is, only the territory under the ROC's jurisdiction.[31] Rhetorically, therefore, he removed some of the ambiguity concerning the traditional connection of the Republic of China to mainland China and suggested that Taiwan itself was a state.

What was going on here? Was he simply trying to appeal to the more fundamentalist members of his party in the run-up to legislative elections, contests in which DPP voters could vote for candidates of the more radical Taiwan Solidarity Union? Or was he laying the rhetorical groundwork for reintroducing the issues of title and territory into a revised constitution? Recall that Chen fenced off those sovereignty issues because a "consensus has yet to be reached." Might he seek to create a consensus later where none existed on May 20? Recall also that Chen had spoken of defining and interpreting the issue of the ROC's territory. Might he favor "clarification" of the national title and territory in the constitution? On the title, for example, might he keep the term "Republic of China" but add the word "Taiwan" in parentheses? Recall finally that Chen signaled in his inaugural address that future rounds of revision might include sovereignty questions.

The second question concerns the procedural and political circumstances under which Chen might secure the kind of radical change in the constitution that would provoke the PRC. Recall that, as described in chapter 6, revision is not easy. The first step is securing passage of a change in the Legislative Yuan, where at least three-fourths of that body (169 members of 225) must be present to vote and three-fourths of those present must vote "yes."

Hitherto, the second step has been ratification by the National Assembly, whose membership would reflect the ratio of party support in a specially called election and where a simple majority vote was required to approve amendments. But the process began to change somewhat in August 2004, when the Legislative Yuan took up a long-standing proposal to reduce the size of the legislature and to shift from election districts that had several representatives to districts with only one. As part of this exercise, however, the Legislature Yuan also agreed to change part of the process for approving constitutional amendments. It preserved its own, central role in the first stage but changed the second. If the National Assembly approves the August 2004 amendments when it presumably meets in the summer of 2005, the second stage of ratification of *future* amendments—including the major constitutional revision that Chen Shui-bian promised to undertake later in his second term—will require approval by 50 percent of all eligible voters through a referendum. (In effect, the National Assembly will be asked to vote itself out of business.)[32]

In spite of this change, a strong case can still be made that the Taiwan political system prevents constitutional revisions that do not command broad support among political parties and the public and that, because opinion on the island is fairly evenly divided, the sort of change that Beijing might find fundamentally provocative will not occur. There is the quorum problem in the Legislative Yuan: if the pan-Blue parties control more than one-fourth of the seats, they can block revision by simply not permitting a quorum. Similarly, requiring half of the eligible voters to approve amendments through a referendum poses some challenges. The number of eligible voters for the 2004 presidential election was around 16.5 million; half of that would be 8.25 million. Around 13 million voters cast ballots in that election. Chen Shui-bian secured 6.5 million votes. If 13 million people were to vote in a referendum, the 8.25 million votes required for passage would amount to about 63 percent of ballots cast.[33] The reality is that opinion on the island is divided on the fundamental issue of how to cope with an increasingly powerful China and a lot of less fundamental ones as well. The "sense of shared destiny," of which Chen spoke in his inaugural address, does not yet exist on Taiwan. Inferentially, therefore, a proposal that did not have pan-Blue support could not get through the legislature and might fail in a ratification referendum.

The third question concerns the balance of power in the Legislative Yuan, for which an election was held in December 2004. The conventional expectation during the fall of 2004 was that the pan-Green parties would sustain the momentum created in the presidential election and secure a small majority but not one large enough to enable them to amend the constitution at will. In the event, the pan-Blue camp ended up with 113 of 225 seats (one less than in 2001) and the pan-Green got one more. The main shift in seats came within the pan-Blue camp, with the KMT gaining eleven and the PFP losing twelve seats. In terms of share of the vote, the pan-Blue camp received 46.7 percent of total votes cast and the pan-Green camp got 43.5 percent, which represented a net increase of 0.5 percent for the former and 2.3 percent for the latter compared with results in 2001 (the share won by independents dropped commensurately). There were competing explanations for the outcome. One focused on mistakes the pan-Green camp made in coping with the dynamics of the multimember-seat system, particularly its failure to allocate votes among its various candidates. The other was that voters—particularly middle-of-the-road voters—were increasingly concerned about Chen Shui-bian's overall approach, as reflected in his renewed appeals to the dark-Green segment of the political spectrum. Thus those voters abandoned the DPP out of concern over where Chen was taking Taiwan. Both factors had an impact, but the latter is probably more significant. Because of public anxiety, the pan-Green parties will have even less freedom of action in the Legislative Yuan than if they had won a slim majority.[34]

The fourth question concerns the firmness and unity of the pan-Blue parties. Losing the March presidential election had been a serious blow, prompting some serious soul searching and calls for Lien Chan and James Soong to give up their leadership positions and their parties to merge. Multiple defeats had sapped the coalition's will to oppose, particularly when Chen succeeded in putting it on the defensive. He had twice maneuvered the pan-Blue camp into a position in which it was politically difficult to resist him. The first occasion was in November 2003, when it shifted course on whether to undertake a constitutional revision at all. The second was in August 2004, regarding amendments on the size of the legislature and the use of a referendum for final ratification. In both episodes, it had decided that it had to avoid any public perception that it was against reform. As Hsu Yung-ming of the Academia Sinica's Institute of Social Sciences put it after the second episode: "Whether to pass the constitutional amendments is a game of 'chicken' for the political parties. The party who first shrinks will lose the game."[35] In this context, therefore, there are two ways that Chen and the pan-Green camp can secure pan-Blue cooperation on constitutional revision. The first is to make it so palatable substantively that there is no reason for opposition. The other is to make opposition so distasteful politically that the Blue parties decide not to mount a resistance. One result of the legislative election was to stiffen the spine of the KMT segment of the pan-Blue camp.

Events took a turn in February 2005, when Chen Shui-bian and James Soong, leader of the People First Party, reached an accord that promised some degree of cooperation between the DPP and the PFP. In their joint declaration, Chen Shui-bian reaffirmed the pledges in his second inaugural address. He and Soong stressed the primacy of the ROC constitution, the sovereign character of the ROC, the need for any change in the status quo to be approved by Taiwan's people, and the importance of both improving cross-Strait relations and ensuring Taiwan's defense. The Chen-Soong declaration sent shockwaves through both the KMT, which could no longer count on having a legislative majority on every issue, and more radical elements in the pan-Green camp, which regarded Soong as the enemy.

Yet the political impact of cooperation between the DPP and the PFP is to enforce the tendency toward moderation. The price for Chen's alignment with Soong is to abjure initiatives that would be provocative to China. Presumably, if Chen reneged on his commitments, he would lose Soong's support. And the PFP's members of the Legislative Yuan do not solve Chen's problem when it comes to constitutional revision. The KMT's seventy-nine seats are enough to block even a coalition of all other parties. Indeed, Chen's decision to pursue Soong may have reflected a practical decision on his part to secure a legacy by passing legislation that the PFP would support rather than pursue a more ambitious constitutional agenda.[36]

The fifth question is what China would regard as a *casus belli.* Beijing's position was clarified somewhat in the fall of 2004. Through the summer some PRC sources had complained about Taiwan policy steps that reflected, in Beijing's mind, continuing "de-Sinification" in Taiwan; the increasing use of the name "Taiwan" in Taipei's diplomatic activities was raised as an example. Moreover, its public statements betrayed no appreciation that Chen had shifted his position on constitutional revision, assuming instead that a new charter through referendum only was still his goal. For example, in August 2004 Wang Zaixi, deputy director of the Taiwan Affairs Office, pointed to Chen's proposal for "a timetable for moving toward 'Taiwan independence' by bringing into existence a new 'constitution' in 2006 and implementing a new 'constitution' in 2008" as evidence that "separation aimed at 'Taiwan independence' has become a real crisis, and cross-Strait relations are on the brink of danger"—ignoring that this was no longer what Chen proposed. China, it appeared, was still focused on the fact of constitutional revision rather than the content.[37]

Yet Beijing did not react publicly to the late August passage of an amendment that would require a referendum to ratify future constitutional changes, perhaps because passage by the Legislative Yuan remained the primary stage. And in late September, after the third plenary session of the Sixteenth Party Congress, an "authoritative person" in the PRC revealed that Beijing had less sense of urgency about Taiwan. On constitutional revision in particular, that person warned:

> The Taiwan authorities must not engage in "de jure Taiwan independence." If through the method of "constitutional amendment" or "creation of a new constitution," the Taiwan authorities were to announce that the "territory" of the "Republic of China" only includes Taiwan, Penghu, Jinmen, and Mazu, then in fact Taiwan has declared "'de jure' independence." Under these circumstances, the mainland will have no other choice but to use force to settle the issue.[38]

On the basis of this statement at least, it is the content of amendments, not their mere passage, that will be the standard by which China would judge Chen's intentions.

The antisecession law that China's National People's Congress (NPC) passed on March 14, 2005, raised new questions about what kind of constitutional revision Beijing could tolerate. President Hu Jintao took a modestly hopeful stance when he called on Chen Shui-bian to fulfill "his commitment of not seeking 'legalization of Taiwan independence' through 'constitutional reform.'" But others did not sound so hopeful. In explaining the law right before its passage, Wang Zhaoguo, vice-chairman of the NPC's standing committee, said that among Taiwan's alleged secessionist activities, "we should be particularly watchful that the Taiwan authorities are trying to use so-called 'constitutional' or 'legal' means through 'referendum' or 'constitutional reengineering' to back up their secessionist attempt." Yu

Keli, director of the Institute of Taiwan Studies of the Chinese Academy of Social Sciences, associated "constitutional reform" with the separation of Taiwan from China, thus meeting one of the law's conditions for the use of "non-peaceful means."[39] All these formulations suggested that China might equate significant constitutional changes with separatism. Moreover, the very vagueness of the law itself concerning the definition of those three conditions creates some uncertainty over what Beijing is prepared to tolerate. For example, if in the summer of 2005 Taiwan's National Assembly approves the constitutional amendment instituting a popular referendum as the second stage of approving future constitutional amendments, might Beijing regard that step as a "major incident entailing Taiwan's secession from China" (the second condition in the law)?

In short, some of the scenarios for Chen Shui-bian's constitutional project are benign. There is the distinct possibility that it could run out of steam, because of effective pan-Blue opposition and the daunting hurdles that the constitutional revision process erects. Or Chen might choose to content himself with relatively modest changes that could secure pan-Blue support and therefore could be made through the established amendment process without raising sovereignty concerns. Such outcomes are not impossible, even with a pan-Blue majority in the legislature. The United States would not oppose such reforms, and it would encourage China to accept them.

Yet other, more destabilizing scenarios cannot be ruled out. The issue of whether Beijing would tolerate moderate constitutional change is clouded by the passage of the antisecession law. China's interests *seem* to lie in following the moderate approach that was emerging in the early fall of 2004. It could conclude that improvement of Taiwan's domestic institutions does not cross the line that it has drawn. Although Chinese leaders would still believe that Chen is intent on total separation and would regard limited constitutional revision as only a slowdown in a trend that will still continue, they would also conclude that China's fundamental interests had not been threatened and, perhaps, that the Taiwan public might turn against the pan-Green camp in 2008. Beijing would thus avoid a severe challenge, which it certainly does not want, and Taiwan might get a better political system, which it desperately needs.[40]

On the other hand, China continued to worry that Chen would find some way to push the envelope, even after the legislative elections arguably constrained his choices. That anxiety plus the Chinese system's inability to stop a proposal once it had gathered momentum led to the enactment of the antisecession law even when it was probably no longer necessary.[41] Those factors plus the law's ambiguities produce the possibility of future miscalculation on Beijing's part. Finally, circumstances can be imagined that would lead Chen Shui-bian to return to the course he charted during the election campaign—collapse of the Chen-Soong entente, renewed pressure from pan-Green radicals, and so on—and thereby prompt an aggressive Chinese response. But continuation of a more centrist stance seems more likely.

Some sort of communication between Beijing and Taipei would serve stability and, if necessary, facilitate crisis management. Resuming dialogue through either the SEF-ARATS mechanism or through a secret channel would be conducive to cooperation on this and many other issues. But Beijing again has set tough preconditions for contact, so it seems unlikely, at least in public. Appearing to give in to Chen, particularly after he had predicted during the campaign that China had no choice but to do so, would be a blow to its credibility. A private channel would be a good alternative, but Chinese mistrust may be too great. Yet it is precisely because mistrust is so deep that communication is necessary. China's desire to extract political concessions from Chen outweighs the practical need to prevent conflict. It is making a volatile situation even more unstable.

Under these circumstances, the United States will have to stay involved to protect its interests in peace and stability. The approach will be the same: dual deterrence—warnings and reassurance for both Beijing and Taipei. Within that context, the challenge will be to define a zone of accommodation between Beijing and Taipei concerning constitutional revision. That entails ensuring that Chen Shui-bian's inaugural commitments are upheld and that Taipei has a proper appreciation of how Beijing is likely to react— or overreact—to its initiatives. It requires helping Beijing to define what it cannot accept and adopt a reasonable attitude toward the rest. And it should include encouraging the two sides to engage with each other and so take more responsibility for security in the Strait. The Bush administration's approach during late 2003 and the first half of 2004 is a case in point: persuading Chen Shui-bian to use the established process and focus on governmental reform and counseling Beijing to focus on the content of constitutional change rather than the fact of it. If either side is unwilling to enter that zone of accommodation, then U.S. firmness is required. Taiwan's democracy fundamentally depends on the U.S. security umbrella, so Washington has the right and obligation to state its views when democracy and security conflict. A China that would use force against Taiwan poses a challenge to U.S. credibility and to the peaceful external environment that China requires to continue to grow economically and ensure social stability.

Beyond Constitutional Revision: Stabilization

Even if Chen Shui-bian's proposal for constitutional revision is managed in a manner that avoids conflict—and even if the substantive and aggravating obstacles to a settlement of the Taiwan Strait issue remain—stabilization of the situation should be a high priority. It is too fraught with uncertainty and the potential for miscalculation to be ignored. The leaders on each side mistrust each other and are prone to miscalculation. The development of a distinctive Taiwanese identity will continue, particularly if Beijing continues through its actions to alienate the island's public. The PRC's growing military power will feed Taiwan's nationalism even as it may deter a breakout, and over time it may create the temptation to bring Taiwan to heel and force it into a political settlement. Politics in both places will rear its head again in late 2007 and early 2008, and Beijing will host the Summer Olympics later in 2008.[42]

A Formal Agreement

One way to do bring about stabilization would be through a formal agreement between the two sides. Kenneth Lieberthal has been developing proposals for such an agreement since the late 1990s. The latest version was published in *Foreign Affairs* in the spring of 2005.[43]

Because a cross-Strait conflict is possible and settlement of the dispute probably impossible for decades to come, Lieberthal's current solution to the problem is to eliminate what each side fears. What China fears, he says, is that Taiwan will cross the "independence red line." What Taiwan fears is that China will attack. The core of a stabilization agreement would "consist of credible commitments to take the issues of independence and the use of force off the table."[44] This long-term bargain would be reinforced by a variety of steps: consideration of greater international space for Taiwan; military confidence-building measures; and more cross-Strait political and economic exchanges, including visits of political leaders, to reduce mutual mistrust.

As Lieberthal acknowledges, there are many elements of his proposal that remain to be operationalized. Although the proposal goes part way in addressing what each side fears, is there any certainty that it will capture what they might fear in 2015 or 2025? And since it would likely be impossible to anticipate for purposes of an agreement every conceivable form that a violation of the agreement might take, who would decide whether a violation occurred? If China would agree not to use force to change Taiwan's status, are there other ways that force or the threat of force—intimidation—might be used?

Even in general terms, the proposed framework has defects. Some are conceptual. Even though the purpose of the agreement would be to somehow set aside the sovereignty issue, it would come up when the format for negotiations was debated, as the two sides sought to define what the other was to not do—declare independence (Taiwan) and use force (China)—and as any agreement was implemented. It would surface as the two sides tried to work out the terms and conditions for Taiwan's participation in international organizations and the status of visiting political leaders; Taiwan would want to maximize its sense of sovereignty and Beijing would seek to minimize it. More broadly, how could Taiwan be assured, as it would want to be, that its claim to sovereignty would be taken seriously in any later political negotiations, after Chinese power had grown even more? On the security side, what Taiwan fears is not just China's threat to use force but also China's acquisition of advanced military equipment—which certainly would continue.

Other problems have to do with process. Who would negotiate for each side? Would China demand Taiwan's reaffirmation of the one-China principle before talks on the framework began? Is it reasonable to expect that Taiwan's Legislative Yuan would approve such an arrangement, as it would have to do? What would be the role of the United States in promoting such an agreement? Would it need to mediate between Taipei and Beijing or pressure Taiwan to negotiate, both of which actions the Reagan administration pledged that Washington would not take? And what would be the U.S. responsibility if Taiwan's political system took actions that Beijing regarded as violations of the understanding?

As these questions suggest, such a framework, in spite of its efforts to address the fears of each side, does not succeed in allaying the concerns of each that the other will renege on its commitments. Moreover, Taipei is unlikely to undertake any agreement that fosters fears of U.S. abandonment.

Functional Equivalents

The problem with the Lieberthal proposal is not its attempt to stabilize and bound the Taiwan Strait situation, for the danger that he seeks to address is a real one. The difficulty perhaps is that he seeks to embody reciprocal obligations in a formal agreement, wherein it would be impossible to allay every concern and close every loophole in the text. The way out may be to forge the functional equivalent of an interim agreement. The goals would be the same: ease mutual fears, reduce unpredictability and mistrust, enhance mutual confidence, and offer incentives for cooperation. But the steps would be taken through a process other than a negotiated accord.

The steps that might be taken to stabilize the tenuous cross-Strait situation are fairly obvious. Some are part of Lieberthal's proposal (as well as being relevant to a full solution of the dispute): restoration of dialogue; creation of a secret, authoritative communications channel; reassuring policy declarations; military confidence-building measures; removal of obstacles to economic relations (regarding direct transportation, for example); restraint on arms acquisitions; and an expanded international role for Taiwan. The problem is how to create a process that will bring them about.

The discussion in previous chapters on the obstacles to resolving the Taiwan Strait issue laid primary blame on Beijing. The PRC has pursued the one-country, two-systems concept, which is inappropriate in the Taiwan context; misinterpreted and overreacted to Lee Teng-hui's and Chen Shuibian's resistance to the formula; and sought to pressure Taiwan diplomatically, politically, and militarily. Moreover, it has not used the two sides' economic interdependence and Taiwan's democracy to its advantage by making positive appeals to the island's public.

That same approach undermines the effort to stabilize the situation in the absence of a resolution of the dispute. Consequently, if China wants to reduce its uncertainty about Taipei's intentions and simultaneously enhance the prospects for unification, it needs to take significant measures to improve the environment of cross-Strait relations. These measures do not mean explicit acceptance of Taiwan's claim that it is a sovereign entity, but they represent steps in that direction. They also are likely to have a positive impact on Beijing's image on the island, which is in its interests.

In the security realm, for example, it is China that has resisted agreeing to confidence-building measures (CBMs) on the false grounds that they are undertaken only between states and because it believes that its interests are better served by destroying Taiwan's confidence than building it.[45] China's inclusion of CBMs in its statement right before Chen's inauguration is a welcome move, though it still insists that Taiwan would have to make unacceptable concessions even to begin discussions. China is setting the pace with respect to military acquisitions, a pace that Taiwan is finding hard to match. Beijing has leeway, therefore, to announce a unilateral suspension of the production and deployment of missiles and the acquisition of other advanced systems that might be used against Taiwan. Because such a move would reduce the sense of threat on the island, it would have a direct impact on choices that the Taipei government, including the legislature, made on future weapons procurement. It would also affect Washington's definition of Taiwan's defense needs.

Economically, China has blocked direct transportation links more than Taiwan by insisting on a negotiation mechanism (private associations) that the Chen administration has rejected because it fears the implications for any future political negotiations. Taipei has been willing to have government officials negotiate on the links under the nominal aegis of private bodies, but until early 2005 Beijing dismissed that possibility because it did not wish to provide Chen with a political victory before Taiwan's 2004 presidential and legislative elections. Once they had taken place, Beijing accommodated Chen's suggestion on process, and direct charter flights were arranged for the 2005 lunar new year. Transportation links should be broadened through the same negotiating mechanism, which protects the political equities of each side.

In the international arena, China's quarantine of Taiwan has hurt its image in the eyes of the island's public. The dispute is not over whether Taiwan is a separate state with rights of membership in international organizations for which statehood is required but over the question of Taiwan's participation in the work of these institutions in a capacity other than state-member. Again, for Beijing to allow Taiwan's participation—perhaps as an observer—would not undermine its principles.

Politically, China needs to undertake a fundamental reassessment of the one-country, two-systems formula, because its approach to the sovereignty issue is likely to remain a nonstarter for Taiwan. Even the fact of such a reassessment would inspire confidence in Taiwan.[46]

Beijing, of course, would see little value in these proposals; it would fear that Chen Shui-bian would take advantage of its goodwill, pocket the concessions, and proceed with his "separatist" agenda. However, China might wish to use them to appeal to Taiwan's public. What it would seek in return for these gestures is a firm and credible assurance that Taipei will not do what it most fears—move toward independence.

Such an understanding may be unlikely, given the misunderstandings and missed opportunities of the last fifteen years. But it will be impossible without some sort of communication between Beijing and Taipei. It is only through dialogue that Beijing can lay out for Taipei what actions it believes are separatist and why; only through dialogue can Taipei describe its intentions and why some of those actions are not in fact separatist. If convergence is possible on these issues, then the two sides can perhaps work out a roadmap of sequenced steps to stabilize the cross-Strait situation, reduce their mutual insecurity and the danger of war, reduce mistrust, and enhance the possibilities for mutually beneficial interaction. The result might in fact be an "interim agreement." What is important, however, are the substantive building blocks of stability and reassurance and the process by which they are formed.

Chapter 5 used the Prisoner's Dilemma game as a metaphor to convey the difficulties of reaching a mutually beneficial resolution of the Taiwan Strait issue. In the language of game theory, each side will benefit objectively from cooperation (a settlement) but so fears that the other side will defect (choose not to cooperate and so increase its own vulnerability) that it opts for a suboptimal status quo. The dynamic in Prisoner's Dilemma is also relevant in a situation of economic interaction and political hostility plus militarization. Chapter 9 introduced the technique of reciprocal and conditional concessions (tit for tat) as a way for the two parties to get to an optimal solution even in a climate of mistrust. The same sort of tit-for-tat interchange can turn a tenuous status quo into stable coexistence. For that to happen, Beijing must be willing to talk to Taipei and to broaden its view of the issue. Dialogue would best be undertaken directly and without preconditions. If that is temporarily not possible, then the United States might provide intellectual facilitation. Yet the goal should be to get Washington out of the middle as soon as possible.

An Opening Window of Opportunity?

If domestic politics on both sides have complicated the search for a cross-Strait settlement since the late 1990s, the year 2005 offers an uncommon opportunity. The PRC leadership transition was concluded in the fall of 2004, when Jiang Zemin stepped down from his last major position, chairmanship of the Central Military Commission. Hu Jintao has since headed all three institutional hierarchies: party, government, and military. Although that does not give him and the rest of the fourth-generation leadership a free hand, they now have a freer hand. Similarly, the December 2004 legislative election in Taiwan was the last island-wide election for central-level offices until late 2007 and early 2008. The balance of power between the pan-Green and pan-Blue camps is clearer, and the imperatives of an imminent electoral campaign need not preoccupy leaders' attention or distort their approach to China. Moreover, the coming adoption of a system of single-member districts for a majority of legislative seats should, over time, give politics a more centrist cast.

An easing of political pressures does not, of course, mean that the two sides will seize the opportunity created thereby. Nor does it guarantee that either will demonstrate the substantive creativity needed to sustain momentum.

But it is not a trivial matter. Because politics can poison the atmosphere in which Beijing and Taipei operate, the rare opportunities that do exist should be seized.

A Role for the United States?

What should the United States do to promote stabilization? That it has an interest in doing so is indisputable; its stake in regional peace and stability is too great to permit the vectors of negative cross-Strait interaction from meeting. And Beijing's and Taipei's perceptions—or misperceptions—of the U.S. role in a crisis will become part of the calculus of each.

As in the case of facilitating a settlement, an U.S. role is likely to be limited. There is, of course, the question of whether Beijing and Taipei would both trust Washington over time to play the role of intermediary. For example, instability will be the outcome if the consensus on Taiwan is that the United States is somehow imposing an arrangement on it. If there is to be a stabilizing understanding between the two sides, it will be more durable if they reach it on their own.

Yet there may be a role for the United States at the beginning of the process, in order to break down some of the mistrust between the two sides and so smooth the way for them to come together at their own table. Intellectual facilitation—privately describing for one side the views of the other without the noise of public debate—is probably the most feasible modality.

Self-Strengthening for Taiwan

There is another set of priorities for managing the Taiwan Strait issue. Even if Taiwan pursues a course that does not back Beijing into a corner, it should also strengthen itself in a variety of areas as China's power continues to grow. Indeed, it should strengthen itself even if there is promise of a settlement.

Taiwan cannot avoid a choice concerning China. Located only ninety miles from a potential great power, it is a victim of geography. It also is a victim of economic fundamentals: the inevitable increase in wages on the island, the vast supply of cheap labor on the mainland, the adjustments to membership in the World Trade Organization, and the demands of a globalized system for low-cost, high-quality goods. Individuals and companies have an array of options from which to choose. For the island as a whole, the basic yet overly simplified choice is between accommodating or resisting Chinese power. A variant of that choice, which tends to be the default selection, is accommodating China economically and resisting politically.

Complicating matters is the messy discourse on choices that is common on Taiwan. For example, the alternatives used in the most common public opinion polls (for example, unification now; status quo now, unification later; permanent status quo; status quo now, independence later; and independence now) are not very helpful. They neither define what terms like unification, independence, and the status quo mean nor describe the likely consequences of each choice in terms of military danger and economic gains and losses. Moreover, to not make a choice is also a choice.

A related yet more clear-cut issue is whether to make choices from a position of strength or a position of weakness. There is probably little debate that choosing from a position of weakness is undesirable and that Taiwan should strengthen itself if it is to make good choices. However, there might be consensus on the areas where self-strengthening should occur but debate on how to achieve it.

A threshold question is whether to focus on issues of symbols or substance. There is an all-too-present tendency in any Chinese culture to focus on the former and downplay the latter. Chapter 6 discussed the politics of words on Taiwan. To be sure, symbols can have a substantive value. Look, for example, at the power that the PRC gains by being recognized by most of the countries of the world and by conducting its diplomatic relations from buildings called embassies—and the satisfaction that Taiwan gets from taking away one of Beijing's diplomatic partners. Yet symbols have their limits, and to assume that they alone convey power is an unfortunate illusion for a country in Taiwan's position. To think that the island's problems will be solved by such exercises as changing its title from "China" or "Republic of China" to "Taiwan" may make a statement (a dangerous one perhaps) and create some sense of psychological security. But it cannot substitute for the hard work of making the island stronger in real terms.

Economically, there is no doubt broad agreement that Taiwan needs to strengthen itself in order to maintain a globally competitive niche and to guarantee attractive employment for the population. As companies move production offshore, even though they retain the higher-skill positions at their headquarters, there will be an inevitable loss of jobs on Taiwan. Advanced manufacturing can take up some of the slack. But the greatest opportunity lies in building a knowledge- and service-based economy. That in turn requires making a number of institutional changes. If the economy is to be knowledge-based, government must effectively protect knowledge—intellectual property rights. Taiwan has thrived on producing goods based on the technology of others. Its competitive advantage lies now in producing technology itself to embed in the goods produced, whether in Taiwan, in China, or elsewhere. Protection of knowledge in turn requires a stronger legal system that will enforce those rights and impose disincentives to piracy. A stronger judiciary can also constrain corruption in government procurement. A second key element of a service-based economy is a strong and agile financial sector, which also is needed for advanced manufacturing. Another is direct transportation links with China, to which political factors—some understandable—have been a barrier. Taiwan has many talented entrepreneurs and outstanding companies. To continue to excel, they need the right policy environment. A weak, uncompetitive Taiwan economy means a weak negotiating position vis-à-vis China.

In terms of security, there is a mainstream understanding that China's military power is growing and that Taiwan needs to catch up; a minority discounts the threat because of the mutual interests that come with extensive cross-Strait economic interaction. There is less comprehension of the specifics of the island's defense posture. The facts are that if Taiwan were attacked—and even if the United States decided to intervene—the armed forces would have to hold on for a few weeks before U.S. forces were mobilized and fighting with them. Thus Taiwan needs sophisticated military equipment, both to deter a PRC attack and to provide strategic endurance should deterrence fail. The United States has agreed to provide much of what Taiwan needs, but the island's political system has been slow to mobilize and allocate the resources for the necessary weapons systems. Moreover, institutional reform (in the areas of command and control, doctrine, personnel, training, logistics, and so on) must accompany procurement advances.[47] Software must improve with hardware. Here too, the progress has been slow, primarily because the challenges are daunting. Yet continuing effort will be required to ensure that, within the limits of Taiwan's resources and the parameters of its democratic system, the armed forces will be strong. For certain, a weak military increases the risk of intimidation.

The *least* effective way to strengthen Taiwan's security would be to significantly shift the emphasis of its military strategy from one that is essentially defensive and anchored in alliance with the United States to one that has a much greater offensive component. The logic of those who argue for a shift is that the acquisition of capabilities that can threaten military, population, and infrastructure targets on the mainland will deter Beijing from undertaking military action against Taiwan. However tempting and symbolically satisfying this option may be, it is simply not feasible. There are daunting political obstacles to acquiring offensive assets from foreign sources (pressure from China on third countries) and serious budgetary and technological ones to indigenous production. And the underlying assumption—that the mere possession of some offensive capabilities would deter China because Beijing would have to take them seriously in a war-fighting context—is flawed. As Gregg Rubenstein notes: "Given the differences in the magnitude of territory and resources available to both sides, it is simply inconceivable for Taiwan to compete—let alone prevail—with China in a force/counterforce exchange. A deployment of counterforce capabilities by Taiwan unsupported by appropriate defense preparations would be—and would be readily seen as—a hollow façade instead of a real defense."[48] The mere decision by Taiwan to acquire offensive capabilities would compound the security dilemma from China's point of view—by making it easier for the former to take provocative political initiatives and defend against a military response—and give it a greater incentive to preempt. Finally, because the United States is the ultimate guarantor of its security, Taiwan must ensure that there is no strategic divergence that might lead Washington to conclude that its de facto ally is entrapping it in a conflict that it prefers not to fight.

Diplomatically, therefore, Taiwan's priority is to improve its ties with the United States, which were frayed during the island's 2004 presidential campaign. President Chen took initiatives that augmented at least the possibility of increasing tensions and the potential for conflict with China and thereby called into play the security commitment of the United States. Yet he took those initiatives without consulting Washington. Private advice to show restraint was ignored, culminating in President Bush's December 2003 public rebuke. Concern mounted that Taiwan might draw the United States into an unwanted conflict. Several steps should be taken to remedy this situation. First of all, there should be a shared understanding of the cause of the 2003–04 difficulties. Second, Taiwan should make the decisionmaking process with regard to national security and foreign policy more coherent so that the appropriate senior officials review political initiatives. Third, both sides should enhance mutual confidence by picking individuals to conduct relations who have a reputation for moderation and reasonableness. Fourth, high-level dialogue, authorized by the president on each side, should be energized. In short, a strained relationship with Washington puts Taipei at a disadvantage with Beijing. Another way that Taiwan could strengthen itself diplomatically is to improve its substantive performance in those international organizations in which it does have membership, such as the WTO. Achieving the status of member is an important achievement, but it should be consolidated through tangible contributions to the work of those institutions.

Next, Taiwan's public needs a clearer understanding of the legal identity of its governing authorities. The sovereignty issue infuses cross-Strait disputes and reverberates into domestic policy disputes. Yet there is little understanding of what is at stake in the sovereignty issue and why, in some instances, following a pragmatic course of accelerating interdependence might be more beneficial than pursuing a rigid definition of sovereignty. As a result, those in the government who are responsible for defending the ROC's sovereignty are permanently on the defensive. Over the medium term and assuming that ultimately political negotiations will occur with the PRC, there should be public debate on what aspects of sovereignty are important to preserve and why. Taiwan will have only itself to blame if it makes mindless concessions to China on the nature of its government and on how it is a part of China. Conversely, it has a lot to lose by holding rigidly to positions that public discussion would reveal to be inconsistent with Taiwan's situation and a globalized economy. In 2000, there was an attempt to forge a consensus on cross-Strait policy, of which Taiwan's legal identity was a core element, but the pan-Blue parties chose not to participate. Yet their position on that issue is not fundamentally different from that of the pan-Green camp. With political will, the two coalitions could find much on which to agree.[49]

The most important field of self-strengthening concerns Taiwan's democratic system. Chapter 6 described some of the weak points of the island's political order and how it might find it difficult to take "yes" for an answer even if Beijing offered an acceptable arrangement. A number of reforms are needed to ensure that the political system reflects the public will better than it does today. The constitutional amendments of August 2004 were a significant start. Moving to single-member districts for the electoral system for the legislative branch will, over time, give centrist views stronger representation than marginal ones. Yet much more needs to be done: ending the constitutional disjunction between the president and the premier, to create more coherent policy formulation in the executive branch; streamlining decisionmaking in the Legislative Yuan so that small minorities cannot block proposals that enjoy significant consensus; restricting opportunities for conflict of interest, particularly in the legislature, where members use their position to secure private or political gain; strengthening the judicial system; and encouraging more professionalism in the mass media so that it would serve the public more than commercial interests.

Obviously, political reform is very difficult because it affects the power of the people who must make the change. Yet it is important for its own sake and to ensure that Taiwan makes good choices on cross-Strait relations. Self-strengthening in all five areas will foster psychological strength, and a sense of self-confidence will be essential if Taiwan is to stand up for its core interests. A lack of confidence will place it at the mercy of Beijing and render it overly dependent on the United States.

12

Choices Ahead

To make policy is to make choices—often in an environment of uncertainty from a set of unfavorable alternatives, and sometimes with dire consequences. The Taiwan Strait dispute is no exception. Each of the parties concerned—China, Taiwan, and the United States—faces a complex set of choices as it seeks to promote its objectives or at least to prevent disaster. Disaster has loomed and has been avoided a couple of times in the last twenty years. It is likely to loom again. Pessimists worry that it will be increasingly difficult to control the trajectories of Taiwanese nationalism and Chinese antiseparatism and that conflict is all but inevitable. Optimists believe that the growing tensions, though serious, still can be contained and that in the proper environment the two sides can reach a modus vivendi and perhaps settle their differences.

Whether the task is crisis management, stabilization, or resolution, it is essential to understand the nature of the dispute. To misunderstand why there is a disagreement in the first place only ensures bad policy choices, often with serious consequences. This analysis has sought to describe and explain in depth the Taiwan Strait issue and why it is so difficult to resolve. It is a paradoxical sort of quarrel, in that cross-Strait relations are both mutually beneficial and potentially dangerous. The two sides already gain a lot from their multifaceted interaction—in business, education, sports, cultural affairs, philanthropy, and so on. Why does that not offer a basis for political reconciliation? Why does each side fear that the other will take actions that threaten its fundamental interests and therefore hedge against that possibility by accelerating its acquisition of advanced weapons systems? Through design, accident, or miscalculation, the cross-Strait dispute could erupt in war. It would be a war that the United States would probably end up fighting.

Frustrating any negotiated solution are two substantive issues: sovereignty and security. Beijing and Taipei fundamentally disagree over whether the Taiwan government would possess sovereignty within a political union of the two sides. Taipei says that it should. Beijing's consistent approach would deny Taiwan sovereign status, leaving it a subordinate entity. Complicating the dispute is China's tendency to interpret opposition to the one-country, two-systems formula as opposition to unification itself. In Beijing's mindset, it has transmuted a disagreement over *how* Taiwan might be a part of China into a dispute over *whether* Taiwan sees itself as part of China.

On security, Beijing fears that Taiwan will take a political initiative that threatens its fundamental interests and national mission; therefore it strengthens China's military forces to deter such an action and to be able to respond should deterrence fail. Taiwan regards this military buildup as proof of Beijing's malevolent intentions. Their mutual mistrust makes each side reluctant to let its guard down and show goodwill for fear that the other will only pocket the gesture and ask for more. As a result, even starting a reconciliation process is difficult. Complicating matters, Taiwan relies on its de facto alliance with the United States to deter any PRC aggression, which China sees as proof of hostile intentions on the part of both Taipei and Washington. If there were negotiations to resolve the dispute, Taiwan would be very reluctant to give up U.S. support unless it had a high degree of confidence that it was no longer necessary.

These two issues form a two-stranded conceptual knot that will have to be untied if there is to be a negotiated settlement. Taiwan in particular sees a link between the two issues, in that it may be considered less deserving of security assistance from other countries if it is not regarded as a sovereign entity.

Aggravating matters—tightening the knot—are three other factors. The first is the impact of domestic politics in each country. In Taiwan, there is a strong Taiwanese identity and significant fear of outsiders. Some Taiwanese have advocated making the island a separate country, and the Democratic Progressive Party, the primary vessel of Taiwan's sense of identity, has wrestled with how much emphasis to place on promoting independence as a goal. It played down that objective in order to elect Chen Shui-bian as president in 2000 and because of the island's economical dependence on the mainland. Still, the combination of separate identity and fear of China ensures broad opposition to the one-country, two-systems formula. On the PRC side, Taiwan has been an issue in elite conflict, and some leaders try to gain political advantage by attacking the Taiwan policy of their colleagues. The leadership sometimes feels constrained by nationalistic pressures from the public.

Politics also affects whether a settlement, if concluded, could actually be ratified in Taiwan. Some elements of the settlement would probably have to take the form of constitutional amendments, which in turn require the support of most of the island's political parties to clear the supermajority threshold. However difficult, securing such broad support would help ensure that an agreement would endure.

The second aggravating factor is the decisionmaking system on each side. In both Beijing and Taipei, policy formulation on the cross-Strait issue is centralized and personalized. Each side is prone to misperception and miscalculation.

The third aggravating factor is the zero-sum leverage game. Each side competes for international support, particularly from the United States. In addition, China has sought to influence Taiwan's domestic politics, but there is little that Taiwan can do to influence Chinese politics.

If this is the problem, how can Taiwan, China, and the United States structure their choices to prevent tensions and conflict in the short term, stabilize the situation in the medium term, and explore the possibility of resolving the dispute in the long term?

In the short term, Taiwan needs to decide what kind of constitution it really needs and China must assess what sort of Taiwan charter it can accept. There is a zone of mutual restraint in which a new constitution is restricted in scope to the reform of domestic political institutions—that is, it focuses on domestic sovereignty and sets aside matters of Westphalian and international sovereignty. That would be good for Taiwan, in that it would get a better system of government, and it should be something that Beijing could tolerate, because it would not substantively affect its core interests.

To achieve that outcome, several things must happen. First of all, President Chen Shui-bian must resist the impulses of the fundamentalists in his party to go beyond domestic political reform and use a constitutional revision to address Taiwan's legal relationship with China, particularly in a way that might lead Beijing to conclude that permanent separation is about to occur and any hope for unification is lost. He needs to reassure China on a continuing basis that his goal is what he says it is: creating a government that better reflects the will of Taiwan's people. China must distinguish between the fact of a new Taiwan constitution and its content—and ensure that its decisionmaking system does not overinterpret in a negative way what is happening. And the United States will have to both work with Taiwan's leaders to shape the new document so that it preserves a clear focus on domestic political reform and counsel China that its core interests are not being hurt as a result. It will need good communications channels with each side and internal policy consensus that this is the course of action that best protects U.S. interests.

For the medium-term goal of stabilization, the objective is both to reduce the fear and uncertainty that Beijing and Taipei each feel toward the other and to foster stronger confidence that peaceful coexistence is possible. Taipei must reassure Beijing that it is not bent on permanent separation and that there are some models of unification that it could accept if they were put on the table. Beijing should mitigate the negative impact that its military buildup, diplomatic isolation strategy, and united front tactics have on its image in the eyes of Taiwan's people and so strengthen the Chinese dimension of their identity. That would require the PRC to reverse some long-standing policy priorities, such as blocking Taiwan's observership in the World Health Organization and other international institutions, refusing military confidence-building measures, and demanding that the three links be negotiated in a way that threatens Taiwan's view of itself as a sovereign entity. Above all, it will require that China no longer set political preconditions for cross-Strait dialogue. High-level, authoritative interaction can clarify intentions and enhance confidence. And given that neither side finds it easy to assume the goodwill of the other, dialogue can provide a venue wherein a roadmap of conditional and reciprocal steps can be drawn up. Because of that mutual mistrust, the United States might play a useful role in clarifying each side's clear understanding of the other's goals. A formal stabilization agreement might be possible, but the substance of such an accord—its functional equivalent—is more important than the agreement itself. Returning to a point in chapter 11, a more stable cross-Strait environment would give Taiwan the opportunity to strengthen itself economically, diplomatically, conceptually, militarily, politically, and psychologically.

If China and Taiwan can keep tensions to a minimum in the short term, if they can stabilize their relations in the medium term, and if Taiwan can gain the confidence that comes from self-strengthening, then the two sides can again contemplate the possibility of forging a broad, enduring settlement of their dispute. Their shared and parallel interests are not trivial. The costs of conflict would be severe, and conflict cannot be ruled out even if the situation is stabilized. As this volume has demonstrated, however, there should be no illusions that a settlement will be easy. Addressing the sovereignty and security issues will require concessions from both sides, but particularly from China. (For a variety of reasons, Beijing, not just Taiwan, needs to be more flexible and creative about how power is organized within the Chinese state—that is, about the nature of its domestic sovereignty.) Both will have to resist the temptation to seize easy—and self-destructive—diplomatic or political advantage. In order to mitigate aggravating factors and reach consensus on substantive issues and to limit the corrosive effects of mutual mistrust, the two sides will have to create an approach to negotiations in which substance and process reinforce each other and so enhance the prospects for progress. In this complex and difficult exercise, the United States can play only a limited role, because neither Beijing nor Taipei can be expected to let it play a mediating role and because its contribution to Taiwan's security makes it a party to the dispute—and exacerbates the island's fear of abandonment. Some sort of intellectual facilitation is probably the most useful and acceptable contribution that the United States can make. And even if negotiators can draft a settlement, the Taiwan political system in its current polarized and paralyzed state probably would not be able to take "yes" for an answer—all the more reason to reform that system. Whether it is tension control, stabilization, or settlement, it is essential that China and Taiwan talk to each other. Erecting political obstacles to dialogue makes making and preserving peace more difficult.

Cross-Strait relations have been a graveyard of missed opportunities. China's failure to understand Lee Teng-hui's objection to the one-country, two-systems model and its refusal to enter into dialogue in 2000 are only the most obvious examples. But there are others, on both sides.

One reason that opportunities are missed is because Beijing and Taipei both believe—or at least hope—that time is on their side. China thinks that its growing economic and military power will sooner or later force Taiwan to negotiate on its terms, if only it can avoid a separatist breakout in the meantime. Some in Taiwan believe that democratization on the mainland will put it in a much better bargaining position vis-à-vis Beijing, if only it can, with U.S. help, preserve its de facto independence until then. Yet each side's hope is based on a flawed assumption. Increasing cross-Strait economic integration will create even greater anxiety in some parts of the Taiwan population about political capitulation, and Taiwanese identity in some form is a permanent feature of the island's political life. Democratization in China will probably come slowly and gradually and may foster a more, not less, ideological approach to unification. The belief of each that time is on its side probably makes a stalemate between the two more likely, which is not a bad outcome if it is a stable stalemate. More dangerous is the conclusion in either China or Taiwan—or both—that time favors its adversary. For some forces in Taiwan to conclude that the only way to secure the future is to go for independence while China is relatively weak and constrained by the Olympics—or for the PRC to judge that preemptive military action is needed to keep the door to unification from closing—is to invite unnecessary conflict. Instead of recklessness or naiveté, both sides have the option of shaping the current situation to maximize their shared interests and minimize the risk of a foolish conflict. The choice is theirs to make.

A Final, Personal Note

I did not intend to focus my professional attention on Taiwan and its relations with China. Although my parents served in Taiwan as missionaries in the late 1960s and although my wife and I lived in Taipei in 1975 and adopted our daughter in Taiwan, I was purposefully inattentive to the obvious political restrictions of that time and to the Kuomintang's halting experiments with political reform, which were not readily apparent but led ultimately to the democratization of the late 1980s. My substantive focus at that time was politics on the Chinese mainland, not on Taiwan. My doctoral thesis did address KMT rule, but as it occurred on the mainland in the 1920s and 1930s. Taiwan was not an object of interest in and of itself.

My first real immersion in the politics of Taiwan began in the summer of 1983 when I went to work for U.S. Representative Stephen Solarz, chairman of the House Subcommittee on Asia and the Pacific. Promoting human rights and democracy on Taiwan was one of Steve's causes, which he pursued with his customary dedication and vigor. On the staff of the subcommittee, I provided support as he sought to expose KMT repression, get dissidents out of jail, make the case that Taiwan was ready for democracy, hold hearings, pass resolutions, and serve as a beacon of hope for the *dangwai* opposition.[1] I was the point of contact on his staff for his Taiwanese American friends, who were in self-imposed exile in the United States and wanted to bring change in Taiwan by participating in the American political system. They became my friends, and even though we disagreed sometimes on whether the KMT could lead the process of democratization and whether de jure independence was in the interest of Taiwan and the United States, I deeply admired the love they had for their native land. I was also the point of contact with *dangwai* dissidents who visited the United

States looking for support. Steve Solarz was one of the people to whom they looked, and I made sure that they got the recognition and backing they wanted. Among the calling cards I have from that period is one for a dissident lawyer who had spent time in prison on a questionable libel suit: Chen Shui-bian.

From that congressional vantage point, I was a keen observer of and minor participant in the momentous changes of the late 1980s. I organized a subcommittee hearing on the murder of Henry Liu by agents of the Taiwan security services, an atrocity that moved Chiang Ching-kuo to accelerate the political liberalization process—and just in time, for he was in failing health. When, in violation of law, the *dangwai* announced on September 28, 1986, that it was forming the Democratic Progressive Party, I quickly drafted a press release that Solarz, Representative Jim Leach, Senator Claiborne Pell, and Senator Edward Kennedy issued, calling on the KMT not to crack down; I learned later that Chiang had no intention of suppressing the new party. I was in Taiwan with Solarz in January 1988, days after the death of Chiang Ching-kuo, and we met with his new, untested successor, Lee Teng-hui. And so on. As the decade turned, China experienced the tragedy of Tiananmen Square and its repressive aftermath, but Taiwan was proving that a Chinese society could make the transition to democracy and still preserve stability.

Steve Solarz left Congress at the end of 1992, and I went to work for Lee Hamilton, who had just become chairman of the House Foreign Affairs Committee. He focused more on the U.S. relationship with China and how to put it back on track after Tiananmen, and my work shifted accordingly. Although the Taiwanese American community had successfully stimulated congressional support for democratization, it was less able to elicit enthusiasm for its other goal, independence. And many of the activists returned home to participate directly in the island's politics, becoming legislators and county magistrates.

Taiwan's salience grew again in 1995. The frustration of the island's public with its PRC-inspired exclusion from the international community was beginning to boil over, and Lee Teng-hui decided to give voice to that frustration—and thereby improve his chances in the 1996 presidential election. He would visit the United States. He engineered an impressive campaign to gain support in Congress for the idea and to mount pressure on the Clinton administration to give him permission. I shared the administration's opposition to the idea, but I also understood early on that Congress would win the fight. The impulses of Taiwan's democracy had pushed against the limits of Beijing's narrow tolerance, and the United States was caught right in the middle.

That summer, after Lee's visit to Cornell University, I left Congress and moved to the intelligence community, taking the position of national intelligence officer for East Asia. From that vantage point, I watched the missile crisis of March 1996, when there was a chance that accident or miscalculation would produce a conflict in the Taiwan Strait. I realized then that the United States could not take peace for granted and would have to work harder if it was to protect its interest in peace and security. I came gradually to the conclusion that I could serve that cause better as a diplomat than as an analyst, and in September 1997, I was privileged to be named chairman and managing director of the American Institute in Taiwan, based in Washington, D.C.

In that capacity, I was part of the team that formulated Taiwan policy and helped in the day-to-day conduct of a relationship that, although unofficial in form, is robust in substance. I participated in meetings of American and Taiwan officials (both civilian and military), represented the U.S. government on the ground during transits by senior Taiwan leaders, and was among those who served as the public voice of the United States. Because mine was nominally an unofficial position, I could speak more fully about the details of U.S. policy. I often traveled to Taiwan at sensitive times. I briefed Taiwan leaders after Jiang Zemin's 1997 visit to the United States and Bill Clinton's 1998 visit to China. I was sent in July 1999 to register U.S. concern about Lee Teng-hui's special state-to-state formulation; in December 1999 to announce that Washington had a neutral stance on the 2000 presidential election; and right after the 2000 election, with Lee Hamilton, to check signals with Chen Shui-bian. During those visits, having the Taiwan public see that I had delivered messages from the United States often was as important as the messages themselves. I stayed at AIT as the relationship grew closer during the first eighteen months of the Bush administration and, in a bit of lucky timing, departed just before it began to deteriorate.

Because I had only bit parts in the drama of Taiwan's relations with the United States, I deliberately chose to make this a book of policy analysis rather than a memoir. Yet what I learned during almost two decades in the U.S. government does infuse this volume. And running through it is a thread of empathy for the people of Taiwan: Minnan, Hakka, and mainlanders; old and young; women and men; pro-Green and pro-Blue parties; politicians, officials, businessmen, farmers, soldiers, scholars, and students. This was a population that until the 1990s was not party to fundamental decisions about its fate but had to accept the decisions of imperial bureaucrats, Japanese colonials, KMT officials, or U.S. administrations. For several decades, the great majority was subject to harsh repression and cultural orthodoxies, at the hands of both Japan and the KMT. A few protested and were jailed or killed for their pains. A number went abroad. Most suffered in silence, while channeling their energies into creating wealth and a better life for their children. At the same time, in response to repression, that majority clandestinely nurtured a non-Chinese sense of themselves. Once the political system was democratized, there erupted aspirations long suppressed: to express their Taiwan identity; to receive international respect; and not to cede the power of choice to others. In addition, there was ambivalence about China, which for some was so profound that it translated into a desire to make Taiwan a completely separate country.

For a variety of reasons, the people of Taiwan long ago became, in a sense, wards of the United States. Their complex history and aspirations, their security, and their governments' penetration of the U.S. political system became a part of U.S. foreign policy. And although popular Taiwan wishes get refracted through the priorities of officials and politicians, at the end of the day it is to the people of the island that the United States bears a responsibility.

There are things that the United States can do to carry out that responsibility and some things that Taiwan's people will have to do for themselves. We must work within the dynamics of Taiwan's dependence on the United States, appreciating both its overconfidence that American support is automatic and unqualified and its sense of vulnerability to the possibility that Washington will sell it out again. We therefore must reassure at the same time that we dissuade. And we must listen carefully, in the Chinese phrase, to "the sound beyond the strings" (*xianwai zhi yin*). Ultimately, however, the Taiwan people are most dependent on the quality of their democratic system. They are ill-served by a system that makes decisions based on a distorted reflection of the popular will, one that cannot make decisions supported by the mainstream because small minorities can call the tune. Neither excessive dependence on the United States nor a defective system of government serves the public good. After a checkered past, let us hope that Taiwan's people get the political system—and the future—that they truly deserve.

Notes

Note: Access to the Foreign Broadcast Information Service (FBIS) is restricted to certain U.S. government employees and contractors. Access to its publicly available version, the World News Service, is by subscription only. All FBIS sources noted here are available through the author.

Chapter One

1. The spelling of Chinese names in this book is romanized according to the pinyin system used in the People's Republic of China, except for the names of individuals in Taiwan who have their own preference (for example, Lee Teng-hui) and names that have a long-established form in another system (for example, Chiang Kai-shek, Chiang Ching-kuo, Taipei).

2. The situation is a bit more complicated than this statement suggests. Taiwan has a small aboriginal population, members of tribes that have lived on the island for millennia. With the arrival of outsiders from China, these groups shrank through assimilation, disease, and warfare. Moreover, immigrants from China before the twentieth century were from three different groups. Two groups, from south Fujian (*Minnan*, literally "southern Fujian"), came from two prefectures—Zhangzhou and Quanzhou—and long retained a loyalty to those localities. A third group, the Hakka (*Kejia*), came from the upland areas of the western Fujian and eastern Guangdong provinces. Even today, they regard themselves as a distinct group. In Taiwan, the term Taiwanese is usually associated with the *Minnan* people. When "Taiwanese" or "native Taiwanese" is used outside the island, it often refers to all three groups.

Chapter Two

1. For excellent discussions of Taiwan's early absorption into the Chinese cultural world, see John Robert Shepherd, *Statecraft and Political Economy on the Taiwan Frontier, 1600–1800* (Stanford University Press, 1996); Eduard B. Vermeer, "Up the Mountains and Out to the Sea: The Expansion of the Fukienese in the Late Ming Period," in *Taiwan: A New History*, edited by Murray A. Rubinstein (Armonk, N.Y.: M. E. Sharpe, 1999), pp. 45–83; and John E. Wills Jr., "The Seventeenth-Century

Transformation: Taiwan under the Dutch and the Cheng Regime," in *Taiwan: A New History*, pp. 84–106. For an account of Taiwan's Sinicization through the history of one family, see Johanna Menzel Meskill, *A Chinese Pioneer Family: The Lins of Wufeng, Taiwan, 1729–1895* (Princeton University Press, 1979).

2. Robert Gardella, "From Treaty Ports to Provincial Status, 1860–1894," in *Taiwan: A New History*, edited by Rubinstein, pp. 163–200; and Harry J. Lamley, "Taiwan under Japanese Rule, 1895–1945: Vicissitudes of Colonial Rule," in *Taiwan: A New History*, pp. 201–60.

3. Lamley, "Taiwan under Japanese Rule"; and George H. Kerr, *Formosa: Licensed Revolution and the Home Rule Movement, 1895–1945* (University Press of Hawaii, 1974).

4. For the Nationalist and Communist views of Taiwan in the late 1930s, see Frank S.T. Hsiao and Lawrence R. Sullivan, "The Chinese Communist Party and the Status of Taiwan," *Pacific Affairs* 52 (Fall 1979): 446–67. For U.S.-ROC interactions concerning Taiwan's fate and Roosevelt's decision, see Richard C. Bush, "The Wartime Decision to Return Taiwan to China," in *At Cross Purposes: U.S.-Taiwan Relation since 1942* (Armonk, N.Y.: M. E. Sharpe, 2004), pp. 3–39.

5. For the best single volume on U.S.-Taiwan relations after 1945, see Nancy Bernkopf Tucker, *Taiwan, Hong Kong, and the United States, 1945–1992: Uncertain Friendships* (New York: Twayne Publishers, 1994). For the immediate postwar period, see Steven Phillips, "Between Assimilation and Independence: Taiwanese Political Aspirations under Nationalist Chinese Rule, 1945–1948," in *Taiwan: A New History*, edited by Rubinstein, pp. 275–319; George H. Kerr, *Formosa Betrayed* (London: Eyre & Spottiswoode, 1965); and Lai Tse-han, Ramon H. Myers, and Wei Hou, *A Tragic Beginning: The Taiwan Uprising of February 28, 1947* (Stanford University Press, 1991).

6. On the U.S. response to the 2-28 uprising, see my "Difficult Dilemmas: The United States and Kuomintang Repression, 1947–1972," in *At Cross Purposes*, pp. 40–84. On Washington decisionmaking at the end of the Chinese civil war, see David M. Finkelstein, *Washington's Taiwan Dilemma, 1949–1950* (George Mason University Press, 1993).

7. When peace treaties were concluded in 1952, Japan, under U.S. pressure and in accordance with the notion that Taiwan's status was undetermined, renounced sovereignty over Taiwan but did not transfer it to another party.

8. On the U.S.-ROC alliance, see John W. Garver, *The Sino-American Alliance: Nationalist China and American Cold War Strategy in Asia* (Armonk, NY: M. E. Sharpe, 1997); and Robert Accinelli, *Crisis and Commitment: United States Policy toward Taiwan, 1950–1955* (University of North Carolina Press, 1996).

9. The best political history of postwar Taiwan is Denny Roy, *Taiwan: A Political History* (Cornell University Press, 2003). For several contemporaneous perspectives on KMT rule in the early 1960s, see Mark Mancall, ed., *Formosa Today* (New York: Praeger, 1964). For the experience of a Taiwanese opponent of the regime, see Peng

Ming-min, *A Taste of Freedom: Memoirs of a Formosan Independence Leader* (New York: Holt, Rinehart, and Winston, 1972). For an inside look at Chiang Ching-kuo's role, see Jay Taylor, *The Generalissimo's Son: Chiang Ching-kuo and the Revolutions in China and Taiwan* (Harvard University Press, 2000). On the impact of U.S. economic aid, see Thomas B. Gold, *State and Society in the Taiwan Miracle* (Armonk, N.Y.: M. E. Sharpe, 1997).

10. For U.S.-ROC conflicts over the United Nations problem, see my "The Status of the ROC and Taiwan, 1950–1972: Explorations in United States Policy," in *At Cross Purposes*, pp. 85–123.

11. For an excellent study of the reorientation of U.S. relations with China and Taiwan and their strategic context, see Robert S. Ross, *Negotiating Cooperation: The United States and China, 1969–1989* (Stanford University Press, 1995). For background on the Shanghai Communiqué, the normalization communiqué, and the Taiwan Relations Act, see "The Sacred Texts of United States–China–Taiwan Relations," in *At Cross Purposes*, pp. 124–78. For the "I will not sell you down the river" statement, see James C. H. Shen, *The U.S. and Free China: How the U.S. Sold Out Its Ally* (Washington: Acropolis Books, 1983), p. 51.

12. For the evolution of Taiwan's political system during the 1970s and early 1980s, see Edwin A. Winckler, "Institutionalization and Participation on Taiwan: From Hard to Soft Authoritarianism?" *China Quarterly* 99 (September 1984): 481–99. On the impact of even limited elections on the political system, see Shelley Rigger, *Politics in Taiwan: Voting for Democracy* (N.Y.: Routledge, 1999).

13. For the 1972–73 challenge, see Mab Huang, *Intellectual Ferment for Political Reforms in Taiwan, 1971–1973* (University of Michigan Center for Chinese Studies, 1976).

14. For my reasons for this conclusion, see "The Sacred Texts of United States–China–Taiwan Relations," in *At Cross Purposes*, pp. 152–60.

15. On the 1982 communiqué, see "The Sacred Texts of United States–China–Taiwan Relations," in *At Cross Purposes*, pp. 160–75.

16. See "Congress Gets into the Taiwan Human Rights Act," in *At Cross Purposes*, pp. 179-218

17. Roy, *Taiwan: A Political History*.

18. For Chiang Ching-kuo's response to the challenges of the 1980s, particularly his reasons for beginning democratization, see Taylor, *The Generalissimo's Son*, pp. 377–430; Andrew J. Nathan and Helena V. S. Ho, "Chiang Ching-kuo's Decision for Political Reform," in *Chiang Ching-kuo's Leadership in the Development of the Republic of China on Taiwan*, edited by Shao-chuan Leng (Lanham, Md.: University Press of America, 1993), pp. 31–61; and Philip Newell, "President Chiang Ching-kuo and Taiwan's Transition to Democracy," *Harvard Studies on Taiwan: Papers of the Taiwan Studies Workshop*, 1 (Fairbank Center for East Asian Research, Harvard University, 1995), pp. 64–88.

19. For the story of Lee Teng-hui's political reform, see Linda Chao and Ramon

H. Myers, *The First Chinese Democracy: Political Life in the Republic of China on Taiwan* (Johns Hopkins University Press, 1988).

Chapter Three

1. "Survey Shows Half of Top 1000 Taiwan Companies Investing in Mainland," *China Post*, April 24, 2003 (Foreign Broadcast Information Service [FBIS], CPP20030424000231 [June 13, 2003]); Tain-Jy Chen and C. Y. Cyrus Chu, "Cross-Strait Economic Relations: Can They Ameliorate the Political Problem?" in *Taiwan's Presidential Politics: Democratization and Cross-Strait Relations in the 21st Century*, edited by Muthiah Alagappa, (Armonk, N.Y.: M. E. Sharpe, 2001), p. 218.

2. "2004 Nian Liangan Maoyi Touzi Qingkuang," Ministry of Commerce of the People's Republic of China, Department of Taiwan, Hong Kong, and Macao Affairs, January 25, 2005 (http://tga.mofcom.gov.cn/aarticle/d/200501/20050100338068.html); "Taiwan 2004 Exports to China Hit U.S.$61.6 Billion, Central News Agency (CNA), March 17, 2005 (FBIS, CPP20050317000210).

3. You Tien Hsing, *Making Capitalism in China: The Taiwan Connection* (Oxford University Press, 1998).

4. Ibid. Details about the geographic division of tasks can be found on page 68.

5. Rupert Hammond-Chambers, "The Emerging Technology Triumvirate: China, Taiwan, and the United States," speech to the China Forum, Johns Hopkins School of Advanced International Studies, February 20, 2002.

6. Chin Chung, "Division of Labor across the Taiwan Strait: Macro Overview and Analysis of the Electronics Industry," in *The China Circle: Economics and Technology in the PRC, Taiwan, and Hong Kong*, edited by Barry Naughton (Brookings, 1997).

7. Ibid., pp. 181–82.

8. Ibid., pp. 189–90.

9. Terry Cooke, "Cross-Strait Economic Ties and the Dynamics of Globalization," in *Cross-Strait Economic Ties: Agent of Change, or a Trojan Horse?* Asia Program Special Report 118 (Washington: Woodrow Wilson International Center for Scholars, February 2004), p. 9.

10. "Taiwan Job Seekers Eyeing Opportunities in Mainland China," CNA, June 15, 2001 (FBIS, CPP20010615000155 [March 15, 2005]); Fu-kuo Liu, "Uncertain Prospect of Present Cross-Strait Relations: A Taiwanese Perspective, *International Journal of Korean Unification Studies* 13, no. 2 (2004): 56.

11. "Searching for a Way Out, Chinese Brides Look across Taiwan Strait," *Washington Post*, October 14, 2004, p. A26.

12. Tse-Kang Leng, "Economic Globalization and IT Talent Flows across the Taiwan Strait," *Asian Survey* 42 (March-April 2002): 230–50.

13. "Taiwan, Mainland Curators Meet over 2,500-Year-Old Bronze Artifacts," CNA, June 8, 2001 (FBIS, CPP20010608000072); "Taiwan Pilgrims Make First Direct

Cross-Strait Voyage via Kinmen," CNA, June 8, 2001 (FBIS, CPP20010608000085); "Political Barrier Hinders Cross-Strait Learning Exchanges," CNA, June 14, 2001 (FBIS, CPP20010614000201); "Cross-Strait Adult Education Symposium Held in Taipei," CNA, June 13, 2001 (FBIS, CPP20010613000152); "Number of Taiwan People Studying at Mainland Colleges Tops 3,000," CNA, June 6, 2001 (FBIS, CPP20010606000147); "Taiwanese Donate Marrow to Save on Chinese Mainland," Xinhua (New China News Agency), June 13, 2001 (FBIS, CPP20010613000132); "Cross-Straits Sports Exchanges Frequent but Confined by Politics," CNA, June 18, 2001 (FBIS, CPP20010618000108); "Forty-one Taiwan Cyclists Return to Kinmen by Ship Directly from Xiamen," CNA, June 24, 2001 (FBIS, CPP20010624000056); "Taiwan Culture Official Visits Shanghai, Calls for End to 'Opium War Complex,'" CNA, June 23, 2001 (FBIS, CPP20010623000054); "Taiwan, Mainland Maritime Rescue Centers Maintain Close Contact," CNA, June 7, 2001 (FBIS, CPP20010607000076); "SEF Notifies ARATS about Rescued Fishermen," CNA, June 25, 2001 (FBIS, CPP20010625000075); "One Hundred Seventy-five Illegal Mainland Chinese Immigrants Repatriated," CNA, June 27, 2001 (FBIS, CPP20010627000138); "PRC Reports Taiwan Returns Eight Hijackers," Xinhua, June 28, 2001 (FBIS, CPP20010628 000106); "China Repatriates Four Criminals Wanted by Taiwan," *Renmin Ribao* (*People's Daily*), June 28, 2001 (FBIS, CPP20010628000073); all accessed October 20, 2003.

14. "The Poll of Cross-Strait Relations and National Security in 2003." The questionnaire was administered December 27, 2002. For the item concerning travel, the number of valid responses was 1,225. For the item on work, study, business, and so on, the number was 1,216. Communication to author from Emerson Niou, Duke University, October 20, 2003.

15. T. J. Cheng, "China-Taiwan Economic Linkage: Between Insulation and Superconductivity," in *Dangerous Strait: The U.S.-Taiwan-China Crisis*, edited by Nancy Bernkopf Tucker (Columbia University Press, 2005), pp. 104–16; Denny Roy, "Cross-Strait Economic Relations: Opportunities Outweigh Risks," Asia-Pacific Center for Security Studies Occasional Papers Series, April 2004 (www.apcss.org/Publication/Occasional%20Papers/Cross-Strait%20Economic%20Relations.pdf. [February 28, 2005]).

16. This is the conclusion of Chen-yuan Tung in "China's Economic Leverage and Taiwan's Security Concerns with Respect to Cross-Strait Economic Relations," Ph.D. dissertation, Johns Hopkins University, May 2002.

17. The analysis that follows is based in part on my "Lee Teng-hui and Separatism," in *Dangerous Strait*, edited by Tucker, pp. 70–92.

18. Sheng Lijun, *China's Dilemma: The Taiwan Issue* (New York: I. G. Taurius, 2001), pp. 89–92.

19. For the message, see *Beijing Review*, January 5, 1979, pp. 16–17.

20. For Ye's nine points, see Stephen P. Gibert and William M. Carpenter, *America and Island China* (Lanham, Md.: University Press of America, 1989), pp. 288–90.

21. See "The Taiwan Question and the Reunification of China," Taiwan Affairs Office and Information Office, State Council, August 1993, reprinted in John F. Copper, *Words across the Taiwan Strait: A Critique of Beijing's "White Paper" on China's Unification* (Lanham, Md.: University Press of America, 1995), p. 83. For some reason, this statement was not included in Deng's *Selected Works*.

22. "An Idea for the Peaceful Reunification of the Chinese Mainland and Taiwan" (remarks made June 26, 1983), *Selected Works of Deng Xiaoping* (Beijing: Foreign Languages Press, 1994), pp. 40–41.

23. "'One Country' Is Premise and Basis of 'Two Systems,' Scholar Says," Xinhua, February 22, 2004 (FBIS, CPP20040222000061 [February 23, 2004]). Moreover, Deng Xiaoping had made clear a few months before that the "local inhabitants" who ran Hong Kong had to be "patriots"; see "One Country, Two Systems" (remarks made June 22–23, 1984), *Selected Works of Deng Xiaoping*, volume 3, pp. 70–71.

24. Lee would soon add another element: the PRC's international quarantine of Taiwan.

25. Tse-kang Leng, "State, Business, and Economic Interaction across the Taiwan Strait, *Issues and Studies* 31 (November 1995): 40–58.

26. Author's interview with Lin Bih-jaw, then the vice president of National Chengchi University and previously deputy secretary general of the Office of the President, February 24, 2003; author's interview with Chu Yun-han, senior fellow of the Institute of Political Science at Academia Sinica, Taipei, and professor of political science at National Taiwan University, March 3, 2003; Zou Jingwen, *Li Denghui Zhizheng Gaobai Shilu (Record of Revelations on Lee Denghui's Administration)* (Taipei: INK, 2001), pp. 182, 194–5. This work is a retrospective account of Lee's presidency written with his cooperation.

27. Lee Teng-hui, "Opening a New Era for the Chinese People, Inaugural Address by the Eighth-Term President of the Republic of China, May 20, 1990," in *Creating the Future: Towards a New Era for the Chinese People* (a government compilation of speeches, statements, and so forth by Lee) (Taipei: Government Information Office, 1992), pp. 7–9; also in *Li Denghui Zongtong Xiansheng Qishijiunian Yenlun Xuanaji (Selected Opinions of President Lee Teng-hui, 1990)* (Taipei: Government Information Office, 1991), pp. 53–54.

28. For the secret talks between Taipei and Beijing, see Zou, *Li Denghui Zhizheng Gaobai Shilu*, pp. 192–204.

29. From "Relations across the Taiwan Straits," Mainland Affairs Council, July 1994, reprinted in Copper, *Words across the Taiwan Strait*, p. 110; Zou, *Li Denghui Zhizheng Gaobai Shilu*, p. 183.

30. "Guidelines for National Unification," *Creating the Future*, pp. 159–61.

31. "Termination of the Period of National Mobilization for the Suppression of the Communist Rebellion," *Creating the Future*, pp. 37–62; also in *Kaichuang Weilai: Maixiang Zhonghua Minzu di Xinshidai (Creating the Future: Striding toward a New Era of the Chinese Nation)* (Taipei: Government Information Office, 1992), pp. 65, 67, 70.

32. Hungdah Chiu, "The Koo-Wang Talks and the Prospects for Building Constructive and Stable Relations across the Taiwan Strait," in *Sino-American Relations at a Time of Change*, edited by Gerrit W. Gong and Bih-jaw Lin (Washington: Center for Strategic and International Studies, 1993), pp. 8–9.

33. Chiu, "The Koo-Wang Talks," pp. 10–11.

34. Author's interview with Chu Yun-han, March 3, 2003; "The Taiwan Question and the Reunification of China," in Copper, *Words across the Taiwan Strait*, p. 83.

35. For a PRC account of the discussions that led up to the "1992 consensus," which includes the formulations used by each side, see "ARATS, SEF Reached Consensus in July 1992," Xinhua, September 8, 1999 (FBIS, FTS19990914000977 [November 7, 2004]).

36. Democratization on the mainland apparently was receding as an essential requirement in Lee's approach to unification.

37. For Lee's view that international space and cross-Strait relations were positively reinforcing, see Lee Teng-hui, *The Road to Democracy: Taiwan's Pursuit of Identity* (Tokyo: PHP Institute, 1999), pp. 96–98. For the rhetorical combat on Taiwan's role in the international community, see "The Taiwan Question and the Reunification of China" and "Relations across the Taiwan Straits," in Copper, *Words across the Taiwan Strait*. Neither offered new ideas.

38. Steven Goldstein, "The Rest of the Story: The Impact of Domestic Politics on Taiwan's Mainland Policy," *Harvard Studies on Taiwan*, vol. 2 (1998), pp. 62–90. Lee had sought to dampen Taiwanese suspicions of his cross-Strait initiatives by appointing Taiwanese to lead the Mainland Affairs Council, with supervisory responsibility over the Straits Exchange Foundation, which was staffed by mainlanders; see David Reuther, "The Straits Exchange Foundation: A Study in Policy Flexibility," *Washington Journal of Modern China* 2 (Summer 1996): 68–88.

39. "Transcript of a Press Conference Held after President Lee's visit to the Southeast Asian Countries," February 16, 1994, from a no-longer-operative website of the Office of the President established during Lee Teng-hui's tenure, accessed May 13, 2000 (hereafter cited as the OOP website; all documents from this site are in the author's files); Lee, *Road to Democracy*, p. 52. Author's interview with Lin Bih-jaw, February 24, 2003.

40. Author's interview with Chu Yun-han, March 3, 2003; Goldstein, "The Rest of the Story," p. 72.

41. Author's interview with Chu yun-han, March 3, 2003.

42. "Report on the State of the Nation Given at the Second Extraordinary Session of the Second National Assembly," January 4, 1993, OOP website [May 9, 2000]; "International Press Conference," May 20, 1993, OOP website [May 13, 2000]; "Transcript of a Press Conference Held after President Lee's Visit to the Southeast Asian Countries" (February 16, 1994), in Lee Teng-hui, *Jingying Da Taiwan* (*Managing Great Taiwan*) (Taipei: Yuanliu Publishing, 1995), pp. 423–46; "Report on the State of the Nation Given at the Fourth Extraordinary Session of the Second National

Assembly," May 19, 1994, OOP website [May 13, 2000]; "Written Responses to Questions Submitted by Mr. K. F. Owen, Editor of *Sunday Times*, Johannesburg," October 10, 1994, OOP website [May 13, 2000]. The skepticism about one China comes from my interview with Chiao Jen-ho, February 26, 2003. Note that Lee and his government were using two different concepts to describe the ROC and the PRC and their relationship to China. On one hand, he referred to China as divided; on the other, he insisted that the ROC was a sovereign state, in effect a successor to the Qing dynasty, as was the PRC. But there is either one divided state, China, or two successor states. Taiwan officials appeared to resolve the contradiction both by blurring it with the assertion that the ROC and the PRC were "political entities" and by saying that "one China" referred not to a state but a "historical, geographical, cultural, and racial entity." See "Relations across the Taiwan Straits," in Copper, *Words across the Taiwan Strait*, p. 110.

43. Issued in August 1993 by the Taiwan Affairs Office and the Information Office of the State Council.

44. "Shemma Wenti Dou Keyi Taolun: Qian Qichen Fuzongli Jieshou 'Huashengdun Youbao' Jizhe Pan Wen Caifang" ("Anything Can Be Discussed: Vice Premier Qian Qichen Accepts an Inteview by Journalist John Pomfret of the *Washington Post*"), *Shijie Zhishi* (*World Knowledge*) 3 (February 2001): 14; "The Taiwan Question and the Reunification of China," in Copper, *Words across the Taiwan Strait*.

45. "Transcript of a Press Conference Held after President Lee's Visit to the Southeast Asian Countries," pp. 423–46.

46. "Changsuo di Beiai: Sheng wei Taiwanren di beiai" ("A Place of Sorrow: The Sorrow of Being Born a Taiwanese"), in Lee, *Jingying Da Taiwan*, pp. 469–83. For my interpretation, see my "Lee Teng-hui and Separatism," in *Dangerous Strait*, edited by Tucker.

47. Author's interview with Lee Teng-hui, July 31, 2003.

48. "Continue to Promote the Reunification of the Motherland," Xinhua (FBIS, *Daily Report: China*, January 30, 1995, pp. 84–86, CH-95-019).

49. "Text of President's Speech," translated from *Lianhebao* (*United Daily News*, a leading Taiwan newspaper) (FBIS, *Daily Report: China*, April 8, 1995, pp. 77–80, CH-95-068). Lee's reference to the eighty-four-year existence of the ROC was apparently the first time that he himself asserted that the ROC had existed since 1912, as the NUC had done in August 1992.

50. See, for example, Robert L. Suettinger, *Beyond Tiananmen: The Politics of U.S.-China Relations, 1989–2000* (Brookings, 2003), pp. 200–63; John W. Garver, *Face Off: China, the United States, and Taiwan's Democratization* (University of Washington Press, 1997); Suisheng Zhao, ed., *Across the Taiwan Strait: Mainland China, Taiwan, and the 1995–1996 Crisis* (New York: Routledge, 1999), particularly the essays on the PRC perspective; Michael D. Swaine, "Chinese Decision-Making Regarding Taiwan, 1979–2000," in *The Making of Chinese Foreign and Security Policy in the Era of Reform*, edited by David Michael Lampton (Stanford University Press, 2001), pp. 289–336; Robert S. Ross, "The 1995–96 Taiwan Strait Confronta-

tion: Coercion, Credibility, and the Use of Force," *International Security* 25 (Fall 2000): 87–123; and Tai Ming Cheung, "Chinese Military Preparations against Taiwan over the Next Ten Years," in *Crisis in The Taiwan Strait,* edited by James R. Lilley and Chuck Downs (National Defense University Press, 1997); Allen S. Whiting, "China's Use of Force, 1950-1996, and Taiwan," *International Security* 26 (Fall 2001): 120–23.

51. Suettinger, *Beyond Tiananmen,* pp. 219–20.

52. See Ross, "The 1995–96 Taiwan Strait Confrontation."

53. "Reportage on Li's Visit to Cornell University: Text of 9 June Cornell Speech," CNA, July 9, 1995 (FBIS, OW1006051095). In his Cornell speech, Lee spoke in general and routine terms about cross-Strait relations.

54. "Text of President Li Teng-hui's Inaugural Speech" (May 20, 1996), Broadcast Corporation of China, FBIS, *Daily Report: China,* CH-96-098. For details on popular sovereignty, identity, and Taiwan's role in China, see my "Lee Teng-hui and Separatism," in *Dangerous Strait,* pp. 84–87.

55. "President Lee's Foreign Policy Address," *Topics* (magazine of the Taipei American Chamber of Commerce), August 1997, pp. 34–40. Jiang Zemin replayed old themes himself in his political report to the Communist Party's Fifteenth Congress. He also stressed Beijing's opposition to "splittist tendencies" on the island and refused to renounce the use of force or to talk to the "handful of people who stubbornly cling to the position of independence of Taiwan." See "Jiang Zemin's Political Report," Beijing Central Television, September 12, 1997 (FBIS, *Daily Report: China,* OW1209033297).

56. "Closing Remarks to the Thirteenth Plenum of the National Unification Council," July 22, 1998, in *President Lee Teng-hui's Selected Addresses and Messages: 1998* (Taipei: Government Information Office, 1999), pp. 113–20.

57. "VOG Interviews Li Teng-hui," *Zhongyang Ribao* (*Central Daily News,* the newspaper of the KMT), July 10, 1999 (FBIS, OW12007135899 [July 12, 1999]). Lee may have used this interview to lay out his views because the "German model" of one nation, two states used from 1972 to 1991 was close to what he thought was appropriate for Taiwan and the PRC.

58. Author's interview with Lee Teng-hui, July 31, 2003.

59. "President Lee's Foreign Policy Address, *Topics,* pp. 36, 39; "Response to Questions Submitted by Bruce W. Nelan, Senior Editor for *Time Magazine,*" in *President Lee Teng-hui's Selected Addresses and Messages: 1998,* pp. 78–101.

60. "The One-China Principle and the Taiwan Issue," *Beijing Review,* March 6, 2000, p. 20.

61. See, for example, James Crawford, *The Creation of States in International Law* (Oxford: Clarendon Press, 1979), pp. 31–71.

62. Jacques deLisle, "The Chinese Puzzle of Taiwan's Status," *Orbis* 44 (Winter 2000): 48–51.

63. Shelley Rigger, *From Opposition to Power: Taiwan's Democratic Progressive Party* (Boulder, Colo.: Lynne Rienner Publishers, 2001), p. 131.

64. Ibid., pp. 131–32.

65. Ibid., pp. 121–22.

66. For a hint of this trend, see Rwei-Ren Wu, "Toward a Pragmatic Nationalism: Democratization and Taiwan's Passive Revolution," in *Memories of the Future: National Identity Issues and the Search for a New Taiwan,* edited by Stéphane Corcuff (Armonk, N.Y.: M. E. Sharpe, 2002), pp. 210–11.

67. "Taiwan Stands Up: Advancing to an Uplifting New Era" (Chen Shui-bian Inaugural Address), May 20,2000 (www.president.gov.tw/2_special/520/e_index.html [March 24, 2004]).

68. "PRC Taiwan Affairs Offices Issue Statement on Chen Shui-bian Inauguration Speech," Xinhua, May 20, 2000 (FBIS, CPP20000520000060 [March 24, 2004]).

69. For a commentary on the need for caution in negotiating with the PRC, written retrospectively by one of the few officials from Lee Teng-hui's Presidential Office whom Chen Shui-bian retained, see Chang Jung-feng, "Be Mindful of Negotiating Tactics," *Taipei Times,* November 17, 2004 (www.taipeitimes.com/News/edit/archives/2004/11/17/2003211449 [November 24, 2004]).

70. "Taiwan President Accepts 'One China, Respective Interpretations,'" CNA, June 27, 2000 (FBIS, CPP20000627000121 [March 24, 2004]).

71. "Chen Has Gone Too Far This Time," *Taipei Times,* June 29, 2000 (www.taipeitimes.com/News/edit/archives/2000/06/29/41885 [November 11, 2004]); "Chairperson Tsai Ing-wen at the June 28, 2000, Press Conference," Mainland Affairs Council (www.mac.gov.tw/english/index1-e.htm [March 24, 2004]).

72. "Presidential Press Conference," June 20, 2000 (www.president.gov.tw/1_president/e_subject-06a [March 24, 2004]); Mark Landler, "Risking China's Ire, Taiwan Leader Questions Unification," *New York Times,* September 2, 2000, p. 3. Beijing read Chen's statement as "in essence, advocating the separatist stand of 'Taiwan Independence.'"

73. Department of Defense, *Annual Report on the Military Power of the People's Republic of China: Report to Congress Pursuant to the FY 2000 National Defense Authorization Act,* May 28, 2004 (hereafter cited as *2004 Pentagon Report*), p. 7 (www.defenselink.mil/pubs/d20040528PRC.pdf [June, 1 2004]); David Shambaugh, *Modernizing China's Military: Progress, Problems, and Prospects* (University of California Press, 2003), pp. 307–27.

74. "President Chen's Cross-Century Remarks," December 31, 2000 (www.president.gov.tw/php-bin/prez/showenews.php4. [March 24, 2004]).

75. "I Am Already at the Table for a Dialogue: Interview with Chen Shui-bian," *Sekai Magazine,* February 2001, pp. 45–46. I am grateful to Tomohiko Taniguchi for the translation of this passage.

76. From Li's point of view, Taiwan's people wanted to be totally separate from China, ruling out any possibility of future integration. Various Taiwan figures compete to define what the public's wishes are; in this case, Li probably was wrong. Li

Thian-Hok, "Chen Sent Beijing the Wrong Message," *Taiwan Communique*, April 2001 (www.taiwandc.org/twcom/96-no3 [March 24, 2004]).

77. With the exception of the unique case of Lee Teng-hui's 1995 visit, it has been U.S. government practice to permit Taiwan's president, vice president, premier, and vice premier to stop in the United States only on the way to some other country. During their "transit," activities are kept private and low-key to observe the principle that U.S. relations with Taiwan are unofficial. Beginning in May 2001, the administration of George W. Bush offered transit treatment that was less restrictive than that of previous administrations.

78. "Taiwan President on Opening 'Direct Links' With China; Military's Role," CNA, May 10, 2002 (FBIS, CPP20020510000182 [March 24, 2004]); "President Chen Delivers the Opening Address of the 29th Annual Meeting of the World Federation of Taiwanese Associations via Live Video Link," August 3, 2003 (www.president.gov.tw/php-bin/prez/showenews.php4 [March 24, 2004]). Nor was *yibian yiguo* a new formulation that suddenly sprang from Chen's imagination. He had used it in his 2000 campaign, and it was actually a saying in opposition circles as early as the 1980s. The purpose was to mock the pretensions of the PRC and ROC (KMT) governments that they were legitimate *guo* when their treatment of their respective populations was anything but legitimate. Communication to author from Stephen Schlaikjer, November 11, 2004.

79. See, for example, "He Who Plays with Fire Spreading the Notion of 'One Country on Each Side' Shall Get Burnt," *Wenhuibao* (a communist newspaper in Hong Kong), August 5, 2002 (FBIS, CPP20020805000020 [July 9, 2003]).

80. "A Conversation with Chen Shui-bian, the President of the Republic of China on Taiwan," E-Notes, Foreign Policy Research Institute, January 22, 2003 (www.fpri.org/enotes/20030122.asia.sicherman.chenshuibian [March 27, 2004]).

81. "Interview with Taiwanese President Chen Shui-bian," *Washington Post*, October 10, 2003 (www.washingtonpost.com/ac2/wp-dyn/A9815-2003Oct10?language [October 11, 2003]); "Defensive Referendum," *Taipei Times,* December 3, 2003 (FBIS, CPP20031203000191 [December 3, 2003]); "Taiwan President Rejects One China 'Myth,'" *China Post*, December 22, 2003 (FBIS, CPP20031222000195 [December 22, 2003]); "TSU Proposes Name Change for Taiwan in Planned Referendum," CNA, December 3, 2003 (FBIS, CPP20031203000148 [December 3, 2003]).

82. "The One-China Principle and the Taiwan Issue," *Beijing Review*, March 6, 2000, p. 20.

83. "PRC Taiwan Affairs Offices Issue Statement on Chen Shui-bian Inauguration Speech," Xinhua, May 20, 2000 (FBIS, CPP20000520000060 [July 8, 2004]); Xinhua and *Renmin Ribao*, "Dangerous Provocation—Criticizing Chen Chui-bian's Separatist Remarks," Xinhua, August 6, 2002 (FBIS, CPP20020806000049 [July 8, 2004]).

84. Washington tended to focus on the increased tensions that followed Lee's statement rather than on substance of what he said.

85. "Taiwan Predicts Peking Will Come Around, Interview Conducted by Mr.

Arnaud de Borchgrave, Editor-at-Large of the *Washington Times*, published July 10, 1991," in *Creating the Future*, p. 98.

86. "*Zhongguo Shibao* Investigative Report," *Zhongguo Shibao* (*China Times*, a leading Taipei newspaper), December 12, 2000 (translation in author's files); "Li Teng-hui Defends State-to-State Relationship," *Zhongguo Shibao*, September 1, 1999 (FBIS, CP9909010005 [September 1, 1999]); author's interview with Lin Bih-jaw, February 24, 2003. It is interesting to speculate whether the announcement that PRC leaders reportedly intended to make was in fact an earlier version of "The One-China Principle and the Taiwan Issue," the "white paper" ultimately issued in February 2000.

87. The other parts were democratization, restrictions on economic interaction with the mainland, fostering a Taiwan identity, pragmatic diplomacy, and a left-center political coalition.

88. "Lee Teng-hui Says Name Should Be Changed to Taiwan and the Island Should Join the United Nations" and "Promoting a New Constitution! Lee Teng-hui Addresses U.S. Senators in Teleconference," both from TVBS Cable News Channel, October 8, 2004 (FBIS, CPP20041009000204); Lee Teng-hui, "Becoming a Normal Country," *Taipei Times*, October 28, 2002 (FBIS, CPP20021028000135); both accessed September 26, 2004.

89. "Strait Talk: The Full Interview," *Time*, February 16, 2003 (www.time.com/time/nation/article0,8559,591348,00 [March 7, 2004]). Chen's statement about unity leading to separation and separation leading to unity is an echo of the beginning lines of the *Romance of the Three Kingdoms*, a popular traditional Chinese novel. The reference here is analogous to referring to Hamlet's soliloquy as the classic statement on indecisiveness. See Luo Guanzhong, *Three Kingdoms: China's Epic Drama*, trans. and ed. by Moss Roberts (New York: Pantheon, 1976), p.1. The usual rendering of the title is *Romance of the Three Kingdoms*.

90. "Don't Let 'One China Spell' Hinder Cross-Strait Ties: Adviser," CNA, June 23, 2003 (FBIS, CPP20030623000147 [July 8, 2004]).

91. Beijing's approach toward territories that have not yet been reunified bears some similarities to its approach to key social groups within the PRC. Just as the one-country, two-systems proposal grants home rule but preserves the status of the central government as the exclusive sovereign, so too social groups are allowed some measure of autonomy as long as they serve the goals of the Chinese Communist Party and do not threaten its authority. For a case study, see H. Lyman Miller, *Science and Dissent in Post-Mao China: The Politics of Knowledge* (University of Washington Press, 1996). Some members of the group in question—natural scientists—believed that although they should support the central task of modernization, the norms of their profession required that they have the freedom to take a critical stance toward the regime. The CCP believed that their position exceeded tolerable limits.

Chapter Four

1. "PFP Issues Six-Point Stance on Cross-Strait Ties," Central News Agency (CNA), August 25, 2000 (Foreign Broadcast Information Service [FBIS], CPP20000825000145).

2. For a fascinating account of the European political order, which culminated in the dominance of the sovereignty concept, see Hendrik Spruyt, *The Sovereign State and Its Competitors: An Analysis of Systems Change* (Princeton University Press, 1994). Other sources on the concept include Hedley Bull, *The Anarchical Society* (Columbia University Press, 1977), p. 8; Hurst Hannum, *Autonomy, Sovereignty, and Self-Determination: The Accommodation of Conflicting Rights*, rev. ed. (University of Pennsylvania Press, 1990), p. 15. The summary of the sovereignty principle comes from Stephen D. Krasner, *Sovereignty: Organized Hypocrisy* (Princeton University Press, 1999), p. 11.

3. James Crawford, *The Creation of States in International Law* (Oxford: Clarendon Press, 1979), pp. 36, 26–27.

4. Krasner, *Sovereignty*, pp. 4, 11–25.

5. Nor are the four types equally relevant to the different dimensions of authority and control. Domestic sovereignty is concerned with both. Interdependence sovereignty focuses on control but not authority. The last two—international and Westphalian—are keyed to authority but not control. See Krasner, *Sovereignty*, p. 4.

6. Robert H. Jackson, *Quasi-States: Sovereignty, International Relations, and the Third World* (Cambridge University Press, 1990), p. 21. Jackson notes that historically states were recognized as such once they had demonstrated the capacity to meet the qualifications that were later enshrined in the Montevideo Convention—that they were "empirical realities before they were legal personalities" (see p. 34).

7. Hungdah Chiu, ed., *China and the Question of Taiwan: Documents and Analysis* (New York: Praeger, 1973), p. 345; Stephen P. Gibert and William M. Carpenter, eds., *America and Island China: A Documentary History* (Lanham, Md.: University Press of America, 1989), p. 208.

8. Krasner, *Sovereignty*, p. 11; Hannum, *Autonomy, Sovereignty, and Self-Determination*, p. 15. In any event, if the intent had been to have the adjective *duli* (independent) apply to "state" rather than "sovereignty," it would have been rendered differently in Chinese.

9. Although in the 1930s neither Mao nor Chiang demanded the return of Taiwan, unlike Manchuria, their positions changed—for Chiang in 1942 and for Mao in 1943. See Richard C. Bush, "The Wartime Decision to Return Taiwan to China," in *At Cross Purposes: U.S.-Taiwan Relation since 1942* (Armonk, N.Y.: M. E. Sharpe, 2004), pp. 10–13.

10. For the classic statement of this thesis, see Lung-chu Chen and Harold D. Lasswell, *Formosa, China, and the United Nations* (New York: St. Martin's Press, 1967).

11. Mongolia had been part of the Chinese empire. In 1924, before the KMT regime became the government of China, the government accepted the emergence

of Mongolia as a separate country. Chiang Kai-shek reneged on that commitment; Mao Zedong reaffirmed it.

12. "The President Grants an Interview to *Los Angeles Times* of the United States," Office of the President, February 8, 2004 (FBIS, CPP20040203000077 [February 15, 2004]). If Chen had merely referred to jurisdiction rather than territory, this would not have been such a controversial statement.

13. Jacques deLisle, "The Chinese Puzzle of Taiwan's Status," *Orbis* 44 (Winter 2000): 51–52.

14. For one example, written in 1979, see Crawford, *The Creation of States in International Law*, pp. 146–152.

15. On the cold war security relationship, see Nancy Bernkopf Tucker, *Taiwan, Hong Kong, and the United States, 1945–1992: Uncertain Friendships* (New York: Twayne Publishers, 1994). On economic issues, see Thomas B. Gold, *State and Society in the Taiwan Miracle* (Armonk, N.Y.: M. E. Sharpe, 1997).

16. Stanley Roth, speech to the Asia Society, January 11, 2001 (www.state.gov/www/policy_remarks/2001/010111_roth_uspolicy [March 24, 2004]).

17. Some have suggested that the second element of this formula represents a major concession by Beijing, an acceptance of an essential equality of the two sides. Yet that is an overinterpretation. First of all, the phrase "belong to one China" does not convey the sense of equality that the phrase "are both parts of one China" does. Moreover, the reference is to geographic entities, not political ones. A key element of Beijing's approach—that the ROC government does not exist—has not changed.

18. Taiwan officials are aware of analyses of PRC negotiating behavior—such as that of Richard H. Solomon in *Chinese Negotiating Behavior: Pursuing Interests through 'Old Friends'* (Washington: United States Institute of Peace Press, 1999)—and the specific observation that Beijing always tries to get its negotiating adversary to accept certain principles at the outset, after which the negotiations are more than half over because the principles then define how everything else is handled. See, for example, Chang Jung-feng, "Be Mindful of Negotiating Tactics," *Taipei Times*, November 17, 2004 (www.taipeitimes.com/News/edit/archives/2004/11/17/2003211449 [February 10, 2005]). Chang was an official in both the Lee Teng-hui and Chen Shui-bian administrations.

19. For a perceptive Taiwan analysis of the Hong Kong political system, see Byron S. J. Weng, "'One Country, Two Systems' from a Taiwan Perspective," *Orbis* 46 (Autumn 2002): 713–31.

20. To paraphrase Carl Becker, *The History of Political Parties in the Province of New York* (University of Wisconsin Press, 1969; first published 1909), p. 22. There was some pressure on freedom of the press in 2003–04, a time when public opposition to PRC and Hong Kong government policies grew.

21. This section is based in part on the secondary literature on the political system of postreversion Hong Kong, some examples of which are cited; on a series of

interviews that I conducted there with government officials and political scientists in February 2003; and on conversations with Dr. Wilson Wai-ho Wang of Chinese University of Hong Kong.

22. "Speech at a Meeting with the Members of the Committee for Drafting the Basic Law of the Hong Kong Special Administrative Region," April 16, 1987, *Selected Works of Deng Xiaoping, 1982–1992*, vol. 3 (Beijing: Foreign Languages Press, 1994), pp. 218–20. For another Deng discussion of the need for patriots to lead Hong Kong, see "One Country, Two Systems" (talk given June 22–23, 1984), *Selected Works of Deng Xiaoping*, vol. 3, pp. 70–71.

23. Siu-kai Lau, ed., *The First Tung Chee-hwa Administration* (Hong Kong: Chinese University Press, 2002), pp. xxvi, xxvii, xxxii.

24. Shui Hing Lo, *Governing Hong Kong: Legitimacy, Communciation, and Political Decay* (Huntington, N.Y.: Nova Science Publishers, 2001), p. 166.

25. Ibid., 174.

26. Anthony B. L. Cheung, "The Changing Political System: Executive-Led Government or 'Disabled' Governance?" in *The First Tung Chee-hwa Administration*, edited by Lau, p. 49.

27. Hsin-chi Kuan and Siu-kai Lau, "Between Liberal Autocracy and Democracy: Democratic Legitimacy in Hong Kong," *Democratization* 9 (Winter 2002): 58. Even the liberal dimension of Kuan and Lau's formula seemed in some jeopardy in 2002 and 2003. The SAR government proposed national security legislation pursuant to Article 23 of the Basic Law, raising questions about its commitment to preserving civil liberties, the nature of Hong Kong citizenship, and the distinction between two systems in one country. The government's lack of transparency exacerbated public anxiety more than was probably necessary and gave new life to a debilitated opposition. The denouement was a massive demonstration on July 1, 2003, when half a million people protested the legislation. The SAR government then backed down and withdrew the legislation, and the opposition intensified the calls for more democracy and universal suffrage.

28. Also, there was never a military dimension in the Hong Kong case. The PRC had overwhelming power and the British were never prepared to fight for the territory.

29. In this regard, China's requirement that Hong Kong enact national security legislation pursuant to Article 23 of the Basic Law is relevant, for the net effect of that legislation would have been to make illegal, among other things, the formation of any group in the SAR that would advocate independence from China.

30. "Qian Qichen Proposes 'Seven-Point' Plan for 'One Country, Two Systems' for Taiwan," *Wenhuibao*, July 13, 2001 (FBIS, CPP20010713000050 [July 8, 2004]).

31. For the fullest development of this point, see Ralph N. Clough, *Cooperation or Conflict in the Taiwan Strait?* (Lanham, Md.: Rowman & Littlefield Publishers, Inc., 1999).

32. Rupert J. Hammond-Chambers, "The Emerging Technology Triumvirate:

China, Taiwan, and the United States," speech, China Forum, Paul H. Nitze School of Advanced International Studies, Johns Hopkins University, February 20, 2002.

33. Wang Mingyi, "Mainland Affairs Council: Non-Governmental Organizations May Represent Taiwan in Direct Shipping Talks with Mainland," *Zhongguo Shibao* (*China Times*), May 23, 2002 (FBIS, CPP20020523000059 [May 24, 2002]).

34. Ibid.; "Long Time Coming," *Taipei Times*, October 10, 2003 (FBIS, CPP20031010000150 [July 10, 2004]); and David G. Brown, "Strains over Cross-Strait Relations," *Comparative Connections*, January 2004 (www.csis.org/pacfor/cc/0304Qchina_taiwan [March 17, 2004]). The legislation provoked criticism from the Straits Exchange Foundation, which hitherto had been solely responsible for discussions with China, but only when China was willing to talk; see "SEF Chief Criticizes Revisions to Statute Dealing with China," *Taiwan News*, October 21, 2003 (www.etaiwannews.com/Taiwan/2003/10/21/1066699228 [October 23, 2003]).

35. John C. C. Deng, "How Will Taiwan Interact with Mainland China under WTO?" talk at Center for Strategic and International Studies, Washington, February 6, 2002; "Cross-Straits Financial Supervision Should be at Hands of Trade Associations: Spokesman," Xinhua (New China News Agency), November 12, 2003 (FBIS, CPP20031112000120); Yang Yung-nien, "Cross-Strait Crime Fight Hindered by Politicking," *Taipei Times*, November 1, 2003 (FBIS, CPP20031104000204); "Government Should Be Involved in Cross-Strait Disease Control: MAC," CNA, February 13, 2004 (FBIS, CPP20040213000105 [February 18, 2004]); Bo Tedards, "A Light Shines through WTO Haze," *Taipei Times*, November 26, 2001 (www.taipeitimes.com/News/edit/archives/2001/11/26/113197 [July 9, 2004]).

36. My thinking on European integration has been shaped most by Andrew Moravcsik, *The Choice for Europe: Social Purpose and State Power from Messina to Maastricht* (Cornell University Press, 1998). On parliaments' loss of power, see Shirley Williams, "Sovereignty and Accountability in the European Community," in *The New European Community: Decisionmaking and Institutional Change*, edited by Robert O. Keohane and Stanley Hoffmann (Boulder, Colo.: Westview Press, 1991), pp. 155–76.

37. Robert Rotberg, *Cyprus after Annan: Next Steps toward a Solution*, World Peace Foundation Report 37 (Cambridge, Mass: World Peace Foundation and John F. Kennedy School of Government, 2003) pp. 6, 7; "Greek Cypriot Leader calls UN Plan Unworkable," *Financial Times*, April 8, 2004; "Cyprus Must Not Miss This Chance to Reunify," *Financial Times*, April 8, 2004; "Cash Warning to Greek Cypriots over Peace Plan," *Financial Times*, April 16, 2004; and "'No' Vote Spoils Celebratory Mood over EU Enlargement," *Financial Times*, April 26, 2004. All *Financial Times* items were accessed July 27, 2004 (www.ft.com). The Turkish Cypriots won a victory of sorts: the EU decided to reward their support of the agreement by granting them economic assistance—and denying it to the Greek Cypriots—and by taking steps to end its international isolation and strengthen its autonomy. See "EU

Envoys Rush through Deal to Help Northern Cyprus," *Financial Times*, April 24, 2004; and "Brussels Tries Once More to End Isolation of Northern Cyprus," *Financial Times*, July 8, 2004. Both *Financial Times* items were accessed July 27, 2004 (www.ft.com). A United Nations role in the Taiwan Strait issue is, of course, unlikely because Beijing wishes to preserve the basic principle that it is an internal, not an international, issue.

38. Jacques deLisle, "Varieties of Sovereignty and China: Challenges and Opportunities in the Cross-Strait Relationship: A Conference Report," E-Notes, Foreign Policy Research Institute, July 1, 2002 (www.fpri.org/enotes/asia.20020701. delisle.sovereigntychina.html [June, 23, 2002]).

39. Coincidentally, Chen Shui-bian has used a house metaphor to describe cross-Strait relations, though not in as complex a way as done here. In July 2001, in an interview with the *Washington Times*, Chen offered an analogy to explain why Taiwan objected to the one-country, two-systems model. He said that it was like "a neighbor coming over to our home and very roughly saying, 'I want your house. But please be assured that you can still live in the house and you can use part of the furniture.' But, it is clear that this house does not belong to the neighbors. It belongs to us and it is a product of years of hard work, hard-earned money, and we purchased this house, and this is a very unreasonable demand, for this neighbor has contributed nothing to buy this house. Neither has the neighbor done anything toward purchasing the furniture." See "Chen Shui-bian Calls Chinese Plan 'Unacceptable,'" *Washington Times*, July 16, 2001, p. 9.

Chapter Five

1. Robert Jervis, *Perception and Misperception in International Politics* (Princeton University Press, 1976), p. 62.

2. John H. Herz, "Idealist Internationalism and the Security Dilemma," *World Politics* 2 (January 1950): 158.

3. Jervis, *Perception and Misperception in International Politics*, pp. 58–84.

4. Robert Jervis, "Cooperation under the Security Dilemma," *World Politics* 30 (January 1978): 186–214.

5. Glenn H. Snyder, "The Security Dilemma in Alliance Politics," *World Politics* 36 (July 1984): 461–95.

6. Again, Jervis, *Perception and Misperception in International Politics*, is the *locus classicus*.

7. Patrick Tyler, *A Great Wall: Six Presidents and China* (New York: Public Affairs, 1999), p. 269.

8. Zhang Zuqian, "National Defense Modernization and the Taiwan Problem," *Zhanlue Yu Guanli* (*Strategy and Management*), December 30, 1999 (Foreign Broadcast Information Service [FBIS], CPP29999215999116 [February 22, 2000]).

9. See Richard Bush, "Helping the Republic of China to Defend Itself, " in *A*

Unique Relationship: The United States and the Republic of China under the Taiwan Relations Act, edited by Ramon H. Myers (Stanford, Calif.: Hoover Institution Press, 1989), pp. 79–118.

10. On Taiwan's nuclear weapons efforts, see David Albright and Corey Gay, "Nuclear Nightmare Averted," *Bulletin of the Atomic Scientists* 54 (January-February 1998) (www.thebulletin.org/past_issues/054_001.htm [February 22, 2005]).

11. Thomas J. Christensen, "The Contemporary Security Dilemma: Deterring a Taiwan Conflict," *Washington Quarterly* 25 (Autumn 2002): 12–13. Christensen is the scholar who has most successfully applied the concept of the security dilemma to East Asia and explored its implications for Taiwan. See also his "China, the U.S.-Japan Alliance, and the Security Dilemma in East Asia," *International Security* 23 (Spring 1999): 49–80; and "Posing Problems without Catching Up: China's Rise and Challenges for U.S. Security Policy, *International Security* 25 (Spring 2001): 5–40.

12. On the importance in traditional Chinese military thought of "awing" one's adversary into submission, see Alastair Iain Johnston, *Cultural Realism: Strategic Culture and Grand Strategy in Chinese History* (Princeton University Press, 1995). On Taiwan's tendency to see U.S. arms as symbols of American political support, see Michael D. Swaine, *Taiwan's National Security, Defense Policy, and Weapons Procurement Process* (Santa Monica, Calif.: RAND, 1999), pp. 31–35.

13. "Shemma Wenti Dou Keyi Taolun: Qian Qichen Fuzongli Jieshou 'Huashengdun Youbao' Jizhe Pan Wen Caifang" ("Anything Can Be Discussed: Vice Premier Qian Qichen Accepts an Inteview by Journalist John Pomfret of the *Washington Post*"), *Shijie Zhishi* (*World Knowledge*) 3 (February 2001): 14.

14. There are a number of accounts of the crisis. See, for example, Robert L. Suettinger, *Beyond Tiananmen: The Politics of U.S.-China Relations, 1989–2000* (Brookings, 2003), pp. 200–63; John W. Garver, *Face Off: China, the United States, and Taiwan's Democratization* (University of Washington Press, 1997); Suisheng Zhao, ed., *Across the Taiwan Strait: Mainland China, Taiwan, and the 1995–1996 Crisis* (New York: Routledge, 1999), particularly the essays on the PRC's perspective; Michael D. Swaine, "Chinese Decision-Making Regarding Taiwan, 1979–2000," in *The Making of Chinese Foreign and Security Policy in the Era of Reform*, edited by David Michael Lampton (Stanford University Press, 2001), pp. 289–336; Robert S. Ross, "The 1995–96 Taiwan Strait Confrontation: Coercion, Credibility, and the Use of Force," *International Security* 25 (Fall 2000): 87–123; Allen S. Whiting, "China's Use of Force, 1950–1996, and Taiwan," *International Security* 26 (Fall 2001): 120–123; and Tai Ming Cheung, "Chinese Military Preparations against Taiwan over the Next 10 Years," in *Crisis in The Taiwan Strait*, edited by James R. Lilley and Chuck Downs (National Defense University Press, 1997), pp. 45–71.

15. Garver, *Face Off*, pp. 4–5, 13, 22–23.

16. Ross, "The 1995–96 Taiwan Strait Confrontation," p. 94.

17. See Richard Bush, "Taiwan Policy-Making since Tiananmen: Navigating through Shifting Waters," and Jim Mann, "Congress and Taiwan: Understanding the

Bond," both in *Making China Policy: Lessons from the Bush and Clinton Administrations*, edited by Ramon H. Myers, Michel C. Oksenberg, and David Shambaugh (Lanham, Md.: Rowman & Littlefield, 2001).

18. "Full Text of Taiwan President Chen Shui-bian's Inauguration Speech on 20 May 2000," China Television Company, May 20, 2000 (FBIS, CPP20000520000042); "PRC Taiwan Affairs Offices Issue Statement on Chen Shui-bian Inauguration Speech," Xinhua (New China News Agency), May 20, 2000 (FBIS, CPP20000520000060).

19. "Dangqian Guoji Guanxi Yanjiuzhong de Ruogan Zhongdian Wenti" ("Certain Major Issues in Studying Current International Relations"), *Guoji Zhanwang* (*International Forecast*), February 15, 2001, p. 7; Chen Shui-bian, *Xiangxin Taiwan: Ahbian Zongtong xiang Renmin Baogao* (*Believe in Taiwan: President Ah-Bian Reports to the People*)(Taipei: Yuanshen Chubanshe, 2004), p. 27; "CNA Cites 18 Jan Interview with Chen Shui-bian on Cross-Strait Ties, Referendum," Central News Agency (CNA), January 18, 2004 (FBIS, CPP20040118000055 [January 24, 2004]).

20. David Shambaugh, *Modernizing China's Military: Progress, Problems, and Prospects* (University of California Press, 2003), pp. 222–24; Stockholm International Peace Research Institute, "Transfers of Major Conventional Weapons to China, 1994–2003" (http://web.sipri.org/contents/armstrad/trend_ind_CHI_94-03.pdf [July 27, 2004]).

21. Council on Foreign Relations (CFR), *Chinese Military Power: Report of an Independent Task Force Sponsored by the Council on Foreign Relations* (New York: 2003), pp. 24, 26, 38–39; Department of Defense, *Annual Report on the Military Power of the People's Republic of China: Report to Congress Pursuant to the FY 2000 National Defense Authorization Act* (hereafter cited as *2004 Pentagon Report*), May 28, 2004, pp. 7, 46–47 (www.defenselink.mil/pubs/ d20040528PRC.pdf [June, 1 2004]).

22. Ibid.

23. CFR, *Chinese Military Power*, pp. 56–58; *2004 Pentagon Report*, pp. 16–17, 26–28.

24. *2004 Pentagon Report*, pp. 6, 23, 34–46; CFR, *Chinese Military Power*, pp. 27–29, 41–56.

25. *2004 Pentagon Report*, pp. 25–26; CFR, *Chinese Military Power*, p. 41.

26. CFR, *Chinese Military Power*, pp. 25–29; *2004 Pentagon Report*, pp. 48–50. David Shambaugh downplays the PLA's ability to bring Taipei to heel through the invasion or blockade, even without American intervention; see *Modernizing China's Military*, pp. 307–27.

27. Michael O'Hanlon, "Why China Cannot Conquer Taiwan," *International Security* 24 (Fall 2000): 54.

28. For Chinese doctrinal writings on coercion strategies, see Thomas J. Christensen, "Contradictory Messages on Deterrence: Zhanyixue and Taiwan Scenarios," in *The PLA Revolution in Doctrinal Affairs: Zhanyixue and Beyond*, edited by James Mulvenon and David Finkelstein (Santa Monica, Calif.: RAND, 2005, forthcoming).

29. *2004 Pentagon Report*, pp. 18–20.

30. Michael D. Swaine, "China's Military Posture," in *Power Shift: China and Asia's New Dynamics*, edited by David Shambaugh (University of California Press, 2005, forthcoming).

31. "The One-China Principle and the Taiwan Issue," Xinhua, February 21, 2000 (FBIS, CPP20000221000057 [March 25, 2004]).

32. "Official with Taiwan Affairs Office on the Bottom Line for Use of Force," *Renmin Wang* (*People's Daily* online), January 15, 2004 (FBIS, CPPP20040105000073 [February 12, 2004]).

33. "Fan Fenlie Guojia Fa Quanwen" ("Full Text of the Anti-Secession Law"), March 14, 2005, (http://.tw.people.com.cn/GB/14810/3240911 [March 14, 2005]).

34. CFR, *Chinese Military Power*, pp. 24–26; *2004 Pentagon Report*, p. 7.

35. *2004 Pentagon Report*, pp. 7, 11, 48. Other assessments of the PRC's military modernization that focus the emergence of coercive options against Taiwan include Mark A. Stokes, *China's Strategic Modernization: Implications for the United States* (Carlisle Barracks, Pa.: Strategic Studies Institute, U.S. Army War College, 1999); Lyle Goldstein and William Murray, "Undersea Dragons: China's Maturing Submarine Force," *International Security* 28 (Spring 2004): 161–96; Michael A. Glosny, "Strangulation from the Sea," *International Security* 28 (Spring 2004): 125–60. Tom Christensen warns that although China lacks the capacity to conduct even coercive campaigns until at least the middle of the 2000–10 decade and that although it would likely understand the risk of using force to challenge unwanted political initiatives from Taipei, it might decide that time is not on its side and that coercion supplemented by asymmetric strategies would be necessary. See Christensen, "Posing Problems without Catching Up," pp. 42–44.

36. See, for example, the publications of the Chinese Council of Advanced Policy Studies (www.caps.org.tw), the journal *Taiwan Defense Affairs*, and Martin Edmonds and Michael M. Tsai, *Defending Taiwan: The Future Vision of Taiwan's Defence Policy and Military Strategy* (London: RoutledgeCurzon, 2003).

37. "Defense Report: Republic of China," Taiwan Ministry of National Defense, July 2002 (http://163.29.3.66/whitepaper.pdf [March 11, 2005]).

38. "Military Threat," *Taipei Times*, December 20, 2003 (FBIS, CPP200312000002 [March 9, 2004]). In September 2004, the Ministry of National Defense predicted that China would gain the advantage regarding capabilities beginning in 2006 if Taiwan did not upgrade its assets and that the imbalance would be become clear by 2008. See "PRC Would Most Likely Invade Taiwan in 2012, MND Warns," *Taiwan News*, September 23, 2004 (FBIS, CPP20040923000195 [September 23, 2004]).

39. "Quadrennial National Security Estimate Report," (Taipei: Foundation of International and Cross-Strait Studies, 2004), pp. 42–43, 45, 50, 62.

40. "Beijing's Hostility toward Taiwan," results of surveys sponsored by the Mainland Affairs Council from April 1998 to April 2004 (www.mac.gov.tw/english/

english/pos/9305/9305e_7.gif [February 22, 2005]). The poll surveyed 1,600 Taiwan adults aged twenty or older.

41. "Take the Initiative to Promote and Upgrade Taiwan-U.S.-China Relations," *Lianhebao (United Daily News)*, February 23, 2002 (FBIS, CPP20020223000006 [February 26, 2002]).

42. Michael D. Swaine, "Deterring Conflict in the Taiwan Strait: The Successes and Failure of Taiwan's Defense Reform and Military Modernization Program," *Carnegie Papers* 46 (July 2004), p. 22 (www.ceip.org/files/pdf/ CP46.SWAINE. final.PDF [July 7, 2004]).

43. "Survey on Taiwanese Public Perception of Cross-Strait Security," commissioned by *Shangye Zhoukan (Business Weekly)*, conducted by the Election Study Center of National Chengchi University, and released July 22, 2004; project consultants, Yun-han Chu and Philip Yang (http://taiwansecurity.org/IS/2004/ BW-Poll-220704.ppt [February 22, 2005]). The center interviewed 1,811 people aged twenty or older.

44. These results are clouded by a certain vagueness in the questions. How constitutional change might occur and its content would affect the PRC response.

45. Ross, "The 1995–96 Taiwan Strait Confrontation," p. 123; Chas. W. Freeman Jr., "Preventing War in the Taiwan Strait," *Foreign Affairs* 77 (July-August 1998): 7.

46. Project for the New American Century, "Statement on the Defense of Taiwan," August 20, 1999 (http://newamericacentury.org/Taiwandefensestatement.htm [July 11, 2003]).

47. "U.S. Hits Obstacles in Helping Taiwan Guard against China," *Washington Post*, October 30, 2003, p. A1.

48. This latter shift did prompt some criticism from those who favored greater equidistance and ambiguity in U.S. policy. Robert Ross, for example, argued that "instead of welcoming the benefits of deterrence, the George W. Bush administration has developed policies that contribute to conflict by unnecessarily challenging China's interests in Taiwan." See Robert S. Ross, "Navigating the Taiwan Strait: Deterrence, Escalation Dominance, and U.S.-China Relations," *International Security* 27 (Fall 2002): 82.

49. Statement of Richard P. Lawless, U.S.-China Economic and Security Review Commission, *Hearing on Military Modernization and Cross-Strait Balance*, 108th Cong., 2d sess., February 6, 2004, pp. 11–12.

50. "Shemma Wenti Dou Keyi Taolun," p.13.

51. Wang Weixing, "The United States and Taiwan Start a Quasi-Military Alliance," *Shijie Zhishi*, July 1, 2002 (FBIS, CCP20020717000147 [July 6, 2002]). For another example of "defend unification by force," see Xi Yang, "An Exercise of the Taiwan Military to 'Defend Independence' by Force," *Dagongbao*, May 27, 2002 (FBIS, CPP20020527000018 [June 13, 2002]). Another author charged that the U.S. goal was to "maintain Taiwan's status quo so that Taiwan can be the United States' per-

manent strategic resource in the Western Pacific" and to be ready to launch a joint defense operation in the event of war: see Guo Siren, "Joint Monitoring Targeting Mainland Using Many Different Methods of Cooperation," *Huanqiu Shibao* (*Global Times*), September 14, 2001 (FBIS, CPP20010919000064 [September 24, 2001]).

52. Peng Weixue, "United States and Taiwan Step Up Military Collaboration to Protect 'Taiwan Independence,'" *Renmin Wang*, April 23, 2003 (FBIS, 20030423000041 [July 9, 2003]); Wang Weixing, "Substantial Changes Witnessed within Taiwan's Armed Forces," *Liangan Guanxi* (*Cross-Strait Relations*), July 1, 2003 (FBIS, CPP20030717000169 [July 25, 2003]).

53. Yu Keli, "'State-to-State Relations' Is the Core of the Taiwan Authorities' Present Mainland Policy," *Taiwan Yanjiu* (*Taiwan Research*), March 20, 2002 (FBIS, CPP200206000197 [July 9, 2002]).

54. Xu Bodong, "Denial of One-China Principle Means Opting for 'War,'" *Dagongbao*, January 4, 2002 (FBIS, CPP20020107000050 [January 9, 2002]).

55. Xinhua and *Renmin Ribao*, "Dangerous Provocation: Criticizing Chen Chuibian's Separatist Remarks," Xinhua, August 6, 2003 (FBIS, CPP20020806000049 [July 9, 2003]). Chen's remarks also unnerved Washington, which wished to avoid cross-Strait tensions at a time that it needed China's cooperation on foreign policy issues like North Korea. It certainly did not wish to be drawn into an unnecessary conflict. The Bush administration moved quickly to reassure Beijing and reduce tensions. For the retrospective judgment, rendered by Taiwan specialist Xu, see "Mainland Taiwan Issue Experts Visit the United States to Get to Know Sino-Relations, US Policy toward Taiwan," Zhongguo Xinwen She (China News Agency), September 29, 2003 (FBIS, CPP20030929000159).

56. Huang Hai and Yang Liu, "Military Experts on War to Counter 'Taiwan Independence': Six Prices; War Criminals Cannot Escape Punishment," *Renmin Wang*, December 3, 2003 (FBIS, CPP2003120300036 [March 10, 2004]).

57. For an articulate Taiwan discussion of which side was being more provocative, see Holmes Liao, "Referendum—Taiwan's Provocation?" *China Brief*, July 1, 2003 (www.jamestown.org/publications_details.php?volume_id=19&issue_id=678 &article_id=4748 [March 13, 2003]).

58. Statement of Richard P. Lawless, p. 12.

59. "Chinese President Is Optimistic about Relations with the U.S.," *New York Times*, August 10, 2001, p. A1.

60. "PRC Taiwan Affairs Offices Issue Statement on Chen Shui-bian Inauguration Speech"; "Li Teng-hui Stresses No National Unification Timetable," CNA, July 22, 1998 (FBIS, DRCHI07221998001067 [July, 12, 2004]).

61. Bonnie S. Glaser, "Sustaining Cooperation, Security Matters Take Center Stage," *Comparative Connections*, January 2003, Center for Strategic and International Studies Pacific Forum (www.csis.org/pacfor/cc/0204Qus_china.html [July 12, 2004]).

62. Jacques deLisle, "Varieties of Sovereignty and China: Challenges and Oppor-

tunities in the Cross-Strait Relationship: A Conference Report," E-Notes, Foreign Policy Research Institute, July 1, 2002 (www.fpri.org/enotes/asia.20020701.delisle. sovereigntychina.html [February 22, 2005]).

63. "An Idea for the Peaceful Reunification of the Chinese Mainland and Taiwan" (remarks made June 26, 1983), *Selected Works of Deng Xiaoping* (Beijing: Foreign Languages Press, 1994), pp. 40–41; "Shemma Wenti Dou Keyi Taolun," p. 14.

64. "*Liaowang* Article Expounds One-Country, Two-Systems Concept," *Renmin Ribao (People's Daily)*, July 26, 1991 (FBIS, *Daily Report: China*, p. 62, CHI-91-147).

65. The United States might face something of a dilemma, depending how a settlement was arranged. The Taiwan Relations Act authorizes the executive branch to "make available to Taiwan such defense articles and defense services in such quantity as may be necessary to enable Taiwan to maintain a sufficient self-defense capability." Yet the decision here would be made more on political grounds than on legal ones: this provision provides ample flexibility to define Taiwan's needs as minimal.

66. Alastair Iain Johnston, "Is China a Status Quo Power?" *International Security* 17 (Spring 2003): 55.

67. I am grateful to Tom Christensen for reinforcing this point.

68. When it comes to avoiding war, the meanings of defection and cooperation differ from those pertaining to reaching a settlement. Here, cooperation takes the form of mutual restraint, in which Taiwan avoids political initiatives that threaten Beijing's fundamental interests and China eschews the use of force. Defection would be each abandoning restraint: Taiwan declares independence or China uses force, or both.

Chapter Six

1. Steve Tsang, "A Sustainable Basis for Peace between China and Taiwan," *American Asian Review* 20 (Winter 2002): 66.

2. For the immediate postwar period, see Steven Phillips, "Between Assimilation and Independence: Taiwanese Political Aspirations under Nationalist Chinese Rule, 1945–1948," in *Taiwan: A New History*, edited by Murray A. Rubinstein (Armonk, N.Y.: M. E. Sharpe, 1999). For a discussion of mainland Chinese as seen by Taiwanese as the "Other," told from the perspective of a PRC Chinese, see Hai Ren, "Taiwan and the Impossibility of the Chinese," in *Negotiating Ethnicities in China and Taiwan*, edited by Melissa J. Brown (Berkeley, Calif.: Institute of East Asian Studies, 1996), pp. 75–97.

3. George H. Kerr, *Formosa Betrayed* (London: Eyre & Spottiswoode, 1965), p. 97.

4. On the 2-28 incident see Kerr, *Formosa Betrayed*; and Lai Tse-han, Ramon H. Myers, and Wei Hou, *A Tragic Beginning: The Taiwan Uprising of February 28, 1947* (Stanford University Press, 1991). The passage cited is from *A Tragic Beginning*, p. 183.

5. Phillips, "Between Assimilation and Independence," p. 277.

6. *Renquan zhi Dao: Taiwan Minzhu Renquan Huigu* (literally, *The Road of Human Rights: A Retrospective on Taiwan's Democracy and Human Rights*; English published title, *The Road to Freedom*) (Taipei: Wu-shu tu-shu Publishing, 2002), table, Post-War Taiwan Political Cases, pp. 17–24.

7. Robert Edmondson, "The February 28th Incident and National Identity," in *Memories of the Future: National Identity Issues and the Search for a New Taiwan,* edited by Stephane Corcuff (Armonk, N.Y.: M. E. Sharpe, 2002), p. 30.

8. Lee Teng-hui promoted a constitutional amendment that stripped the provincial government of most of its power in order to undermine James Soong Chu-yu, who was challenging Lee's chosen successor, Lien Chan. Chen Shui-bian has proposed an amendment that would abolish the provincial government altogether.

9. Alan M.Wachman, *Taiwan: National Identity and Democratization* (Armonk, N.Y.: M. E. Sharpe, 1994), p. 108; Maurice Meisner, "The Development of Formosan Nationalism," in *Formosa Today*, edited by Mark Mancall (New York: Praeger, 1964), p. 158.

10. Hill Gates, "Ethnicity and Social Class," in *The Anthropology of Taiwan Society*, edited by Emily Martin Ahern and Hill Gates (Stanford University Press, 1981), pp. 241–81; Mark Mancall, "Introduction: Taiwan: Island of Resignation and Despair," in *Formosa Today*, edited by Mancall, p. 26; Meisner, "The Development of Formosan Nationalism," pp. 155, 157.

11. Myron L. Cohen, "Being Chinese: The Peripheralization of Traditional Identity," in *The Living Tree: The Changing Meaning of Being Chinese Today*, edited by Wei-ming Tu (Stanford University Press, 1995), p. 132; Emily Martin Ahern, "The Thai Ti Kong Festival," in *Anthropology of Taiwan Society*, edited by Ahern and Gates (quoted passage on p. 425).

12. Su Bing, *Taiwan's 400 Year History: The Origins and Continuing Development of the Taiwanese Society and People* (Washington: The Taiwanese Cultural Grass Roots Association, 1986), p. 59. For an account of these views from the early 1960s, see Meisner, "The Development of Formosan Nationalism." Even Lee Teng-hui himself, a member of the KMT until 2000, regarded the party as a *wailai de zhengquan*—literally, "a regime come from outside," sometimes translated "alien regime."

13. Stéphane Corcuff, "Taiwan's 'Mainlanders,' New Taiwanese?" in *Memories of the Future*, edited by Corcuff, p. 169.

14. Wachman, *Taiwan: National Identity and Democratization*, p. 119–24. For a fascinating discussion of how social and political experience (rather than ancestry or cultural norms) shape identity—in this case for Taiwan's plains aborigines—see Melissa J. Brown, *Is Taiwan Chinese?: The Impact of Culture, Power, and Migration on Changing Identities* (University of California Press, 2004).

15. Alan M. Wachman, "Competing Identities in Taiwan," in *Taiwan: A New History*, edited by Rubinstein, pp. 17–80. For a recent poll, see Yun-han Chu, "Taiwan's

National Identity Politics and the Prospect of Cross-Strait Relations," *Asian Survey* 44 (July–August 2004): 502.

16. "International Press Conference," May 20, 1993, from a no-longer-operative website of the Office of the President established during Lee Teng-hui's tenure (hereafter cited as OOP website; all documents from this site are in the author's files.) In February 1994, Lee said: "I believe that before we do anything else, Taiwan has to get its own house firmly in order. If Taiwan's identity is not completely clear to its people, how can we deal with mainland China?" See "Transcript of a Press Conference Held after President Lee's visit to the Southeast Asian Countries," February 16, 1994, OOP website [May 13, 2000]. In an interview I had with Lin Bihjaw, a former aide of Lee's, on February 24, 2003, he confirmed this bulwark strategy.

17. On Lee and *gemeinschaft*, see Christopher Hughes, *Taiwan and Chinese Nationalism: National Identity and Status in International Society* (New York: Routledge, 1997), pp. 97-100. Lee used the Chinese term *shengming gongtongti* (literally, "living community") to translate *gemeinschaft*. On curriculum reform, see Christopher Hughes and Robert Stone, "Nation-Building and Curriculum Reform in Hong Kong and Taiwan," *China Quarterly* 160 (December 1999): 977–91; Stéphane Corcuff, "The Symbolic Dimension of Democratization and the Transition of National Identity under Lee Teng-hui," in *Memories of the Future*, edited by Corcuff, pp. 83–92.

18. On Taiwanese anxieties in the 1980s, see interview with David Reuther, in *China Confidential: American Diplomats and Sino-American Relations, 1945–1995*, edited by Nancy Bernkopf Tucker (Columbia University Press, 2001), p. 428. I am grateful to Reuther for reminding me of these points. On "enemies within" today, see Denny Roy, "Taiwan's Threat Perceptions: The Enemy Within," Asia-Pacific Center for Security Studies Occasional Papers Series, March 2003 (www.apcss.org/Publication/Occasional%20Papers/OPTaiwanThreat.pdf [November 11, 2003]), 3.

19. Steve Chen, "In Media, Ethnic Manipulation," *Taipei Times*, November 21, 2003 (Foreign Broadcast Information Service [FBIS], CPP20031121000176 [December 14, 2003]).

20. For the 2004 poll, "Survey on Taiwanese Public Perception of Cross-Strait Security," commissioned by *Shangye Zhoukan* (*Business Weekly*), conducted by the Election Study Center of National Chengchi University, and released July 22, 2004; project consultants, Yun-han Chu and Philip Yang (http://taiwansecurity.org/IS/2004/BW-Poll-220704.ppt [July 23, 2004]). For the correlation of identity trends to ethnicity and so on, see Ho Szu-yin and Liu I-chou, "The Taiwanese/Chinese Identity of the Taiwan People in the 1990s," *American Asian Review* 20 (Summer 2002): 29–74. See Chu, "Taiwan's National Identity Politics and the Prospect of Cross-Strait Relations," p. 501, for the methodological concerns about the MAC surveys.

21. Gunter Schubert, "Taiwan's Political Parties and National Identity: The Rise of an Overarching Consensus," *Asian Survey* 44 (July-August 2004): 554.

22. Communication to author from Emerson Niou, October 20, 2003. The idea

that individual Taiwan people carry around both Chinese and Taiwanese identities raises the issue of whether, given the island's growing integration in world culture, there may be a cosmopolitan identity as well. On this point, see Hughes and Stone, "Nation-Building and Curriculum Reform in Hong Kong and Taiwan."

23. Robert Marsh, "National Identity and Ethnicity in Taiwan: Some Trends in the 1990s," p. 158; Rwei-Ren Wu, "Toward a Pragmatic Nationalism: Democratization and Taiwan's Passive Revolution," p. 211; and Chia-lung Lin, "The Political Formation of Taiwanese Nationalism," p. 227, all in *Memories of the Future*, edited by Corcuff; Schubert, "Taiwan's Political Parties and National Identity," p. 537; Chu, "Taiwan's National Identity Politics and the Prospect of Cross-Strait Relations," p. 506; and Shelley Rigger, "Disaggregating the Concept of National Identity" (originally presented at a WWICS Asia Program event entitled "The Evolution of a Taiwanese Identity"), *Asia Program Special Report* 114 (Washington: Woodrow Wilson International Center for Scholars, August 2003), pp. 17–21. Prior statements of the view that identity does not ipso facto lead to independence are found in Wachman, *Taiwan: National Identity and Democratization,* especially pp. 103–04, 127–28; and Hughes, *Taiwan and Chinese Nationalism,* pp. 99–103, 127–08.

24. The results of the MAC polls, "Survey on Taiwanese Public Perception of Cross-Strait Security," can be found at the MAC website, www.mac.gov.tw.

25. Chu, "Taiwan's National Identity Politics and the Prospect of Cross-Strait Relations," pp. 503–06.

26. See "Congress Gets into the Taiwan Human Rights Act," in Richard Bush, *At Cross Purposes: U.S.-Taiwan Relation Since 1942* (Armonk, N.Y.: M. E. Sharpe, 2004), pp. 179–218.

27. For a case study of the dilemma in action, see Tun-jen Cheng and Yung-ming Hsu, "Issue Structure, the DPP's Factionalism, and Party Realignment," in *Taiwan's Electoral Politics and Democratic Transition: Riding the Third Wave,* edited by Hung-mao Tien (Armonk, N.Y.: M. E. Sharpe, 1996), pp. 137–73. The debate within the *dangwai* mirrored a similar one within the regime. Moderates on each side needed the cooperation of the other to succeed, as did the more radical forces. The initial stages of democratization only made the dilemmas more complicated.

28. The following account is based on Shelly Rigger, *From Opposition to Power: Taiwan's Democratic Progressive Party* (Boulder, Colo.: Lynne Rienner Publications, 2001), pp. 120–38.

29. Wilson Tien, "The DPP's Position on Cross-Strait Relations," in *Breaking the China-Taiwan Impasse,* edited by Donald S. Zagoria (Westport, Conn.: Praeger Publishers, 2003), pp. 69–70. Chen also signaled this flexibility in his 2004 inaugural speech, in which he did not rule out any future cross-Strait outcome for Taiwan as long as it had the Taiwan people's approval and in which he made particular reference to the European model of integration. See "President Chen's Inaugural Address, 'Paving the Way for a Sustainable Taiwan,'" Government Information Office, May 20, 2004 (www.gio.gov.tw/taiwan-website/4-oa/20040520/2004052001 [May 30, 2004]).

30. For the two documents, see "The Taiwan Question and the Reunification of China," Taiwan Affairs Office and Information Office, State Council, August 1993; and "Relations across the Taiwan Straits," Mainland Affairs Council, July 1994, reprinted in John F. Copper, *Words across the Taiwan Strait: A Critique of Beijing's "White Paper" on China's Unification* (Lanham, Md.: University Press of America, 1995).

31. Steven Goldstein, "The Rest of the Story: The Impact of Domestic Politics on Taiwan's Mainland Policy," *Harvard Studies on Taiwan*, vol. 2 (1998), pp. 62–90; David Reuther, "The Straits Exchange Foundation: A Study in Policy Flexibility," *Washington Journal of Modern China* 2 (Summer 1996): 68–88.

32. On the problem of corruption, which got worse during the 1990s, see Michael Ying-mao Kau, "The Power Structure in Taiwan's Political Economy," *Asian Survey* 36 (March 1996): 287–305; and Ying-mao Kao, "Structural Transformation of Taiwan Politics," *Harvard Studies on Taiwan*, vol. 2 (1998), pp. 118–140.

33. For an interesting account of the Taiwan shoe industry's migration to China, see You-Tien Hsing, *Making Capitalism in China* (Oxford University Press, 1998). For the government-business conflict over transportation links, see Ralph N. Clough, *Cooperation or Conflict in the Taiwan Strait* (Lanham, Md.: Rowman & Littlefield, 1999), p. 94.

34. Yu-Shan Wu, "Does Chen's Election Make Any Difference? Domestic and International Constraints on Taipei, Washington, and Beijing," in *Taiwan's Presidential Politics: Democratization and Cross-Strait Relations in the 21st Century*, edited by Muthiah Alagappa (Armonk, N.Y.: M. E. Sharpe, 2001), pp. 167–79.

35. These are provisions in the act governing relations between the peoples of Taiwan and the mainland, promulgated on October 29, 2003; communication to author from Alexander Huang, November 29, 2003.

36. Shelley Rigger has shaped my thinking on the efficacy of Taiwan's democratic system. See, for example, her "The Unfinished Business of Taiwan's Democratization," in *Dangerous Strait: The U.S.-Taiwan-China Crisis*, edited by Nancy Bernkopf Tucker (Columbia University Press, 2005), pp. 16–43.

37. Larry Diamond, *Developing Democracy: Toward Consolidation* (Johns Hopkins University Press, 1999), pp. 109–110.

38. On the KMT's reliance on factions, see Joseph Bosco, "Faction versus Ideology: Mobilization Strategies in Taiwan's Elections," *China Quarterly* 137 (March 1994): 28–62; Bosco, "Taiwan Factions: Guanxi, Patronage, and the State in Local Politics," in *The Other Taiwan*, edited by Murray A. Rubinstein (Armonk, N.Y.: M. E. Sharpe, 1994), pp. 114–44; and Ming-tong Chen, "Local Factions and Elections in Taiwan's Democratization," in *Taiwan's Electoral Politics and Democratic Transition*, edited by Tien, pp. 174–92.

39. See Shelley Rigger, *Politics in Taiwan: Voting for Democracy* (New York: Routledge, 1999); and Bosco, "Taiwan Factions."

40. From 1996 through 2004, presidential elections on Taiwan were held every

four years and legislative elections every three. If the National Assembly approves the constitutional amendments that the Legislative Yuan approved in August 2004, both types would occur every four years.

41. For a good summary of these issues, see Yun-han Chu, "Democratic Consolidation in the Post-KMT Era: The Challenge of Governance," in *Taiwan's Presidential Politics*, edited by Alagappa, pp. 88–114.

42. "Taiwan President Accepts 'One China, Respective Interpretations,'" Central News Agency (CNA), June 27, 2000 (FBIS, CPP20000627000121 [March 24, 2004]); "Chen Has Gone Too Far This Time," *Taipei Times*, June 29, 2000 (www.taipeitimes.com/News/edit/archives/2000/06/29/41885 [November 11, 2004]).

43. As will be seen, moreover, there were suspicions that the opposition was working in league with China to undermine Chen.

44. For a discussion of the Legislative Yuan, see Don Shapiro, "The Still-Evolving Legislative Yuan, *Topics*, April 2003, pp. 41–44.

45. Despite the change on investment policy, businesses still complained that there was more emphasis on management than on opening.

46. David L. Hall and Rogert T. Ames, *Thinking Through Confucius* (State University of New York Press, 1987), p. 269; William Theodore De Bary, Wing-Tsit Chan, and Burton Watson, comps., *Sources of Chinese Tradition*, vol. 1 (Columbia University Press, 1960), p. 51.

47. "Taiwan Considering Adding 'Taiwan' to Passport," CNA, May 18, 2001 (FBIS, CPP20010518000165); "Taiwan to Introduce New Passport," Agence France-Presse, December 15, 2001 (FBIS, CPP20011215000049); "Several Taiwan Personalities Voice Opposition to Adding Word 'Taiwan' to Passport," Xinhua (New China News Agency), June 22, 2001 (FBIS, CPP20010622000067); "PRC Official Cautions Taiwan on Planned Passport Title Change," Xinhua, June 27, 2001 (FBIS, CPP20010627000); all accessed October 4, 2004.

48. "Decision to Add 'Taiwan' to Taiwan Passport Cover Draws Mixed Reaction," CNA, January 13, 2002 (FBIS, CPP20020113000028 [October 4, 2004]). On the early history of FAPA, see "Congress Gets into the Taiwan Human Rights Act," in Bush, *At Cross Purposes*.

49. "New Addition to Taiwan Passport Cover Is Final Proposal: Minister," CNA, January 14, 2002 (FBIS, 20020114000120); "Controversy Continues over New Taiwan Passport Cover," CNA, January 14, 2002 (FBIS, CPP20020114000106); "Gao Siren Exposes Chen Shui-bian's Ulterior Motives," *Wenhuibao*, January 16, 2002 (FBIS, CPP20020116000067); all accessed October 4, 2004.

50. "Legislative Committee Calls for 'Taiwan Passport,'" CNA, May 30, 3002 (FBIS, CPP20020530000164); "Foreign Ministry to Stick to Passport Cover Reform Plan: Spokesman," CNA, June 4, 2002 (FBIS, CPP20020604000096); "MOFA Sticks to 'Issued in Taiwan' on New Version of Passports," CNA, July 11, 2002 (FBIS, CPP20020711000); "MOFA Delays Passport Proposal," *Taipei Times*, July 18, 2002

(FBIS, CPP20020711000069); "New Taiwan Passport Will Remain Unchanged: MOFA," CNA, September 20, 2002 (FBIS, CPP20020920000156); "'Taiwan' Passport Issue Still Up In the Air: Taiwan Foreign Ministry," CNA, February 18, 2003 (FBIS, CPP20030218000076); all accessed October 4, 2004.

51. "Taiwan Passports to Bear 'Taiwan' on Cover," CNA, June 12, 2003 (FBIS, CPP20030612000226); "Foreign Ministry to Brief Legislators on 'Taiwan' Passports," *Taipei Times*, June 12, 2003 (FBIS, CPP20030612000192); both accessed October 4, 2004.

52. "Transcript of Interview with Chen Shui-bian," *Financial Times*, December 16, 2003 (www.ft.com [December 16, 2003]).

53. For a good summary of the sources of Chen's initiatives, see David G. Brown, "China-Taiwan Relations: Pernicious Presidential Politics," *Comparative Connections*, October 2003 (www.csis.org/pacfor/cc/0303Qchina_Taiwan [March 13, 2004]).

54. Yu-shan Wu, "Taiwan's Domestic Politics and Cross-Strait Relations," *China Journal* 53 (January 2005).

55. On the consistency of support for the status quo (around 50 percent), see the results of the poll ("Survey on Taiwanese Public Perception of Cross-Strait Security") commissioned by the Mainland Affairs Council, which can be found at its website, www.mac.gov.tw. A problem with these polls, of course, is that they do not define the status quo. The public's conception of the status quo could change, but the surveys would show continuing support.

56. Specifically, seniority consciousness in the pan-Blue camp deemed Ma to be too junior, not only because of his age (which happened to be close to Chen Shui-bian's) but also because older officials around Lien Chan believed that they would be ineligible for positions in a Ma administration. The KMT's coalition with the PFP also hurt Ma's chances. PFP chairman Soong Chu-yu would insist on being on the ticket, but he, like Ma, was a mainlander, and a Hunanese at that. A two-mainlander ticket is not feasible given Taiwan's ethnic politics.

57. "Downsizing," *Taipei Times*, August 24, 2004 (www.taipeitimes.com/News/front/archives/2004/08/24/2003199977 [August 24, 2004]). For the text of the amendments, see "Xiuzheng Zhonghua Minguo Xianfa Zengxiu Tiaowen Diyitiao, Dierhtiao, Disitiao, Diwutiao ji Dibatiao Tiaowen; bing Zengding Dishierhtiao Tiaowen" (Text of the Revision of Articles 1, 2, 4, 5, and 8, and Added Article 12 of the Additional Articles of the Republic of China Constitution), August 23, 2004 (http://lis.ly.gov.tw/npl/fast/04105/930823 [September 15, 2004]).

58. Robert L. Suettinger, *Beyond Tiananmen: The Politics of U.S.-China Relations, 1989–2000* (Brookings, 2003), pp. 224–25, 245–46, 262–63; John W. Garver, *Face Off: China, the United States, and Taiwan's Democratization* (University of Washington Press, 1997); You Ji, "Changing Leadership Consensus: The Domestic Context of War Games," in *Across the Taiwan Strait: Mainland China, Taiwan, and the 1995–1996 Crisis*, edited by Suisheng Zhao (New York: Routledge, 1999), pp. 77–98; Michael

Swaine, "Decision-Making Regarding Taiwan," in *The Making of Chinese Foreign and Security Policy in the Era of Reform*, edited by David Michael Lampton (Stanford University Press, 2001), pp. 319–27; Tai Ming Cheung, "Chinese Military Preparations against Taiwan over the Next Ten Years," in *Crisis in the Taiwan Strait*, edited by James R. Lilley and Chuck Downs (National Defense University Press, 1997); Andrew Scobell, "Show of Force: Chinese Soldiers, Statesmen, and the 1995–1996 Taiwan Strait Crisis," *Political Science Quarterly* 115 (Summer 2000): 227–46.

59. Cheng Li, *China's Leaders: The New Generation* (Lanham, Md.: Rowman & Littlefield, 2001), particularly chapter 6.

60. Zong Hairen, ed., *Disidai (The Fourth Generation)* (New York: Mingjing chubanshe [Mirror Publishers], 2002), pp. 72–73.

61. Ibid., pp. 318–20.

62. Qian Qichen, "Zuguo Shixian Tongyi di Weida Mubiao Yiding Nenggou Shihxian" ("We Certainly Can Reach the Great Goal of Achieving Complete Reunification of Our Motherland"), January 28, 2000 (www.gwytb.gov.cn/ jiang8d/jiang8d0/asp?jbd_m_id=69); Qian Qichen, "Zaori Wancheng Zuguo Tongyi Daye: Shixian Zhonghua Renmin Weida Fuxing" ("Complete the Great Task of National Reunification Soon: Realize the Great Revival of the Chinese Nation"), January 22, 2001 (www.gwytb.gov.cn/jiang8d/jiang8d0/ asp?jbd_m_id=79); Qian Qichen, "Jianchi 'Hoping Tongyi, Yiguo Liangzhi' Jiben Fangzhen: Nuli Tuijin Liangan Guanxi Fazhan" ("Adhere to the Basic Policy of 'Peaceful Unification, One Country, Two Systems': Vigorously Promote the Development of Cross-Strait Relations"), January 28, 2002 (www.gwytb.gov.cn/ jiang8d/jiang8d0/asp?jbd_m_id=89); Qian Qichen, "Liangan Tongbao Tongxin Xishou: Wancheng Zuguo Tongyi erh Nuili Douzheng" ("Compatriots on Both Sides of the Strait, Vigorously Struggle with One Heart and Linked Hands to Complete the Motherland's Reunification") (www.gwytb.gov.cn/jiang8d/jiang8d0/ asp?jbd_m_id=99); all accessed March 25, 2004.

63. On Jiang's ability to retain influence even as he gave up his party and government posts, see Joseph Fewsmith, "The Sixteenth Party National Congress: The Succession That Didn't Happen," *China Quarterly* 173 (March 2003): 1–16.

64. For an elaboration of this conclusion, see Yun-han Chu, "Power Transition and the Making of Beijing's Policy towards Taiwan," *China Quarterly* 176 (December 2003): 960–80.

65. "Jiang Puts Hard Line to the Test in China," *Washington Post*, May 31, 2004, p. A1. See also Robert L. Suettinger, "Leadership Policy toward Taiwan and the United States in the Wake of Chen Shui-bian's Reelection," *China Leadership Monitor* 11 (Summer 2004) (www.chinaleadershipmonitor.org/20043/rs [October 16, 2004]).

66. Charles Tilly, *Coercion, Capital, and European States* (Cambridge, Mass.: Blackwell Publishers, 1992), p. 116.

67. John Fitzgerald, "The Nationless State: the Search for a Nation in Modern

Chinese Nationalism," *Australian Journal of Chinese Affairs* 33 (January 1995): 75–104 (cited passage on p. 76).

68. James Townsend, "Chinese Nationalism," *Australian Journal of Chinese Affairs* 27 (January 1992): 114; Frank Dikotter, "Racial Identities in China: Context and Meaning," *China Quarterly* 138 (June 1994): 404–12; Lei Yi, "Xiandai de 'Huaxia zhongxingguan' yu 'minzhu zhuyi'" ("Modern 'Sinocentrism' and 'Nationalism'"), in *Zhounguo Ruhe Miandu Xifang* (*How China Faces the West*), edited by Xiao Pang (Hong Kong: Mirror Books, 1997), pp. 49–50, cited in Peter Hayes Gries, *China's New Nationalism: Pride, Politics, and Diplomacy* (University of California Press, 2004), p. 8; Edward Cody, "China Gives No Ground in Spats over History," *Washington Post*, September 22, 2004, p. A25.

69. Townsend, "Chinese Nationalism," p. 118; Barry Sautman, "Anti-Black Racism in Post-Mao China," *China Quarterly* 138 (June 1994): 413–37; Alaister Iain Johnston, "The Correlates of Nationalism in Beijing Public Opinion," Harvard University, 2003; and "Racial 'Handicaps' and a Great Sprint Forward," *New York Times*, September 8, 2004, p. A4.

70. Frank S. T. Hsiao and Lawrence R. Sullivan, "The Chinese Communist Party and the Status of Taiwan," *Pacific Affairs* 52 (Fall 1979): 458–64; "Vice Premier Qian Qichen Stresses When Attending Discussion of Taiwan Delegation, Upholding the One-China Principle is the Basis for Cross-Strait Dialogue," Xinhua, March 8, 2001 (FBIS, CPP20010308000148 [March 24, 2004]).

71. Zhu Chengxiu, "On Li Denghui's Certain Remarks," Xinhua, June 18, 1994 (FBIS, CHI-94-118).

72. Edward Friedman, "Chinese Nationalism: Challenge to U.S. Interests," in *The People's Liberation Army and China in Transition*, edited by Stephen J. Flanagan and Michael E. Marti (Washington: National Defense University Press, 2003), p. 97.

73. "Watch Out for Li Teng-Hui's Words and Deeds about 'Taiwan Independence,'" *Wenhuibao*, June 16, 1994 (FBIS, CHI-94-119); Hua Ji, "A Marionette in U.S. Double-Faced Policy," *Renmin Ribao* (*People's Daily*), June 11, 1995 (FBIS, HK13066144895).

74. On humiliation and victimization, see Suisheng Zhao, "Chinese Nationalism and Its International Orientations," *Political Science Quarterly* 115 (Spring 2000): 5, 7; and Gries, *China's New Nationalism*, pp. 45-52, 69-85. For the quoted passage, see Geremie Barmé, "To Screw Foreigners Is Patriotic: China's Avant-Garde Nationalists," *China Journal* 34 (July 1995): 233. Chinese history, as presented for popular audiences, is often selective and distorted, and it ignores cases in which China's difficulties were the result of its own leaders' mistakes; see "China's Textbooks Twist and Omit History," *New York Times*, December 6, 2004, p. A10.

75. "People's Daily and Xinhua Commentary on Li Teng-hui's Cornell Speech," Xinhua, July 23, 1995 (commentaries published on July 24, 1995) (FBIS, OW2307111095).

76. Based on Yongnian Zheng, *Discovering Chinese Nationalism in China: Mod-*

ernization, Identity, and International Relations (Cambridge University Press, 1999), pp. 97–100; Edward Friedman, "Chinese Nationalism: Challenge to U.S. Interests," pp. 92–98.

77. Edward Friedman, "Anti-Imperialism in Chinese Foreign Policy," in *China and the World: Chinese Foreign Relations in the Post–Cold War Era*, edited by Samuel S. Kim (Boulder, Colo.: Westview Press, 1994), pp. 60–74, Gries, *China's New Nationalism*, pp. 43–53; Townsend, "Chinese Nationalism," p. 129; Edward Friedman, "Reconstructing China's National Identity: A Southern Alternative to Mao-Era Anti-Imperialist Nationalism," *Journal of Asian Studies* 53 (January 1994): pp. 67–91; David S. G. Goodman, "Structuring Local Identity: Nation, Province, and County in Shanxi During the 1990s," *China Quarterly* 138 (December 2002): 837–62.

78. On the point that the regime's propaganda has fostered the very nationalistic attitudes that now constrain it, see Nicholas D. Kristof, "The China Threat?" *New York Times*, December 20, 2003, p. A19. Gries, *China's New Nationalism* is particularly effective in demonstrating the authenticity of popular sentiments.

79. Joseph Fewsmith and Stanley Rosen, "The Domestic Context of Chinese Foreign Policy: Does Public Opinion Matter?" in *Making of Chinese Foreign and Security Policy*, edited by Lampton, pp. 158–169; Suisheng Zhao, "Chinese Nationalism and Its International Orientations," *Political Science Quarterly* 115 (Spring 2000): 5–10.

80. Johnston, "The Correlates of Nationalism in Beijing Public Opinion."

81. This section draws extensively on Fewsmith and Rosen, "The Domestic Context of Chinese Foreign Policy," pp. 151–90.

82. Fewsmith and Rosen, "Domestic Context of Chinese Foreign Policy," pp. 158–72; Suisheng Zhao, "Chinese Intellectuals' Quest for National Greatness and Nationalistic Writing in the 1990s," *China Quarterly* 152 (December 1997): 725–45. Some of the replacements for cosmopolitanism are actually of Western origin (postmodernism, deconstructivism, and so forth); others have strong Chinese roots.

83. Of course, nationalist appeals are sometimes made not solely to advance foreign policy objectives but also as a legitimate way of advocating more controversial goals such as political reform. See Michael J. Sullivan, "The 1988–1989 Nanjing Anti-African Protests: Racial Nationalism or National Racism," *China Quarterly* 138 (June 1994): 438–57.

84. Gries's *China's New Nationalism* takes the 1999 demonstrations as its point of departure.

85. David M. Finkelstein, "China Reconsiders Its National Security: The Great Peace and Development Debate of 1999" (Alexandria, Va.: Project Asia, CNA Corporation, December 2000), pp. 5–7.

86. Ibid., pp. 16–18.

87. Ibid., p. 6. This mode of politics is reminiscent of the phenomenon of *qingyi* in the imperial system, when officials and degree holders were allowed to submit memorials to the throne that evaluated government policy on the basis of Confucian orthodoxy. For a Qing dynasty case, see Lloyd E. Eastman, *Throne and Mandarins:*

China's Search for a Policy During the Sino-French Controversy, 1880–1885 (Harvard University Press, 1967), especially pp. 16–29.

88. Fewsmith and Rosen, "Domestic Context of Chinese Foreign Policy," pp. 176–77.

89. Suettinger, *Beyond Tiananmen,* pp. 384–85.

90. Zhao, "Chinese Nationalism and Its International Orientations," p. 23.

91. Zheng, *Discovering Chinese Nationalism in China,* pp. 145–47.

92. Fewsmith and Rosen, "Domestic Context of Chinese Foreign Policy," pp. 172–87.

Chapter Seven

1. Alastair Iain Johnston, "China's Militarized Interstate Dispute Behaviour 1949–1992: A First Cut at the Data," *China Quarterly* 153 (March 1998): 7; Robert S. Ross, "The 1995–96 Taiwan Strait Confrontation: Coercion, Credibility, and the Use of Force," *International Security* 25 (Fall 2000): 118. For interpretations stressing China's rationality, see Allen S. Whiting, *China Crosses the Yalu: The Decision to Enter the Korean War* (Stanford University Press, 1960), and Whiting, *The Chinese Calculus of Deterrence* (University of Michigan Press, 1975).

2. Johnston, "China's Militarized Interstate Dispute Behaviour," pp. 27–29; Shu Guang Zhang, *Mao's Military Romanticism: China and the Korean War, 1950–1953* (University Press of Kansas, 1995); Shu Guang Zhang, *Deterrence and Strategic Culture: Chinese-American Confrontations, 1949–1958* (Cornell University Press, 1992); Chen Jian, *China's Road to the Korean War* (Columbia University Press, 1995); and Chen Jian, *Mao's China and the Cold War* (University of North Carolina Press, 2001). The classic work on misperceptions is Robert Jervis, *Perception and Misperception in International Politics* (Princeton University Press, 1976).

3. Michael D. Swaine, "Chinese Decision-Making Regarding Taiwan, 1979–2000," in *The Making of Chinese Foreign and Security Policy in the Era of Reform,* edited by David Michael Lampton (Stanford University Press, 2001), pp. 289–336.

4. "Hu Jintao to Meet Chairmen of Taiwan Businessmen's Associations on 25 December," *Wenhuibao,* December 25, 2003, (Foreign Broadcast Information Service [FBIS], CPP20031225000017 [June 12, 2004]); Wang Yuyan, "PRC Leading Group for Taiwan Affairs Restructured. Hu Jintao Is the Head," *Lianhebao* (*United Daily News*), May 29, 2003 (FBIS, CPP20030529000071 [June 5, 2003]).

5. Swaine, "Chinese Decision-Making Regarding Taiwan," pp. 307–09.

6. Ibid.," p. 309; Ning Lu, *The Dynamics of Foreign-Policy Decisionmaking in China* (Boulder, Colo.: Westview Press, 1997), p. 76. Chen Youwei, a former PRC diplomat, identifies several pathologies in Beijing's decisionmaking: reading the worst intentions into an adversary's actions; ideological ossification; divorce from reality; faulty intelligence; and the "celestial mentality" that assumes an air of self-importance. See Chen Youwei, "China's Foreign Policy Making as Seen through Tiananmen," *Journal of Contemporary China* 12 (November 2003): 715–22.

7. Swaine, "Chinese Decision-Making Regarding Taiwan," p. 309.

8. Su Ge, *Meiguo duihua zhengce yu Taiwan wenti* (*The China Policy of the United States and the Taiwan Question*) (Beijing: Shijie zhishi chubanshe [World Knowledge Publishing], 1998).

9. Su Ge, *Meiguo duihua zhengce yu Taiwan wenti*, pp. 20–27, 103–147, 156 (quoted passage), 291, 792, 304–309.

10. Zong Hairen, ed., *Disidai* (*The Fourth Generation*) (New York: Mingjing chubanshe [Mirror Publishers], 2002), p. 320.

11. "The One-China Principle and the Taiwan Issue," Xinhua (New China News Agency), February 21, 2000 (FBIS, CPP20000221000057 [December 22, 2004]).

12. Xu Jiatun, *Xu Jiatun Xianggang Huiyilu* (*Xu Jiatun's Hong Kong Memoir*)(Taipei: Lianhebao, 1993), pp. 238, 324–25.

13. Zou Jingwen, *Li Denghui Zhizheng Gaobai Shilu* (*Record of Revelations on Lee Denghui's Administration*)(Taipei: INK, 2001), pp. 196–97.

14. Jiang Zemin's Political Report, Chinese Central Television (the official PRC television network), September 12, 1997 (FBIS, OW1209033297 [March 3, 2004]).

15. "PRC State Council Official Welcomes Talks with Taiwan DPP," Zhongguo Tongxunshe (China News Agency), December 1, 1997 (FBIS, CRCHI12011007000989 [February 22, 2004]).

16. "Chen Shui-bian and Lee Teng-hui Are of Same Ilk," *Dagongbao*, December 1, 1999 (FBIS, FTS19991201000566 [February 22, 2004]).

17. "Experts Believe Taiwan to Face Continued Turbulent Political Situation," Zhongguo Tongxunshe, March 23, 2000 (FBIS, CPP20000323000141); Dan Wenbin, "Viewing the Taiwan Strait Situation after the Election," *Wenhuibao*, March 25, 2000 (FBIS, CPP20000327000057); both accessed February 22, 2004.

18. "He Who Plays with Fire Spreading the Notion of 'One Country on Each Side' Shall Get Burnt," *Wenhuibao*, August 5, 2002 (FBIS, CPP20020805000020 [July 9, 2003]).

19. Zong, ed., *Disidai*, p. 319.

20. Hu Lingwei, "Taiwan Shehui Luanxiang Congsheng di Yuanyin Fenxi" ("Analysis of the Reasons for Proliferating Chaos in Taiwan Society"), in *Jingxin Mianbi* (*Facing Obstacles with Peace of Mind*)(Shanghai: Taiwan Institute of East Asian Studies, 2004), pp. 92–95.

21. There is a recognition in the PRC that KMT repression created alienation and hostility among the Taiwanese and that ethnic division resulted (see Zeng Qinghong's comment in Zong, ed., *Disidai*, pp. 318-19). But the analysis is not taken to the next step, the formation of a separate identity.

22. See, for example, Robert L. Suettinger, *Beyond Tiananmen: The Politics of U.S.–China Relations, 1989–2000* (Brookings, 2003), pp. 200–63; John W. Garver, *Face Off: China, the United States, and Taiwan's Democratization* (University of Washington Press, 1997); the authors in Suisheng Zhao, ed., *Across the Taiwan Strait: Mainland China, Taiwan, and the 1995–1996 Crisis* (New York: Routledge, 1999),

particularly You Ji, "Changing Leadership Consensus: The Domestic Context of War Games," pp. 77–98; Swaine, "Chinese Decision-Making Regarding Taiwan"; Ross, "The 1995–96 Taiwan Strait Confrontation"; Allen S. Whiting, "China's Use of Force, 1950–1996, and Taiwan," *International Security* 26 (Fall 2001): 120–23; and Tai Ming Cheung, "Chinese Military Preparations against Taiwan over the Next 10 Years," in *Crisis in The Taiwan Strait*, edited by James R. Lilley and Chuck Downs (Washington: National Defense University Press, 1997).

23. As noted in chapter 6, there is disagreement on the role of the PLA in decisionmaking during 1995 and 1996. Some scholars suggest that it was one participant in a rolling consensus. Others conclude that the military actually forced a more robust response to Lee's trip than would have otherwise been the case. In a more recent, general assessment, Jing Huang says that there are differences between civilian and military leaders but attributes them to institutional priorities: civilians focus on containing crises; generals prefer to show strength and resolve (which could exacerbate the crisis); see Jing Huang "The PLA's Role in Policymaking under the New Leadership," paper prepared for "PRC Policymaking in the Wake of Leadership Change," Center for Strategic and International Studies, Washington, October 31, 2003, page 13. David Finkelstein, in his paper for the same conference, states that the precise PLA role is basically unknown; see his "The Role of the PLA in the Chinese Policymaking Process."

24. Garver, *Face Off*, p. 24.

25. Edward Friedman, "The Prospects of a Larger War: Chinese Nationalism and the Taiwan Strait Conflict," in Zhao, *Across the Taiwan Strait*, p. 261.

26. In March 1995, I warned officials of the PRC's embassy in Washington that Congress would succeed in pressuring Clinton into granting a visa. This small signal was likely ignored, even though it came from someone whom the embassy at the time regarded as friendly and knowledgeable about how Congress operated.

27. Ross, "The 1995–96 Taiwan Strait Confrontation," p. 118. For a more recent assessment of the 1995–96 events that emphasizes the benefits, see "Peace Will Prevail Only When the Two Sides of the Taiwan Strait Are Reunified: An Interview with Maj. Gen. Huang Bin, Noted Military Strategist on the Mainland," *Dagongbao*, May 13, 2002 (FBIS, CPP20020513000048 [February 28, 2004]). At the time of the interview Huang was on the staff of China's National Defense University.

28. The analysis that follows is based on my "PRC Foreign Policy and Security Behavior," *Journal of International Security Affairs* 4 (Winter 2003): 77–88.

29. "Xinhua Cites Clinton Remarks on Embassy Bombing," Xinhua, May 8, 1999 (FBIS, FTS19990508000903); "Clinton Sends Letter of Apology to Jiang Zemin," Xinhua, May 10, 1999 (FBIS, FTS19990510001965); both accessed March 16, 2002. When the United States is on daylight saving time, as it was in May 1999, Beijing time is twelve hours ahead of that on the U.S. East Coast.

30. "*Renmin Ribao* Commentator on Embassy Bombing," *Renmin Ribao*, May 9, 1999 (FBIS, FTS19990509000110); "Commentary Condemns NATO Attack on

Embassy, Xinhua, May 10, 1999 (FBIS, FTS19990510000141); "Commentary on NATO Explanation on Attack," Xinhua, May 10, 1999 (FBIS, FTS19991510000169); all accessed March 16, 2002. Generally, the Xinhua commentator articles were harsher than that of *Renmin Ribao* (*People's Daily*), perhaps because the news agency lost personnel in the bombing.

31. "PRC Missile Experts Say Embassy Attack 'Premeditated,'" Xinhua, May 10, 1999 (FBIS, FTS19990510000407 [March 16, 2002]).

32. "Ministry Spokesman Announces Decisions on Ties with US," Xinhua, May 10, 1999 (FBIS, FTS19990510000725); "Further on Tang Jiaxuan 'Representations' to Sasser," Xinhua, May 10, 1999 (FBIS, FTS19990510000806); "Qin Huasun Addresses Press Prior to UNSC Meeting on NATO," Xinhua, May 10, 1999 (FBIS, FTS19990510001988); all accessed March 16, 2002.

33. The extent of debate within the leadership on how to respond to the embassy bombing is not known.

34. Unless otherwise noted, this account is based on John Keefe, "Anatomy of the EP-3 Incident, April 2001" (Alexandria, Va.: CNA Corporation, January 2002). At the time of the incident, Keefe was a special assistant to the U.S. ambassador to the PRC, Joseph Prueher.

35. "CCTV Carries FM Spokesman's Comments on U.S. Military Plane Incident," Chinese Central Television, April 1, 2001 (FBIS, CPP20010401000065 [March 24, 2002]). The broadcast was at 10:20 p.m. It is sometimes said that the Chinese stance on the incident was a response to a statement by Admiral Dennis Blair, the U.S. Commander in the Pacific. But Blair's statement came *after* the first Zhou-Prueher meeting, by which time the Chinese had already locked in their basic position.

36. Bonnie S. Glaser and Phillip C. Saunders, "Chinese Civilian Foreign Policy Research Institutes: Evolving Roles and Increasing Influence," *China Quarterly* 171 (September 2002): 615.

37. For an example of that restraint in operation, one in which PRC Taiwan specialists argue for "calmness" in Beijing's response to Chen Shui-bian's August 2002 "two countries on each side" statement, see "Roundup: Chen Shuibian's Blunt Remarks Stir Up Turmoil, Mainland Experts Call on Making a Counterattack with Rationality and Calmness," Zhongguo Tongxunshe, August 9, 2002 (FBIS, CPP20020809000090). Presumably, the scholars' public advice was similar to what they were telling officials, and it can be inferred that the officials listened.

38. Robert L. Suettinger, "China's Foreign Policymaking Process," paper prepared for "PRC Policymaking in the Wake of Leadership Change," Center for Strategic and International Studies, Washington, October 31, 2003.

39. This section is based in part on Michael D. Swaine and James C. Mulvenon, *Taiwan's Foreign and Defense Policies* (Santa Monica, Calif.: RAND Center for Asia-Pacific Policy, 2001), pp. 77–90.

40. Ibid., pp. 88–89; author's interview with Lin Bih-jaw, February 24, 2003.

41. Zou, *Li Denghui Zhizheng Gaobai Shilu*, pp. 263–311.

42. Author's interview with Lee Teng-hui, July 31, 2003.

43. Zou, *Li Denghui Zhizheng Gaobai Shilu*, pp. 222–23.

44. "NSC Official on Li's 'State-to-State' Remark," *Zhongguo Shibao* (*China Times*), July 14, 1999 (FBIS, OW1407125199 [August 16, 2003]).

45. Zou, *Li Denghui Zhizheng Gaobai Shilu*, pp. 23, 25–26.

46. Ibid., 226–27. According to Lee's memoir, Su was briefed in early July, but it may have been late June since Su was in the United States in time for a conference around July 4 and briefed Stanley Roth on July 6.

47. "*Zhongguo Shibao* Investigative Report," *Zhongguo Shibao*, December 12, 2000 (translation in author's files); "Li Teng-hui Defends State-to-State Relationship," *Zhongguo Shibao*, September 1, 1999 (FBIS, CP9909010005 [September 1, 1999]); author's interview with Lin Bih-jaw, February 24, 2003. It is interesting to speculate on whether the announcement that PRC leaders reportedly intended to make was in fact an earlier version of "The One-China Principle and the Taiwan Issue," the white paper ultimately issued in February 2000.

48. Zou, *Li Denghui Zhizheng Gaobai Shilu*, pp. 227–29.

49. "Quadrennial National Security Estimate Report," Foundation of International and Cross-Strait Studies (Taipei, 2004), p. 52.

50. "Consensus," *Taipei Times*, August 7, 2002 (FBIS, CPP20020807000163); "Misunderstanding," *Taipei Times*, August 7, 2002 (FBIS, CPP20020807000164); both accessed August 6, 2004.

51. "Losing Confidence," *Taipei Times*, May 28, 2003 (FBIS, CPP20030528000238); "Selection List: Taiwan Press 22-23 May 03," reference to May 22, 2003, article in *Ziyou Shibao* (*Liberty Times*) (FBIS, CPP20030523000003); both accessed August 6, 2004.

52. "Inside Story of President Chen's New Constitution Proposal," *Xin Taiwan* (*New Taiwan*), no. 393, October 4-10, 2003 (FBIS, CPP20031007000107 [August 6, 2004]).

53. "Plan B," *Taipei Times*, November 30, 2003 (FBIS, CPP20031201000227); "Taiwan: 'Hard-Core DPP' Forced Chen into Defensive Referenda," *Taipei Times*, December 4, 2003 (FBIS, CPP20031204000186); "Taiwan President's Office Quiet on Reported Visit by U.S. Official," *Taipei Times*, December 3, 2003 (FBIS, CPP20031203000192); all accessed August 6, 2004.

Chapter Eight

1. Myra Lu, "Study Suggests Yueh Ancestry," *Taiwan Weekly*, May 4, 2001; "DNA Analysis Reveals 'Taiwanese' Originated in Mainland China," Xinhua (New China News Agency), December 14, 2001 (Foreign Broadcast Information Service [FBIS], CPP20011214000043 [December 14, 2001]). Each set of results is off the point. The social and cultural makeup of the people of southern Fujian is a regional variation of the larger Chinese society and culture. That a genetic link between Taiwan's abo-

rigines and people on the mainland creates a political connection between the two is like saying that North and South America are connected to East Asia because the ancestors of Native Americans originated there.

2. See my "The Status of the ROC and Taiwan, 1950–1972: Explorations in United States Policy," in *At Cross Purposes: U.S.-Taiwan Relation since 1942* (Armonk, N.Y.: M. E. Sharpe, 2004), pp. 85–123. Ironically, the United States was flexible in the 1960s on the ROC's status in the international system while Taiwan was rigid. When Taipei began proposing flexible approaches in the 1990s, the United States was locked into its position that the PRC was the sole legal government of China.

3. "Taiwan Hails World Semiconductor Council Membership," Central News Agency (CNA), April 18, 1998 (FBIS, DRCHI04181998000119 [July 12, 2004]); "Hong Kong, Macau Unlike Taiwan with Regards to WTO: MOFA," CNA, November 27, 2001 (FBIS, CPP20011127000127 [November 27, 2001]); "PRC FM Spokesman Urges Taipei to Change Error in Title of WTO Representatives," Xinhua, May 27, 2003 (FBIS, CPP20030527000224 [May 27, 2003]); "Taiwan Asked to 'Downgrade Status' at WTO," *Taipei Times*, May 27, 2003 (FBIS CPP20030527000279 [May 27, 2003]); "Opposition Parties Condemn Beijing over WTO Title Change Issue," CNA, May 27, 2003 (FBIS, CPP20030527000178 [May 27, 2003]); "Political Obstacles Prevent Taiwan Joining WTO's GPA," CNA, August 23, 2003 (FBIS, CPP20030823000036 [July 12, 2004]); "'Taiwan' to Make Sizable Donation to WHO," *Taipei Times*, May 16, 2002 (FBIS, CPP20020516000156 [May 16, 2002]).

4. "Beijing Pushes for Change in Taiwan's Designation in OIE," CNA, February 15, 2004 (FBIS, CPP20040215000021 [February 18, 2004]); "After APEC, No More Mr. Nice Guy," *Taipei Times*, October 21, 2001 (FBIS, CPP20011121000122 [October 22, 2001]); "Economics Ministers from Beijing, Taipei Hold Talks in Shanghai," CNA, October 16, 2001 (FBIS, CPP20011016000243); John C. C. Deng, "How Will Taiwan Interact with Mainland China under WTO?" speech at the Center for Strategic and International Studies, Washington, February 6, 2002; "Beijing Rejects Cross-Strait Direct Links Talks under WTO Framework," CNA, December 5, 2001 (FBIS, CPP20011205000080 [December, 5, 2001]); "Taiwan Hopes to Use 'WTO Mechanism' to Avert Steel Dispute with China," CNA, March 27, 2002 (FBIS, CPP2002032700002222 [March 27, 2002]); "Taiwan to Discuss Steel Issues with PRC through WTO Mechanism," CNA, June 18, 2002 (FBIS, CPP20020618000208 [June, 18, 2002]).

5. "Further on Shi Guangsheng Saying FTA with Taiwan Means 'Political Trouble,'" Xinhua, June 21, 2002 (FBIS, CPP20020621000048 [June 21, 2002]).

6. "Name Change Unacceptable to Taiwan Veterinarian Association," CNA, November 23, 2001 (FBIS, CPP20011123000130 [November 23, 2001]); "Government Opposes Change of Local Lions Club to 'China, Taiwan,'" CNA, April 23, 2002 (FBIS, CPP20020423000156 [April 23, 2002]).

7. See Chen Shui-bian, *Xiangxin Taiwan: Ahbian Zongtong xiang Renmin Baogao* (*Believe in Taiwan: President Ah-Bian Reports to the People*)(Taipei: Yuanshen Chubanshe, 2004), p.24.

8. "Qian Qichen Addresses Taiwan Affairs Officials on Cross-Strait Issues," Xinhua, March 24, 2000 (FBIS, 20000324000091 [August 23, 2003]); Qian Qichen, "Certain Major Issues in Studying Current International Relations," *Guoji Zhanwang* (*International Forecast*), February 15, 2001 (FBIS, CPP20010316000195).

9. This discussion is based on Leo F. Goodstadt, "China and the Selection of Hong Kong's Post-Colonial Elite," *China Quarterly* 163 (September 2000): 721–40. On Anson Chan, see Sze-yuen Chung, *Hong Kong's Journey to Reunification: Memoirs of Sze-yuen Chung* (Hong Kong: Chinese University Press, 2001), pp. 233–36. It should be noted that the British in the 1970s and 1980s pursued a similar strategy: co-opting the wealthy through a set of consultative mechanisms as an alternative to other, more inclusive institutions.

10. See Goodstadt, "China and the Selection of Hong Kong's Post-Colonial Elite," for the manifestation of the united front in appointments.

11. This section is based on Shui-hing Lo, *Governing Hong Kong: Legitimacy, Communication, and Political Decay* (Huntington, N.Y.: Nova Science Publishers, 2001), pp. 222–25. The cited passages are on p. 223 and p. 225. For a different view of the Hong Kong media that emphasizes the impact of economic factors, see Tuen-yu Lau and Yiu-ming To, "Walking a Tight Rope: Hong Kong's Media Facing Political and Economic Challenges since Sovereignty Transfer," in *Crisis and Transformation in China's Hong Kong*, edited by Ming K. Chan and Alvin Y. So (Armonk, N.Y.: M. E. Sharpe, 2002), pp. 322–42.

12. David Zweig, "Democratic Values, Political Structures, and Alternative Politics in Greater China," Peaceworks 44 (Washington: United States Institute of Peace, July 2002), p. 18.

13. For an excellent account of the role of the interaction among the DAB, FTU, NTAS, and KFA during election campaigns, see Shiu-hing Lo, Wing-yat Wu, and Kwok-fai Wan, "The 1999 District Councils Elections," in *Crisis and Transformation in China's Hong Kong*, edited by Chan and So, pp. 151–55.

14. On the united front strategy in action in elections, see Lo, Wu, and Wan, "The 1999 District Councils Elections," pp. 139–65; the cited passages are on pages 153 and 154. On the 2000 LegCo elections, Lo concludes: "First, the DAB was able to mobilize full support from its solid supporters by utilizing a triangular alliance with the FTU and united front organizations at various districts. . . . Second, the DAB constantly enjoys sufficient financial support from pro-Beijing organizations and the coordination work of the Liaison Office. . . . Third, the FTU provided manpower, logistical support, and coordination work for the DAB in the 2000 LegCo elections. . . . United front organizations played a decisive role in the 2000 LegCo elections." See Lo, *Governing Hong Kong*, pp. 199–200.

15. Lyman P. Van Slyke, *Enemies and Friends: The United Front in Chinese Communist History* (Stanford University Press, 1967), p. 3; *Selected Works of Deng Xiaoping, 1982–1992*, vol. 3 (Beijing: Foreign Languages Press, 1994), p. 219.

16. On the Hong Kong opposition, see Shui-hing Lo, "Political Opposition, Co-optation, and Democratization," in *Political Order and Power Transition in Hong*

Kong, edited by Li Pang-kwong (Hong Kong: Chinese University Press, 1997), pp. 127–58, especially pp. 149–58; and Lau Siu-kai and Kuan Hsin-chi, "Hong Kong's Stunted Political Party System," *China Quarterly* 172 (December 2002): 1010–28 (cited passage on p. 1016).

17. "Hong Kong Reminded That China Is in Charge," *Washington Post*, February 20, 2004; "Beijing Says Only 'Patriots' Are Fit to Rule Hong Kong," *New York Times*, February 21, 2004; Christine Loh, "Patriot Missives," CLSA Asia-Pacific Markets, Hong Kong, March 3, 2004 (www.civic-exchange.org/publications/2004/Patriot%20Missives.doc [March 4, 2004]).

18. "China's Changing Role in Local Polls," *Taiwan News*, November 26, 2001 (FBIS, CPP20011126000196 [November 27, 2001]); "Chen Shui-bian Says PRC Tries to Influence Elections in Taiwan," Agence France-Presse, May 16, 2002 (FBIS, 20020516000002 [May 17, 2002]); "China Reportedly to Allow Taiwan's KMT to Establish Mainland Office," Agence France-Presse, September 10, 2001 (FBIS, CPP20010910000101 [September 10, 2001]); "Lin Chia-lung Says Communist China Is Trying to Buy Up Taiwan Radio Stations," *Zhongshi Wanbao* (Internet version of evening "Express" edition of *Zhongguo Shibao* (*China Times*), October 6, 2004 (FBIS, CPP20041006000162 [October 13, 2004]).

19. Zhu Yuanfeng, "Observation after Elections: Causes of KMT Decline and Ways to Remedy," *Wenhuibao*, December 6, 2001 (FBIS, CPP20011206000073 [December 11, 2001]).

20. Chen Yunlin, "Reunification of the Two Sides of the Taiwan Strait Is Our Common Wish," *Liangan Guanxi* (*Cross-Strait Relations*), January 1, 2001 (FBIS, CPP20010118000175 [August 23, 2003]).

21. Bonnie S. Glaser, "China's Taiwan Policy: Still Listening and Watching," Center for Strategic and International Studies Pacific Forum, *PacNet Newsletter* 33, August 17, 2001 (www.csis.org/pacfor0133.htm [accessed August 15, 2003]); "KMT Denies U.S. Report of Interference in Cross-Strait Affairs," *Taipei Times*, August 15, 2001 (FBIS, CPP20010815000150 [August 20, 2001]).

22. "Taiwan Worried about 'Undermining' Effect of NGOs," *Taipei Times*, September 27, 2001 (FBIS, CPP20010927000134 [September 27, 2001]). Jiang used the term "patriotic" in his "eight points" Taiwan statement of January 1995.

23. "Qian Qichen Proposes 'Seven-Point' Plan for 'One Country, Two Systems' for Taiwan," *Wenhuibao*, July 13, 2001 (FBIS, CPP20010713000050 [July 8, 2004]).

24. "Text of Qian Qichen Speech on Taiwan," Xinhua, January 24, 2002 (FBIS, CPP20020124000121 [January 24, 2002]); "Beijing Rebukes Democratic Progressive Party for Closing to Contacts," *Dagongbao*, January 31, 2002 (FBIS, CPP20020131000039 [February 4, 2002]); "PRC's ARATS on Cutting Contacts with Taiwan's DPP Members Pushing Independence," *South China Morning Post*, February 5, 2002 (FBIS, CPP20020205000089 [February 5, 2002]).

25. "Shi Guangsheng: PRC Not to Tolerate Pro-Independence Taiwan Businessmen in PRC," *Hong Kong iMail*, March 14, 2001 (FBIS, CPP200103000102 [March

14, 2001]); "Beijing Blocks 'Hsin Pao,' Lin Hsing-chih's Works and Stirs up Disturbance at International Book Exhibition," *Pingguo Ribao* (*Apple Daily*), August 30, 2000 (FBIS, CPP20000830000051 [September 6, 2000]).

26. T. J. Cheng, "China-Taiwan Economic Linkage: Between Insulation and Superconductivity," in *Dangerous Strait: The US-Taiwan-China Crisis*, edited by Nancy Bernkopf Tucker (Columbia University Press, 2005), pp. 104–112.

27. Ibid, p. 104.

28. Christopher Hughes, *Taiwan and Chinese Nationalism: National Identity and Status in International Society* (New York: Routledge, 1997), pp. 115–18.

29. "*Lien-ho Pao* Interviews PRC Vice Premier Qian Qichen on Three Direct Links," *Lianhebao*, October 17, 2002 (FBIS, CPP20021017000055 [September 16, 2003]).

30. "Taipei Mayor Calls for 'Depoliticization' of Three Links Issue," CNA, October 18, 2002 (FBIS, CPP2002101859); "Taiwan Fully Prepared for Direct Links Talks: Premier," CNA, October 17, 2002 (FBIS, CPP20021017000107); "Taiwan to 'Observe' China's Position in Light of Qian's Comments, *Taipei Times*, October 19, 2002 (FBIS, CPP20021021000175); "Poll Finds 61 Percent Favor Direct Transport Links with Mainland China," CNA, October 19, 2002 (FBIS, CPP2002101900004); "Direct Cross-Strait Links Lead to New Middle-of-the-Road Line," *Lianhebao*, October 22, 2002 (FBIS, CPP20001024000203); Xing Zhigang, "Flexible Wording Bid for Three Links," *China Daily*, October 18, 2002 (FBIS, CPP20021018000094); and "PRC, Taiwan Businessmen Pressure Taipei to Lift Ban on 'Three Links,'" *China Daily*, October 18, 2002 (FBIS, CPP20021018000089); all accessed September 16, 2003. Also, Cecilia Fanjiang, "Qian's Remark Sparks Speculation in Taipei," *Taipei Journal*, November 1, 2002.

31. This account is based primarily on David G. Brown, "The Shadow of SARS," *Comparative Connections*, July 2003 (www.csis.org/pacfor/cc/0302Q/china_taiwan.html [July 2003]). Daphne Fan provided valuable research assistance.

32. "Taiwan Seeks Greater China Cooperation on SARS," *Taiwan News*, March 27, 2003 (www.etaiwannews.com/Taiwan/2003/03/27/1048725985.htm [July 2003]); "Three Taiwan Experts Visiting China after Spat over SARS," Agence France-Presse, April 8, 2003 (FBIS, CPP20030409000090 [July 2003]).

33. "Taiwan Willing to Work with China in Preventing SARS," CNA, April 19, 2003 (www.etaiwannews.com/Taiwan/2003/04/19/1050717903.htm [July 2003]); "SCTAO, ARATS Responsible Persons Call on Both Sides of Taiwan Strait to Strengthen Cooperation in Preventing, Controlling Atypical Pneumonia," Xinhua, April 28, 2003 (FBIS, CPP20030428000194 [July 2003]).

34. Brown, "The Shadow of SARS"; "Chronicle of Cross-Strait Relations, March 1–April 30, 2003," *Exchange*, Mainland Affairs Council, June 2003; "Stay Away from China, Activists Say," *Taiwan News* (www.etaiwannews.com/Taiwan/2003/05/22/1053565143.htm [July 2003]); "Taiwan Investment on Mainland up 43 Percent Year on Year," Xinhua, June 21, 2003 (FBIS, CPP20030621000067 [July 2003]);

"Mainland China-Bound Investment from Taiwan Slows over SARS," CNA, June 20, 2003 (FBIS, CPP20030620000176 [July 2003]); "MAC Beckons Taiwan Investors to Return from Mainland China," CNA, June 6, 2003 (FBIS, CPP20030606000101 [July 2003]); "MOEA Plan to Lure Back Taiwan Businessmen on Mainland to be Unveiled," CNA, June 7, 2003 (FBIS, CPP 20030607000060 [July 2003]); "KMT Officials Say SARS Can Enhance Local Investment," *Taipei Times*, May 12, 2003 (www.taipeitimes.com/ News/taiwan/archives/2003/05/12/205645 [July 2003]).

35. Brown, "The Shadow of SARS"; "WHO Representative at SARS Forum Says Taiwan 'Province of China,'" Xinhua, April 23, 2003 (FBIS, CPP200030423000170 [July 2003]); "PRC Health Ministry Spokesman Pledges Cooperation with Taiwan," Xinhua, May 2, 2003 (FBIS, CPP20030502000198 [July 2003]).

36. "Taiwan's Exclusion from WHO 'Serious Danger' to Global Health," CNA, March 20, 2003 (FBIS, CPP20030320000328 [July 2003]); "Politics Matters More Than Health to WHO," *Taiwan Journal*, April 4, 2003 (FBIS, CPP20030403000277 [July 2003]); "Taiwan Health Minister Says Keep Politics Out of Health Issues," *Taiwan Journal*, April 25, 2003 (FBIS, CPP20030425000256 [July 2003]); "Government to Review Cross-Strait relations in Wake of SARS Outbreak," CNA, May 19, 2003 (www.taiwanheadlines.gov.tw/20030420/20030520p4.htm [July 2003]).

37. "ARATS Sends Letter to SEF on Donation of Anti-SARS Goods to Taiwan," Xinhua, May 23, 2003 (FBIS, CPP20030523000137 [July 2003]); "SEF Rejects ARATS Offer of SARS Help," CNA, May 25, 2003 (FBIS, CPP20030525000030 [July 2003]).

38. On Chen's decision, see "Taiwan President's 20 May Speech to DPP, Calls for Referendum on WHO," Democratic Progressive Party WWW, May 20, 2003 (FBIS, CPP20030520000178 [July 2003]). For a good expression of Taiwan resentment over China and SARS (one that is not necessarily fair to the WHO), see Mark Mehta, "Beijing Plays Political Games, WHO Fiddles while Health Care in Taiwan Burns," *Taiwan Journal*, July 11, 2003. On the opposition's dilemma, see "Bianzheng beiqing mincui pin xuanzhan" ("The Chen Government Uses Victimization and Populism to Fight the Election Campaign"), *Zhongyang Ribao (Central Daily News)*, May 29, 2003 (http://tw.news.yahoo.com/2003/05/29/polity/cdn/4016897.html [July 2003]). Politics reared its head again in late May when a doctor associated with the PFP was invited at Beijing's request to a SARS conference in Malaysia. He came under withering attack, and James Soong counseled him to return home. See "PFP Legislator's Comments at WHO Conference Do Not Represent Taiwan," CNA, June 17, 2003 (FBIS, 20030617000219 [July 2003]).

39. Brown, "The Shadow of SARS"; "AIT Director Paal Tells Chen U.S. Is against Referendum on Any Issue," *Lianhebao*, June 21, 2003 (FBIS, CPP20030621000194 [July 2003]); "AIT Director Denies Reports on His Comments on Taiwan Referendum," CNA, June 25, 2003 (FBIS, CPP20030625000198 [July 2003]).

40. For a proposal on how the SARS crisis might have induced cooperation rather than conflict, see Alastair Iain Johnston, "Here's How a Tiny Virus Can Help Improve Cross-Strait Ties," *Straits Times* (Singapore), May 17, 2003.

41. "A Conversation with Chen Shui-bian, the President of the Republic of China on Taiwan," E-Notes, Foreign Policy Research Institute, January 22, 2003 (www.fpri.org/enotes/20030122.asia.sicherman.chenshuibian [March 25, 2004]).

42. For a summary of PRC involvement in the 2004 contest, see Chih-cheng Lo, "The China Factor in Taiwan's Presidential Election," Taiwan Perspective E-Paper 6, Institute for National Policy Research, February 26, 2004 (www.inpr.org.tw).

43. On Beijing's legal, psychological, and media leverage and the combined effect of its united front strategy and its military buildup in fostering Taiwan's insecurity, see Jiann-fa Yan, "Only Peace and Democracy Can Smash the Menace of China's 'Three Types of Warfare,'" Taiwan Perspective E-letter 37, Institute for National Policy Research, September 1, 2004 (www.tp.org.tw/letter/story.htm?id=20003746).

Chapter Nine

1. Stephen R. Weissman, *A Culture of Deference: Congress's Failure of Leadership in Foreign Policy* (New York: Basic Books, 1995); Barbara Hinckley, *Less than Meets the Eye* (University of Chicago Press, 1994); Rebecca K. C. Hersman, *Friends and Foes: How Congress and the President Really Make Foreign Policy* (Brookings, 2000).

2. For good accounts, see James Mann, "Congress and Taiwan: Understanding the Bond," in *Making China Policy: Lessons from the Bush and Clinton Administrations*, edited by Ramon H. Myers, Michel C. Oksenberg, and David Shambaugh (Lanham, Md.: Rowman & Littlefield, 2001), pp. 207–11; and Robert L. Suettinger, *Beyond Tiananmen: The Politics of U.S.-China Relations, 1989–2000* (Brookings, 2003), pp. 212–17.

3. See my "Taiwan Policy Making since Tiananmen: Navigating through Shifting Waters," in *Making China Policy*, edited by Myers, Oksenberg, and Shambaugh, pp. 179–200.

4. Chan Li-fang, "The New National Defense Strategy of the White House Does Not Back [Taiwan] in Reality," *Zhongyang Ribao (Central Daily News)*, June 12, 2001 (Foreign Broadcast Information Service [FBIS], CPP20010612000029 [June 12, 2001]); "Take the Initiative to Promote and Upgrade Taiwan-US-China Relations," *Lianhebao (United Daily News)*, February 23, 2002 (FBIS, CPP20020223000006 [February 26, 2002]).

5. Colin L. Powell, "Remarks at Conference on China-U.S. Relations," Texas A&M University, College Station, Texas, November 5, 2003 (www.state.gov/secretary/rm/2003/25950.htm [July 18, 2004]).

6. "Shemma Wenti Dou Keyi Taolun: Qian Qichen Fuzongli Jieshou 'Huashengdun Youbao' Jizhe Pan Wen Caifang" ("Anything Can Be Discussed: Vice Premier Qian Qichen Accepts an Interview by Journalist John Pomfret of the *Washington Post*"), *Shijie Zhishi (World Knowledge)* 3 (February 2001): 14.

7. "China Summons U.S. Ambassador to Protest Taiwan Defense Minister's U.S. Visit, Others," Xinhua (New China News Agency), March 16, 2002 (FBIS,

20020316000109 [March 16, 2002]); He Yijian, "Villain's Design Is Obvious to All—Comment on U.S. Obstinate Invitation to Tang Yao-ming to Visit U.S.," *Jiefang Junbao* (*People's Liberation Army Daily*), March 21, 2002 (FBIS, 20020322000004 [March 22, 2002]); "A 'Slip of the Tongue' or 'Misguided Mentality?'" *Wenhuibao*, April 6, 2002 (FBIS, CPP20020406000019 [April 8, 2002]).

8. Suettinger, *Beyond Tiananmen*, p. 232.

9. Bonnie S. Glaser, "Sustaining Cooperation: Security Matters Take Center Stage," *Comparative Connections*, January 2003 (www.csis.org/pacfor/cc/0204Qus_china.html [March 29, 2005]); "PRC FM Tang Jiaxuan Meets Powell, Discusses Taiwan, DPRK, Iraq Issues," Xinhua, January 20, 2003 (FBIS, CPP20030120000044 [June 12, 2004]). In September 2000, PRC foreign minister Tang Jiaxuan complained that Bill Clinton criticized Chen Shui-bian in a private meeting with Jiang Zemin and then publicly denied the statement; "Tang Jiaxuan Criticizes U.S. on Taiwan Issue, Clarifies Clinton Remarks," *Ming Bao*, September 13, 2000 (FBIS, CPP20000913000015 [September 13, 2000]).

10. Powell, "Remarks at Conference on China-U.S. Relations."

11. "Keeping Watchful Eye on U.S. Presidential Elections; Taiwan Leaning a Little More Towards Bush," *Zhongguo Shibao* (*China Times*), September 12, 2004 (FBIS, CPP20040912000025 [September 13, 2004]).

12. See my "The Sacred Texts of United States-China-Taiwan Relations," in *At Cross Purposes: U.S.-Taiwan Relation since 1942* (Armonk, N.Y.: M. E. Sharpe, 2004), pp. 124–78.

13. Chen Shui-bian, *Xiangxin Taiwan: Ahbian Zongtong xiang Renmin Baogao* (*Believe in Taiwan: President Ah-Bian Reports to the People*) (Taipei: Yuanshen Chubanshe, 2004), p. 18.

14. "Basic Human Rights," *Taipei Times*, December 12, 2003 (FBIS, CPP20031212000250); "On the Road," *Taipei Times*, December 15, 2003 (FBIS, CPP20031215000210); both accessed July 19, 2004.

15. Shi Lujia, "Halting 'Taiwan Independence' Separatist Activities Is the Key to Preserving Taiwan Strait Peace and Stability," Xinhua, May 30, 2004 (FBIS, CPP20040530000022 [July 20, 2004]).

16. For an analysis of these documents, see my "The Sacred Texts of United States-China-Taiwan Relations."

17. Secretary of State Colin Powell said in a press interview in October 2004 that "Taiwan is not independent. It does not enjoy sovereignty as a nation, and that remains our policy, our firm policy" (www.state.gov/secretary/rm/37361). That could be interpreted as applying more to Taiwan's place in the international system than to cross-Strait relations, but the Taiwan government was upset nonetheless; see "President Chen: Will Not Tolerate Such Remarks by Powell," *Ziyou Shibao*, October 28, 2004 (FBIS, CPP20041028000082); Laurence Eyton, "Taiwan Reels from Powell's Anti-Sovereignty 'Goof,'" *Asia Times Online*, October 30, 2004 (www.atimes.com/atimes/China/FJ30Ad03 [November 15, 2004]).

18. The "six assurances" refers to pledges that the Reagan administration made to Taipei at the time of the August 1982 communiqué. The United States assured Taipei that it had not agreed to set a date for ending arms sales; had not agreed to hold prior consultations with the PRC on arms sales; had not agreed to revise the Taiwan Relations Act; had not altered its position regarding sovereignty over Taiwan; would not play any mediation role between Taipei and Beijing; and would not exert pressure on Taiwan to enter into negotiations with the PRC.

19. Nancy Bernkopf Tucker has contributed to my thinking on the merits of strategic ambiguity. See her "Strategic Ambiguity or Strategic Clarity" in *Dangerous Strait: The U.S.-Taiwan-China Crisis* (Columbia University Press, 2005), pp. 186–211.

20. For the most explicit articulation of this point of view, see the testimony of William Kristol, House Committee on International Relations, *The Taiwan Relations Act: The Next Twenty-Five Years*, 108th Cong., 2d sess., April 21, 2004 (www.newamericancentury.org/taiwan-20040421).

21. This is the fundamental theme of my *At Cross Purposes*.

22. This theme is most effectively developed in Thomas J. Christensen, "The Contemporary Security Dilemma: Deterring a Taiwan Conflict," *Washington Quarterly* 25 (Autumn 2002): 7–21.

23. In the late Carter and early Reagan administrations, some U.S. officials believed that the new context created by normalization of the U.S.-PRC relationship plus Beijing's one-country, two-systems formula might produce a settlement and transform Washington's role.

24. For a brief discussion of dual deterrence by two individuals who served in the Clinton administration at the time of the 1995–96 crisis, see Ashton B. Carter and William J. Perry, *Preventive Defense, A New Security Strategy for America* (Brookings, 1999), p. 113.

25. Lee Teng-hui, *The Road to Democracy: Taiwan's Pursuit of Identity* (Tokyo: PHP Institute, 1999), p. 130.

26. The PRC regarded Washington's efforts to prepare for the possibility of a Chen presidency as evidence that it was working to bring about that outcome.

27. See David Shambaugh, "Facing Reality in China Policy," *Foreign Affairs* 90 (January-February 2001): 51–52. In January 2002, Richard Holbrooke argued that after September 11 the strategic estrangement that had existed in U.S.-PRC relations since Tiananmen had ended and that it was time to create a new basis for positive partnership. He proposed a fourth communiqué that would "update the relationship based on a new realism." Concerning Taiwan, he suggested using the "side-by-side" approach of the Shanghai communiqué and expressed the hope that the new document would "perhaps help Taiwan open a more productive dialogue with the mainland." Such an exercise would not be focused on Taiwan but would certainly affect Taiwan, probably in a negative way. See Richard Holbrooke, "A Defining Moment with China," *Washington Post*, January 2, 2002, p. A13.

28. Timothy Crawford, "Pivotal Deterrence and the Kosovo War: Why the Holbrooke Agreement Failed," *Political Science Quarterly* 116 (Winter 2001–02): 499–523 (cited passage on p. 502).

29. "Overview of U.S. Policy toward Taiwan," testimony of James A. Kelly, House Committee on International Relations, *The Taiwan Relations Act: The Next Twenty-Five Years*, 108th Cong., 2d sess., April 21, 2004 (www.state.gov/p/eap/rls/rm/2004/31649pf.htm [April 22, 2004]).

30. On the difference between strategic ambiguity and conditional commitments, see Thomas J. Christensen, "Clarity on Taiwan: Correcting Misperceptions on Both Sides of the Strait," *Washington Post*, March 20, 2000, p. A17.

Chapter Ten

1. Jacques deLisle, "Varieties of Sovereignty and China: Challenges and Opportunities in the Cross-Strait Relationship: A Conference Report," E-Notes, Foreign Policy Research Institute, July 1, 2002 (www.fpri.org/enotes/asia.20020701.delisle.sovereigntychina.html [June 27, 2002]).

2. Ibid.

3. See, for example, "Official of Relevant Central Department Discloses to This Paper: The Title of the Country May Be Discussed by Recognizing the One-China Principle," *Wenweibao*, November 5, 2001 (Foreign Broadcast Information Service [FBIS], CPP20011105000059 [November 5, 2001]). The official described the talks of the early 1990s as reflecting no difference between the central and regional authorities or as holding the talks "under the leadership of a given common administrative body." That is very different from the PRC's recognizing that the government in Taipei was of an essentially equal status.

4. Stephen D. Krasner, *Sovereignty: Organized Hypocrisy* (Princeton University Press, 1999), p. 11.

5. International Crisis Group, "Taiwan Strait IV: How an Ultimate Political Settlement Might Look," Asia Report 75 (February 26, 2004) (www.crisisweb.org/home/index.cfm?id=2524&l=1 [February 27, 2004]).

6. "President Chen's Cross-Century Remarks," December 31, 2000 (www.president.gov.tw/php-bin/prez/showenews.php4 [March 24, 2004]).

7. Li Thian-Hok, "Chen Sent Beijing the Wrong Message," *Taiwan Communique*, April 2001 (www.taiwandc.org/twcom/96-no3 [March 24, 2004]).

8. Byron S. J. Weng, "Modes of National Integration," based on paper presented at the Symposium on Comparison of National Sovereignty and Integration Models, Lung-chu Chen New Century Foundation, Taipei, February 24, 2001 (www.dsis.rog.tw/peaceforum/papers/2001-04/O0104001e.htm [January 24, 2003]; David Huang, "'Integration's the Key to Strait Woes," *Taipei Times*, February 13, 2001 (www.taipeitimes.com/News/edit/archives/2001/02/23/73496 [July 14, 2004]).

9. "Taiwan KMT Chairman Lien Chan Proposes Cross-Strait Confederation," Central News Agency (CNA), January 4, 2001 (FBIS, CPP20010104000074); "KMT Unveils Position Paper on 'Confederation,'" CNA, July 7, 2001 (FBIS, CPP20010707000071). Lien later had to abandon his plan of putting the confederation idea on the agenda for the KMT's Sixteenth Party Congress; "Lien Chan Shelves Proposal for Cross-Straits Confederation," *Taipei Times*, July 26, 2001 (FBIS, CPP20010726000185); all accessed October 13, 2003.

10. "NPC Spokesman: China Opposes 'Confederation' System in Solving Taiwan Issue," Xinhua (New China News Agency), March 4, 2001 (FBIS, CPP20010304000048); "Official Says Federation/Confederation Concepts Negotiable under One-China Principle," *Zhongguo Shibao (China Times)*, March 31, 2001 (FBIS, CPP20010402000002); both accessed October 13, 2003. Also John Pomfret, "Jiang Has Caution for U.S.; China's Leader Says Taiwan Arms Deal Would Spur Buildup," *Washington Post*, March 24, 2001, p. 1.

11. Hua Qing: "'Splittism' Is Hidden behind the 'Integration Theory,'" *Liaowang*, March 26, 2001 (FBIS, CPP20010402000100 [July 14, 2004]).

12. "'Confederation' Concept Snubbed by Mainland Scholar," CNA, June 29, 2001 (FBIS, CPP20010629000061); "PRC Expert Rejects Federation, Confederation Models for Taiwan," Xinhua, March 27, 2002 (FBIS, CPP20020327000104); both accessed October 13, 2003. For Beijing, the confederation proposal was no doubt just a little too close to the neuralgic special state-to-state formulation of Lee Teng-hui and may have been jeopardized by the ambiguity of the term *guo* in Chinese ("nation," "country," "state").

13. See Strategic Studies, School of Public Policy and Management, Tsinghua University, "The Cross-Taiwan Strait Relations: Past Present, and Future," December 2003, pp. 28–31; cited passages on p. 29.

14. "PRC Official Says Confederation System Cannot Be Used for Reunification," *Zhongguo Shibao* (Internet version), January 5, 2001 (FBIS, CPP20010105000035 [October 13, 2003]).

15. "*Liaowang* Article Expands One-Country, Two-Systems Concept," *Renmin Ribao*, July 26, 1991 (FBIS, *Daily Report: China*, p. 62, CHI-91-147).

16. This section is based on Kenneth W. Allen, "Military Confidence-Building Measures across the Taiwan Strait," in *Investigating Confidence-Building Measures in the Asia-Pacific Region*, Henry L. Stimson Center Report 28, edited by Ranjeet K. Singh, May 1999 (www.stimson.org/japan/pdf/cbmapstraits.pdf [September 9, 2003]); and Bonnie S. Glaser, "Cross-Strait Confidence Building: The Case for Military Confidence-Building Measures," in *Breaking the China-Taiwan Impasse*, edited by Donald S. Zagoria (Westport, Conn.: Praeger Publishers, 2003), pp. 155–82.

17. Ministry of National Defense ROC, "Defense Report Republic of China"(www.mnd.gov.tw).

18. Glaser, "Cross-Strait Confidence Building," p. 164.

19. "Taiwan Affairs Office of CPC Central Committee, Taiwan Affairs Office of

State Council Are Authorized to Issue Statement on Current Cross-Strait Relations," Xinhua, May 17, 2004 (FBIS, CPP20040517000076 [May 30, 2004]).

20. See, for example, Robert A. Manning and Ronald N. Montaperto, "The People's Republic and Taiwan: Time for a New Cross-Strait Bargain," *Strategic Forum* 103 (February 1997).

21. The following discussion is based on the international relations literature on "cooperation," wherein adversaries choose to pursue the objective interests they have in common despite their subjective mistrust that the other will cheat and exploit their goodwill. Interested readers should see Robert Axelrod, *The Evolution of Cooperation* (New York: Basic Books, 1984); Kenneth A. Oye, ed., *Cooperation under Anarchy* (Princeton University Press, 1986), especially Oye, "Explaining Cooperation under Anarchy: Hypotheses and Strategies," pp. 1-24.

22. Kenneth Lieberthal, "Cross-Strait Relations," in *China under Jiang Zemin*, edited by Hung-mao Tien and Yun-han Chu (Boulder, Colo.: Lynne Rienner, 2000), pp. 165–82. For a later version of the Lieberthal proposal (discussed in chapter 11), see Kenneth Lieberthal, "Preventing a War over Taiwan," *Foreign Affairs* 84 (March-April 2005): 53–63.

23. "Taiwan FM on 'Diplomatic Truce' with PRC," *Zhongguo Shibao*, June 6, 2000 (FBIS, CPP20000666606000042 [June 6, 2000]).

24. This discussion is based on Robert D. Putnam, "Diplomacy and Domestic Politics: The Logic of Two-Level Games," *International Organizations* 42 (Summer 1988): 427–60.

25. Ma defines the 1992 consensus as "respective interpretations" and the one-China principle as the underlying premise of the ROC constitution; see Ying-jeou Ma, "Taiwan's Approach to Cross-Strait Relations," Aspen Institute (www.aspeninstitute.org/AspenInstitute/files/CCLIBRARYFILES/FILENAME/0000000253/China Ma.pdf [September 7, 2003]).

26. "Truth That Dare Not Speak Its Name," *Taipei Times*, June 21, 2004 (FBIS, CPP20040621000164 [November 10, 2004]).

27. "Looking Beneath the Surface of the 'One China' Question," ROC Government Information Office, March 1997.

28. Yun-han Chu, "Making Sense of Beijing's Policy toward Taiwan: The Prospect of Cross-Strait Relations during the Jiang Zemin Era," in *China under Jiang Zemin*, edited by Tien and Chu, pp. 193–214.

29. Zou Jingwen, *Li Denghui Zhizheng Gaobai Shilu (Record of Revelations on Lee Denghui's Administration)*(Taipei: INK, 2001), pp. 194–97.

30. Ibid., pp. 198–201.

31. Ibid., pp. 202–03.

32. Uri Savir, *The Process: 1,100 Days That Changed the Middle East* (New York: Random House, 1998); Yossi Bellin, *Touching Peace: From the Oslo Accord to a Final Agreement* (London: Weidenfeld & Nicolson, 1999); quoted passage on p. 78.

33. The discussion in these two paragraphs is based on Dennis Ross's assessment

of the Middle East peace process in the 1990s; see Ross, *The Missing Piece: The Inside Story of the Fight for Middle East Peace* (New York: Farrar, Straus, and Giroux, 2004), pp. 759–800.

34. "Presidential Press Conference," July 31, 2000 (www.president.gov.tw/1_president/e_subject-06c1 [March 27, 2004]); "A Conversation with Chen Shui-bian, the President of the Republic of China on Taiwan," E-Notes, Foreign Policy Research Institute, January 22, 2003 (www.fpri.org/enotes/20030122.asia.sicherman.chenshuibian [March 27, 2004]).

35. Ross, *The Missing Piece*, pp. 268, 772.

36. Alternatively, there is the possibility that over time the PRC's basic strategy will work and that mainland economics will trump Taiwan's political principles and military insecurity.

Chapter Eleven

1. "Fan Fenlie Guojia Fa Quanwen" ("Full Text of the Anti-Secession Law"), March 14, 2005 (http://.tw.people.com.cn/GB/14810/3240911 [March 14, 2005]).

2. Michael D. Swaine, "China's Military Posture," draft chapter in *Power Shift: China and Asia's New Dynamics*, edited by David Shambaugh (University of California Press, 2005, forthcoming), p. 8–9.

3. On coercive strategies, see Mark A. Stokes, *China's Strategic Modernization: Implications for the United States* (Carlisle Barracks, Pa.: Strategic Studies Institute, U.S. Army War College, 1999); Lyle Goldstein and William Murray, "Undersea Dragons: China's Maturing Submarine Force, *International Security* 28 (Spring 2004): 161–96; Michael A. Glosny, "Strangulation from the Sea," *International Security* 28 (Spring 2004): 125–60.

4. Jonathan Pollack has outlined three different ways in which the PRC might use ballistic missiles against Taiwan. The first way is to create a demonstration effect, as in the exercises of 1995–96, either as warnings to Taipei to desist from specific actions or as coercion short of war to induce changes in Taiwan's political behavior. The second way is as part of an overtly coercive attack with specific targets in mind but short of full-scale war against Taiwan. The third way is as part of a full-scale military campaign to overwhelm Taiwan, in the opening phases of which missiles would play a pivotal role. See his "Short-Range Ballistic Missile Capabilities," in *If China Attacks Taiwan: The Military Balance and Decision-Making across the Taiwan Strait*, edited by Steve Tsang (London: Routledge, 2005, forthcoming).

5. "Text of PRC's Taiwan Affairs Office News Conference on Taiwan Election, More," CCTV-4, April 14, 2004 (Foreign Broadcast Information Service [FBIS], CPP20040414000027 [April 19, 2004]).

6. U.S.-China Economic and Security Review Commission, *Hearing on Military Modernization and Cross-Strait Balance*, 108th Cong., 2d sess., February 6, 2004, p. 59; see also Jacques deLisle, "Taiwan's Referenda, Constitutional Reform, and the

Question of Taiwan's International Status," E-Notes, Foreign Policy Research Institute, February 6, 2004 (www.fpri.org/enotes/20040325.taiwanreferendum.delisle [March 25,2004]).

7. Lee Wei-pin, "Zhang Nianchi Says Defensive Referendum Can Lead to Permanent Separation of the Two Sides of the Taiwan Strait," *Wenweibao*, December 5, 2003 (FBIS, CPP20031205000033 [December 30, 2003]); Zhang Nianchi and Zhong Yan, "Zailun Gongtou yu Liangan Guanxi" ("More on the Referendum and Cross-Strait Relations"), *Shangxia Qiusuo* (*Searching from Top to Bottom*) (Shanghai: Shanghai Institute of East Asian Studies, 2003), pp. 81–82; "Luo Yuan Reiterates Once Again: The Day of 'Taiwan Independent' [sic] Is the Day of Declaration of War," Zhongguo Xinwen She (China News Agency), November 18, 2003 (FBIS, CPP20031113000146 [November 19, 2003]).

8. Michael Swaine, "Trouble in Taiwan," originally published in *Foreign Affairs* 83 (March-April 2004): 39–49; also available at www.ceip.org./files/Publications/2004-02-03-MichaelSwaine-TroubleinTaiwan.asp?from=pubdate [March 1, 2004].

9. Nor is it clear how authoritative those views were. They were conveyed to Americans by Chinese scholars. With the exception of the article by Zhang Nianchi cited above, there was little in the way of systematic and public Chinese analysis of the legal impact of constitutional revision.

10. During the campaign, Chen was explicit that the reason he favored a new constitution was that the existing amendment process required too broad a consensus and so produced outcomes that did not reflect the will of the people. See "Transcript of Interview with Chen Shui-bian," *Financial Times*, December 16, 2003 (www.ft.com [December 16, 2003]). The U.S. government at this time was signaling that changing the constitution through an extraconstitutional process would "definitely cause concerns and affect how the outside world views Taiwan." See "U.S. Senior Official Said There Are No Trust Problems between the Leaders of Taiwan and the United States," *Ziyou Shibao* (*Liberty Times*), February 14, 2004 (FBIS, CPP20040217000023 [March 8, 2004]).

11. On that process, see Ch'ien Tuan-sheng, *The Government and Politics of China: 1912–1949* (Stanford University Press, 1950), pp. 316–24.

12. For recent evidence, see Yung-ming Hsu, "'Identity Problem' Is Not Political," *Taipei Times*, November 22, 2004 (FBIS, CPP20041122000201 [November 28, 2004]), which cites a poll in which 70 percent of the public regarded Taiwan "as a sovereign and independent nation" and only 15 percent disagreed.

13. "Strait Talk: The Full Interview," *Time*, February 16, 2003 (www.time.com/time/nation/article0,8559,591348,00 [March 7, 2004]).

14. "Chen Shui-bian Discusses Issue of Referendum with LA Times," Office of the President (www.president.gov.tw), February 8, 2004 (FBIS, CPP20040209000077 [February 15, 2004]).

15. "Transcript of March 29, 2004, *Washington Post* interview with Chen Shui-bian" (www.washingtonpost.com/wp-dyn/articles/A33322-2004Mar29.html [April

25, 2004]). At play here may have been a desire on Chen's part to meet the various criteria for statehood in international law, particularly the one concerning a well-defined territory (see chapter 4). To assert that the ROC government possesses sovereignty rests on its association with the territory of Taiwan and its associated islands. Recall that this was probably Lee Teng-hui's motivation when he announced his "special state-to-state relations" formulation in 1999. Indeed, Jacques deLisle predicted that a new constitution will affirm in various ways that Taiwan meets all the criteria for statehood (territory, population, effective government, capacity to conduct international relations, and a claim of statehood); see deLisle, "Taiwan's Referenda, Constitutional Reform, and the Question of Taiwan's International Status."

16. "Transcript of March 29, 2004, *Washington Post* interview with Chen Shui-bian." Chen's most interesting idea, which has potential implications for cross-Strait relations, concerned the rights of Taiwan's indigenous peoples: "We believe that the relationship between the government and the indigenous ethnic groups is a relationship of a new partnership and a relationship of quasi-country-to-country relations. Namely, there is one country within a country."

17. Kenneth Lieberthal, "Dire Strait: The Risks on Taiwan," *Washington Post*, January 8, 2004, p. A23.

18. "Announcement of Election Results on Taiwan," Office of White House Press Secretary, March 26, 2004 (http://lists.state.gov/SCRIPTS/WA-USIAINFO.EXE?A2=ind0403d&L=WF-EASIA&P=R13566 [March 28, 2004]); "Chinese FM Talked with Powell via Phone, FM Spokesman Confirms," Xinhua, March 23, 2004 (FBIS, CPP20040323000211 [March 28, 2004]).

19. Derek Mitchell, "Taiwan's Election: A Wake-Up Call to China, *PacNet Newsletter*, March 24, 2004 (http://csis.org/pacfor/pac0412.pdf [March 27, 2004]) (source of the quoted passage); Harvey Feldman, "Taiwan Vote Demands a Softer Stance by Beijing, *Los Angeles Times*, March 24, 2004, p. B13; Ralph A. Cossa, "Taiwan's Elections: Time for Diplomatic Gestures from Beijing?" *PacNet Newsletter*, March 16, 2004 (http://csis.org/pacfor/pac0411.pdf [March 27, 2004]); "Overview of U.S. Policy toward Taiwan," testimony of James A. Kelly, House Committee on International Relations, *The Taiwan Relations Act: The Next Twenty-Five Years*, 108th Cong., 2d sess., April 21, 2004 (www.state.gov/p/eap/rls/rm/2004/31649pf.htm [April 22, 2004]).

20. "Overview of U.S. Policy toward Taiwan."

21. Ibid. Even less coded were the not-for-attribution comments of administration officials. For the best example, see "Bush to Chen: Don't Risk It," *Far Eastern Economic Review,* May 20, 2004, p. 28.

22. "President Chen's Inaugural Address, 'Paving the Way for a Sustainable Taiwan,'" Government Information Office, May 20, 2004 (www.gio.gov.tw/taiwan-website/4-oa/20040520/2004052001[May 30, 2004]).

23. Here, Chen was echoing themes from Lee Teng-hui, who had argued on a number of occasions that the people of Taiwan were a *gemeinschaft*, a collectivity that

shared a common destiny. And during the 1998 Taipei mayoral election, he referred to Ma Ying-jeou, the KMT candidate who hailed from Hunan and was born in Hong Kong, as a "new Taiwan person."

24. "Yao Chia-wen Helps Bian Get Out of Inauguration Speech Bind," *Lianhebao* (*United Daily News*), May 21, 2004 (summarized in FBIS, CPP20040521000227), and "Constitutional Reform Plan Generates Heat," *Taipei Times*, May 22, 2004 (FBIS, CPP20040524000245), both accessed July 16, 2004; "Chen Tells FAPA He Hasn't Backtracked," *Taipei Times*, May 26, 2004 (www.taipeitimes.com/News/taiwan/archives/2004/05/26/2003156987), and Randall G. Schriver, "U.S.-China Relations: 15th Anniversary of the Tiananmen Crackdown," statement before the Congressional Executive Commission on China, June 3, 2004 (www.state.gov/p/eap/rls/rm/2004/33126), both accessed June 18, 2004. Yao's point about "national designation" does not take into account Chen's indirect reaffirmation of the pledges of his first inaugural address, one of which was not to change the national title.

25. "Taiwan Affairs Office of CPC Central Committee, Taiwan Affairs Office of State Council Are Authorized to Issue Statement on Current Cross-Strait Relations," Xinhua (New China News Agency), May 17, 2004 (FBIS, CPP20040517000076 [May 30, 2004]). Note that the PRC offer of military CBMs reverses the position described in chapter 9, that they were only appropriate between sovereign states. More broadly, there was some optimism on Taiwan at the time of Chen's inauguration that cross-Strait progress was actually possible because of the overlap between things that Chen had proposed—and the language he used—and the areas of progress laid out in the TAO statement. Yet given the Chinese preconditions, such optimism was hardly warranted.

26. "Expose 'Taiwan Independence' beneath the Packaging" [on a *Renmin Ribao* (*People's Daily*) commentator article], Xinhua, May 25, 2004 (FBIS, CPP20040525000167 [June 20, 2004]); "*Renmin Ribao* Publishes Signed Article, Pointing Out That Chen Shui-bian's 20 May Speech Is 'Taiwan Independence' Rhetoric with a Hidden Agenda," Xinhua, June 10, 2004 (FBIS, CPP20040610000114 [June 11, 2003]).

27. "Beijing Urged to Get Tougher with Taipei," *Straits Times*, June 3, 2004; "More on PRC Official Says Pro-Independence Taiwan Businessmen Not Welcome," Agence France-Presse, June 16, 2004 (FBIS, CPP20040616000057 [June 17, 2004]); "Halting 'Taiwan Independence' Separatist Activities Is the Key to Preserving Taiwan Strait Peace and Stability," Xinhua, May 30, 2004 (FBIS, CPP20040530000022 [June 20, 2004]).

28. Zhang Nianchi, "Public Opinion in the Background Is More Important than the Election Outcome," *Dagongbao*, March 22, 2004 (FBIS, CPP20040322000075); Zhang Nianchi, "A New Line on Taiwan Needs to Be Formulated," *Mingbao*, March 25, 2004 (FBIS, CPP20040325000069); Zhang Nianchi, "Zhang Nianchi: Encouragement Should Be Given if (Chen Shui)-Bian Pledges 'Four Noes and One Will Not,'" *Mingbao*, May 15, 2004 (FBIS, CPP20040515000039); and "Chinese Scholar

Says Hu Jintao Definitely Will Create New Concepts to Resolve Taiwan Issue," *Lianhe Zaobao* (*United Morning News*), November 23, 2004 (FBIS, CPP20041123000068); all accessed November 25, 2004. Also see "Cross-Taiwan Strait Crisis in 2003–2004: Its Causes, Prospects, and Preventive Approaches to a New Crisis," Shanghai Center for RimPac Strategic and International Studies, September 3, 2004, pp. 38, 40. Li Jiaquoan, former head of the CASS Taiwan Studies Institute, also admitted that China "has not been able to change the minds of the people of Taiwan through propaganda, nor has it been able to blunt the will of Taiwan independence elements through intimidation" and asserted that "we should reexamine ourselves in this respect, adopt resolute policy decisions, have the courage to face reality, and employ both strategies in light of the situation." See Li Jiaquan, "How to Face Deep-Seated Cross-Strait Contradictions," *Dagongbao*, April 3, 2004 (FBIS, CPP20040403000025).

29. "Lee Hung-hsi: Taiwan Has a Chance of Achieving the Goal of Establishing a New Constitution in Four Years," *Ziyou Shibao*, July 2, 2004 (FBIS, CPP20040702000202); "Lee Teng-Hui's Vision for Reform Compatible: Aide," *Taipei Times*, July 30, 2004 (FBIS, CPP20040730000183); and "Lee Teng-hui Says Name Should be Changed to Taiwan and the Island Should Join the United Nations," TVBS, October 8, 2004 (FBIS, CPP20041008000204); all accessed October 29, 2004. "Why Not Annex the U.S.?" *Taipei Times*, October 14, 2004 (FBIS, CPP20041014000154 [October 15, 2004]).

30. "*Renmin Ribao* Publishes Signed Article."

31. "CNA Transcript of President Chen Shui-bian's Address at National Day Rally," Central News Agency (CNA), October 10, 2004 (FBIS, CPPP20041010000021).

32. For the amendments, see "Xiuzheng Zhonghua Minguo Xianfa Zengxiu Tiaowen Diyitiao, Dierhtiao, Disitiao, Diwutiao ji Dibatiao Tiaowen; bing Zengding Dishierhtiao Tiaowen" ("Text of the Revision of Articles 1, 2, 4, 5, and 8 and Added Article 12 of the Additional Articles of the Republic of China Constitution"), August 23, 2004 (http://lis.ly.gov.tw/npl/fast/04105/930823 [September 15, 2004]).

33. Results of the 2004 Election, website of the Central Election Commission (http://210.69.23.140/cec/vote421.asp?pass1=A2004A0000000000aaa [October 23, 2004]).

34. "Taiwan Election Watch: Summary of LY Election 'Results,'" December 11, 2004 (FBIS, CPP20041211000110 [December 11, 2004]). For competing interpretations, see "In Taiwan Ballot, Ties with Beijing Seem to be a Winner," *New York Times*, p. A1; John J. Tkacik Jr., "'Wholesale' Disaster for Taiwan's DPP," *Asia Times Online*, December 15, 2004 (www.atimes.com/atimes/China/FL15Ad02.html [December 22, 2004]). The most thorough analysis is Shelley Rigger, "Making Sense of Taiwan's Legislative Election," E-Notes, Foreign Policy Research Institute, January 4, 2005 (www.fpri.org/enotes/20050104.asia.rigger.taiwanlegislativeelection.html [January 4, 2005]).

35. "Amendment Raises Hopes for a New Constitution," *Taipei Times*, August 24, 2004 (FBIS, CPP20040824000168 [October 23, 2004]).

36. "Report Outlines Chen-Soong Declaration," *Lianhe Wanbao* (*United Evening News*), February 24, 2005 (FBIS, CPP20050224000148).

37. "Sun Ya-fu: Taiwan Must Not Provoke the Mainland Again and Again," *Dagongbao*, September 7, 2004 (FBIS, CPP20040907000040); "State Council Taiwan Affairs Office Spokesman Answers a Reporter's Questions on Chen Shui-bian's Recent Separatist Remarks and Deeds Concerning 'Taiwan Independence,'" Xinhua, September 21, 2004 (FBIS, CPP20040921000231); "Wang Zaixi Urges: Rein in 'Taiwan Independence' Separatist Activities and Safeguard Peace and Stability in the Taiwan Strait," Xinhua, August 6, 2004 (FBIS, 20040806000196 [August 10, 2004]).

38. "Beijing's Authoritative Person Analyzes Fine-Tuning of Policy on Taiwan," *Dagongbao*, September 25, 2004 (FBIS, CPP20040925000027). It may be significant that this new "red line" was drawn after Jiang Zemin stepped down from the chairmanship of the Central Military Commission.

39. "PRC President Hu Sets 'Four-Point Guideline' on Cross-Straits Relations: 'Full Text,'" Xinhua, March 4, 2005 (FBIS, CPP20050304000234); "Full Text of Explanations on Draft Anti-Secession Law," Xinhua, March 8, 2005 (FBIS, CPP20050308000042); "PRC Think Tank Grants Interview on Three Red Lines," *Lianhebao*, March 9, 2005 (FBIS, CPP20050309000149).

40. In this scenario, constitutional revision would be a means of strengthening the sovereignty that Taiwan already possesses rather than making a new country (in Krasner's terms, it would improve domestic sovereignty).

41. On the decisionmaking concering the antisecession law, see Bonnie Glaser, "The Anti-Secession Law and China's Evolving Taiwan Policy," Taiwan Perspective e-Paper 67, March 21, 2005 (www.tp.org.tw [March 29, 2005]).

42. Insightfully, Yu-shan Wu describes a scenario in which the limits on an exclusively Taiwan identity recede, the PRC's growing power alienates more than it deters, the firewall between identity and de jure independence disappears, and the tendency of the island's politicians to promote radical solutions outweighs the efforts of the United States to counsel caution. See his "Taiwanese Nationalism and Its Implications: Testing the Worst-Case Scenario," *Asian Survey* 44 (July-August 2004): 614–25.

43. Kenneth Lieberthal, "Preventing a War over Taiwan," *Foreign Affairs* 84 (March-April 2005): 53–63.

44. Ibid., pp. 60–61.

45. Bonnie S. Glaser, "Cross-Strait Confidence Building: The Case for Military Confidence-Building Measures," in *Breaking the China-Taiwan Impasse*, edited by Donald S. Zagoria (Westport, Conn.: Praeger Publishers, 2003), p. 164.

46. As noted above, in 2004 some PRC scholars called for such a shift.

47. For one example of needed institutional reform, see Gregg Rubenstein, "Defense Acquisition Strategies for Taiwan," *Taiwan Defense Affairs* 3 (Summer 2003): 9–29.

48. Rubenstein, "Defense Acquisition Strategies for Taiwan," p. 21. Moreover, Taiwan would certainly lack the intelligence resources for offensive weapons to be effective.

49. In its campaign policy paper, the pan-Blue parties insisted on "sovereignty, equal footing, and peaceful interaction," noting that the ROC had been an independent, sovereign state since 1912; the two sides of the Taiwan Strait were ruled separately and were not subordinate to each other; the ROC's international space should be protected; and the PRC should renounce the use of force and remove its missiles targeting Taiwan. See "How to Improve Relations between the Two Sides of the Taiwan Strait," March 10, 2004, memorandum provided by the KMT-PFP office in Washington, D.C.

Chapter Twelve

1. For more detail on that story, see my "Congress Gets into the Human Rights Act," in *At Cross Purposes: U.S.-Taiwan Relation since 1942* (Armonk, N.Y.: M. E. Sharpe, 2004), pp. 179–218.

Index

Agriculture, 102

American Institute in Taiwan (AIT), 254

Antisecession law (PRC 2005), 121, 326

APEC. *See* Asia-Pacific Economic Cooperation

Arafat, Yassir, 292

ARATS. *See* Association for Relations across the Taiwan Strait

Arms sales to Taiwan: advanced arms from U.S. and France, 44; Bush administration's approval, 68; Chinese demand for U.S. to cease, 23–24, 110, 113, 136, 253, 276, 278; decline in defense spending, 134; defensive weapons, 4, 112; from former Soviet countries, 112; inflammatory nature of, 130; and negotiated settlement possibility, 294–95; Reagan's reduction of, 251; Taiwanese public's view of, 124; U.S. law authorizing, 22

ASEAN Regional Forum, 229

Asia Foundation, 63

Asia-Pacific Economic Cooperation (APEC), 160, 227, 228

Association for Relations across the Taiwan Strait (ARATS), 41, 45, 63, 101, 200–01, 228, 238, 263, 293, 294

Background of China-Taiwan dispute, 3–4, 14–26

Barmé, Geremie, 191

Belgrade embassy of China, accidental NATO bombing of, 194–95, 197, 213–14

Bellin, Yossi, 291

Blue camp: and election of 2004, 176, 178–79, 198, 324; formation of, 169–70; and relations with PRC, 233–35

Bodin, Jean, 83

Bombing of Belgrade embassy of China, 194–95, 197, 213–14

Bush, George W.: change from Clinton policy, 68, 129, 248, 262; Jiang trying to involve in Taiwan issue, 136, 250; on modernization of Taiwanese military, 134; reinforcing status quo between China and Taiwan, 2, 129–30, 248–53, 255, 262, 309; on Taiwan's contribution to Global Fund, 228; trying to restrain Taiwan, 243, 309, 337

Bush, Richard C., professional background, 345–48.

Cairo Conference, 16

Cairo Declaration (1943), 85, 86

Cai Tongrong, 174, 175

Carter, Jimmy, 21–22, 110, 251, 254, 257, 260

Cassidy and Associates, 49, 247